DEMOCRACY AND MONARCHY

IN

FRANCE

FROM THE INCEPTION OF THE GREAT REVOLUTION TO THE OVERTHROW OF THE SECOND EMPIRE

BY

CHARLES KENDALL ADAMS

Professor of History in the University of Michigan

"Mauern seh' ich gestürzt, und Mauern seh' ich errichtet,
Hier Gefangene, dort auch der Gefangenen viel.
Ist vielleicht nur die Welt ein grosser Kerker? Und frei ist
Wohl der Tolle, der sich Ketten zu Kränzen erkiest?"
GOETHE.

NEW YORK
HENRY HOLT AND COMPANY
1874

JOHN F. TROW & SON, PRINTERS,
205-213 EAST 12TH ST., NEW YORK.

Maclauchlan, Stereotyper,
145 & 147 Mulberry St., near Grand, N. Y.

TO

ANDREW D. WHITE, LL.D.,

PRESIDENT OF CORNELL UNIVERSITY.

MY DEAR FRIEND:

I have long regarded it as the most fortunate circumstance of my collegiate life, that during the five years of your active service as Professor of History in the University of Michigan, I was in the same institution, pursuing either under-graduate or post-graduate studies. To the inspiration of your lectures and your advice, more than to any other cause, I owe my fondness for historical study. I therefore ask for the privilege and the honor of connecting your name with the publication of this volume. In dedicating it to you, I have the double pleasure of doing it at the same time in grateful acknowledgment of personal benefits, and in hearty recognition of most valuable services in the cause of higher education.

Heartily yours,

C. K. A.

CONTENTS.

PREFACE.

In the winter of 1872–'3, I delivered a course of University Lectures on the Politics of France since the Great Revolution, and the studies begun in the preparation of those lectures have resulted in the present volume.

At the time when the work was undertaken, there was everywhere prevalent a more or less general astonishment at the political weakness of France, as displayed after the outbreak of the Franco-German War. In the course of lectures referred to, it was my effort to show that the present political character of the French people is the legitimate result of certain doctrines and habits that have been taking root in the nation during the past hundred years. The same purpose has animated the preparation of the present volume.

It seems to me that every genuine student of history must feel that there is no more potent political truth than this, that the present has its roots running far back into the past, and that it draws its life from the ideas and institutions that have gone before, just as certainly as the vegetation of to-day receives its nourishment from the decaying remains of preceding organic life. I think that one of the most extraordinary examples in illustration of this truth, is to be found in the modern political life of France. Moreover, the lesson taught by this example is as valuable as it is extraordinary; for it brings vividly before us the general truth, that while, on the one hand, the present is the child of the past, on the other, it is in its turn to be the parent of the future.

What the political rôle of France is hereafter to be, it were idle to predict. I think every one that follows these pages through, and assents to the positions taken, will agree with me in the belief that the great present need of France is the destruction of what I have called the revolutionary spirit; and that if this destruction is impossible (as very likely it is), the need next in importance is the establishment of such a government as will make the revolutionary spirit powerless. So long as this revolutionary spirit is dominant, every effort for the establishment of liberty is likely to result in anarchy; and anarchy, it must be confessed, is worse than tyranny. Something, whatever it is, that the nation can agree to *for a permanent form of government*, is, of all things, what is needed; and I can but think that the positions taken by President MacMahon, to maintain his power at all hazards to the end of his legal term, are, in spite of many objectionable features, in the general interest of this necessary permanence. It is quite possible that this course will result in the accession of the Prince Imperial; but that the nation would be content to accept permanently of anything better than some form of Napoleonism, bad as every form of it is, seems to be growing more and more improbable.

Two of the chapters of this volume, the one on *The Rise of Napoleonism*, and the one on *Universal Suffrage under the Second Empire*, were published, in a somewhat abridged form, in the *North American Review* in 1873. The courteous permission of Messrs. J. R. Osgood & Co. to republish them, is gratefully acknowledged.

I would also express my gratitude to my friend and colleague, Professor Henry B. Hutchins, to whom I am indebted for valuable suggestions and assistance in the final preparation of the work for the press.

C. K. A.

UNIVERSITY OF MICHIGAN,
September, 1874.

INTRODUCTORY.

"All questions of political institutions are relative, not absolute, and different stages of human progress not only *will* have, but *ought* to have, different institutions: government is always either in the hands, or passing into the hands, of whatever is the strongest power in society; and what this power is, does not depend on institutions, but institutions on it."—*Mill, Autobiography*, p. 162.

"Colui che lascia quello che si fa per quello che si doveria fare, impara piuttosto la rovina che la perservazione sua."—*Machiavelli, Il Principe*, Cap. XV.

DEMOCRACY AND MONARCHY IN FRANCE.

CHAPTER I.

INTRODUCTORY.

AT the beginning of the late Franco-German war, the prediction was more or less common in France, in England, and in the United States, that the advance of Napoleon III. would be little less than a repetition of the Jena campaign, and that within sixty days the French eagles would be in possession of Berlin. It was within less than sixty days that the French armies were shattered in pieces, and the French emperor was a prisoner of war. How completely had men of ordinary political intelligence, almost everywhere, been deceived in their estimation of the comparative strength of these two hostile nations!

As the war progressed, it became more and more certain that the government which, fifty years before, had been one of the weakest, was now the strongest power in Europe, and that the one which, in the time of Napoleon I., had been the strongest, was, under Napoleon III., apparently one of the weakest.

Now what is the history of this mutual exchange of strength and weakness? How does a nation become strong? How does a nation lose the strength which it has once acquired?

These are questions which it would be presumptive to attempt to answer in full; and yet each of the nations to which I have just referred has characteristics which have exerted a definite and powerful influence, and which, I believe, may be studied with profit. Let us glance at some of the most prominent of them.

The brilliant historian of the Restoration begins his history with these words:—"I scarcely exceed the middle age of man, yet I have already lived under ten dominations, or ten different governments, in France. Between infancy and maturity I have witnessed ten revolutions—ten cataracts, by which the spirit of modern liberty and the stationary or obstructive spirit have endeavored by turns to descend or to remount the declivity of revolutions."

Had Lamartine written his history in 1873, instead of 1849, he might have made his figure still more impressive. During the eighty years and more which have elapsed since the outbreak of the Great Revolution, France has had no less than fifteen distinct governments, every one of which has been the direct or indirect result of revolution. The old monarchy was first succeeded by a democratic monarchy, and then by a pure ochlocracy. Following this there was a republic, which, in turn, gave way to the military government. This assumed three distinct forms: that of a republican consulate, that of a life consulate or elective monarchy, and that of a hereditary empire. The government of the Restoration followed, and was in turn overthrown to make way for the Napoleonic rule of the Hundred Days. The Bourbons were reinstated only to be driven from the stage by the House of Orleans in 1830; the Orleans Dynasty was displaced by a second republic; and this latter, after three years, gave way to a second consulate and a second empire. Then came the military rule of Gambetta, only to be followed by the provisional administrations of Thiers and McMahon.

Each of these governments, moreover, presented to the nation a constitution formed in its own likeness. The law of nature was generally reversed; for in almost every instance the government, instead of being the child of the constitution, was its parent. To the democratic monarchy corresponds the constitution of the 14th of September, 1791; to the republic, that of the 15th fructidor of the year III.; to the limited consulate, that of the 22d frimaire of the year VIII.; to the consulate for life, the *Senatus Consultum* of the 16th thermidor of the year X.; to the empire, that of the 14th floréal of the year XII.; to the Restoration, the Charter of June 14th, 1814; to the Hundred Days, the *Acte Additionel* of April 22d, 1815; to the accession of the House of Orleans, that of the 9th of August, 1830; to the Revolution of 1848, that of September 4th of the same year; and to the second empire, the *Senatus Consultum* of January 14th, 1852. To use a figure of the old Duc de Broglie, some of these constitutions were still-born, others immediately slew the authors of their existence, others committed suicide; and yet they all have a place in French history, not for their intrinsic merit but rather for the purpose of illustrating that condition of affairs which has made so much turbulence possible.

Take another view of the same period. During the whole of this time the Great Revolution has been before the eyes or in the minds of the French people. It has been a sort of dream, a confused souvenir in the national memory. In every one of those revolutionary movements just named the people hoped to realize the full fruition of the ideas and principles on which that great upheaval was founded. But they have constantly failed to see more than one of the two sides of the Revolution. That great event represents not only the destruction of the old monarchic despotism and the creation of armies whose victorious tread was heard in every quarter of Europe save in England; it represented the creation of a general revolutionary spirit, which, if uncontrolled by predominating elements of stability, is as much worse for a nation than absolutism, as anarchy is worse than tyranny. And what *is* the prevalence of a revolutionary spirit in a nation? In answer it must be said that it is nothing less than the claim of the ignorant and the passionate to sit in authoritative judgment on every act of the government. Now such a claim must evidently be injurious just in proportion to its strength. As a general truth, it may be said that ignorance, especially when united with strong passion, chafes under restraint and tries to resist it. But no government can long exist without imposing such restraint, and therefore every good government is more or less unpopular, whenever it becomes necessary to control masses of people who are ignorant and whose ignorance is set on fire by passion. Nothing is more familiar to even the most cursory reader of history than the fact that some of the best of rulers have been least beloved, and that some of the worst have been most popular. The cause of this seeming paradox is in the fact that in turbulent times good government means restraint, while bad government means anarchy: in every nation, therefore, when the anarchic, or, what is the same thing, the revolutionary spirit is strong, any government whatever that is worthy the name of government will be more or less unpopular. Unite poverty with ignorance and passion, and then take away from them that respect for law and order which the revolutionary spirit always destroys, and you have the most difficult elements to control that can ever tax the energies of any government. Poverty, ignorance, and passion always abound; when, therefore, the anarchic spirit is generally prevalent, good government is well-nigh, if not indeed quite, impossible.

Now, looking at the matter historically, what has been the spirit of the leading minds in France since the Great Revolution? Not to enter at this time into details, it may be said that the prevailing spirit of what may be called the predominant elements of society has been one of chronic discontent. I say *chronic* discontent, because the spirit to which I refer has not shown itself once or twice only, but has pervaded to a great extent the whole course of French history ever since the beginning of the present century. Speaking historically, it may be said that whenever the nation has a republican form of government there is a large faction which not only prefers monarchy, but, for the purpose of setting it up, is ready to overthrow the government which exists. Whenever in turn royalty assumes the rule, there is an equally powerful faction seeking opportunities to rise up for its overthrow. The incoming governments have generally been popular for a time; but, if they have chanced to have in them the elements of stability, their popularity has ceased, and passionate admiration has given way and been followed by equally passionate execration. The controlling elements in the nation, beset with the vision of 1789, have, in every new emergency, entrusted the power to that species of government which at the moment gave most reason for the hope that it would apply and develop the principles of the Revolution. The result has been one of almost unvarying uniformity. The new government, either selfishly, or, as has sometimes occurred, in the real interests of the nation, has uniformly extended its powers, that is to say, has consolidated and perfected the restoration of a substantial authority. At the expiration of a dozen years, more or less, the people find, or think they find, that they have been deceived; discontent becomes rife; some faction or other gets the public ear; the government is overturned, and instantly one of another kind is established, which only makes haste to imitate in its life and its death the example of its predecessor. In this way it has occurred that since 1789 France has had ten or twelve different governments which have resulted simply from *coups de force*—governments not a single one of which has been the spontaneous expression of the sober national will—ten or twelve governments which have been usurpations, and usurpations, too, in the precise and scientific sense of the term. Upon an average, once in seven or eight years, violence has overthrown the established authority and created in its place a new government, which was in turn to be destroyed by the very hand which had created it. No history has been so variable; and yet its very variety has been monotonous.

In order to appreciate the extent to which this substitution of force for law has been carried, one must consider not only the revolutions that have been successful, but also those that have failed. In addition to the events already enumerated, there have been no less than fifteen insurrections that have actually broken out, besides a still greater number that have been suppressed or prevented when on the point of committing the first overt act. Then, too, we are not to forget the violent measures committed either by the government or against it in disregard of the regular processes of law. Call to mind the massacres of September, the death of Louis XVI., the Reign of Terror, the death of the Duc d'Enghien, the Massacres of 1816, the 2d of December, 1851, the Massacres of the Commune in 1871, the Infernal Machine under the Consulate, the attempt of Louvel just after the Restoration, those of Alibaud, Fieschi, and others under Louis Philippe, and of Orsini under Napoleon III. These facts, taken together, are quite enough to justify the declaration of Janet, that for the last eighty years France seems to have been abandoned to the domination of Siva, that fierce god of destruction whom the people of India adore and whom the mystic prophecy of Joseph de Maistre has made so real to the nation. One would not be much amiss in saying of France as Petrarch said of Verona, that, Acteon-like, she has been torn by her own dogs.

It need, perhaps, hardly be said, and yet the fact is important, that such a tendency to turbulence is destructive of all healthy national growth. A nation, like an individual, that is always changing its policy and its method of life, may properly be said to lose its personality. In France there has been so ready a disposition to brush aside old forms, often apparently for the simple reason that they are old, that one could almost believe that the highest ambition of the nation had been, at each new crisis, to forget the past and to begin the erection of the political structure completely anew. While the other great nations of Europe have been making slow but steady progress in paths that have been worn by years and centuries of historic sequence, the French have seemed to be chiefly desirous of breaking out of the path which at the moment they happened to be in, to be ever on the watch for some means of overthrowing the existing government. There has been a manifest want of that continuity of political method which is essential to a complete development of national personality, and which can only result from an organic and historic growth. Hence, it has happened, that whenever a new crisis has arisen, instead of attempting to harmonize the requirements of the time with the usages and traditions of the previous national life, the policy has been rather to ignore those traditions and to settle the difficulties at hand by the application of such abstract principles of political philosophy as at the moment happened to be dominant.

Now, this revolutionary spirit, this spirit whose

chief characteristic would seem to be that it is habitually and from principle fonder of that which it has not than of that which it has, is probably the most important fact of modern French history. As we proceed, I think it will become apparent that this revolutionary spirit is at once an important cause and an important result; a result of certain ideas which came to be more or less prevalent at the time of the Revolution, and a cause of much of that weakness which France revealed to the astonished world in the course of the late war.

Now, in the way of contrast with these characteristics, let us look for a moment at those of Prussia. The Prussian government has always been of a severe type, and sometimes it has been grossly tyrannical; and yet as a historical fact, the loyalty of the people to the reigning house and the prevailing methods of government, has been earnest and uninterrupted. During all the vicissitudes of its history, the government has retained its hold upon the people, and the people, by the exercise of a steady policy, have wrested from their rulers one right after another, until at last a parliamentary government, which is substantially free, has been established. Liberty in Prussia has been a growth rather than a creation, and a very slow growth at that. It began in an absolutism, in many respects like that of the Normans in England; and the history of England from the time of the Conquest to the present, has in Germany been more closely imitated than that of any other nation. While France has been spending its energies in attempting to leap at a single bound into a political condition similar to that of England, Germany has been content to follow—if need be, afar off—evidently in a kind of all-sufficing conviction that a steady pace, even though a slow one, if in the right direction, would finally bring the nation to the desired goal.

The spirit to which I refer finds good illustration in the Prussian Reform Bill of 1872. This important constitutional measure was designed to extend the sphere of local self-government in the rural districts. Having passed the Lower House, it was defeated by the peers; whereupon the King, after the English method, appealed to the country by dissolving Parliament and ordering a new election. The bill was passed a second time by the representatives, but the House of Lords still held out. The King then resorted to his prerogative, and created a sufficient number of new peers to carry the measure in a constitutional manner. Thus the Prussian Reform Bill of 1872 followed in the footsteps of the English Reform of forty years before.

But there are other characteristics of France and Germany which, by way of contrast, are scarcely less worthy of our attention. Foremost among them is the general question of education,—not merely the amount and quality of education afforded by the schools, but the whole of that system of preliminary training which these nations demand of a man before he is regarded as fitted for the business of life.

We in America all admit, though I think in a somewhat apathetic manner, that the safety of the nation depends in great measure upon education, as well as upon morality. We have devoted large energies to the education and elevation of the masses, but I fear that we have sometimes forgotten that the masses are always directed by the few, and that consequently it is no less essential that the few be in every way qualified for giving the *best* direction, than that the masses be qualified to recognize and accept such direction. We have heard much of generous legislative provisions for education in the United States, and perhaps on the whole the credit which our country has received, has been fairly earned; and yet it has to be admitted, that, while millions have been bestowed on our common schools, our higher institutions of learning have received next to nothing. While our common schools have been amply provided for, the most of our colleges and universities have been left as beggars, solely dependent upon the precarious benefactions of private generosity. If, here and there, an institution has gained a respectable standing without the aid of such private munificence, it has been the result of exceptional good management on the part of its board of control, rather than of any legislative liberality. * The conse-

* Many of those who talk much of the liberality with which our higher institutions are endowed by private individuals, seem to be quite

quence of this general policy has been what one would have been led to anticipate. While we have in our various professions large numbers of men of respectable culture, I fear it must be said we have, as compared with the larger European nations, very few men of what may be called great culture. When difficult problems of state are to be solved, therefore, they are always more or less liable to fall into the hands of men whose qualifications, to speak within bounds, entitle them to no very high respect.

There is in our country another tendency on which the recent history of France and Germany throws a flood of light. I refer to a general inclination to rush prematurely into the active and responsible work of life. This comes in great part

ignorant of the amounts expended on similar institutions in other countries. Too much in praise of such generosity cannot be said; and yet the fact remains that the whole amount of money furnished to our colleges and universities is lamentably meagre. This becomes strikingly apparent when the incomes of our institutions are compared with those of other countries. The Physiological Laboratory alone at Leipsic has an income of $40,000, and admits to its privileges but twelve students. The Natural History Department of the British Museum has an annual income of $100,000. The Zoölogical Society of London (which attends to the keeping of live animals solely for the purpose of studying their peculiarities) has an income varying from $100,000 to $125,000. The Kew Garden in London (which does a similar work for botany) has also $100,000 annually. The Zoölogical Society at Amsterdam expends $50,000; the Zoölogical Gardens at Hamburg, $30,000; the Berlin Aquarium (devoted to aquatic animals only), $50,000; the Jardin des Plantes, $200,000; the Museum at Edinburgh, $50,000; the College of Surgery at London (exclusively devoted to human and comparative anatomy), $60,000; the Imperial Geological Institute in Vienna, $40,000. These examples, purposely taken for better illustration, from a single department of liberal culture, might be indefinitely extended.

from those popular opinions concerning higher education to which I have alluded. There is a law that is more unchangeable than the laws of the Medes and the Persians; it is the law which establishes the correspondence of demand and supply. So long as men of small culture and men of no culture find easy access to the high, if not the highest, political stations in the gift of society, we may be sure that the men knocking most vigorously at our political doors will be our political charlatans. It is greatly to be feared that until a more healthy and enlightened public opinion on this subject shall come to prevail, a change for the better will be looked for in vain. When such men come to feel that for them there is no high place of political honor, the preparation of those who aspire to public life will be more complete and more satisfactory.

I wish not to be misunderstood. It is one of the glories of our country, that it affords rare opportunities for the encouragement of those who would rise from obscurity to honor. This we have heard at least as often as every Fourth of July. I am by no means disposed to question the truth of the assertion. The question of importance, however, is not whether men can rise, or whether they will attempt to rise; it is rather at what level will they be content to stop. I think no one can compare the average statesman of to-day with the man of similar rank seventy-five years ago, without an oppressive sense of the political degeneracy that has taken place. The generation which framed the Constitution and wrote the Federalist, has had no political successor. Surely, the reason is not that men have had fewer opportunities as time has progressed! Jefferson was a frontiersman, whose wife, at the time of their marriage, as Mr. Parton assures us, could only reach his log-house on horseback; and, yet, when he took his seat in the Continental Congress, though far from being the most learned man there, he was a proficient naturalist, a mathematician able to calculate an eclipse, and a master of four languages.*

If public opinion would to-day be content with nothing short of the highest moral and intellectual attainments, it is certain that within a few years the preparation of those who aspire to public life would be of a far higher order.

Now, in regard to the general worth of this care-

* It is a great mistake to suppose that self-made men are in any sense peculiar to our own country. There is not a nation in Western Europe that has not been largely ruled by such men during the past three hundred years. It was but the other day that the English papers told us how Richard Bethell went to college a poor boy; how from the age of seventeen he supported himself; how he rose to the highest position in the legal profession, and finally how, as Lord Chancellor, presiding over the entire nobility of Great Britain, he died a peer of the realm. The case of Lord Tenterden is another example to illustrate the same fact. Beginning life as the son of a country barber, without friends or influence to aid him, he ended it as Lord Chief Justice. For any who may think that with the aid of party machinery all these things were and are possible, it needs perhaps to be said, that, when Tenterden was offered the position of King's Counsel, he declined it from distrust of his own ability, and that finally, he was taken from his life of patient and unassuming labor and raised to the bench by his political opponents.

ful preliminary training, there comes an occasional lesson which we do well to heed. The war of the Rebellion was a case in point. It is generally remembered that early in the struggle a hue and cry was raised against our Military Academy at West Point. Those who predicted that the war would be terminated in a few months found, at the close of the first year, that the end was apparently as far off as ever. It is singular that so many failed to appreciate the magnitude of the struggle. It should have been generally foreseen that the South, with the advantage, not only of ample preparation, but also of a defensive policy, would be able to offer a resolute and a protracted resistance. Those political sages and editorial generals who found their predictions disappointed, fell to throwing the blame upon our military officers; and when one new man after another was raised to the head of the army, only to disappoint the nation, and be returned into obscurity, the outcry, which at first had been turned against individuals only, was directed against the whole class. Some of the most influential journals in the country appear to have seriously attempted in 1862 and '63 to make the nation believe that the man without the training afforded by West Point was likely to be a better soldier and a better general than the man with that training. In consequence of this absurdity, we had our era of civilian generals. Luckily, however, it took but a short time to satisfy even the most unreasonable, and our civilians gave way to men who seemed divinely called to the double work of putting an end to the war, and of showing to the American people that, if they have a special and difficult work to do, that work is likely to be best done by men who have received the most thorough training for it. When it turned out that Grant and Sherman and Sheridan and Thomas and Meade and the other great soldiers, South as well as North, were men who had all submitted to the rigors of a military training, there was no one found bold enough to renew the proposition to abolish our national Military Academy. It was apparent to everybody, that we must either abandon all thought of war in future, or we must sustain and enlarge our school for the education of officers.

But since the close of our war there has been brought to the attention of the world a far more luminous example in illustration of the same general truth. I refer, of course, to the Franco-German War of 1870. The results of that contest have been so momentous in shaping the subsequent history of the nations involved, that they are apt to overshadow all other considerations, if indeed they do not completely monopolize our attention. There is another fact, however, which, to the person studying that struggle, is even more important. I refer to the peculiar character of the war as a result rather than as a cause; to those systems of general training which gave to the Germans, on the one hand, both overwhelming strength and masterly skill, and to the French, on the other, not only weakness in the field but also corruption and imbecility in the Cabinet. Nothing can be more important to the student than a contemplation of these facts as results of certain causes. Let us look at them for a moment, beginning with Germany.

Whence came all this strength and all this skill? Glance, for a moment, at their growth as a historical fact. At the beginning of this century Prussia, though in name a kingdom, in fact, was hardly more than a province. No nation in modern times has been more completely crushed and overidden than was Prussia in her wars with Napoleon I. After the battle of Jena, she was obliged to surrender nearly half of all her territory and reduce her army to forty thousand men. But even in disaster, the characteristics of the nation and the people were distinctly visible. There was no blustering, or defying, or court-martialling of officers, or repudiating of monarchs; but instead, an earnest endeavor to learn the causes of the misfortune, and to remove them as speedily as possible. Through the efforts of Stein and Scharnhorst and their coadjutors a thorough transformation was wrought, not only in the army, but also in the civil service and in the system of education.

First of all, it was maintained that as the army was to exist for the good of all and for the protection of all, its burdens ought to fall upon all; these burdens, moreover, were interpreted to mean not only taxes, but actual service. From the king's sons, therefore, down to the sons of the poorest peasant, every man of able body was to be trained in the use of arms. The government took every young man, whether his rank were high or low, straightened him up, pulled back his shoulders, put a musket into his hands, required of him three or four hours of daily military service for a number of years—in a word, trained him for military work.

Then, too, as all classes, without excepting even the king's sons, were obliged to begin service in the ranks, the uniform of the private soldier was no badge of dishonor. It indicated neither the existence of social rank, nor the want of it. The Prussian army thus became a complete reproduction of Prussian culture. In any one of the Prussian universities scores of private uniforms were to be seen on the lecture-room benches—uniforms belonging to young men who, after doing three or four hours of guard or patrol duty, were carrying on those university studies which were interrupted when the time came for them to enter military service. When a war broke out the university soldiers took the field with the others. It was related by an English correspondent who marched with a company of soldiers to Sadowa, that as the group next him swung along in their ill-fitting uniforms with seventy rounds of ammunition, they relieved the tedium of the march by discussing in their regular order the different dialogues of Plato. We all remember the sensation that was produced in the war of 1870, when the famous *Kutschke Lied*, as an amusement merely of philological students in the army, was published in thirty-two different languages. These incidents amply illustrate the fact that the Prussian army embodies all the characteristics of Prussian culture. When a war breaks out the German throws down his pen, or his book, or his saw, or his hoe, and takes up his musket; in the use of which he has already had the most thorough training. The excellences and defects, therefore, of the German army are precisely those of the community at large, and, so far as I know, for the first time in history, we have a real example of the worth of mind and training in fitting men for carrying on the work of destruction. And what is the result? It is that you may look through the pages in history in vain to find an army out of which it was possible to get so much fighting, and marching, and indeed dying, as was got out of the German army from the moment it fired its first shot across the Rhine. It has been well said that there are some heights of devotion that are beyond the reach of ordinary troops. Ordinary men may be easily led under an excitement to lay down their lives recklessly; but of such a quality of soldiers only a certain amount can be deliberately and openly exacted. An able and a careful writer on the war has declared that if a Prussian commander found it necessary to have the cost of an assault fall on a single regiment, he had no difficulty in getting it to march to certain destruction, not blindly or hilariously like madmen, but calmly and deliberately like men who had made up their minds that it was their business to die, and that it was equally important that they should not get themselves killed one moment earlier than was necessary, nor one moment later.

Moreover, to this statement it ought to be added that the deliberate heroism of the troops was even less conspicuous than that general intelligence, that omnipresent promptitude, that universal "*knowing how to do it*," which everywhere characterized their movements. This peculiar quality became note-worthy even before the troops were in the field. Less than a week was required after the declaration of war for the mobilization of the army. Dr. Kapp wrote to the *Nation* that in passing from Cologne to Berlin he counted sixty-three military trains, not a single one of which was behind time. The whole of the Second Army Corps of 150,000 men was transferred from Berlin to Neukirchen, more than four hundred miles, in fifty hours; and every one of the hundred and fifty trains arrived punctually to the minute.

This spirit of punctuality and obedience was everywhere manifest during the movements in the field. From the beginning to the end of the war, while their enemies were committing blunder after blunder, not a German corps arrived at its destination too late to-accomplish its purpose.

Now, all these achievements are not to be considered the mere result of a levy *en masse* under the command of a great military genius; they are rather an application to military affairs of the whole intelligence of a nation of extraordinary mental and moral culture. They are the result of no qualities that can be drilled into an army in a month or a year; but of those which are interwoven with the very tissue of the nation's thinking and feeling. They came not from the genius of a few alone; but rather from the genius of the few, united with the superior training and culture of the many. They are the fruit of an application to military affairs of the actual *character* of the nation.

But what is this Prussian culture of which I speak? In general, it may be answered that it consists of those attainments which are acquired by the universal adoption of the truth, that whether you want a man for war or for peace, for a profession or for a trade, there is no way in which you can make so much of him as by training him, and training him not in parts, but as a whole; and furthermore, that in all the contests of life, other things being equal, the trained men are sure to attain the highest success. On this theory, not as a simple sentiment, but as a solid foundation on which to rear the whole fabric of society, the law-makers of Germany went to work.

First of all, they said to every parent: "You must have every child of yours in school from the age of six to the age of fourteen; to neglect this obligation is a crime against the state, and will be punished by law." Then to the child they said: "Whatever business or profession you desire to follow in life, for that you must thoroughly fit yourself, either as an apprentice, or as a professional student." And this was no mere vague generality. It was saying to the child: "If you would be a teacher of common schools, you must not only have a good common-school education, but you must also serve an apprenticeship of three years in a normal school, whose business is, not to teach, but to teach how to teach." It was saying to him: "If you aspire to any position as teacher in a gymnasium or university, there is one condition with which you must first of all comply. You must spend eight or nine years in a gymnasium" (equivalent to eight or nine years in an American academy and an American college); "after which, you must devote at least three years to the study of your profession in a university." They said to him, "Without those twelve years of preliminary training, eight or nine of which are collegiate, and three or four of which are professional, you can receive no degree, and until you have received a degree, you can collect no fee for legal advice; you can write no prescription; you can have no place as instructor in the smallest gymnasium in the land." In a word, all the professions were, and are, closed, except to men of such culture as comes from a complete course of collegiate and professional training.

Now of all these exactions, what is the result? Undoubtedly a considerable number of men are kept from the professions who would, in spite of any deficiencies in their early training, have risen to positions of honor and influence. And yet it must not be forgotten that although such men may be lost to a given profession, they are not, by the fact of their exclusion from that profession, lost to society as a whole. The same energy and ability which would have carried them over high obstacles, in case they had been permitted to make the attempt, is likely to achieve a similar success in some other calling. It is indeed doubtful whether the world will ever be the loser from the fact that any given man, though even a genius, is prevented by law from taking a short cut to either of the professions. In case of such prohibition, he is likely either to follow the prescribed course, or be equally useful in another vocation. But even if it were to be admitted that in some instances such a law imposes a harmful restraint, it would still remain true, that its general influence is vastly to elevate the respective trades and professions. It interferes often with the wishes, and sometimes even with the interests, of individuals; but it contributes to the welfare of society as a whole. While it makes it impossible for the individual to collect a fee which he has not fairly earned, it protects society from a vast amount of sheer impositions.

In no country have these good results been so conspicuous as in Germany. They now show themselves as the fruit of a very long continued policy, and are not to be misunderstood. It is a matter of universal notoriety that the professional men of Germany in all positions are great scholars and powerful thinkers. There are no fields of knowledge which they are not among the first to explore; no heights of speculation which they do not climb; no depths of reason which they do not penetrate; no hard problem over which they do not faithfully toil. Their keenness is equal to their comprehensiveness; and their love of what is thorough is only exceeded by their hatred of what is sham and slipshod. In the universities their attainments excite the admiration of students from all other countries, if indeed they do not fill them with despair. Their devotion to the work in hand is equally remarkable, whether they dedicate their energies to the genealogy of words, or the chemical analysis of fixed stars. In the whole range of liberal culture, it would, perhaps, not be easy to name a single branch of study in the prosecution of which there might not be found some German who, by the general consent of his profession, would be regarded as the foremost authority of his time. Professor Seeley, of the University of Cambridge, admitted and expressed it all, when he sweepingly said: "As a rule, good books are in German."

Now these are the results of that severe habit of training to which I have referred—a habit which lays its commands on all the vocations and employments of German society. It has not only made the little province into a duchy, the duchy into a kingdom, and the kingdom into the foremost power of Europe; but it has made such a race of scholars and thinkers, that if one desires the most complete and exact information on any subject whatever, one is likely to find it nowhere but in some one of the German universities. The German system of education, as a mere element of national strength, it is, perhaps, impossible to over-estimate.

Now, in the way of contrast, let us look for a moment at the system of education in France. Much might be said in regard to the kind of instruction given as compared with that of the German schools, but it will be enough in this connection to refer to a few facts as historically revealed.

When the great revolution broke out in France the nation had about 25,000,000 inhabitants. There were in the country five hundred and sixty-two *colleges*, or schools where classical instruction was given. In these schools there were 72,747 pupils. It was in these schools that young men of every rank and for every career had been trained. Here had been formed in the seventeenth and eighteenth centuries, that varied society of France, whose progress in all the paths of civilization, save the political and the religious, was so rapid and so brilliant. But the Revolution swept all these institutions away. The professors were dispersed; the property was sold. When, at the close of the revolutionary *régime*, men began to look about for means of reviving the schools, it was found that the corporations devoted to public instruction had ceased to exist, and that the ancient endowments had been scattered to the winds.

It was not long before the painful consequences of this misfortune made themselves felt. It was found that with the means the desire had disappeared also. Dr. Chalmers once eloquently said that there is this difference between the material and the intellectual wants of man: while the former pursue their satisfaction with unwearied ardor, the latter, if left to themselves, become feeble and torpid. The hungry man struggles to procure for himself food by any effort and at any risk; while the man who has no moral or intellectual culture is content to do without it; and the more complete his intellectual destitution, the less sensible is he of his want. So it was in France. When the means of gratifying the intellectual appetite was removed, the cravings of that appetite came soon to be no longer felt. The few private schools that were established presented no allurements save to the rich and the more ambitious. The great mass of the French people, for more than forty years before Louis Philippe ascended the throne, had no educational privileges whatever, and, worse than all, they came more and more to have no intellectual appetites. Under the reign of Louis Philippe, it is true, great efforts were made to create a favorable reaction. The department of Public Instruction was placed in the hands of men like Guizot and Villemain; and under the guidance of their genius a great change was made for the better. And yet, after all their efforts, continued through eighteen years, the people in 1848 had so imperfectly recovered from the loss of their schools, that with a population of 36,000,000 they had in their high schools only 69,341 pupils, whereas, in 1789, with a population of only 25,000,000, the number of pupils had been as high as 72,747. In other words, at the outbreak of the Revolution the proportion of the pupils in the *colleges* to all the inhabitants of the country, was one in every three hundred and forty-two; while in 1848 the proportion was only one in every five hundred and nineteen. The significance of these facts, in themselves considered, is perhaps striking enough, and yet their full force will be felt only when we remember the educational tendency of the age. While all the other nations of Europe have been making great advances toward more light and more culture, France has been actually retreating into intellectual darkness. That there are in France great scholars of which the nation has just reason to be proud, there is, of course, no disposition to deny, for any such denial would be untruthful and absurd; but to say that the general culture which comes from a severe training in the schools is a characteristic of the French people of the present generation, would be a declaration as much at variance with the statistics as it would be contrary to the results of all discriminating observation.

Furthermore, on this subject there is no lack of positive evidence. The report of the French Minister of Public Instruction for 1865 shows that of those conscripted in the preceding year 30.40 per cent. could neither read nor write.* From a similar report made to the Prussian Parliament in 1869, it is found that of the soldiers enrolled, not simply in Prussia, but in all Germany, during the previous year, the number of those in a similar condition of illiteracy amounted to but 3.80 per cent., while in the kingdom of Saxony the proportion was only seventeen one hundredths of one per cent.†

It is not necessary, in this connection, to say more in detail concerning the condition of the masses of the French people. It is enough that we have the most important elements of the political problem before us. Thirty per cent. of all the male inhabitants of France are unable to read; universal suffrage so firmly established that its expediency is no longer a practical question; a revolutionary spirit that is permanently content with nothing,—

* M. Taine in his work on Universal Suffrage, has put the proportion of the illiterate still higher. He says that of every hundred persons of the male sex there are *thirty-nine* who cannot read or write; and that, as the illiterate belong almost exclusively to the rural population, it may fairly be estimated, that of the rural voters fully one-half are destitute of even the rudiments of an elementary education. *Du Suffrage Universel et de la Manière de voter*, p. 16.

† In comparison with these figures it is interesting to note the proportion of illiteracy in the United States. According to the *Report of the Commissioner of Education for* 1872, p. 963, the proportion of illiterate male adults for the country is 17.15. In South Carolina it ranges as high as 56.28; while in New Hampshire it is only 3.73. In Massachusetts it is 7.97; in Michigan, 6.04.

these are the factors which the reader should keep constantly in mind. The growth of this revolutionary spirit, and its method of dealing with the hard political questions that from time to time present themselves, will constitute not the least important part of our study. As we progress, I think we shall see how the political ideas engendered by the Revolution could only be salutary in case of general intelligence and virtue; how, in the absence of these, the lowest classes in the exercise of their newly acquired privileges took possession of the nation, and then turned it over without guarantee into the hands of an unscrupulous despotism; how the shocked and indignant virtue of the nation called for a return to the *régime* of peace and development; how the government in the hands of the bourgeoisie was enabled for a time to control the masses, which were at once brutalized by ignorance and inflamed by ideas inherited from the Revolution; how, in 1848, the masses, a second time, took possession of the government, only to pave the way for a second despotism; how, by the suffrage of ignorance and vice the Napoleonic dynasty was restored and confirmed; how, by a network of frauds and deceptions, the people were entrapped into the belief that they were enjoying a representative government, while in fact they were living under the most dangerous form of despotism; and, finally, how, when the moment of severe trial came, the political fabric crumbled into dust, as if for a warning to the nations.

THE PHILOSOPHERS OF THE REVOLUTION.

"French Philosophism has arisen; in which little word how much do we include! Here, indeed, lies properly the cardinal symptom of the whole widespread malady. Faith is gone out; scepticism has come in. Evil abounds and accumulates; no man has faith to withstand it, to amend it, to begin by amending himself; it must even go on accumulating."—*Carlyle, French Revolution*, vol. I. p. 13.

"If I were to give a Scriptural genealogy of our modern popular writers, I should say that Rousseau lived twenty years, and then begat Bernardin de St. Pierre; that Bernardin de St. Pierre lived twenty years, and then begat Chateaubriand; that Chateaubriand lived twenty years, and then begat Victor Hugo; and that Victor Hugo, being tempted of the devil, is begetting every day."—*De Tocqueville, Memoir and Remains*, vol. II. p. 116.

CHAPTER II.

THE PHILOSOPHERS OF THE REVOLUTION.

THE history of France during the present century is the heritage of the Revolution and of the causes by which the Revolution was produced. Let us look briefly at some of those causes, and then at some of the ideas which in the course of the Revolution came to prevail.

Previous to the reign of Louis XIV., the political elements of French society had settled into three distinct divisions more or less antagonistic to one another. These elements—the crown, the nobility, and the people—struggled each for an ascendency over the other two. The people had little consciousness of political rights, little political education, and little interest in the general affairs of the country; they were, therefore, in no condition to wage an equal political warfare with their enemies. Nothing but an alliance with either the crown or the nobility could insure their political safety.

In Germany the people were becoming more and more allied in their interests with the nobility, so that the latter were becoming strong enough to defy the power of the Emperor. The consequence of this alliance was that the petty governments into which the Empire was divided secured for themselves a constantly increasing power, and were finally enabled to gain a complete independence.*

A similar alliance took place in England under King John. The nobles were able to enlist the sympathies and the support of the people in their cause against the King, and the result was the Great Charter and the Constitutional Liberty which England has since enjoyed.

In France, however, the alliance was of a different nature. Under the feudal system there sprang up between the nobles and the people a violent antagonism, and this was soon followed by a similar hostility between nobility and royalty. The people found that they had no guarantees with which to protect themselves against the rapacity of the feudal lords so long as the feudal relations were maintained, and consequently they everywhere attempted to find relief in revolt. Roughly stated, the result of the general attempt to throw off the feudal yoke was the system of free cities. The nobles for their part, saw that in their feudal castles they could easily and successfully defy royalty; and moved by the same ambition that inspired their brethren across the Rhine, they attempted to establish a similar independence. But they soon discovered that they were between two fires. The kings on the one side and the people on the other recognized the common interests of their cause.

* For a good portrayal of the influences which led to this separation of the German States, *v. Häusser's Deutsche Geschichte, Einleitung.*

It came about at length that a more or less effective alliance was established. From the death of Charles VII., in 1461, to the accession of Louis XIV., in 1643, the internal history of France was little more than one long war between the nobles and their remaining feudal adherents, on the one hand, and the kings, supported with more or less fidelity by the people, on the other. Recall to mind the gibbet and cages of Louis XI., the campaigns and executions of Henry IV., the treatment of the Parliament of Paris and of the nobles in revolt by Richelieu—wherever one looks, one sees that the heaviest blows and the sharpest thrusts of royalty were directed against the *nobles*, and that at the same time it was in the *kings* that the people found their firmest allies and their best friends. It must not be supposed that the kings were desirous of securing the liberties of the people; such was certainly not the fact. They simply found the people the most convenient weapons with which to fight their most formidable enemies.

In the reign of Louis XIV., however, much of this was changed. The nobles had been so weakened by the blows of Richelieu and the craft of Mazarin that they had no longer hope of securing independence, and no longer power to make themselves feared. But they were still gentlemen of elegance, and could adorn a court even if they could not win a battle. The King was ambitious to gather from every source, within and without the realm, all that would add to the grace and the distinction of his reign. Poets and orators and artists made haste to devote themselves to his service. There were no heights of adulation to which they did not climb—no depths of mire in which they did not bedraggle the garments of their genius. When all the wits of that age of wit were burning incense and singing pæans to *le grand monarque*, was there any reason why the nobles, now that their old position was hopelessly gone, should stubbornly maintain an obscure silence? The King easily won them over to his power. Elegant lords and ladies were now flitting about in the gay *salons* of Paris and Versailles; and the alliance of royalty and nobility was complete.

Meantime, alas for the common people! The wars of the Alliance and the Succession desolated the land. The industries were crippled. Taxation, from which the nobility and the clergy were practically exempt, was multiplied, until increased taxation brought no increase of revenue. As had occurred at Rome after the last Punic war, so now in France, the rich and the poor were divided asunder, and the dividing line, which at first was merely an imaginary thing, became a chasm, and finally a great gulf which no man could cross. As the rich became richer, and the poor poorer, the class of yeomanry,—that very class which carried the Roman Eagles to the Tyne and the Euphrates, which, under Edward III. of England, had threatened to make all France subject to the English crown, and which, under the white plume of Navarre had reduced to allegiance all the enemies of the French crown,—that great middle class which is the bone and sinew of every robust nation, in the age of Louis XIV. and Louis XV. practically ceased to exist. France was hopelessly divided into two parts, one of which had its type in the splendors of the court, and the other in the squalor of the hovel. The whole system tended to endow the upper class with all privileges without exacting any corresponding service in return; to exhaust the lower classes by taxation without conferring upon them any corresponding political rights.* Two-thirds of the soil was owned by a few nobles and great land-holders, while the remaining one-third was divided among nearly 4,000,000 peasant owners. From so small a field as each of these possessed, it was impossible to gain a living. Millions of the people came to have no other food than bread, with a little lard and gruel.†

* The contrast between the luxury of the rich and the indigence of the populace is placed in a glowing light by VON SYBEL in his *Geschichte der Französische Revolution.* Among other interesting things, he shows that in the ministry of Colbert, while only 60,400 hands were employed in the manufacture of woollens, 17,300 were employed in the manufacture of laces; and that while the manufacture of *soap* was of the value of only 18,000,000 francs a year, that of *hair powder* was no less than 24,000,000.

† Historians of this period have often conveyed the impression, if they have not directly asserted, that one of the most formidable difficulties in France grew out of the fact that the laws were exclusively in the hands of the nobility and the church. It is certain, however, that such was not the fact. The best of all authorities on the subject, Arthur Young, assures us that about a third of the land was in the pos-

It is not necessary to attempt the portrayal of the wrongs of the French people during that cruel eighteenth century; it is enough for my purpose to indicate what I believe to be their leading cause; and perhaps to add that the union of royalty and aristocracy continued through a full century, and that during all that period the people were ground as between the upper and the nether millstone. Buckle has remarked, apparently not without reason, that if ever there existed a government that was radically and inherently bad, it was the government of France in the eighteenth century, and that the delay of the Revolution is one of the most striking proofs afforded by history of the force of established habit and of the tenacity with which humanity clings to old associations.

While the mass of the people, thus despoiled and enslaved, were accumulating a stock of bitterness and ferocity to be poured out on some future day of national reckoning, there were other powers at work which it is necessary now to consider. I mean the principal currents of national thought,—that peculiar literature of the time which made upon the nation so deep and so permanent an impression.

To the writers of that age it is difficult and per-

session of small proprietors. Turgot himself plainly showed that one of their most serious difficulties arose, not from the fact that their lands were undivided, but from the fact that the subdivision was carried too far. On the same subject, and on the indigence of the poor, *v.* De Tocqueville, *L'Ancien Régime, p.* 60; and COCHUT in *Revue des Deux Mondes*, Sept., 1848.

haps even impossible to attach too much importance, for whether we consider them as simply gathering into system the loose thoughts that were at the time floating among the people, or whether we regard them purely as the originators of the methods of thought that came to be generally adopted, the fact remains that they furnished both the ground and the justification of the events that followed. Of these writers there were four that may be regarded as typical of the whole class. They exerted an influence which in this connection deserves to be somewhat carefully noted. I mean Helvetius, Condillac, Voltaire, and Rousseau.

In the year 1758 Helvetius published his *De L'Esprit*, a book which is generally considered the ablest and most influential work on morals produced in France during the last century. The work sustains the same relation to ethics that Atheism does to the Christian religion. The author sets out with the declaration that the difference between man and other animals is simply the difference in their external form; that if Nature, instead of giving us hands and flexible joints, had terminated our limbs with hoofs like those of a horse, we should have remained wanderers on the earth, chiefly anxious to find our needful supply of food, and to protect ourselves against the attacks of wild beasts.* That the structure of our bodies

* "Si la nature, au lieu des mains et des doigts flexibles, eût terminé nos poignets par un pied de cheval; qui doute que les hommes, sans art, sans habitation, sans défence contre les animaux, tout occupés du

is thus the sole cause of our superiority over the beasts, he argues from the fundamental doctrine that our thoughts are simply the product of two faculties which we have in common with the beasts, namely, the faculty of receiving impressions from external objects, and the faculty of remembering those impressions. From these premises it was easy to deduce the conclusion, that inasmuch as our sensibility and memory are fundamentally the same as those of all other animals, they would remain as useless as those of all other animals, were it not for the external peculiarities for which we are so eminently distinguished.* It must be, therefore, that to those external peculiarities we owe everything that is most valuable. To take any other view is to allow ourselves to be deceived by conventional expressions and by the prejudices of ignorant men. Furthermore, memory, he asserted, is only one of the organs of sensibility †; and judgment is only a sensation. ‡

soin de pourvoir à leur nouriture et d'éviter les bêtes féroces, ne fussent encore errants dans les forêts commes les troupeaux fugitifs ?" —*Oeuvres de Helvétius*, *London*, 1781, vol. I. p. 2.

* "Ces facultés, que je regarde comme les causes productrices de nos pensées, et qui nous sont communes avec les animaux, ne nous fourniraient cependant q'un très-petit nombre d'idées, si elles n'étaient jointes en nous à une certaine organisation extérieure."—*Oeuvres de Helvétius*, vol. I. p. 2.

† "En effet la mémoire ne peut être qu'un des organes de la sensibilité physique."—*Oeuvres*, vol. I. p. 4.

‡ "Je conclus que tout jugement n'est qu'une sensation."—*Oeuvres*, vol. I. p. 4: also "*Juger* n'est jamais que *sentir*," p. 7.

From these premises Helvetius argued that all our notions of virtue and duty must be tested by reference to our senses; in other words, by the gross amount of physical enjoyment which they afford. The loftiest virtues as well as the meanest vices are *caused*, not simply *indicated*, by the pleasure we find in their exercise. All our emotions spring directly from our physical sensibilities; and, as our sensibilities are dependent upon the outer world, it follows that everything that we have, and everything that we are, we owe to the objects which surround us. In short, man is nothing and can be nothing except what he is made by the circumstances in which he is placed.*

The general tendency of this system of reasoning is too manifest to require any lengthy discussion. It will answer our purpose to indicate one or two of the most curious conclusions to which it directly led. If it be true that there are no virtues except in those objects and actions which minister to the pleasure of our senses, it follows as a necessary corollary that in order to possess the highest virtue we have but to abandon ourselves most completely to the gratification of our appetites and passions. Again, if it be true that man is nothing except what he is made by the objects which surround

* "La conclusion générale de ce Discours, est que tous les hommes, communément bien organisés, ont en eux la puissance physique de s'élever aux plus hautes idées; et que la différence d'ésprit qu'on remarque entre eux, dépend des diverses circonstances dans lesquelles ils se trouvent placés, et de l'education differente qu'ils recoivent."—*Oeuvres*, vol. I. p. 407.

him, it follows that if he finds he is not what he desires to be, his effort should be to change those surrounding objects, since it is these that compel him to be what he is. If those objects are political forms, the political forms should be changed or swept away. If they are the demands of the church, the church must be condemned. If they spring from the restraints of any system of religious belief even, such a system can only contribute to the unhappiness of the race. Thus the system of Helvetius carried out to its natural conclusions furnishes a logical justification, at once, for atheism and for revolution. It does even more than that: it not only establishes them, but it sanctifies them and even makes them a solemn duty, since it founds them upon the requirements and conditions of a severe system of morals. Finally, as if to leave no allurement unused, it completes its attractions by urging the superiority of the passions over the intellect, and by advocating their encouragement and license.*

The extent of the influence of these doctrines can be estimated only after an inquiry concerning the manner in which they were received. In our own day such a work could have no appreciable influence, for it would have no readers except among those who have already thrown off the conventional

* Chaps. VII. and VIII. of Discours III. are devoted to proving "La supériorité d'ésprit des gens passionés, sur les gens sensés," and that "On devient stupide, dès qu'on cesse d'être passioné."—*Oeuvres*, vol. I. pp. 187 et 193.

restraints of respectability. In France, however, during the last century the case was far otherwise. The tone of society was such that it seized with avidity for its justification and encouragement a work of such ability and character.* The consequence was that the *De L'Esprit* of Helvetius not only secured for its author a European reputation, but it increased in influence, especially in France, down to the end of the century. Surin, though a zealous opponent of Helvetius, declares that "strangers the most eminent for their dignity and their culture desire to be introduced to a philosopher whose name is spoken in all parts of Europe." † Brissot, who wrote twenty years and more after the publication of *De L'Esprit*, says that the system of Helvetius was in the greatest vogue.‡ Turgot refers to it as a system that was praised "with a kind of fury," § and Georgel declares that the book was to be found on every table. ‖ In referring to the popularity of the work, Cousin speaks of it as having established itself, almost without combat, in all the ranks of society and in the *salons* of the capital, so that Madame Dudeffant, a person who represented

* Cousin has well expressed the fact in saying, "Le siècle de Louis XV. se reconnut dans l'ouvrage d'Helvétius."—*Hist. de la Philos.*, I. Série, vol. III. p. 201.

† *Biog. Univ.*, vol. XX. p. 33.

‡ *Mémoires*, vol. I. p. 339.

§ *Oeuvres*, vol. IX. p. 297.

‖ "Ce livre se trouvait sur toutes les tables."—*Mémoires*, vol. II. p. 256.

the intelligence of her epoch, could say with truth, "The success of the book of Helvetius is not surprising: he is the man who has told the secret of everybody." *

These references might be reinforced by others drawn from the various branches of French literature of that period; but it is unnecessary. Enough has been said to indicate the powerful hold which the system of Helvetius had upon the different ranks of French society. It is sufficient that we have seen the general character of the work, and that for fifty years before the outbreak of the Revolution, it was the code of morals most generally accepted by the French people.

Four years before the publication of his *De L'Esprit*, had appeared the ablest work of the greatest French metaphysician of the last century.†

I refer to the celebrated treatise of Condillac on the Sensations. Setting out from the great work of Locke on the Human Understanding as a starting-point, and rejecting one-half of Locke's theory, Condillac wrought out a system of the

* *Hist. Mod. Philos., Trans. by Wight.*, vol. I. p. 61.

† "Condillac représente en France la Philosophie du dix-huitième siécle comme Descartes représente celle du dix-septième." (*Cousin, Premiers Essais de Philosophie*, p. 128.) "Condillac est le métaphisicien français du XVIII siécle. (*Hist. de la Philos.*, I. Série, vol. III. p. 83. "Traité des Sensations, sans comparaison, le chef-d'œuvres de Condillac." (*Hist. de la Philoso.*, II. Série, vol. II. p. 77.) "The first writer who undertook the expounding of Locke's philosophy was Condillac, a writer who is universally placed at the head of the whole modern school of French sensationalism."—*Morell's Hist. of Mod. Philos.*, p. 194.

purest sensationalism. His effort, as he plainly declared, was to show by the most subtle course of reasoning that all our knowledge is the product of sensations.*

Cousin sums up the characteristics of the system by saying that it is "sensation transformed, becoming successively conscience, memory, attention, all our faculties, and engendering all our ideas." † Condillac's method of argument it is unnecessary to trace, except in the briefest possible outline. While Locke distinguished two sources of our ideas—sensation and memory—Condillac affirmed that memory is but another form of sensation, ‡—is, indeed, in its principle, only sensation itself,—is less the source of our ideas than the channel in which our ideas flow. It follows, then, that everything which we know is the result of sensation; in other words, of the impression made upon us by the external world. § Accordingly, Nature is the

* "Le principal objet de cet ouvrage est de faire voir comment toutes nos connaissances et toutes nos facultés viennent des sens, ou, pour parler plus exactement des sensations : car, dans le vrai, les sens ne sont que cause occasionelle. Ils ne sentent pas, c'est l'ame seule qui sent à l'occasion des organes ; et c'est des sensations qui la modifient, qu'elle tire toutes ses connaissances et toutes ses facultés."—*Oeuvres de Condillac*, vol. III. p. 3.

† *Premiers Essais de Philosophie*, p. 139.

‡ La mémoire n'est donc que la sensation transformée."—*Oeuvres de Condillac*, vol. III. p. 17.

§ "Il resulte de cette vérité, que la nature commence tout en nous: aussi ai-je démontré que, dans le principe ou dans le commencement, nos connaissances sont uniquement son ouvrage, que nous ne nous instruissons que d'après ses leçons ; et que l'art de raissoner consiste à continuer comme elle nous a fait commencer."—*Oeuvres*, vol. III. p.

beginning of all, and it is to Nature that we owe all our knowledge.

Now observe how completely these conclusions harmonize with those of Helvetius. If it be true that all our ideas are formed by sensation alone, then we are what we are from the nature of those objects about us, from which our sensations are divided. If it be true that the distinguishing characteristics of humanity lie in the peculiarities of sensation, must we not conclude that morality consists simply in being true to the demands and suggestions of sensation? The logic is relentless. It comes then to this: we are *morally bound* to obey the impulses created within us by the objects with which we come in contact,—and what is that but saying that the only moral obligation which rests upon us is to be immoral?

We may be tempted to think, for the moment, that a course of reasoning which leads to so paradoxical a conclusion must have carried with it very little power of conviction; but no greater mistake could be made. Whatever may be thought of the philosophical merit of Condillac's theories, there can be no denying that they were urged and enforced by a closeness and severity of reasoning which was altogether extraordinary. Cousin,

178. Also, "La nature n'avait donc qu'un moyen de lui faire connaitre son corps, et ce moyen était de lui faire apercevoir ses sensations, non comme des modifications de son ame mais comme des modifications des organes qui en sont antant de causes occasionelles." —*Ibid.* p. 179.

though a hostile critic, has declared, as already stated, that Condillac was the one French metaphysician of the last century, and that of his works, the *Traité des Sensations* was beyond all comparison the ablest. In fact, the metaphysical work of Condillac was received with a *fureur* quite similar to that which had displayed itself on the publication of the work of Helvetius on morals.

I have spoken of the characteristics of these works, not for the sake of parading their monstrosities, but in order to show the nature of an influence which for two generations in France was well-nigh irresistible. Without understanding that influence, it is impossible to understand the last three-fourths of a century of French history. Let us inquire, then, briefly what their influence was.

In the first place, it can hardly be doubted that on the progress of science the doctrines of which I have spoken had a stimulating influence of considerable power. As Nature was placed above everything else, it was natural that Nature should receive an extraordinary amount of attention. And this extraordinary devotion to Nature was not left without its rewards. The laws of the radiation and conduction of heat were worked out by Prevost and Fourier; Malus discovered the polarization of light; Lavoisier hit upon the true theory of oxidation and respiration, and was the first to adopt a systematic chemical nomenclature; Buffon and Rouelle prepared the way for a new science by explaining the instability of the earth's surface, while Cuvier made such advances in geology and in comparative anatomy as to entitle him to be regarded as one of the greatest naturalists that Europe has ever produced. Indeed, there was no realm of Nature into which those worshippers of Nature did not push their industry and their intelligence. The result was that France, during the latter half of the eighteenth century, probably added more new truths to our knowledge of the external world than the nation had added during the whole of its previous history.

But what was their influence on religion? Naturally enough, of a character precisely the opposite of that just considered. Indeed, it could not be otherwise. If, as Helvetius declared, all our notions of duty and virtue are to be tested by their relation to the senses, surely it is unreasonable to ask that we obey any other commands than those of our senses. If man be nothing except what he is made by the objects which surround him, he is under no obligations except such as bind him to those objects. If, as Condillac affirmed, our senses are the only factors of our ideas, then we can have no knowledge of anything which is beyond the possible cognition of our senses. If, in fine, Nature be the ultimate source of all, it is merely an absurd contradiction to suppose that there is anything beyond Nature, or back of Nature. The conclusion of all is that there is no God.

Nor was this a mere speculation which took no deep hold of the natures of the people. Many things had occurred to weaken such religious earnestness as they previously may have had. The logic of the new theories was flattering to intelligent minds, and, above all, there was a delicious freedom in feeling that old-time restraints were broken away, and that now there was nothing to be worshipped but the objects which minister to the gratification of the senses. Now notice the result. Burton, in his life of Hume, relates that in 1764 the historian visited Paris, and that at the house of Baron d'Holbach he met a party of the most celebrated Frenchmen then residing at Paris. The Scotchman took occasion to raise a question in regard to the *actual existence* of an atheist. "For my *own* part," said he, "I have never chanced to meet one." "You have been unfortunate," replied Holbach, "but at the present moment you are sitting at table with seventeen of them." Priestly, who visited France ten years later, declared: "All the philosophical persons to whom I was introduced at Paris were unbelievers in Christianity, and even professed atheists." When in 1770 the "*System of Nature*," a work which was generally regarded as the code and hand-book of atheism, was published, it was read and praised by everybody; in the words of Voltaire, by "*des savants, des ignorants, des femmes*." Even the archbishop of Toulouse, in an address to the King in behalf of the clergy, declared, in 1775, that atheism had become the dominant opinion. In short, the fashionable belief of French society during the last part of the last century was that Christianity was a pernicious delusion, and that professing Christians were either hypocrites or imbeciles. It might with entire consistency have adopted as its own the audacious creed of La Mettrie, which has been condensed by a modern historian into these words: "Everything spiritual is a delusion, and physical enjoyment is the highest end of man. Faith in the existence of God is as groundless as it is fruitless. The world will not become happy till atheism becomes universally established. Immortality is an absurdity. The soul perishes with the body of which it forms a part. With death everything is over, *la farce est jouée.* Let us enjoy ourselves as long as we exist, and not throw away any satisfaction." *

But it is time to inquire in regard to the *political* influence of these doctrines.

Perhaps nothing is more familiar to the historical student than the fact that religious and political commotions often go hand in hand. A mistake is sometimes made by supposing that the latter are caused by the former. They are rather the children of the same parent,—not the one the child of the other. This was especially the case in France just before the French Revolution. The same philosophy which manifested contempt for

* Schwegler, *Hist. of Phil.*, p. 207.

existing forms in religion, was equally powerful in supplanting all respect for existing forms in politics. The logic of those political thinkers who had taken their position on the doctrines in morals and metaphysics to which I have referred, when reduced to its simplest form, was as follows: We are, religiously, politically, socially, and individually, what we are made by the objects which surround us. We are not what we desire to be. As we can only change what we are by changing those objects which make us what we are, so we must overthrow those objects before we can become what we desire. Thus the doctrines of the age were not simply the philosophy of atheism; they were also the philosophy of revolution. When the political wrongs of the age are remembered; when we call to mind the financial and social condition of the people; when we see taking firm root in their minds and hearts a philosophy which at once indicates all the causes of their woes and points to a means of escape from them, we see that everything was ready, and that to produce an explosion nothing but an occasion was needed.

Before the occasion arrived, however, other materials, which we must now consider, were added to the mass of combustibles. For the absolute perfection of preparation the influence of Voltaire and Rousseau was still to be supplied.

The extraordinary homage paid to the memory of Voltaire at the time his remains were transferred to the Pantheon in 1791, was hardly more than a just recognition of what he had done for the Revolution.*

When a mere boy, he had felt the hard rigors of the old *régime.* Educated under the direction of dissolute priests, he came to believe as earnestly as he ever believed anything, that all priests were hypocrites, and that Christianity was a deception and a fraud. His quick eye saw with great clearness the abuses of the government, and his quick wit enabled him to expose them. As early as 1716, a satire was published in which the most prominent wrongs of the nation were portrayed. The different members of the court were assailed with an energy and a grace which revealed the hand of a master. On the evidence of a single line Arouet (for he had not yet become Voltaire) was suspected of the authorship, and was accordingly thrown into the Bastile.† He was, how-

* Though Voltaire at the time of his death was the idol of the people, the influence of the church was still such as to exclude his remains from interment in consecrated ground. In 1791 the rod of the priests had been broken, and it was consequently decreed that the remains should be transferred to the Cathedral of French Philosophy. The funeral ceremony was the most magnificent ever given to the memory of a private individual. The march of expiation continued six hours, and was participated in by every member of the National Assembly and every member of the city government. The culmination of this apotheosis was perhaps the graceful stanza of Le Brun:

"O Parnasse, frémis de douleur et d'effroi!
Pleurez, Muses, brisez vos lyres immortelles!
Toi dont il fatigua les cent voix et les ailes
Dis que Voltaire est mort, pleure et repose toi!"

Dictionnaire Universel, vol. 18.

† "J'ai vu ces maux, et *je n'ai pas vingt ans.*" As Arouet was the only *young* poet supposed to be able to produce so good a poem, the critics

ever, innocent of the crime charged, and as he was imprisoned without trial, his hatred of arbitrary power was intensified from a mere sentiment into a real passion. His power and his wit * were already mature, and, from the moment of his release, he let no opportunity escape of making them felt.

In the interests of political liberty, it may perhaps be admitted that Voltaire did good service; at least he would have done good service had he been surrounded by a different atmosphere. The maxims of the old despotism he attacked with a power that was irresistible. That despotism had found its best exponent and defence in the matchless eloquence of Bossuet. The book of this great preacher, entitled "Politics drawn from the Bible," was an able endeavor to justify the maxims of an unlimited monarchy and an unbridled priesthood. It has been called the Catechism of absolution and the Testament of the age of Louis XIV. It was really the embodiment and the consecration of the old *régime* and its worst abuses. The author recalled these abuses and supported them by numerous texts of Scripture. His argument in its nature

and the government at once believed that they had detected the authorship, though no other evidence was produced.

* The Duke of Orleans, informed of Voltaire's innocence, set him at liberty and sent him a liberal sum of money. The wit of the poet's answer shows that he was ready for any emergency: "Monseigneur, je remercie votre altesse royale de vouloir bien continuer à se charger de ma nourriture, mais je la pris de ne plus se charger de mon logement."—*Dic. Univ.*, vol. XVIII. p. 116.

and in its effect was identical with the one which was so familiar to us in the days of slavery. It served to couple absolution and religion together, and in the estimation of many to make them alike obnoxious. Both were vigorously assailed by Voltaire. It was not long before the book of Bossuet was scornfully repudiated by the people; and its influence, even with many of the clergy, was completely destroyed.

In the year 1761 an event occurred which gave Voltaire a national popularity, which his literary genius alone, great as it was, could hardly have secured. The son of a Protestant, by the name of Calas, was found strangled. He had been of a melancholy temperament, and had probably committed suicide. But the father was charged with having committed the deed to get rid of his son. He was put upon trial and was required to prove his innocence; but as this was impossible, eight of his judges against five thought him guilty, and he was accordingly put to death. The remaining members of the family moved to Geneva, where Voltaire became acquainted with the facts of the trial. His indignation was aroused, and he investigated the whole matter. He submitted the results of his inquiries to the judgment of the world. As the facts were revealed, the iniquity of the affair became so notorious that the government was obliged to grant the petition of the family for a new trial. The result was that fifty judges, after carefully examining all the evidence, declared that Calas had been innocent. It was of course something that the name and honor of an innocent man were at length vindicated, although the man himself had already suffered an ignominious death. The real importance of the case, however, is in the fact that it brought Voltaire so prominently before the nation. His eloquent championship of an innocent man introduced him to the sympathies of all the people, and secured for him a favorable hearing. The sympathies of the church had been so enlisted in the case against the Calas family, that Voltaire was able to direct his shots with most telling effect. Nowhere else in all his writings did he attack the church with so much vigor and with such apparent reason as in the treatise called out by this celebrated case.* Beaumarchais, in speaking of the work, refers to it as "the book which contains the most terrible objection that can be raised against religion.† "Why," demanded Voltaire, "do the clergy, who enjoy a fifth of all the property in the state, insist upon making war upon the people? Would you listen to a professor of physics who should be paid for teaching a particular system, and who would lose his fortune in case he should teach any other? Would you listen to a man who preaches humility while he insists upon being called *Monseigneur*, and vol-

* *Traité sur la Tolerance à l'occasion de la Mort de Jean Calas.* --*Oeuvres de Voltaire* (*Beaumarchais edition*), vol. XXX. p. 39.

† *Oeuvres de Voltaire*, vol. XXX. p. 50.

untary poverty while he is accumulating his benefices?" *

The service of Voltaire in the interests of the Calas family illustrates perfectly the spirit with which he treated all questions of a social and political nature. He was strictly a humanitarian; and wherever he saw abuses,—and they were everywhere about him,—he did not hesitate to attack them with all the fervor at his command. There was, moreover, in all his writings a vivacity so sparkling, and an urbanity so exquisite, that he seldom failed to awaken the most hearty and complete sympathy of his readers. The influence of these literary characteristics was encouraged both by his own method of thought, and by the peculiar atmosphere by which he was surrounded. He was, in every sense of the word, a disbeliever; in every system of positive belief he saw what he thought to be so many inconsistencies, that it was impossible for him to adopt any belief whatever. His mind seemed to be constantly on the search for something on which he could flash the fire of his wit; and it happened that at the period when he wrote, the material for the gratification of this quality of his genius was unusually abundant. It was precisely this habit of mind which made it impossible for him to believe ardently in anything. If an atheist is one who believes that there is no God, Voltaire was certainly not an atheist; if, on

* *Oeuvres de Voltaire*, vol. XXX. p. 50.

the other hand, an atheist is one who has no positive belief that there *is* a God, he was an atheist. If asked categorically whether he believed in the existence of a Supreme Being, he probably would have answered in substance: "I don't know, and I know of no way in which I can ascertain." There is a kind of unbelief which is not satisfied with denying, but which asserts its negative as dogmatically as an opponent would assert a positive. Its habit is to assert earnestly that such or such a statement is not true; or that such or such a thing does not exist. There is another species which contents itself with denial; it believes neither in the negative nor the positive; it says practically, "I do not believe that there is a God; neither do I believe that there is not a God; I have no sufficient evidence for a positive faith, one way or the other." Now, of these two species of scepticism, the latter is by far the more dangerous, since it is likely to command by far the greatest influence. In every system of positive belief there are at least apparent difficulties, which, in the hands of a genius, may be made to appear ridiculous; and the more numerous the inconsistencies, the greater the opportunity of the apostle of disbelief. There never was a time in the history of any nation when such opportunities were more numerous than in France during the last century.*

* The only period which bears any considerable resemblance to it, is that which just preceded the Reformation. From a religious point of view, the condition of society at the beginning of the fifteenth century

The condition of French morals, partly created and partly indicated by the philosophers whose works I have just discussed, gave to Voltaire, of course, every encouragement. This state of society, and the peculiar qualities of the author's mind, furnish a complete key to the enormous influence which he was able to exert. They furnish also an explanation of the fact that his influence was comparatively temporary. The man who believes nothing, or, what is the same thing, announces a change of belief fifty times in the course of his life, can have no very permanent influence, whatever may be the qualities of his genius, or whatever may be the extent of his influence on his own generation.*

There can be no possible doubt, however, that these very qualities increased Voltaire's influence on the society of his own time. The tenacity with which the mass of the people always cling to old systems and old names, even after their old faith in them is shaken, is overcome, perhaps, by ridicule more easily than in any other way. Voltaire in early life swore mortal war against the religious man, just as Diderot and Helvetius had sworn against the moral man.† He was not simply un-

was in some respects more deplorable than it was at the end of the eighteenth; from a moral and a political point of view, it was doubtless better.

* "En attendant, souvenez-vous que Voltaire a fait en sa vie une cinquantaine de professions de foi, sans compter ou en comptant celle qu'il fit imprimer à Paris dans tous les papiers publics quelques mois avant sa mort."—La Harpe, *Cours de Littérature*, vol. XVI. p. 56.

† La Harpe, *Cours de Littérature*, vol. XVI. p. 273.

believing; he was impious. He hesitated at nothing; he dealt in calumnies the most outrageous, accusations the most false, and lies the most frequent and enormous. The most sacred things in religion and morals were the favorite objects of his scoffing raillery; and so keen was his wit, so blasting his mockery, that those who professed to cling still to the old doctrines of religion and virtue, were either driven into obscurity or covered with general contempt. The worst of his dramas was the most popular; and the book sure to be found on every drawing-room table in Paris was the one which must now be regarded as the most objectionable.

The negative, or what may perhaps with greater propriety be called the destructive influence of Voltaire, was not altogether unlike that which had long before been exerted by Erasmus. The works of these authors certainly present far more points of difference than points of similarity, and yet in one particular their relation to the times in which they respectively lived were strikingly alike. The work which Erasmus did in preparing the way for the Reformation was quite similar in kind to that done by Voltaire in preparing the way for the Revolution. The work of both was to ridicule that which existed and prepare the way for that which was to come. How well Erasmus did his part is known to all who have read the *Praise of Folly* and the *Colloquies*. But the work of Voltarie was even more effective. Erasmus threw a strong light upon the cunning devices of the monks, and set a large part of Europe to laughing at them; but the light which Voltaire flashed upon the follies of his age, not only made them visible, but it also scorched and blasted them. His was the electric flash; it might be avoided, but it could not be resisted. The only way to be secure was to keep out of its way; and to elude it was either to be insignificant, or to fall into the current of the age and be swept along with it. Indeed, there was no joint in the harness either of religion or government into which he did not thrust his keen lance.

There is one other point in this discussion of Voltaire's influence which must not be passed over. I refer to the amount and variety of his writings. That he was able to produce seventy octavo volumes of such excellence as to entitle them to a permanent rank in French literature would, of itself, be one of the marvels of a literary age; and yet the real wonder is not in the amount of his writings, but in the fact that in all the varieties of literary work to which he turned his attention, save perhaps in what pertained to politics alone, he was the foremost author in France, if not the foremost author of his time. At the age of twenty-four he was conceded to be the greatest poet in France,* and since his death, which occurred at eighty-four, many of the critics maintain that he was the greatest poet that France has ever

* La Harpe, vol. VIII. p. 39, also p. 270.

produced. But great as he was as a poet, as a writer of prose he was even greater. The judgment of La Harpe is, that as a writer on the philosophy of government he was surpassed only by Montesquieu, and as a writer on national history only by Buffon.* Buckle, after a careful analysis of his works, and after a somewhat detailed comparison of his services with those of Niebuhr † declares that "taking him on the whole, he is probably the greatest historian that Europe has yet produced." ‡

In order to complete our estimation of Voltaire's prodigious power, it remains, perhaps, only to add that his popularity was quite equal to his literary merit. Before the beginning of this century fifty editions of his works had been published with an aggregate sale of three hundred thousand copies.

* "Voltaire allait toujours grandissant, et tous les prosateurs, qui avaient occupés le public un moment, s'eclipsaient plus ou moins devant lui. Pour Montesquieu et Buffon leur renommée etait entiére, mais moins populaire que la sienne. Il couvrit la posèie de tout l'eclat qui rejaillissait encore sur elle du beau siede de Louis XIV."—*La Harpe*, vol. VIII. p. 270.

† "I can say with confidence, after a careful comparison of both writers, that the most decisive arguments advanced by Niebuhr against the early history of Rome, had all been anticipated by Voltaire, in whose works they may be found by whoever will take the trouble of reading what this great man has written, instead of ignorantly railing against him."—*History of Civilization*, vol. I. p. 589.

‡ "I have been more particular in stating the immense obligations history is under to Voltaire, because, in England there exists against him a prejudice which nothing but ignorance, or something worse than ignorance, can excuse; and because, taking him on the whole, he is probably the greatest historian Europe has yet produced." —Vol. I. p. 591.

Besides these, there had been separately printed fifty thousand copies of his theatrical works, three hundred thousand copies of the *Henriade*, and about the same number of the *Pucelle* and of the *Romances*.*

Let us recall now, for a moment, what had been accomplished. Helvetius, by a system of specious logic, had undermined the old doctrine of morals, and had taught men that the only obligation resting upon them was to obey the calls of their appetites and passions. Then Condillac, by a system of metaphysics far more able and far more subtle, had convinced the mass of thinking Frenchmen that they owed their condition simply to the nature of the political and religious institutions about them, and that if they would change their condition they had but to overthrow those institutions. But there is, in the mass of humanity, a respect for the venerable which is not easily overcome. Men do not readily attempt to overthrow those institutions which have become sanctified by age. Then, as if for the purpose at once of stinging to death the old forms, and of ridiculing out of existence any such scruples of the people as might still linger, there came forward the dramas and satires of Vol-

* A sufficient idea of the variety and extent of Voltaire's literary work is conveyed, perhaps, by the bare statement that of the Beaumarchais edition there are fifteen volumes of poetry, thirteen of history, three on politics, twelve on metaphysics, and twenty-six on miscellaneous subjects. On the popularity of his works, as indicated by the extent of their sale, v. *Dictionnaire Universel Neuvième édition*, vol. XVIII. pp. 142 et 143.

taire. The work of destruction, in the minds of vast numbers of the people, was thus completed. The soil had been turned over; the old vegetation appeared to be dead; the field was ready for the first new seed that might be thrown in.

It would not be quite true to say that as yet all the work of the writers to whom I have referred was merely negative in its character. The theories of Helvetius and others gave to the passions a tremendous impulse, which was by no means negative, and which ought not to be overlooked. At the same time it may be affirmed that as yet there had appeared no system of human rights that was adequate to take the place of the systems which had been so undermined. The people had acquired a dislike which bordered upon contempt for those which existed, and their passions had been aroused by their wrongs until they were ready to move whenever anything should afford them the needed guidance. They were ready to destroy, but in fact they did not begin the work of political destruction until they had, or at least imagined that they had, something to put in the place of that which they would sweep away. That something was furnished by Rousseau.

It is somewhat singular that one whose life was so full of moral inconsistency, nay, one whose character was, in many ways, so utterly contemptible, should have been able to exert so powerful an influence on the thoughts of his fellow-men. As one reads his writings, one is reminded sometimes of

Burke and sometimes of Job Trotter. He seemed never so well pleased as when parading his sorrows in public, and his whole character, as Mr. Lowell well said of him, seemed to consist of that contemptible mixture which is ready enough to shed tears before man, but which, at the same time, is absolutely devoid of all genuine feeling. He could advise parents pathetically concerning the treatment of their children, and then send his own offspring to a foundling hospital. These contradictions of his nature were everywhere making themselves manifest. His soul was overflowing with sentiment; but his sentiment was of that nervous type which shows itself at one time in tears and at another in the most abject cruelty. In his thoughts he was perpetually dealing with unrealities, and then attempting to apply the results of his reasoning to the hard problems of every-day life. These peculiarities, which are indeed, to a great extent, the peculiarities of the whole school of political sentimentality, made up a character in Rousseau that was the very embodiment and perfection of inconsistency.

But notwithstanding these weaknesses, there can be no doubt that Rousseau's influence was more powerful and more far-reaching than that of any of his contemporaries. In saying this, I remember that he lived in the very age which could boast of the two men who embodied in themselves the greatest literary genius and the highest literary culture of the eighteenth century. The merits of

Rousseau, as a strictly literary man, are not worthy of comparison with those of Burke and Voltaire; and yet, in one respect, he was the superior of them both. In greater measure than any other man of his time, he possessed the art of directing and moulding the thoughts of others. Burke always astonished but never convinced. Voltaire inaugurated a fashion, but it was a fashion of scoffing, of doubting; that is to say, of negation. But Rousseau was the founder of a school. He was the intellectual father of the political sentimentalists of the present century. Chateaubriand, Jefferson, Byron, Lamartine, and Victor Hugo, besides a host of lesser characters, were all his legitimate children.

But abandoning generalities, let us inquire a little more definitely concerning the fundamental character of the system. It begins with the two undeniable assertions that all voluntary actions having for their object good or evil are moral actions, and that all moral actions have their foundation in the reason. Every man is born with the faculty of reason, consequently, everything without reason, be its form what it may, is not a person, but a thing. All law, human and divine, is grounded on the sacred principle that a person can never become a thing, nor be treated as such, without wrong. But the distinction between a thing and a person is that the former may always be used purely and altogether as a means, while the latter must always be included in the end or final cause. For example, we sow a field of grain and reap it; we rear a bullock and slaughter it, simply and solely as a means for the accomplishment of our ends—that is to say, without any obligation on our part to the thing itself. We employ a laborer also as a means, but with this all-important distinction, namely, that it is in accordance with an agreement of reciprocal advantage which includes him as well as us in the end.

Up to this point, Rousseau's positions are doubtless correct; but in his next step there is a fallacy which leads directly to the false conclusions that follow. His position is that, inasmuch as the faculty of reason implies free agency, morality, which is the dictate of reason, gives to every rational being the right of acting under all circumstances as a free agent, and of finally determining his conduct by his own will; and furthermore, that this right is inalienable except by an act of self-forfeiture. The most obvious conclusion to which this position leads, is that no law can be imposed upon an individual until that individual has given his consent to it. This conclusion, startling as it is, Rousseau justifies by a most subtle process of reasoning. He claims that in respect to their reason, strictly so called, all men are equal. The measure of all the other faculties of man, says he, is different in different persons; but the reason is not susceptible of degree, since "it merely decides whether any given thought or action is or is not in contradiction with the rest. It follows that there can be no better reason or more reason in one man than in another; hence what is contrary to the reason of any one man is in its nature essentially and necessarily unreasonable." * It follows, also, that "no individual possesses the right of prescribing anything to another individual, the rule of which is not contained in their common reason," and that society, which is but an aggregate of individuals, can communicate this right to no one. "It cannot possibly," says he, "make that right which the higher and inviolable law of human nature declares contradictory and unjust. But concerning right and wrong, the reason of each and every man is the competent judge; for how else can he be an amenable being, or the proper subject of any law? This reason, therefore, in any one man cannot, even in the social state, be rightfully subjugated to the reason of any other. No individual, nor yet the whole multitude which constitutes the state, can possess the right of compelling him to do anything of which it cannot be demonstrated that his own reason must join in prescribing it." † Rousseau did not shrink from the conclusions to which this process of reasoning led. He boldly stated the problem of a perfect form of government to be, "*to find a form of society in which each one uniting himself with the whole shall yet obey himself*

* For an elaborate exposure of the sophistry of these positions, vide *Coleridge's Works*, vol. II. p. 143–150.

† Oeuvres de Rousseau (Frankfort, 1855), vol. III. pp. 281 and 283.

and remain as free as before." * He did not even hesitate to deny the legitimacy of all representation, but stated boldly that sovereignty cannot be represented for the same reason that it cannot be alienated. "It consists," to use his own words, "essentially in the general will, and the will is not to be represented: it is the same or it is another; there is no middle ground. Deputies of the people are not, and cannot be, the representatives of the people; they are only commissioners, and can decide nothing definitely. Every law which the people has not ratified is null,—it is not a law. The English people think themselves free, but they are grievously mistaken; they are free only during the election of members of parliament. As soon as the election is complete, they are slaves, they are nothing. During the few moments of their liberty, the use which they make of it is such that they deserve to lose it." †

There was another conclusion, to which the positions taken by Rousseau led him, that is even more striking than the one just given. He regarded it as established that "no one is bound to

* "Trouver une forme d'association qui défende et protége de toute la force commune la personne et les biens de chaque associé, et par laquelle chacun, s'unissant à tous, n'obéisse pourtant qu'à lui-même, et reste aussi libre qu'auparavant. Tel est le problème fundamental dont le contrat social donne la solution."—*Du Contrat Social*, Livre I. Chapitre VI.

† *Du Contrat Social*, Livre III., Chapitre XV. The whole of this chapter of the Social Contract should be read by one who would understand the length to which the peculiar views of Rousseau were carried.

obey a law to which he has not given his consent," —in other words, a law which is contrary to his own will.

It is easy to show that this position is fatal to all society. What was my will yesterday, is not necessarily my will to-day. My will does not exhaust itself by a single act. It follows, therefore, that a law which yesterday I approved, to-day I may condemn. But as I am bound by nothing which my will does not approve, and as my will does not now approve of a given law even though I did approve it yesterday, I am no longer bound to obey it. My will is my only master, and I am under no obligation to submit slavishly to laws from which my master bids me to free myself. In his words: "It is absurd that the will should give itself chains for the future." *

Rousseau admitted that his doctrines drove him to the necessity of taking these positions, but he either did not see, or, what is quite as probable, did not choose to admit, the consequences. It seems not to have occurred to him that such principles, if fully carried out, would be destructive, not only of all government, but of all society. It requires but the most elementary reasoning to see

* "Il est absurde que la volonté se donne des chaînes pour l'avenir; il ne dépend d'aucune volonté de consentir à rien de contraire au bien de l'etre qui veut. Si donc le peuple promet simplement d'obéir, il se dissout par cet acte, il perd sa qualité de peuple; à l'instant qu'il y a un maître, il n'y a plus de souverain, et dès lors le corps politique est détruit."—*Du Contrat Social*, Livre II. Chapitre I.; also "La loi d'hier n'oblige pas aujourd'hui," Livre III. Chap. XI.

that if a man cannot be bound by any law or contract to which his own will does not at the moment assent, he is of necessity condemned to an absolute and continued isolation. Such a doctrine, if generally adopted, would introduce an element of dissolution into every fibre and tissue of the body politic; and yet it was so artfully woven into Rousseau's system of political philosophy, that it awakened no alarm whatever.

It cannot be denied that these principles of Rousseau, absurd as they appear to us, were argued and enforced with great power. Coleridge has well remarked that it is always a "bad policy to represent a political system as having no charm but for robbers and assassins, and no natural origin but in the brains of fools and madmen," and the remark may be applied with especial pertinence to our estimation of the political philosophy of Rousseau. Notwithstanding its many absurdities, it was so cunningly wrought out that it had a peculiar fascination for imaginative and gifted spirits. We shall hereafter see something of the extent of its popularity; meanwhile let us consider for a moment the line of argument and exhortation by which his theories were given the appearance of practicality.

He affirms that as soon as the service of the state ceases to be the principal affair of its citizens, the state is near its ruin. Such a deplorable spirit of indifference to state affairs manifests itself in various ways. If it is necessary to go to battle, men pay for substitutes and remain at home. If it is necessary to go to the council of state, they appoint deputies and devote themselves to their own ease and their own interest. By force of money and indolence they can have soldiers ready to fight, and legislators ready to accept of their fighting. It is the bustle of commerce and the arts; it is the avaricious desire of gain; it is the love and effeminacy of elegant ease that substitutes money for personal service and thus threatens the nation's ruin. In a state which is truly free, the citizens accomplish everything with their hands, nothing with their money. Instead of paying to be exempt from their duty, they would rather pay for the privilege of doing it. In a city well constituted, each one hastens to the assemblies; while in a bad government, no one cares to go because no one takes any interest in what is to be done. The reason of this indifference is, on the one hand, that everybody sees that the general will of the whole is not to prevail, and on the other that everybody is absorbed in the conduct of his own private affairs. But such a course is fatal. As soon as any one says of the business of state "Que m'importe?" the state is doomed. The lukewarmness of patriotism, the activity of private interest, the immensity of personal estates, and the abuses of government, have warped our judgment and our imagination respecting the rights of the people and the rights of the government. It is for these reasons that the interests of two orders have been placed in the first and second rank; while the interest of the public as a whole has been placed in the third rank,—has been called the third estate.*

Now, the only remedy for all these evils, declares Rousseau, is that the people arise from their political lethargy and insist upon the restoration of power into their own hands. As already shown, they are under no obligation to obey any law to which they have not consented,—they are indeed under no obligation to obey any statute to which they do not now consent. They must take upon themselves the duty of overthrowing such old laws as are offensive, and of framing such new ones as the circumstances demand.

It will be seen that in these positions there was something far more practical than anything advanced by the writers whose works I have above considered. Here, at last, the French people found something positive and definite as a substitution for those principles which the philosophers had done so much to sweep away. Though the metaphysicians had done everything to convince the people that men are what they are simply as an effect produced upon them by their external surroundings, though the moralists had taught that the only basis of morality is in obeying speedily and conscientiously the calls of the appetites and passions, and though the wits and scoffers had swept

* *Du Contrat Social*, Liv. III. Chap. XV.

almost completely away the lingering respect of the people for everything venerable in church and state, yet it must be said, that in all their teachings there was no practical guidance of the people out of their evils and into what promised to afford them liberty and happiness. It is not altogether strange, therefore, that the masses of the people received the instructions and assurances of Rousseau with an ardor that amounted almost to infatuation. If we remember all their political wrongs, all their physical sufferings, all their bitter hatreds, all their passionate longings, and if, in addition, we call to mind the fact that in all the other writings of the time there was revealed, not a *means* of escape from their present condition, but merely a *justification* of escape, provided such a means should be found, we shall be able at least to form a conjecture with what enthusiasm such words as those of Rousseau were likely to be received. Our conjecture, however, in the absence of most positive testimony, would be likely to fall short of the reality.

But most positive testimony on this subject is not wanting. Hume, when he was in Paris, wrote, concerning Rousseau's popularity: "It is impossible to express or imagine the enthusiasm of this nation in his favor. No person ever so much engaged their attention as Rousseau. Voltaire and everybody else are quite eclipsed by him."* Path-

* Burton's Life of Hume, vol. II. p. 299.

ay in his life of Rousseau declares that when the *Novelle Héloïse* appeared, the circulating libraries found it impossible to supply the demand for the work, though it was loaned out at an enormous rate and *but sixty minutes were allowed for its perusal.** Nor was the popularity of the work merely that which might be indicated by an enthusiastic community over a mere work of fiction. It was generally regarded as in fact a new Gospel to dying men, and it was seized upon with an avidity that stopped not short of absolute fanaticism. Grimm wrote from the capital that the *Dijon Discourse* "wrought a kind of revolution at Paris," † and Napoleon even went so far as to declare to Girardin that "without Rousseau the French Revolution would not have occurred." ‡

But the full influence of Rousseau has been nowhere so well analyzed and portrayed as by Burke in his letter to a member of the National Assembly, written in 1791. This letter is all the more valuable from the fact that it was written before the occurrence of those excesses which marked the Reign of Terror. In speaking of the pernicious doctrines concerning education that were in France taking possession of society, he used these glowing words:

"The Assembly recommends to its youth a study

* "On louait l'ouvrage à tant par jour, ou par heure. Quand il parût on exigeait *douze sous par volume, en n'accordant que soixante minutes pour le lire.*"—*Pathay*, *Vie de Rousseau*, vol. II. p. 361.

† *Correspondence*, vol. I. p. 122.

‡ Lord Holland, *Foreign Reminiscences*, p. 261.

of the bold experimenters in morality. Everybody knows that there is a great dispute amongst their leaders, which of them is the best resemblance of Rousseau. In truth, they all resemble him. His blood they transfuse into their minds and into their manners. Him they study; him they meditate; him they turn over in all the time they can spare from the laborious mischief of the day or the debauches of the night. Rousseau is their canon of Holy Writ; in his life he is their Canon of Polycletus; he is their standard figure of perfection. To this man and this writer, as a pattern to authors and Frenchmen, the foundries of Paris are now running for statues, with the kettles of the poor and the bells of the churches. If an author had written like a great genius on geometry, though his practical and speculative words were vicious in the extreme, it might appear that in voting the statue they honored only the geometrician. But Rousseau is a moralist or he is nothing. It is impossible, therefore, putting the circumstances together, to mistake their design in choosing the author with whom they have begun to recommend a course of studies. Their great problem is to find a substitute for all the principles which hitherto have been employed to regulate the human will and action. They find dispositions in the mind of such force and quality as may fit men far better than the old morality for the purposes of such a state as theirs, and may go much farther in supporting their power and destroying their enemies.

They have therefore chosen a selfish, flattering, seductive, ostentatious vice in the place of a plain duty. When your lords had many writers as immoral as the object of their statue (such as Voltaire and others), they chose Rousseau, because in him that peculiar vice which they wished to erect into a ruling virtue was by far the most conspicuous." *

It may well excite our wonder that a political gospel so full of inconsistencies and absurdities as that of Rousseau found millions of believers. Carlyle has arrayed it as the first of the "Prodigies;" and has shown the fallacy of the *Contrat Social* in a single sentence.† And yet, in view of all the facts, it can hardly be denied that the author exerted a more powerful and a more widespread political influence than any other political writer of the last century. ‡

* *Works of Edwin Burke* (Boston, 1869), vol. IV. p. 25.

† "If all men were such that a mere spoken or sworn contract would bind them, all men were then true men and government a superfluity. *Not what thou and I have promised to each other, but what the balance of our forces can make us perform to each other: that, in so sinful a world as ours, is the thing to be counted on.*"—*The French Revolution*, Part II. Book I. Chap. VII.

‡ Even in Germany the influence of Rousseau was all-powerful. Lessing, after the appearance of the *Discourse*, declared, "It is impossible to speak otherwise than with secret veneration of those lofty ideas and sublime thoughts." Herder dedicated to Rousseau his first poem, and announces him as his guide through life. Kant even forgot his daily walk while reading him; Schiller even went so far as to compare him with Socrates; and Goethe, though his own head seems not to have been turned, gives us a vivid description of his influence over the youth of Germany. Of Rousseau's later influence, so temperate and eminent a writer as Sir Henry Maine (*Ancient Law*, p. 84) speaks in these

To say that these theories of Rousseau were radically wrong and thoroughly pernicious in their political and social influence, is obviously to express but very inadequately the evils which they embodied. Other theories may be thoroughly and fundamentally bad, and yet their evil influence be alleviated or neutralized by external circumstances. But the prime characteristics of Rousseau's doctrines were that they were subversive of all government, future as well as present. He said to Frenchmen, in effect, "Every man is his own absolute master, and the only legitimate law for a man is his own individual will. At no time has any one a right to control him, if he does not give his consent. This will cannot be delegated for the reason that it cannot cease to reside with himself. The consequence is that, speaking strictly, there can be no representative government. The laws may, indeed, be framed by deputies, but they must all be submitted to the people before they can have binding force. If an attempt be made to enforce a statute which the people have not consented to, it is the right and the duty of the people to resist it. If an attempt be made to force away your property, it is cowardly not to resist; if the government endeavor to take away your

terms: "We have never seen in our own generation—indeed, the world has not seen more than once or twice in all the course of history—a literature which has exercised such a prodigious influence over the minds of men, over every cast and shade of intellect, as that which emanated from Rousseau between 1749 and 1762." Carlyle (*Lectures on Heroes, Lecture Fifth*) has written in a similar strain.

liberty by imposing upon you laws to which you do not consent, it is the more cowardly not to resist by so much as liberty is better than earthly possessions. Thus, it will be seen that the doctrines not only make revolution a right, but they also impose it upon the people as a duty,—a duty, too, which it is cowardly not to recognize and act upon."

But the doctrines of Rousseau, as we have already seen, did not end even here. Suppose that a revolution is carried successfully through, and that to-day the government assumes a form that is for the time being entirely satisfactory to the people. But the will of man to-day is not necessarily what it was yesterday; and to-morrow it will not necessarily be what it is to-day. To-day I enter into a contract. To-day this contract is binding upon me, for it has received the endorsement of my free will. To-morrow, however, my will may change, and I may regret the action of to-day. My will of to-morrow is as independent of my will of yesterday, as it is of the will of another person. My will of to-day or to-morrow rises up against the tyranny of my past will and throws off its authority. I am justified in rebelling,—nay, it is my duty to rebel,—whenever my will is not satisfied.

These conclusions, drawn legitimately from the doctrines of Rousseau, are manifestly destructive, not only of all political governments, but also even of all social and commercial life. If there can be no permanency; in other words, if there can be no prospect that what is done to-day will remain until it is changed by a process which is to-day understood and accepted by all concerned, then all legislation is folly, inasmuch as all legislation is for the future, and there is no intelligence able to anticipate what the future may desire. It is not too much to say that the theories of Rousseau leave no standing-place for any political organization whatever. There can be no such absolute freedom of political action as Rousseau demands, without a return to barbarism; — indeed, such absolute freedom *is* barbarism.

I have dwelt at some length upon the most influential writers of the period just before the Revolution, for the reason that I believe their writings contained the germs of those peculiar political evils with which France during the last half century and more has been afflicted. The social and political evils under which the people were staggering when Louis XVI. ascended the throne, numerous and oppressive as they were, cannot with propriety be called the chief causes of the Revolution. They were rather its occasion or its opportunity. They were the rank soil into which these seeds were thrown, and in which they sprang up and bore their bitter fruits.

In every community there is some pervading public sentiment or other that is far more potent for good or for evil than any power which, independent of this public sentiment, is embodied in the statutes. It is difficult, nay it is impossible, under a free government to enforce a law which has not the general sanction of the community to which it is designed to apply. Corruption in government may accumulate and abound until an enraged community rises up in its might to overthrow those in authority. All these facts go to show the superiority of public opinion over written codes. While the laws are the nation's words, public opinion is the nation's character. As we determine the amount of confidence we may safely repose in the words of men only after we have formed an estimate of their character, so we can judge of the condition of society only after we are familiar with the thoughts of the people. What Emerson calls the "tone" or "bent" of society is infinitely more important than its laws; for if the tone is right, the laws, if faulty, may be corrected; while if the tone is bad even good laws will not be enforced. This accords precisely with what Professor Seeley remarks concerning the necessary spirit in an institution of learning. "Nothing," says he, "is more indispensable than an intellectual tone, a sense of the value of knowledge, a respect for ideas and for culture, a scholarly and scientific enthusiasm, or what Wordsworth calls a strong book-mindedness." *

This is but a recognition in an educational institution of that very power to which I would call attention in a nation at large. The thoughts, the feelings, the sentiments of a people are the powers

* *Roman Imperialism, etc.*, p. 210.

which, in monarchies and in republics alike, determine what a nation shall be and the laws which it shall have.

We have seen that the philosophers who wrote just before the revolution broke out, were philosophers of negation. The tendency of all their writings was not to establish or correct, but to destroy; and this destructive tendency, by means of the popularity of their works, came to be thoroughly wrought into the intellectual and political character of the nation.* The consequences of this destructive tendency have been most important. The prevailing tone of French society, and especially of French politics, has been during the whole of the present century what can in no other way be so well characterized as by calling it *revolutionary*. And what can such a spirit accomplish for a nation? An eloquent answer to this question has been given by one who sheds light upon every subject which he considers. Guizot in accounting for the political tone of his lectures on the history of civilization, uses these somewhat melancholy words: "Forgetfulness and disdain of its past is a serious disorder and a great weakness in any nation. Such a spirit

* In speaking of the spirit which pervaded the French writers of the last century, Sir Henry Maine wrote as follows:

"It gave birth, or intense stimulus, to the vices of a mental habit all but universal at the time, disdain of positive law, impatience of experience, and the preference of *à priori* reasoning. In proportion, too, as this philosophy fixes its grasp on minds which have thought less than others and fortified themselves with smaller observation, its tendency is to become strictly anarchical."—*Ancient Law*, p. 88.

can in a revolutionary crisis raise itself in opposition to weak and worn-out institutions; but when this work of destruction is accomplished, if it continues to take no account of the nation's history, if it persuades itself that it has completely broken with the secular elements of civilization, it does not found a new society, but it simply perpetuates the state of revolution. When generations in the momentary possession of the country have the absurd arrogance to believe that it belongs to them alone, and that the past confronting the present is simply death confronting life, when they thus throw off the empire of traditions and the bands which unite the successive generations to one another, they disown not only the distinct and eminent character of the human race, but its high honor and its grand destiny. A people which falls into this gross error falls also into anarchy and abasement, for God does not suffer that Nature and the laws of her works should be misunderstood and outraged with impunity." *

Another influence of the writers whose works we have been considering, and one which ought not to be overlooked, was that which they exercised upon the distinctively religious character of the people. Among the writers of the revolution-

* *Mémoires* (*Édition interdite pour la France*, Leipzig, 1858), vol. I. p. 336. On the same subject of the fatal influence of the *L'Esprit Révolutionaire* in France, see also a very able essay by M. Paul Janet in *Revue des Deux Mondes*, vol. C. p. 721; also, Prevost-Paradol, *La France Nouvelle*, p. 295. Courcelle-Seneuil; *L'Héritage de la Révolution*, p. 217. Gervinus, *Geschichte des 19. Jahrhundert*, 8. Bd. 1 Th. s. 204.

ary period the very name of God was spoken in derision. The editor of a prominent encyclopædia declined an article on God, saying that the belief in a Supreme Being was no longer entertained, and was no longer of interest to the French people. I have already referred to the declaration of an archbishop, that atheism was the accepted creed of the people. There can be no doubt that something of a reaction took place after the close of the Revolution, and yet it is by no means strange that when the belief in God had once completely lost its hold on cultivated minds, it was exceedingly slow in regaining its former position and influence. The religious, or more properly speaking, the irreligious teachings of the philosophers of the eighteenth century are still exciting a powerful influence in the nation. Atheism has not yet gone out of fashion, if indeed it may not be said to be still in the very height of fashion. The followers of Renan and Vacherot are more genteel than the followers of Lacordaire and Hyacinthe, and among the intellectual classes they are probably even more numerous. The tone of French society is proverbially anti-religious. The character of this tone has a powerful influence even on the ecclesiastical assemblies themselves. Questions are admitted into such bodies for discussion, which, by their very nature, show the unsubstantial basis on which the faith of the members rests. In many of their recent meetings the points which have called out the most earnest discussions have not been about articles of the Athenasian creed, or the details of language concerning the sacrament, or the most efficient methods of propagating and spreading the truth, but concerning the existence of the very basis of Christianity itself. The great question, even among themselves, seems to be whether the Christian religion is or is not founded on truth; and if we may judge from the proceedings of the last general synod of the French Protestant Church, we should conclude that of every seven members four think that it is, and three that it is not. In June, 1871, after a prolonged and stormy debate of several days' duration, even a studiously vague and general assertion of the supernatural element in religion was carried in the synod by a majority of only sixty-one to forty-six.* That the declarations of the synod contained no assertions of the divinity of Christ, may be explained by the fact that the assembly contained delegates from all Protestant denominations; but that in any body of representative ecclesiastics of high rank, three out of every seven of its members should be unwilling on a test vote to declare that the Christian religion has a supernatural basis, is a fact which can have no other explanation than that which appears upon its surface.

Such I believe to have been the political and religious influence of the writers whom I have called the Philosophers of the Revolution. Their

* On this subject see Döllinger's *Lectures on the Reunion of the Churches.* Preface, p. xvii; also, *Pall Mall Gazette*, for July 4th, 1872.

work was a work of destruction. They did much to sweep away crying evils, and so far they made their good influence felt and appreciated. But destruction is never a means of growth; the best it can ever do, is to remove hindrances. The author of "Ecce Homo" has remarked that all moral growth comes through admiration. It is not the man who sees nothing but evil in society that advances to a higher life and a nobler virtue; but the one who recognizes a higher standard, admires it and struggles to attain it. A general revolutionary spirit in a nation is a spirit which sees only the evil, and for the sake of curing it is ready to destroy everything. It would burn the house in order to kill the vermin. In France it doubtless destroyed many evils, but it became so thoroughly the habit of the intellectual leaders that it continued its work of destruction long after its wholesome and legitimate labors were finished. The nation has suffered and is still suffering from the prevalence of this spirit more than from any other evil whatever.

THE POLITICS OF THE REVOLUTION.

"Tum Lælius, nunc fit illud Catonis certius, nec temporis unius, nec hominis esse constitutionem reipublicæ."—*Cicero, De Republica,* Lib. ii . 21.

"Ce fus là l'erreur de la Révolution, et en general c'est la faute de l'esprit français de traiter les theories politiques comme des vérités mathematiques, et de leur prêtèr un absolu qu'elles ne comportent pas."—*Laboulage Histoire des États-Unis,* vol. III. p. 292.

CHAPTER III.

THE POLITICS OF THE REVOLUTION.

IN the last chapter I endeavored to present some of the most prominent doctrines of the men whom I called the Philosophers of the Revolution. I shall now attempt to show how these doctrines took form in actual political life, how they have since influenced, and even moulded, the character of French history. It is necessary to prepare the way, however, by one or two general observations.

Chateaubriand has remarked that liberty is a thing which all men long for, which but few understand, and which no one seems able to define. We may not understand precisely its nature, and we may be unable to give to it an adequate definition, and yet we may perhaps be sure that there are certain definite conditions on which alone it can exist. Are there then any fixed peculiarities of good government? Are there any fundamental principles of such government which all men—monarchists, democrats, oligarchs, republicans—can agree upon as necessary? Without doubt, yes, there are many; but for our purpose it will be sufficient to name the one most prominent.

Whatever may be the peculiar relations of the

governing and the governed in any society, it is indispensable to good government that those relations should be defined and understood. If they are not defined, there can be no liberty on the part of the governed, for the reason that there can be no anticipating the course to be pursued by the governing. The same result will ensue if those relations are not generally understood. If, for example, at the present day you go into Russia, you find no difficulty in seeing that the people at large recognize the fact that all the functions of government are in the hands of the Emperor and his subordinates. There is no misunderstanding. The relations of emperor and people are defined and understood. The absolutist finds, therefore, much in the Russian government to excite his admiration. Go, on the other hand, into England at the middle of the seventeenth century, and you find the nation embroiled in a terrible civil war. Why? Was it not because the proper relations of rulers and governed had become enshrouded in doubt, and because the two parties concerned could not agree upon what those relations should be in the future? Moreover, was it not the chief result of that struggle to fix those relations, and to bring king and people in the Declaration of Rights to an agreement concerning them? It comes then to this, that there must be in every nation a certain something —call it a constitution, call it national custom, call it what you will—which restrains and fixes the powers of the government; which defines and guarantees the rights of the governed. In England Parliament seems to be omnipotent. A well-known formula, started by De Lolme, declares that the only limitations of its power are that it cannot convert a man into a woman, or a woman into a man. But, after all, the limitations of parliamentary power are practically innumerable. They suggest themselves to every mind. Notwithstanding the boasted authority of Parliament, there is something back of those powers, something on which those powers rest, something, even, without which those powers could not exist. That something is the universal conviction that there are certain *individual rights* belonging to every person which may not be interfered with by any power; no, not even by Parliament. That conviction everywhere pervades the history of British legislation. It is indeed in the marrow and tissue of the Anglo-Saxon race. That spirit has sometimes been overlooked; it has, indeed, sometimes been asleep; but it has always been in its place, ready to assert its rights; ready, if need be, to destroy its enemies. It is that spirit alone which can justify revolution; that spirit alone which, under peculiar circumstances, not only may justify resistance to the laws, but also may make such resistance a sacred duty.*

But, it is important to bear in mind not only the *existence* of these personal rights, but also the fact that they are *inalienable*, and cannot be represented.

* On the question of ultimate sovereignty, Guizot has some good words in *Hist. of Rep. Govt.*, Lect. VI.

Does the American, or the Englishman, or the German, when he votes for a representative to his national legislature, surrender to that delegate his personal rights? Does he say to the man whom he elects, "By chosing you as my representative I not only delegate to you my political functions, but I also transfer my sovereignty over myself into your hands"? By no means; such sovereignty must remain intact with the individual where it belongs. It can be interfered with by neither king, nor president, nor legislature. In either case such interference is tyranny, and as completely so in one case as in another.

Now, it is for the very purpose of preventing such tyranny, that in all good governments, the legislative, as well as the executive, power of the nation is hedged about with constitutional limitations. A nation as a whole cannot of course be permanently restrained by a constitution, for the reason that the same power which created it may change it, or even sweep it away; the very fact, therefore, that the constitution, whether written or unwritten, puts a restraint upon the legislature, proves that there is a sovereignty in the nation which the people are unwilling to commit to the caprice of legislators.

But how was it in France? The one most potent truth which Rousseau lodged, and lodged permanently, in the French brain, was that the *people* of France are by right the sovereign rulers of France. But it was also his opinion that every representative government is in its own nature a delusion and a snare.* How are those two ideas to be reconciled? It is not quite certain that Rousseau attempted to reconcile them. Be that as it may, his followers did attempt it, and in a manner that has brought countless wars upon the nation. Their simple explanation was that the people, themselves sovereign, by the act of choosing a legislature, transferred their sovereignty to the delegates whom they elected. What was the result? Simply that the National Assembly professed to stand in the place of the nation, not merely to represent the nation, but for all the purposes of sovereignty to be the nation. At first sight this may appear to be not very different from the status of the Parliament of England. In reality, however, the difference is great and radical. In England the Parliament is nothing more than the agent of the people. The simple fact alone that Parliament is sometimes dismissed for the purpose of ascertaining, by means of a new election, the will of the people on some important question, is ample proof that the sovereignty is not lodged with Parliament, but is still with the nation at large. In France, on the contrary, the nation surrendered its sovereignty when it chose the National Assembly. If Louis XIV. could affirm *L'Etat c'est moi*, the National Assembly could make the same declaration with a thousand-fold

* *Contrat Social*, Liv. III. Chap. XV.

more assurance and a thousand-fold more truth. But what followed? With unlimited power in the hands of a body of five hundred men, is the spirit of liberty to be better subserved than with the same unlimited power in the hands of a single individual? On the contrary, the worst tyranny possible is that which is inflicted by a divided, and, for that reason, an irresponsible, power. If a monarch is known to be absolute, the eyes of the people are concentrated upon him, and the very fact throws around him a restraining influence of enormous force. Responsibility, where it is concentrated and recognized, always restrains and makes its possessor conservative. But if the same power be divided, the sense of responsibility is weakened, restraints vanish, and the worst results are to be awaited. The most tyrannical and oppressive governments have not, as a rule, been those which were absolute *in theory*, but those which have been just sufficiently limited in theory to distract the attention of the observer from the true source of the evil. This latter condition was what occurred in France. The people imagined that in allowing the functions of government to be performed by men whom they had elected, they were securing to themselves absolute liberty. But in fact, they secured the very worst form of tyranny that France has ever known. There has probably never been a more oppressive government in Europe than was that of the National Assembly. But its oppression was unfortunately not its worst feature. The saddest circumstance of all was the fact that it was instituted in the name of liberty; that it was believed to subserve the interests of liberty, even while it was doing everything to make liberty impossible. For this reason liberty perished by the very means which had been instituted to establish it. The Assembly proved to be the worst of all tyrannies; the worst, simply because it was founded upon an idea that was recognized and accepted by the mass of the people.

It soon became evident, however, that a government with so many defects and so few merits could not long continue. What was to be done? Was it possible to change the government without sacrificing the principle of national sovereignty? The answer was perfectly easy. If a majority of the electors, which, in fact, is only a minority of the nation, represents the nation; if a majority of the representatives, which is merely a handful of men, has the same privilege, and rules over the nation, is there any reason why the same principle of representation should not be carried still farther,—why, in a word, the Assembly should not delegate its authority to one man by the same process as that by which the nation had transferred its power to the Assembly? This was the logic of the Roman emperors, and it was the logic of the Bonapartes. And there is no resisting it. Who does not see that if a nation may deposit its sovereignty in the hands of five hundred men, it may also deposit it in the hands of one man? There is no error in the reasoning by which the conclusion is reached; all the dangers of the system lie concealed in the premises.

I take it then to be fully established that in every good government, whether a monarchy or a republic, there must be certain rights which no power, either legislative or executive, can infringe upon with impunity. Those rights, moreover, must be sacredly inalienable. There must be no abdication of rights by means of elections. There must be no delegation to a handful of deputies of an absolute control over the national life. As in America, as in England, as in Germany, there must be in operation some system by means of which the great questions affecting the national life may be referred for final decision to the general franchise of the nation. There must be constitutional limitations either carefully expressed, as in the United States, or else unwritten but no less truly existing in the national heart, as in Great Britain; and those limitations must be equally binding upon the legislative and the executive branches of the government.

Now one of the most marked peculiarities of the political life of France is that, although since the Revolution the nation has not been without a written constitution, the constitution, whatever might be its form, has had no binding power upon the representatives. The constitution formed and adopted yesterday by the nation, that is to say, by the representatives of the nation, is to-day judged by the same representatives to be inadequate to the wants of the hour, and accordingly is changed by the same power which formed it. The constitution which to-day is promulgated by the king or the emperor, happens to-morrow to conflict with the wishes of the representatives; and what do we see? Practically a reasoning like this: The sovereignty rests with the people. The people have chosen their monarch. The people are, therefore, superior to their monarch. The people and their representatives are the same. The representatives disapprove the constitution promulgated by the monarch, and therefore, as his superior, they annul it. Thus in every case the overthrow of the constitution seems to come from a confounding of the people and their representatives. The delegates, of course, cannot be bound permanently by any constitution which they themselves have made, nor indeed by any framed and promulgated by a monarch whom they regard as their subordinate.

There is still another element in the politics of the revolutionary period to which I desire to call attention. I mean what I believe to be the political significance of the ideas embodied in the sentiment, "*Liberty, Equality, and Fraternity.*"

That liberty, absolute and unqualified, is incompatible with civilization, and even with organized society of any form, I suppose there is no one to deny. I will presume, therefore, that the devotees of this sentiment meant only that qualified form of liberty which allows of certain necessary restraints. As a matter of fact, the word in its connection doubtless means the largest possible amount of personal freedom consistent with the suppression of anarchy. It means, let us admit, the privilege "of pursuing our own good in our own way, so long as we do not attempt to deprive others of theirs or impede their efforts to obtain it." It means that "each is the proper guardian of his own health, whether bodily or mental or spiritual." It means that "the individual is not accountable to society for his actions in so far as these concern the interests of no person but himself." * It means still further, that in society every person is to be allowed to exert whatever political influence he can without interfering with the similar rights of others.

That a political organization founded on these ideas as its basis would be the best one, or even a good one, for a community of average intelligence and virtue, I think there are many reasons to doubt. Be that as it may, it is certain, as it seems to me, that such a basis of organization would be utterly incompatible with the prevalence of what must be meant by the French meaning of the word Equality. It is unnecessary to give to this word any exact definition in order to show that this statement is strictly true. Whatever Equality

* *Mill on Liberty*, pp. 29 and 181.

may mean, it cannot mean *in*equality, and inequality, political as well as personal, is just what liberty, as Mr. Mill defines it, is sure sooner or later to develop. This fact is so important that I desire not to be misunderstood, and I will therefore illustrate what I mean by one or two examples. Put a hundred men with their families into a wilderness, or on a prairie, and oblige them to make their living. Put them under no political restraints, but give them to the fullest extent that liberty which Mr. Mill so ably and eloquently (but, as I think, somewhat incoherently) advocates. What would be the result? Some would become rich, others would barely get a living, others would die of starvation, or be dependent on their more skilful and fortunate neighbors. To take another example, go into one of our largest cities. Remove to the largest possible extent the restraints of law and of force, that is to say, give to all men the largest possible liberty, and what is the result? It is, and it will always be, that the able and the unscrupulous, by means of a combination of ability and perfidy, will rise, and rise rapidly, above their fellows. If it were possible by some fiat to reduce the people, say of New York or London, in a single day, to an absolute level, how long would that level continue? Not a day, scarcely an hour. Not only would inequality at once begin to show itself, but the rapidity with which it would grow would be in exact proportion to the extent of the liberty with which men of different degrees of tact and ability would be allowed to act.

Take another example, and one not from the imagination but from history. There is no other large country in Europe where liberty during the last two hundred years has been so general and so well guarded as in England. It is certain that in Great Britain people of all classes have, during that period, had greater freedom to act than have the people of any other nationality. The differences between different men and between the circumstances in which different men are placed have there, as nowhere else, been allowed to exert the full measure of their natural influence. The consequence has been a perfectly natural one, though, so far as I know, it has not often been noticed. Nowhere else has the distance between the highest and the lowest classes in society become so enormous as there. While in other countries this distance has been growing less, in England it has certainly been growing greater. More than fifty years ago Hallam gave it as his deliberate opinion that the laboring classes in England at the time when he wrote were relatively in a less comfortable condition than they had been four centuries before; and if that author were living at the present day he would see, I imagine, no reason to change his opinion.*

* "After every allowance, I should find it difficult to resist the conclusion that, however the laborer has derived benefit from the cheapness of manufactured commodities, and from many inventions of com-

No doubt this tendency has been greatly increased by the laws of entail and primogeniture, but they are quite insufficient to account for its existence. They enable a family simply to keep what it gets. The primal cause has been the fact that in England as nowhere else in Europe, men have been protected in their efforts to accumulate fortunes. By this I mean simply that *there* men have had the greatest liberty to exercise the gifts which they may happen to have, and to exercise them under the circumstances in which they may happen to be placed. We may talk about equality, and advocate it as long and as well as we please; the stubborn fact remains, and will always remain, that men are *not* equal, and, moreover, that they cannot be made equal by act of Parliament. This natural inequality in the abilities of men and in the circumstances by which different men are surrounded, *if not interfered with*, becomes greater and greater; and for a reason that finds its expression in the words "to him that hath shall be given, and from him that hath not shall be taken away even that which he hath." In England this

mon utility, he is much inferior, in ability to support a family, to his ancestors three or four centuries ago. I know not why some have supposed that meat was a luxury seldom obtained by the laborer. Doubtless he could not have procured as much as he pleased. But from the greater cheapness of cattle, as compared with corn, it seems to follow that a more considerable portion of his ordinary diet consisted of animal food than at present. It was remarked by Sir John Fontesque that the English lived far more upon animal diet than the French; and it was natural to ascribe their superior strength and courage to this cause."—*Hallam*, *Middle Ages* (New York, 1870), vol. III. p. 353.

inequality has not been interfered with, and the consequence is the rapid tendency to which I have referred. At the beginning of this century the real estate of England was owned by about three hundred and fifty thousand persons. At the present moment more than half of England, Ireland, Scotland, and Wales is declared to be in the possession of one hundred and sixty families.*

In the illustrations which I have given I have not intended to argue either for or against the prevalence of the largest amount of personal and political liberty. It has been my design to show that liberty and equality in any such sense as that embodied in the celebrated French motto cannot go together, and, furthermore, that where there is the greatest amount of liberty, there must necessarily, in the long run, be the least amount of equality. Whether liberty on that account should be opposed is quite another question, and one that has nothing whatever to do with the matter before us. I have dwelt upon the subject merely for the purpose of explaining a certain peculiarity of the French Revolution, which I believe can be so well explained in no other way. Let us see how it is to be applied in the consideration of French politics.

At the outbreak of the Revolution a general

* I confess that I have no other authority for this statement than the newspaper report of the declaration of Mr. Charles Bradlaugh, who was reported to have used these words in his first address in New York: "On our land 160 families own one-half of England, one-half of Wales, and more than one-half of Ireland, and four-fifths of Scotland."—*Address of October 3d*, 1873, *as reported in the Tribune.*

levelling process was inaugurated. Down with the clergy! down with the nobility! down with the prominent men of all classes! was the cry of the people. For a time it seemed as though a man had only to raise his head above the rest in order to have it stricken off. While this levelling process was going on, liberty and equality were equally in favor. The liberty which men exercised was the liberty to destroy their fellows, and the equality which they sought was that which comes not by building up but by putting down. The time came, however, when this process exhausted itself. The former enemies of the people were all subdued, and it was necessary that somebody should fill their places. You may reduce society to a dead level, but you cannot keep it so. It cannot exist without officers and leaders. A ship's crew may mutiny and kill every officer on board. It may, for a time, perhaps enjoy absolute equality of rank and influence. But the moment there is an attempt made to move the vessel, equality vanishes. Somebody must decide what shall be done, and that very fact raises somebody to distinction. It was just so in France. Of course there was no inclination to raise into power the men whom the people had just overthrown; on the contrary, it was but natural that the representatives of the revolutionary ideas should be looked to for guidance. This actually happened; and we accordingly have the wretched spectacle of a nation controlled for years by a succession of feather-brained men, the bad effects of whose fantastic folly it is scarcely possible to exaggerate. These men of "quips and cranks and wanton wiles" were the intellectual children of Rousseau. When their parentage and education are considered, it cannot be regarded strange that instead of making the government the subject of national alteration, they made it an object on which to experiment with their rhetorical and pathetic nonsense. Still further, I think it can be shown that their excesses were the natural product of their beliefs.

When these men of fantasy came into power, like all political dreamers and sentimentalists, they believed, or appeared to believe, in the omnipotence of statutes. In the universal scramble, however, it was soon found that their fellows could not be voted into quiet. That liberty, for which everybody was clamoring, was the right of everybody to object to everything and to resist everything. As there were necessarily more ambitious men out of power than in power, the government at any assignable moment was weaker than the opposition. As those in authority had no right to rule save in the fact that they had been chosen to rule, so their right ceased, or was thought to cease, when the preference of their constituents was changed. At the first exercise of authority irritation ensued. This was followed by recrimination; and at last we behold the most terrible exercise of arbitrary power to be found in modern history. The Reign of Terror was merely the *Contrat Social* put into practice.

Meantime the political dreamers continued to entertain the public with their theories. The notion seems to have been general that if the right political and social machinery could be hit upon, everything would be transformed into order and harmony. In all their speculations there is nothing so pitiable as their utter failure to see that human nature is corrupt and selfish, and that it cannot be made otherwise by any political machinery or any act of Parliament or National Assembly.

Open any one of the more important books of the time, devoted, not to political philosophy, but to the practical politics of the hour, and you will be astonished at the fanaticism there displayed. As examples, look at the works of Mably and Saint-Just. Both of these authors believed honestly that they had discovered an antidote for all the evils under which France was groaning. Mably was a bachelor and a recluse. Never mingling with society, he lived in a little garret, from which he looked out with melancholy eyes upon the world. He saw about him those who were very rich and very corrupt. He soon came to adopt as his creed, "Riches are the condition of corruption, poverty the condition of virtue." Setting out from these postulates, he proceeded to develop a political system, which he recommended to his country for adoption. The children were to be reared in common, in order that public morals might be controlled. He prescribed a national system of philosophy, in order that philosophy might not degenerate into impiety; and a national system of religion, in order that religion might not decline into superstition. As wealth engendered corruption and avarice, he made great wealth impossible by destroying all commercial traffic. He even took the trouble to volunteer some carefully elaborated advice to Americans. He assured our forefathers that, at the beginning of their nationality, they should see to it that their great cities were founded far from the sea-shore; "for," said he, "if your cities are on the sea-shore you will have a great commerce, and the moment you come to have a great commerce you are lost."

Still more bizarre was the political system of Saint-Just. He recommended that the entire youth of the nation should be devoted to two occupations—arms and agriculture. He decided that no dress other than hemp or linen should be allowed, that all should be required to sleep either on the bare ground or upon a bare floor, and that no one should be allowed to eat meat. Finally, in order that the functions of government might not be neglected, it was decided that every citizen should be allowed to vote once a year—the poor by right of their poverty, the rich or land-owners on condition of having raised four sheep in the course of the preceding year. *

* As Laboulaye has pertinently suggested, one is curious to know what Saint-Just would have the land-owners do with their sheep, as the

Now I have referred to Mably and Saint-Just, not because of their inherent importance, but because they are typical examples of a large class of political writers of that time. Our first impulse is to laugh at them, and to regard them as of no serious consequence whatever. And so long as such dreamers are confined to their own chambers, we are right; but the moment they are abroad and have a prospect of getting the government into their hands, it is time to be alarmed. It would be no element in the problem worth consideration, if there were in the state simply two or three or half a dozen insignificant fanatics who believed that political miracles could be wrought simply by voting laws, but the sad fact is that nearly all the controlling minds of France, and indeed a large proportion of the people of France, were under the same delusion. The danger was that these men of fantasy, who believed it possible and easy to regenerate a country simply by voting yes or no, would get the exclusive power of legislation into their hands, and thus convert their preposterous ideas into statutes.

We have now before us the most important elements of the problem which at the end of the last century was thrust upon the French people for solution. We have seen the condition of the nation to be such that revolution of some kind was

people were forbidden either to eat meat or to wear woollen. "Perhaps," he adds, "they were to serve a political purpose as exemplars of obedience and humility."—*États-Unis.*, vol. I. p. 12.

unavoidable. We have seen springing into an all-pervading influence systems of ethics and metaphysics which well-nigh swept away all faith in the ordinary laws of morality and religion. Connected with these systems we have seen growing up, chiefly through the influence of Voltaire, that scoffing and mocking spirit which found its sole delight in the use of ridicule,—that spirit which might appropriately have had for its motto : *Whatever is, is wrong.* Then by the side of this spirit we have seen take its place the political philosophy of Rousseau; a philosophy which not only struck at the vitals of all government, but which, by dint of the eloquence and force with which it was promulgated, came to be accepted as the political creed of a large share of the ablest thinkers of the nation. Finally, we have seen that system which, in disregard of all personal rights, gives absolute power into the hands of the representatives, thus merely transferring absolutism from the throne to the halls of legislation.

We may now inquire how these various ideas have shown their influence on the actual history of the nation. Let us glance at some of the facts of the Revolution.

At length the political condition of France had become so utterly hopeless, that the king in 1789 summoned a meeting of the States-General. The very fact was an acknowledgment of desperation, for since the days of Mary de Medicis, one hundred and seventy-five years before, no monarch had ventured to call the three estates together.

The moment they assembled, it became apparent how vastly, during that hundred and seventy-five years, public sentiment had changed. On the day of the opening ceremonies, half of Paris went to Versailles. When the representatives of the *Tiers-État* appeared, the air resounded with shouts of joy; but the magnificent procession of the clergy and nobility was received with the deepest silence.

Then, too, it was found that the proportion of the deputies of the third estate to the whole number was twice greater than it had ever been before. The representatives of the Tiers-État equalled in number those of both the other orders, though previously the three estates had been represented by numbers about equal. Nor was that all. The king had unwisely neglected to determine whether the respective orders should meet and vote separately, or whether they should constitute a single assembly. The third estate saw that if they were to deliberate and vote separately, they would be overwhelmed by the other two orders; accordingly they insisted on sitting with the clergy and nobility. In this way they secured the full advantage of the superiority of their numbers.

But notwithstanding these facts, it is probable that, if the king and his ministers had acted wisely, the work of the Assembly might have been speedily and peacefully terminated.* The great mass of the representatives had no definite plan of action. They were by no means free from their accustomed reverence for their monarch; they were, therefore, in no condition to resist any thoroughly matured plan of the king, and of the higher orders. The result was what should have been foreseen. The blunders of the king and the vacillating policy of his ministers gave the third estate time to organize their opposition. The clergy and the nobility stubbornly opposed all attempts to constitute a single general assembly. Conferences were attempted, but no progress was made. Thus, days and weeks passed away. At length Abbé Sieyès brought forward a motion, that the time had come to organize the assembly—to summon the other orders for an inspection of elections, and to take no notice of those who remained away,—to proceed, in short, at once to the business before them. This motion of Sieyès was followed with a speech in which were embodied the extremest revolutionary doctrines. "We are, as may be shown by our commissions," said he, "representatives of ninety-six per cent. of the whole nation; the *people* is sovereign: we, therefore, as its representatives, must regard and constitute ourselves as a National Representation."

* Such was the opinion of Mirabeau. Though he was by far the ablest and most influential man in the Assembly, he hesitated to lead on his followers, lest their ignorance and inexperience should lead them to ruin.—*See Von Sybel, Hist. of the Fr. Rev.*, vol. I. p. 59.

This, it is plain to see, was nothing less than a declaration of war between what were thought to be inherent rights and what were actually the existing forms. It was a declaration that the majority must rule; that if the king and the higher classes remained unreasonable, the sovereign people must proceed to administer the government without them. On the 17th of June, amidst the applause of four thousand spectators, the motion of Sieyès was carried almost unanimously. Thus the third estate constituted itself as the National Assembly.

Now the importance of this action can hardly be over-estimated. It was the formal declaration of the representatives of the nation that they were raised above all existing forms to the rank of absolute rulers of France. It was the Revolution. All the rest came in natural order.

But the king and the nobles bestirred themselves, and thought that they might yet circumvent the Assembly. When the deputies of the third estate came to the hall on the 20th of June, they found the doors closed, to make preparations for a royal sitting. It was then that the leaders assembled their followers in the neighboring Tennis-Court, and took that solemn oath which was the beginning of a new era in France,—that oath by which they swore never to separate until they had given to France a free constitution,—an oath by which most of them devoted their own heads as a sacrifice to freedom and their country. Thus Louis

XVI. was deposed, and the National Assembly was placed at once on the throne and in the hall of legislation.

The most important fact to be noted in this connection is that here was the enthronement in absolute power of those various principles and doctrines which we have been considering. I say *enthronement in absolute power*, for the Assembly professed to be controlled by no fundamental law, by no established usage. Instead of finding themselves obliged to conform to a fixed constitution, they found themselves able to frame a constitution which should conform to their wishes and designs.

Now, the importance of this feature of the French Revolution was in the peculiar character of the elements of which the Assembly was constituted—and of the peculiar views which the Assembly entertained. If it be true, as has so often been asserted, that the Revolution formed a new and a mighty era in the history of social science, it is because for the first time in the history of the modern world, if not indeed in the history of the world, ancient or modern, the past was formally renounced in the legislation of the whole people, and a government established, or attempted to be established, on purely speculative principles. This, more than anything else, is the distinctive characteristic of that event, and is what makes it of such vast importance in the study of social history. Both the English Revolution and our own were strictly circumscribed by historical and hereditary custom.

There was nothing on which Pym and Sir John Eliot insisted with more persistency and with more reason than this, that they were contending for privileges which their ancestors had enjoyed and to which they were entitled, not indeed by revolutionary right, but by simple historical right. In the last Parliament of James I., old Sir Edward Coke showed that the rights which they were claiming were embodied in the Great Charter, and that the Great Charter had been confirmed in the course of English history no less than fifty-three times.

Of the same historical character were the discussions previous to the American Revolution. From 1765 to 1776 the whole controversy turned upon what were well called the "muniments and monuments of the past." We insisted that we claimed nothing new, and asked only for what we were ready to show by the record had been confirmed by the possession of at least five hundred years. What we resisted was what we stigmatized as change. We fought for what we called our birthright,—the undoubted privileges of our race, settled upon at Runnymede, and confirmed by the Petition of Right and the Bills of Rights.

But it was far otherwise with the French Assembly in 1789. They set about pulling down the whole polity of France, and building it up again on the principles and policy of their master, Jean Jacques. The Revolution was founded on theories alone; but these were regarded as solid ground, and the delegates proceeded to erect their fabric with as much confidence as though they were building upon the solid foundation of the ages. *

But what was the character of the Assembly? It was very soon manifest that there were three parties struggling for the mastery. The first, that which occupied the extreme right, contained all the uncompromising adherents of the old *régime.* These appeared to be desirous of certain reforms, but in principle they adhered firmly to royalty. Many were men of wealth; and these, of course, had much to lose by revolution. They had an instinctive fear of disturbance; and, therefore, in all aggressive measures they were conservative, while in defensive measures they were violent. They were devoted to principle, but were for the most part quite incapable of sacrificing a single prejudice to the good of king or country. This party gradually declined in numbers and strength, until it dwindled into insignificance under the lead of such men as Maury and Cazalès.

The second party, or Centre, contained the moderate men from both extremes; representatives who were conscious, on the one hand, of the rottenness of the old government, and who were opposed, on the other, to placing the permanent con-

* Ce fûtl à l'erreur de la Révolution, et en general c'est la faute de l'ésprit français de traiter les théories politique comme des vérités mathématiques, de leur préter un absolu qu'elles ne comportent pas."—*Laboulaye, Hist des États-Unis*, vol. III. p. 292.

trol of the country in the hands of the revolutionists. This party probably contained the ablest statesman in the Assembly—men who not only saw all the horrors of the past, but who also were able to foresee and foretell something of the horrors of the future. They accepted the Revolution, not as a permanent right, but as a necessity. They were anxious to reform the old abuses, and then, as speedily as possible, to erect a new political system similar to that which existed in England.

These men, the most prominent and worthy of whom were Lally-Tallendal, Malouet, and Mounier, in less troublesome times would have constituted a reformatory party of admirable spirit and of sufficient power—a party akin to that in England which is equally removed from the conservatism of Disraeli and the radicalism of Sir Charles Dilke. But in revolutionary times, critical reason has little chance before the fiery onset of passion. The moderate party, with all its learning and eloquence, shrunk and withered before the hot blasts of the Revolution.*

* M. de Lally-Tallendal explains the reason of his leaving the Assembly in a letter to a friend, which reveals the condition of that body better than anything else with which I am acquainted. He uses these words:

"Ma santé, je vous jure, rendait mes fonctions impossibles; mais même en les mettant de côté il a été au-dessus de mes forces de supporter de plus longtemps l'horreur que me causait ce sang,—ces têtes, cette reine *presque égorgée*, ce roi, amené *esclave*, entrant à Paris au milieu de ses assassins, et précédé des têtes de ses malheureux gardes. Ces perfides janissaires, ces assassins, ces femmes cannibales,

Then there was the Left, which contained all the radical elements of the revolutionary spirit. Here were found all the worshippers of the Encyclopædists: all the followers of Rousseau, all the believers in the absolute sovereignty of the people, all the opponents of the church and of the aristocracy, all the advocates of a complete transfer of political power to the masses, in a word, all those men who were clamoring for *rights*, and who as yet had no conception of the fact that in a state there are not only *rights* to be enjoyed, but *duties* to be performed.

In every revolution there are to be found men of this character; the peculiarity of the First Revolution was that they were sufficiently strong in numbers and influence to constitute the dominant party in the Assembly. This party held the horrors of the old *régime* ever before their eyes, and they imagined that its destruction could never

ce cri de TOUS LES ÉVÊQUES À LA LANTERNE, dans le moment ou le roi entre sa capitale avec deux évêques de son conseil dans sa voiture, un *coup de fusil*, que j'ai vu tirer dans *un des carrosses de la reine*, M. Bailly appellant cela *un beau jour*,—l'assemblée ayant déclaré froidement le matin, qu'il n'était pas de sa dignité d'aller toute entière environner le roi,—M. Mirabeau disant impunément dans cette assemblée, que le vaisseau de l'état, ,loin détre arrêté dans sa course, s'élancerait avec plus de rapidité que jamais vers sa régénération, M. Bernave, riant avec lui, quand des flots de sang coulaient autour de vous, le vertueux Mounier échappant par miracle à vingt assassins, qui avaient voulu faire de sa tête un trophée de plus: voilà ce qui me fit jurer de ne plus mettre le pied *dans cette caverne d'Authropophages* (the National Assembly) où je n'avais plus de force d'élever la voix, où depuis six semaines je l'avais élevée en vain." Quoted by Burke: *Works*, vol. iii. p. 328.

be too complete. Their mistake was not in a vigorous onset upon the old abuses, but in supposing that everything connected with the former condition of things was a part of the evil. The king, the court, the clergy, the nobility, the parliaments were all alike looked upon with aversion and distrust. Whatever favored these, no matter however indirectly or moderately, received their violent opposition; whatever was opposed to these, no matter however unreasonably, was treated with admiration or indulgence.

This spirit of the Left made itself apparent the moment the great questions of the hour were brought forward for discussion. The most influential man in the party at that time was without doubt Lafayette. He brought forward the Bill of Rights. That famous document may be abbreviated into these three propositions:

All men are free and equal; all men have a right to resist oppression; all sovereignty has its origin with the people, and consequently no individual can exercise authority unless it be entrusted to him by the people.

Now, it is well to observe carefully the import of these propositions. They were not simply a general declaration that all men ought to be educated for self-government, and when so educated ought to have self-government, but they were a bold enunciation of the dogma that the government should be *by* the people, whatever the condition of the people.

One has only to call to mind the fact that, at the moment of which I am speaking, the masses of France were sunk in the deepest ignorance, and the higher orders in unparalleled immorality, to understand how difficult, nay, how impossible, it was there to establish and to maintain such a government. But that was not all, nor, indeed, was it the worst. The Bill of Rights, instead of claiming equality before the law, demanded *actual* equality, and proclaimed the right of every individual to resist every unpopular law. What was this but doing away with every existing government? It was raising to absolute power, not the collective will of the whole community, but the caprice of individual wills. The adoption of the bill by the National Assembly was simply changing the *contrat social* of Rousseau from the abstract to the concrete. It was giving to anarchy the authority and sanction of the statute. It made every violation of law lawful.

This done, there were other questions which obtruded themselves for immediate settlement. In the future government of France, was the legislature to consist of one house or of two houses? The violent revolutionists of the Left clamored loudly for one, and they carried their point, apparently for no better reason than that governments had always found the greatest safety and permanency in two. Then, again, the question arose whether the king was to have any part in the formation of the new constitution. Those who would deny him this right were largely in the minority, but they were again clamorous, while the king's counsellors and friends were weak and divided. Thus again the Extremists were victorious, and the king was deprived of his veto.

In this way the Constitution of 1793 was formed. The National Guard was now under the command of General Lafayette; the National Assembly was practically in the hands of the Extreme Left.

And now what was the result? Scarcely had the Constitution of '93 been launched, when the fatal error of the whole business showed itself. The worst was not simply that unlimited power had now passed into the hands of bad men, as unaccustomed as they were unworthy to yield it,—though that would seem to have been bad enough;—it was that the principles which had been promulgated declared to every man in the realm that he was the judge of his own cause and complaint, and furthermore that he had the same right to rebel against the Assembly that the Assembly had exercised in rebelling against the government of Louis XVI. Then occurred that fierce struggle between the most turbulent elements of the nation, the struggle which history has christened the Reign of Terror.

Of the horrors that ensued it is no part of my purpose to speak. It is in this connection enough to say, that they were sufficient to convince the nation that some form of government was a necessity. Some form of government? Yes, precisely that; for during two years, it is not inaccurate to say there was in France no government whatever. The principle seemed to be that every man was to wield whatever power he could clutch and make himself master of. At length, in 1795, the nation, wearied and crushed, was willing to turn over the formation of a constitution to men of established courage and integrity.

Perhaps the Constitution of 1795 or of the year III., taken as a whole, was the best that France has ever had. And yet at one point it was fatally weak. The nation could not endure the thought of a king, nor was it willing to entrust its fortunes to the hands of a single president. The new constitution, therefore, committed the error of conferring the executive power upon five persons, to be known as a Directory. To make a bad matter worse, the Convention decided that all the members of the Directory should be chosen from a certain one of the political parties. The immediate consequence was that the Directory fell under the control of Barras, one of the most corrupt men of the time; and the advantages that appeared to have been gained were found to be pure chimeras. For the purpose of bringing the country to a condition of rest, or, indeed, for the purpose of giving it a vigorous administration, the new constitution was found to be no more efficient than the old.

France had now tried two constitutions, and

both had failed. It was not altogether strange, therefore, that a reaction took place. A party arose which was bold enough to deny the power of constitutions to work miracles. This new party soon took one step further and began to question whether the state ought to have any constitution whatever.

The mouth-piece of the new political sect was Joseph de Maistre. In 1796, he published his *Considérations sur la France.* The work contained all the spirit and all the disdain of the old *régime.* He had a summary way of settling all difficult questions by announcing his own theories, and then by declaring that all who differed from him were imbeciles. His pet theory was that the people of a nation are politically perpetual children, and that they are to be cared for by kings, as minors are to be cared for by parents. Another notion of his was that a state which has a constitution is no longer free. "You give to yourselves a constitution, and what have you done? You have bound yourselves," he answers, "and, therefore your liberty is gone." It was one of the ideas that Rousseau had advanced, the very idea which keeps savages from civilization.

De Maistre and his school of writers had their followers and their influence; a fact that is chiefly important as showing that no absurdity failed in those days to win to itself disciples.

The practical consequence of all these diverse theories in politics and in philosophy was just what *à priori* we should be led to suppose. The work of *destruction* was one of great ease; a work, indeed, which required, not careful thought, but energetic physical force, and such physical force the Revolution was in every way fitted to provide. The exercise of liberty was so exhilarating, that men under the impulses of it were inspired with a heroism and a power which astonished the whole of Europe. But at length the work of destruction had to cease; something had to be created to be put into the place of that which had been destroyed.

The Republic, before which all Europe trembled, had to be organized in a positive and permanent form; and the form determined upon was the Directory. But no sooner were the Directors in power, than the evil influence of those revolutionary ideas of which I have spoken began painfully to show their influence. The government had at its disposal a formidable army, and perhaps the greatest generals that had appeared in the world since the downfall of Rome, and yet it began to totter the very instant it arose. In its infancy, it was devoured by innumerable diseases; during the whole of its short life it steadied itself with difficulty and seemed on the point of falling under the weight of its follies and vices.

And yet, it would be a mistake to suppose that the Directory fell from want of power. De Tocqueville declares emphatically that it had more power than any of the monarchs under the old *régime*. But his words on this whole subject are so important that I quote them at length:

"After the 18th Fructidor, more power was conferred on the Directory than had ever belonged to the dynasty which the Revolution had overthrown." "The most cruel of the laws of 1793 are less barbarous than many of those passed in 1797, 1798, and 1799. The laws which banished, without trial, the representatives of the people and the newspaper-writers to Guiana; that which authorized the Directory to imprison or transport *at will* any priests whom it should consider dangerous; the graduated income-tax, which, under the name of the forced loan, deprived the rich of the whole of their revenues; and, lastly, the famous law of hostages; have a finished and skilful atrocity that did not belong even to the laws of the Convention, and yet they did not reawaken terror. The men who proposed them were as bold and unscrupulous as their predecessors, and perhaps more intelligent in the devices of tyranny. It is the most striking fact of all, that these measures were voted almost without discussion, and promulgated without resistance. While most of the laws which prepared and established the Reign of Terror were warmly contested and excited the opposition of a great part of the country, the laws of the Directory were silently accepted. But they never could be completely enforced, and (this observation deserves especial attention) the same cause aided their birth and deadened their effect. The Revolution had lasted so long, that France, enervated and dispirited, had neither surprise nor reprobation left to manifest when the most violent and cruel laws were propounded; but this very moral debility made the daily application of such laws difficult. Public opinion no longer lent its aid; it opposed to the virulence of the government a resistance, languid indeed, but on account of its languor, almost impossible to put down. The Directory wasted its strength in this endeavor." *

Such was the feeble and desperate condition of the law-making power; such the languor of public opinion concerning the nature of the laws which were enacted.

But what was the real political condition of the country, not at the moment when the Directory came into power, but after it had been four years in the control of affairs?

An answer can in no other way be so well given as by quoting further the description of De Tocqueville. It is well known that this distinguished author at the time of his death was engaged upon a work which was to be a continuation of *L'Ancien Régime.* After spending many years in the study of the provincial archives of France, he brought to the work of composition an extraordinary sagacity enriched by the most comprehensive knowledge and the most mature re-

* *De Tocqueville, Memoir and Remains,* vol. I. p. 265.

flection. Of the two chapters which were found after the author's death to be in a condition for publication, that on *France before the Consulate* is perhaps the most remarkable that he ever wrote. I know not where, in all historical literature, there is anything better of its kind, unless, perhaps, it be the description, by Thucydides, of the political condition of Greece just before the outbreak of the Peloponnesian war. * The extra-

* Indeed, the resemblance between the condition of Greece at the time alluded to, and the condition of France just before the beginning of the Napoleonic wars, is exceedingly striking. It would require but little alteration in the way of substituting modern, in the places of ancient, names and places, to make of the 82d, 83d, and 84th chapters of the Third Book of Thucydides, the most vivid and most powerful description of French society during the French Revolution ever written. How admirably does the following passage, for example, describe one of the phases of French society: "The states then were torn by sedition, and the later instances of it in any part, from having heard what had been done before, exhibited largely an excessive refinement of ideas, both in the eminent cunning of their plans, and in the monstrous cruelty of their vengeance. The ordinary meaning of words was changed by them as they thought proper. For reckless daring is regarded as courage that is true to its friends; prudent delay, as specious cowardice; moderation, as a cloak for unmanliness; being intelligent in everything, as being useful for nothing. Frantic violence was assigned to the manly character; cautious plotting was a specious excuse for declining the contest. The advocate for cruel measures was always trusted, while his opponent was suspected. He that plotted against another, if successful, was reckoned clever; he that suspected a plot, still cleverer. While struggling by every means to obtain an advantage over each other, they dared and carried on the most dreadful deeds; heaping on still greater vengeance, not only so far as was just and expedient for the state, but to the measure of what was pleasing to either party in each successive case: and whether by an unjust sentence, or condemnation, or on gaining ascendency by a strong hand, they were ready to glut the animosity they felt at the moment. Thus piety was in fashion with neither party; but those who had the luck to effect some odious purpose under fair

ordinary merit of the work, and the fact that it forms so fit a conclusion of what I have been saying, I deem sufficient excuse for quoting it at unusual length:

"No sooner had the sovereign power returned to the *corps legislatif* than universal debility pervaded the administration throughout the country. Anarchy spread from private individuals to officials. No one resisted,—no one obeyed. It was like a disbanding army. The taxes instead of being ill paid were not paid at all. In every direction conscripts preferred highway robbery to rejoining the army. At one time it seemed as though not only order, but civilization itself, were to be overturned. Neither persons nor property, nor even the high-roads, were safe. In the correspondence of the public functionaries of the government, still preserved in the National Archives, is a description of these calamities; for, as a minister of that time said, 'The accounts given to the nation should be reassuring; but in the retreat not exposed to the public eye, where the government deliberates, everything ought to be told.'

"I have before me one of these secret reports, that of the Minister of Police, dated the 30th Fructidor, an. VII. (the 16th September), on the condition of the country. I gather from it that at

pretences were the more highly spoken of. The neutrals among the citizens were destroyed by both parties; either because they did not join in the quarrel, or for envy that they should so escape."—Bk. III. chap. 82.

that time, of the eighty-six departments into which France (properly so called, for I except the recent acquisitions by conquest) was divided, forty-five were abandoned to disorder and civil war. Troops of brigands forced open the prisons, assassinated the police, and set the convicts at liberty; the receivers of taxes were robbed, killed, or maimed; municipal officers murdered, land-owners imprisoned for ransom or taken as hostages, lands laid waste, and diligences stopped. Bands of two hundred, of three hundred, and of eight hundred men overspread the country. Gangs of conscripts resisted everywhere, arms in hand, the authorities whose duty it was to control them. The laws were disobeyed in all quarters; by some to follow the impulse of their passions, by others to follow the practices of their religion; some profited by the state of affairs to strip travellers, others to ring the long-silent church-bells, or to carry the banners of the Catholic faith through the deserted church-yards.

"The means used to suppress disturbances were at once violent and insufficient. We read in these reports that often when a refractory conscript tried to escape from the soldiers, they killed him as an example. The private dwellings of the citizens were continually exposed to domiciliary visits. Moving columns of troops, almost as disorderly as the bands which they pursued, scoured the country and extorted ransoms for want of pay or rations.

"Paris was cowed. She slept, but uneasily and disturbed by fearful dreams. A thousand different prophecies of some terrible outbreak are circulated through the city. Some say a great movement will be made against the Directory, in favor of democracy—others think it will be on the royalist side; a huge fire is to give the signal. Men have been heard to say, 'It is foolish to pay one's rent, for a blow will be struck that will settle every debt; blood will shortly be shed.' Such is the language of the reports."

"It is curious," continues the author, in commenting upon the character of these reports, "to observe the despair into which the sight of this universal confusion throws the reporters; the causes that they assign and the remedies which they propose. The citizens are in absolute apathy, say some; public spirit is utterly destroyed, say others. Here we find it asserted that the brigands find asylums everywhere; in another place it is said that the manœuvres of different parties and the impunity of crime are viewed by patriots with deplorable indifference. A few ask for measures against the supporters of fanaticism; many wish for still more stringent laws against emigrants, priests, and nuns. The greater number are full of astonishment, and consider all that is going on as incomprehensible. The secret disease which surprised the agent of the Directory, the unknown and hidden evil which was sapping the life of authority, was the state of public opinion and public morals,—France refused to obey her government.

"This secret moral resistance sufficed to paralyze a government which had no internal force or vitality. Often in our own day we have seen the executive survive the legislative functions. While the paramount powers in the state were expiring or already overthrown, the subordinate powers still continued to conduct affairs with regularity and firmness. They were times of revolution but not of anarchy. The reason is, that now in France the actual executive government forms, to a considerable extent independently of the sovereign, a special administrative body, with habits, rules and instruments of its own, so that it is able for a certain period to present the phenomenon of a headless trunk still proceeding on its way. Nothing similar existed at the time of which we are speaking. The old authorities were overthrown without any in reality being as yet substituted. The administration was as incoherent and disorderly as the nation; as much without rules, without hierarchy, and without traditions. The Reign of Terror had been able to work with this ill-made and ill-adjusted machinery. To return to it had become impossible, and in the failure of public spirit the whole political machine fell at once to pieces.

"The French nation, after having been passionately attached to liberty in 1789, loved her no longer in 1799, though no other object had engaged her affections. Having at one time bestowed on her a thousand imaginary charms, they now could not see even the merits that she really possessed, they could feel only her inconveniences and her dangers. For the last ten years, indeed, they had found her little else. According to the stormy expression of a contemporary, the republic had been nothing but a restless slavery. At what other period in history had the habits of men been so violently interfered with, and when did tyranny enter so deeply into the details of private life? What feelings and what actions had been left free? What habits or what customs had been respected? The private citizen had been forced to change the days of his work and rest, his calendar, his table of weights and measures, even his terms of speech. While obliged to bear his part in ceremonies which appeared to him ridiculous and profane, he was not allowed to worship except in secret. He broke the law whenever he obeyed his conscience or indulged his taste. I know not if a similar state of things could have been endured for so long by any other nation, but there is no limit to our patience, nor again to our resistance, on different occasions.

"Often during the course of the Revolution the French thought they were on the point of finding a happy termination of this great crisis; sometimes they trusted in the constitution, sometimes in the Assembly, and sometimes in the executive itself. Once or twice they trusted to their own exertions, which is always the last resource. All these hopes had been deceived, all these attempts had been in vain. The march of the Revolution was not arrested. Great changes, indeed, were no longer effected, but a continual agitation was kept up. The wheel, it is true, carried nothing with it, but it seemed likely to go round and round forever.

"It is difficult to imagine, even in these days, the extreme fatigue, apathy, indifference, or rather contempt for politics, into which such a long, terrible, and barren struggle had thrown men's minds. Many nations have presented a spectacle of the same nature, but as every nation brings its own peculiar character into a situation resembling that in which others have been placed, on this occasion the French appeared to abandon themselves to fate, with a feverish, passionate intoxication. Despairing of escape from their misfortunes, they determined not to think about them. The amusements of Paris, says a contemporary, are not now interrupted for a single instant, either by the terrible events that take place, or by the fear of future calamities. The theatres and public places were never so crowded. At Tivoli you hear it said that things will soon be worse than ever; patriotism is sneered at, * and through it all we dance. One of the police reports says, that on the pedestal of the statute of Liberty has been placed this inscription: 'Our Government resembles the Funeral Service; there is no Gloria, no Credo; a long Offertory, and

* "On appelle la Patrie la Patraque." Patraque is slang for an old, worn-out machine or cart.

no Benediction at the end.' Fashion was never so despotic nor so capricious. It was a strange phenomenon that despair revived the frivolity of former times. New features, however, were introduced. Our manners became eccentric, disorderly, in fact, revolutionary; trifles as well as serious things no longer knew rule or limit.

"The last thing abandoned by a party is its phraseology, because, among political parties, as elsewhere, the vulgar make the language, and the vulgar abandon more easily the ideas that have been instilled into it than the words that it has learnt. When one reads the harangues of the time, it seems as if nothing could be said simply. Soldiers are called warriors; wives, faithful companions; children, pledges of love. Duty is never mentioned—virtue takes its place; no one ever promises less than to die for his country and for liberty. The contemptible part is, that most of the orators who delivered these speeches were themselves almost as wearied, as disgusted, and as cold as their hearers; but it is a sad necessity to violent passions in their decline, that long after they have lost all influence over the heart, the expressions that once were natural to them survive. Any one who had derived all his information from the newspapers might have imagined that he lived in the midst of a nation passionately fond of liberty, and interested in public affairs. Their language had never been more inflated, nor their demands more clamorous, than when they were on the eve of fifteen years of silence. To ascertain the real power of the press, attention should be paid, not to what it says, but to the way in which the public listens. Its very vehemence is sometimes a forerunner of its entire extinction; its clamors are often the proof of its perils. It screams only because its audience is growing deaf, and this very deafness makes it safe to silence it." *

To this graphic description of De Tocqueville I shall only add that French society, in this condition, was simply waiting for a master; the only question now was as to who and what that master should be.

* *Memoir and Remains of Alexis De Tocqueville* (English Translation with Additions), London, 1861, vol. I. p. 268.

THE RISE OF NAPOLEONISM.

Δήμου τε αὖ ἄρχοντος ἀδύνατα μὴ ου κακότητα ἐγγίνεσθαι· κακότητος τοίνυν εγγινομένης ἐς τὰ κοινὰ, ἔχθεα μὲν οὐκ ἐγγίνεται τοῖσι κακοῖσι, φιλίαι δὲ ἰσχυραί· οἱ γὰρ κακοῦντες τὰ κοινὰ, συγκύφαντες ποιεῦσι, ταῦτο δὲ τοιοῦτο γίνεται, ἐς ὃ ἂν προστάς τις τοῦ δήμου τοὺς τοιούτους παύσῃ. ἐκ δὲ αὐτῶν θωμάζεται οὗτος δὴ ὑπὸ τοῦ δήμου, θωμαζόμενος δὲ ἀν' ὧν ἐφάνη μούναρχος ἐών.—HERODOTUS, Book III., Chap. 82.

Napoleon, though gigantic in war and in legislation, was imperfect and incoherent in both. He deprived France not only of liberty, but of the wish for liberty; he enveloped her in a network of centralization, which stifles individual and corporate existence, and prepares the way for the despotism of an assembly or of an emperor.—DE TOCQUEVILLE, *Memoir and Remains*, vol. II., p. 108.

CHAPTER IV.

THE RISE OF NAPOLEONISM.

THE most difficult political problems that a nation has to grapple with are those which arise at the close of its civil wars; and the questions then demanding solution are likely to be especially perplexing if the party which threw itself into rebellion has succeeded in winning its cause. A revolution is the result of real or imagined oppression; and oppression, whether real or imaginary, never fits a people or a party for the better exercise of political functions. Whenever a class of people, therefore, which has been long oppressed, finds itself, by reason of the fortunes of war, suddenly raised to a political ascendency, it always finds itself at the same time confronted with difficulties which neither its training nor its experience has qualified it to surmount. To find the enemy and to overwhelm him requires a far less comprehensive talent than that needed to mould the new elements, hostile as well as friendly, into such a government as shall embody the political theories of the victorious party. It is for this reason that many a time a political party, under the lead of a skilful general, has succeeded in completely vanquishing its enemies in the field, only to fall a speedy prey to surprising and overwhelming difficulties in the cabinet. There is nothing plainer than that revolutions, begun in the interests of the common people, have often, even when apparently successful, ended in a more complete centralization and oppression. Perhaps the most remarkable example of this abandonment of the fruits of victory, in modern history, is afforded by France at the close of the great Revolution.

For a long time it was a fond notion with a certain class of writers, especially of French writers, that the government built up by Napoleon I. was but the substantial embodiment and establishment of those principles which impelled the nation into the civil war. Of late, however, the scales have fallen from a great many eyes, and even French historians are coming to estimate in their true character the labors and the permanent influence of the first French Emperor. The great work of Lanfrey alone has been enough to dispel a multitude of illusions. I imagine it would be difficult for any one to follow his volumes through honestly without being profoundly impressed with the fact of the transformation to which I have alluded. At the time when the Revolution was at its fiercest heat, for example, the all-absorbing theory of the revolutionists was that France should not be controlled by any one man, but by the masses of the people at large. In the reign of Napoleon, however, the people were as destitute of power and influence as they had been in the days of Louis XIV. The revolutionists stoutly maintained that the executive branch of the government, no less than the legislative, should be under the control of *the people*; but Napoleon raised himself to power without consulting the will of the people, and then crowned his work of usurpation by re-establishing the principle of hereditary succession. The Revolution designed to give the largest possible power into the hands of a representative legislature; but the Emperor reduced the power of the legislature practically to nothing. In short, during the Revolution we find the people daring everything and suffering everything for the sake of a democratic republic; while in the time of the Empire we find the same people equally enthusiastic in support of an imperial and hereditary monarchy.

But the question at once arises as to how far this change of form was the result of a change of political doctrines. Had the French people abandoned their republican principles as unsound or impracticable; or, on the other hand, had they been deceived into the belief that, while they were having an empire in form, they were in reality enjoying the benefits of a republic? The latter was, without doubt, substantially the fact. Though under Napoleon I., just as later under Napoleon III., the intelligence of the nation saw clearly enough through the thin veil of republicanism, and though it understood perfectly the imperial character of the government, yet it would appear that the common people failed utterly to recognize the impossibility of having a republican government under a hereditary emperor. It may be said that both of the emperors maintained their hold upon the nation through two classes of people,—the first embracing a small but intelligent minority, who believed in an absolute government as the best which the nation could have; the second, made up of the vast but ignorant majority, who were easily deluded into the belief that because they were allowed the right of suffrage, and were occasionally consulted, they were exercising a real influence on the character of the government. With the firm support of the former class in the cabinet, and with the overwhelming numbers of the latter as a kind of ultimate court of appeal, Napoleonism was for a long time able to sustain itself, even in opposition to the great mass of the intelligence of the nation. When at last it gave way, the world expressed its surprise and fell to studying the causes of the disaster. What had long been understood by the most intelligent observers came now, on closer observation, to be generally admitted, namely, that Napoleonism was imperial in character, as well as in name, and furthermore, that it owed its success strictly to its imperial characteristics. So far as it was imperial, it was strong; while so far as it professed to be republican or democratic, it was simply a system of appearances without substance, and of pretence without reality. That it could have retained its place, even as long as it did retain it, if it had not professed democratic principles, there is no reason whatever to believe; but whether it could or could not have done so, of the fact of its essential character, there can no longer be any reasonable doubt. The rise of this fraudulent system out of the ruins of the Revolution it is now my purpose to examine.

At the moment when the first Bonaparte appeared upon the political stage, the Revolution was in its most chaotic condition. The atrocious excesses of the Reign of Terror had deprived the country of the services of the best talent, and the powers of the government had fallen into the hands of men equally remarkable for their brutality and their incapacity. The original purpose of the Revolution seemed to have been entirely forgotten. The *coup d'état* of the Mountain had been a successful attempt of the minority to get control of the majority; it was indeed a virtual abandonment of the principles for which the first blows of the Revolution had been struck. The disorders which arose as a pure result of this action were innumerable, and, from that time on, the nation presents the sad picture of half a score of factions grappling in a death-struggle with one another, not for the sake of principle, but solely for the sake of power.

No party had become so completely triumphant as to be sure of permanent rule; no faction had obtained so exclusive an influence as to discourage the ambition of the aspiring and the violent. And this was not all, nor was it the worst. For reasons which in the last chapter I endeavored to present, there was prevailing in the nation so notable a want of moral tone, as well as so morbid a craving for the sensational, that the people were in no condition to be repelled by the most audacious scrupulousness, or to be shocked by the most atrocious crimes. It would not be easy to imagine a field presenting larger possibilities to a great, bad genius like Napoleon, than that which opened before him during the latter days of the Revolution.

It is a fact of great importance, and one on which Mr. Lanfrey in his recent history has laid great stress, that the education of Napoleon was in closest harmony with the spirit of his country. The "bias of his character," was early fixed, perhaps even at the time of his birth. The island on which the family of Bonapartes had its home, had scarcely emerged from the Middle Ages. Corsica, in its struggle for independence, had fought with an unscrupulous desperation worthy of the most ferocious Italian republic. The Bonapartes were high in rank and influential in society. They threw everything into the contest. But at last the end came; for no amount of heroism and devotion could resist the overwhelming power of France. The last standard of Corsica went down in 1769, and two months after that event Napoleon was born.

But even when France had taken possession of Corsica, the island was by no means subdued.

With that tenacious persistency of opposition which, nearly two thousand years before, had so successfully defied the Romans, the Corsican chiefs threw themselves into the mountain fastnesses, and had to be hunted out one by one. Their struggle was in many respects similar to the struggle of the Saxons against the Normans in England. The contest threatened to be perpetual, and it was in the infancy of Napoleon that this slow work of conquest was going on. Stories of these bloody deeds were the first intellectual food with which the mother, burning with patriotic hatred, fed the precocious imagination of her child. In 1789 Bonaparte wrote to the Corsican chief Paoli: "I was born when my country was sinking; the cries of the dying, the groans of the oppressed, and the tears of despair surrounded my cradle from my birth."

Perhaps these facts were enough to explain Bonaparte's early transformation from childhood into manhood. If it be true, as he himself once affirmed, that men mature suddenly on the field of battle, it is no less the fact that the turmoils of civil war are destructive of all the best characteristics of boyhood. But whether these surroundings were sufficient in themselves to account for his remarkable development or not, the fact remains that in his growth the period of childhood was practically omitted. All testimony agrees that with his first intelligence he manifested an intensity of political feeling such as ordinarily comes only with maturity. It was of an importance which can hardly be over-estimated, that his intensity of character was so early developed, and that his first notions of government were associated with relentless power, rather than with the principles of justice.

This exceptional character of the parentage and infancy of Bonaparte made the first ten years of his life a kind of anachronism. The circumstances and training which influenced his early years were characteristic of the twelfth century rather than of the eighteenth. It is not altogether strange, therefore, that, as his temperament began to unfold itself, it displayed the peculiar characteristics of an imperious leader who had been born and reared in the Middle Ages. Had his lot been cast among the mediæval chieftains of Spain, he would have found congenial spirits among the Laras and the Castroes; had he lived in Italy, he would probably have secured an unenviable immortality by the side of Azzolino da Romano in the *Inferno* of Dante.*

* Could anything describe more exquisitely one of the most striking traits of Napoleon's character than the following anecdote of Azzolino? "Being one day with the Emperor on horseback, with all their people, they laid a wager as to which of them had the most beautiful sword. The Emperor drew from its sheath his own, which was wonderfully garnished with gold and precious stones. Then said Messer Azzolino: 'It is very beautiful, but mine, without any great ornament, is far more beautiful;' and he drew it forth. Then six hundred knights, who were with him, all drew theirs. When the Emperor beheld this cloud of swords, he said, 'Yours is the most beautiful.'"—*Cento Novelle Antiche*, No. 83, as *quoted by Longfellow in Note on Inferno*, xii. 110.

His father had died early, leaving a large family in absolute poverty, and, therefore, both at Brienne and afterward at Paris, where the young student went in 1785, he was obliged to remain completely isolated from society. He soon gained a reputation for being a good scholar in the mathematics, and for being thoroughly unsocial. He was morose, and had no companions. A fair proportion of his working time was spent in the routine of his studies, while his recreation consisted in making himself familiar with the few authors who were to exert an influence on his subsequent life and character.

If one were to select from the whole range of historical literature two books fitted to satisfy the intellectual hunger of so restless, craving, and ambitious a student of war as Napoleon, what would they be, if not Plutarch and the Commentaries of Cæsar? Over these books the young dreamer of military glory spent his days and his nights, until they became woven into the very tissues of his character. Before he left Brienne his ideals were fixed, and those ideals were the military heroes of antiquity. Thus, up to the time when he became an officer in the French army, the influences which unite to make up character had been in his case something entirely foreign to his age and country. Without figure of speech, they might be called barbaric. When Napoleon first began to belong to history, he not only seemed to be, as indeed he pretended to be, but he really was, a barbarian.

And in cultivated society does not genuine barbarism always carry with it a kind of fascination? Culture and morality have so many hesitations, so many misgivings, so many second thoughts, that they often lose the main chance and appear weak, while the simple and intense passions of barbarism strike suddenly and achieve brilliantly. Hence it is that the man of highest culture is often not the man for the direst emergency; hence it is sometimes that, in the most desperate situation, he who feels simply and wills strongly carries off the palm. And it is to such a victor that vulgar society is wont to shout its loudest pæans of praise. France was in just the condition to take up such a character most willingly and most heartily. If there was any one want that was felt more than any other, it was the want of a man with strong feeling, a powerful will, and a commanding intelligence. Napoleon was just such a man of feeling and will, with the addition of a great intellect.

There is one other feature of Napoleon's character which should not be overlooked, for without doubt it was one of the most important elements of his peculiar success. I refer to his freedom from all restraints of morality and good faith. It would doubtless be unreasonable to expect a man trained as Napoleon had been to play the part of a Washington, or perhaps even to understand his true mission. Professor Seeley has somewhere remarked that military government and civil government are so very different things, that a man who has a decided genius for either of them is not likely to excel at the same time in the other. The remark is just, and therefore it might have been predicted with great certainty from the first that Napoleon would turn out to be something of a tyrant; but it was not too much to hope that he would be a tyrant having some fixed belief, devoted to some cause more noble than that of self. He was sure to be narrow-minded and hard, but narrow-mindedness and hardness are not incompatible with fidelity and even generosity. And yet, when we look for these and other moral qualities in Napoleon, they elude our search. His character was fundamentally different from that of common men. We judge of men ordinarily by a moral code, simply because they give evidence of some understanding of virtue and duty. But to apply such a code to the life of Napoleon is simply absurd; as absurd as to apply it to the deeds of children who have not yet any discrimination of right and wrong, or of truth and falsehood. If there had been any ground for doubt on this subject, it has been removed by the recent publication of his works. His despatches and correspondence display the fact that he did not hesitate to resort to the most elaborate falsehood whenever falsehood would best serve his purpose. His ingenuity in misrepresentation amounted to real genius. We soon cease to be astonished at the frequency of his lies, only to be amazed at their audacity and their currency. In his military campaigns he inaugurated a system of pillage unknown in the history of the world since the famous taking of Corinth by the Romans. He robbed the nations not only of their power, but of their works of genius; despoiling them at once of their wealth and of their history and their glory. In the name of expediency he did not hesitate to put to the sword, in cold blood, a disarmed garrison to whom he had just promised protection in case of surrender; and in the same campaign he sought to rid himself by poison of his own wounded soldiers whom it was convenient to leave behind.* When there was anything to be gained, he could talk most pathetically of the sacrifice he was willing to make for the sake of saving a single life; but when the necessity was removed, he had no compunction in ordering a battle and having men killed, merely to afford a spectacle for his mistress.†

* The response of Surgeon Desgenettes to the proposition of Bonaparte is historical: "Sire, my art teaches me to cure men, not to kill them." On the whole subject the reasoning of Lanfrey (vol. I. p. 292 *seq.*) is conclusive.

† These are severe words, but here are two facts on which they are founded. On the 31st of March, 1797, he wrote from Klagenfurth, to the Archduke Charles, a celebrated letter, in which he invited that Prince to earn the title of benefactor of humanity. His army, at the moment, was in danger of annihilation, from the fact that he had pressed on towards the Austrian capital, in expectation of reinforcement from the Army of the Rhine. When he found that the Directory had kept the reinforcements back, and that he was in presence of the most imminent peril, he wrote the letter in which occurs this passage: "If the overtures of peace which I have the honor to make could save the life of a single man, I should feel prouder of the civic crown which would be my reward than of all the mournful glory of military suc-

I referred to Napoleon as being free from all restraints of morality and good faith, and I think the facts fully warrant the phrase. And yet how many there are who profess for Napoleon a profound admiration! Where is there a spirited boy who has not wished that the Emperor had conquered at Waterloo, and who has not felt the blood tingle in his veins with indignation, that such a paragon of power should be sent to languish at St. Helena? But the fact is not difficult to explain. There is a quality in human nature that refuses to be shocked even at the worst crimes, when those crimes attend upon great success. There is something captivating even in lying, when lying becomes a fine art. Crimes which in the vulgar are rewarded with ignominy, awaken a kind of admiration when they are so colossal as to become sublime.

When Napoleon first began to figure in history, his character was fully established. It must be said, moreover, that to the end he was one of the most consistent of men. In proof of this there still exists an essay written in early life, in which his ideas of statesmanship are developed. It reads

cess." These are doubtless noble words, but here is another fact which occurred in the same year, and which will serve as an interpretation. Las Casas, in his *Memorial*, gives it in the words of Napoleon himself: "Walking with her (that is, his mistress) one day, in the midst of our position near the Col de Tenda, the idea suddenly occurred to me that I would let her see something of a battle, and I ordered an attack to be made by the advance posts. We won, it is true, *but the combat could, of course, result in nothing. The attack was a pure fancy, but, for all that, some few men were left on the ground.*"

as though it were the ardent conclusions of a boy who had just read Machiavelli's Prince, and adopted his political theories. His philosophy was already the philosophy of success. He professes to have been in active sympathy with the Girondists until their fall, when his sympathy was transferred to their victorious enemies. He argues that it was an act of good citizenship to join the party of the Mountain, because the Mountain had proved itself the strongest; and if he does not convince his reader of the truth of his proposition, he at least shows with what force the idea had taken possession of his own mind.*

We see, then, the character of Bonaparte when he began to be a power among the turbulent elements of France. Calculating self-interest had completely overwhelmed every other motive. He was free from every scruple and proof against every impetuosity. On the best of terms with the party in power, he was ready to be reconciled with the conquered in case of any sudden reverse of the

* This essay, the *Souper de Beaucaire*, contained sentiments, however, which, at the time he was attempting to rise, were exceedingly troublesome to Bonaparte. When he was arrested, just after the Ninth Thermidor, he gave orders to have all the copies destroyed, and also to have the speeches, which he had made at the Club, ascribed to his brother Lucien, though Lucien at the time was too young to have spoken them. On the Twentieth Thermidor, less than ten days later, as if to give a certificate of political orthodoxy, he wrote: "I was somewhat affected at the fate of the younger Robespierre, whom I liked and whom I believed pure, but I would have poniarded my own father with my own hand, if he had aspired after despotism."—*Lanfrey*, vol. I. p. 39.

wheel of fortune. With the chaotic elements of a revolutionary government before him, and waiting for a master to mould them, this predestined favorite of fortune entered upon his work with no guide but his own genius, and no rule of action but his own ideal of greatness.

The Constitution of the year III., all things considered, was the best that the Revolution produced. The Convention which framed it had become weary of the frenzy and delirium of the multitude. It was a reaction toward a healthful public sentiment, but it was a violent reaction. It closed the Jacobin clubs, it disarmed the faubourgs, it repealed the work of the terrorists, it was, in short, a vigorous effort to return to ways of order and good government.

But that effort, from its very violence, contained in itself immense possibilities of harm. It was able to accomplish its ends only by subduing and muzzling the populace, and by this very act it cut off its own principal support. Thus the Convention, though it left some of the most liberal laws that France has ever possessed, lost its hold upon the multitude. Furthermore, the distrust of the Convention on the part of the populace, and of the populace on the part of the Convention, was completely reciprocal. All power was for the time being in the hands of the Convention, and consequently the Constitution which it bequeathed to the nation was framed so as to give to the executive branch of the government the largest possible independence of the legislature. This was the great defect of the Constitution, and it was a fatal one. There was sure to spring up as a result of this action a violent antagonism between the two branches of the government, and there was no provision for a mediatorial power by means of which it was possible to prevent either an open rupture or a complete submission. Then, too, as if for the purpose of hastening the very evils which they had thus provided for, the Convention decreed that two-thirds of its own number should hold seats in the legislature about to assemble, while one-third only should be newly elected by the people.* This was justly regarded as an insult to the nation. The hostility to the Decrees that had been enacted was most intense. When they were submitted to the popular vote, however, the people of the country districts, with that blind custom which no tyranny provokes them to break through, not only ratified the action of the Convention, but ratified it by a large majority. In explanation of this action, Lanfrey has remarked that, in a choice between known and unknown evils, the masses of the people will invariably embrace the former as the safer of the two. But whether or not this explanation alone is sufficient, Paris did not acquiesce. Her tribunes resounded with most vehement declama-

* The "Decrees," so often referred to in the history of this period, were: first, the declaration that two-thirds of the Convention should sit in the new legislature; and secondly, that these two-thirds should be chosen by the electoral colleges.

tions. At length the people of the capital, finding that their appeals to the nation were in vain, determined to resort to arms.

It was easy for the insurgents to get control of the national guard, which numbered forty thousand men. The army of the Convention numbered only eight thousand. As it became certain that an attack would be made, it was manifestly of the highest importance that the troops of the Convention should be ably commanded. After a long discussion, Barras was chosen commander-in-chief. He had seen the flash of Bonaparte's genius at Toulon, and requested that the young artilleryman might be made his second in command. Napoleon in his memoirs declares that he hesitated long whether to accept the command; not, indeed, as he clearly intimates, because he had any thought as to which side was in the right, but because he was in some doubt which party could be made to succeed.

But he accepted the sword of the Convention. He spent the night in posting his eight thousand troops for the defence of the Tuileries. On the next day, when the National Guard appeared, they found every avenue of approach bristling with cannon. After some hesitation they advanced to the attack, but the artillery of the Convention ploughed their ranks through and through. In an hour after Bonaparte had mounted the saddle the battle was over and the National Guard dispersed. Barras made haste to send in his resignation, and

Bonaparte was appointed General of the Interior. Such was the 13th Vendémiaire.

Now in this struggle the victorious Convention would seem to have been technically in the right, and yet it may be doubted whether the day was not a fatal one for the nation. The country had confirmed by its vote, not only the Constitution, but the Decrees. And yet the opposition which had just shown itself willing to resort to arms was made up of a class which it was by no means safe to alienate. Indeed, it was the very party with which the Convention had just acted, in opposition to the extreme democrats. It included the most enlightened populace of Paris. It embraced the National Guard, nearly the whole of the electoral body of the city, the brilliant middle class, in short the whole of that third estate which had done so much for the nation, and which during the past years had been trodden under foot by the populace of the faubourgs. Suspicion had been thrown on this party by the Decrees at the very moment when they were striving to blot out the remembrance of so many humiliations. They were endeavoring to recover an influence which was justly theirs, when all at once they were overwhelmed by a measure of distrust, and deprived of the fruits of what they regarded as their rightful conquest.

The Convention sustained in one respect much the same relation to the country at large as at a later period did the government of Napoleon III. In a vote taken by the people exercising universal franchise, it could boast of a majority; and yet it had arrayed against it the great mass of the intelligence of the nation, for the reason that it had deprived intelligent men of their legitimate hope of influencing the government. The victory of the 13th Vendémiaire had confirmed this alienation. It was easy to foresee that henceforth a spirit of hostility to the Convention would pervade all the ranks of intelligence in the nation. Driven from the legislative body by the Decrees and their confirmation, the spirit of hostility betook itself to the executive as its stronghold. At the first election the deputies added to the members of the Convention in order to form the legislature were chosen from the hostile party. The Convention replied by calling into the Directory five regicides of a radical type. As neither the legislative nor the executive body had any control over the other, and as they were now in open antagonism, it followed that there was no way of settling the difficulties but by a resort to force. It might have all been avoided if the Convention had simply remembered and acted on one of the most obvious principles of political science. It was enunciated by Aristotle and more fully elaborated by Cicero, that a government, to be efficient and worthy of confidence, must conserve at once the wealth and intelligence of the land, and no subsequent experience has shown that their assertions were ill founded or of limited application. It may be stated as a general truth, that a nation is in the greatest peril when those in power cease to regard these interests, and rely solely upon the most ignorant class for support; and this was just the condition of France when Napoleon took command of the army.

Meantime the 13th Vendémiaire had revealed to the different parties the weight of the sword. On the one hand it had taught authority how, at all hazards, it must rely on the army; on the other, it had shown the army how it could dispose of authority. It thus opened wide the doors to a new military government.

It is of great importance in this connection to notice that the foreign policy of France during the Revolution, had, up to the time of which we are speaking, been purely a defensive one. Since the outbreak in 1789 the country had entrenched itself firmly in the doctrine that every nation should be allowed to control its own internal affairs, and that no foreign power should be permitted, under any circumstances, the privilege of interference. But immediately after the appointment of Bonaparte all was changed. The doctrine which had hitherto been such an element of moral power in the conduct of its foreign relations was cast aside, or, rather, it was reversed. An aggressive policy was adopted, and Italy was destined to feel the first blow.

Nothing is now plainer than that the invasion of Italy by Napoleon, in 1796, was in most positive antagonism with the habit as well as the spirit of the Revolution. It was in no sense a war for principles or for right, but a war for aggrandizement. It was the beginning of a policy of offensive warfare, of which it was impossible to foresee the end. Moreover, Italy was regarded, not as an oppressed nation to be delivered, but as a rich country to be seized.*

The relations of Bonaparte with the Directory during this war afford us admirable material for the study of his character. It is the opinion of Lanfrey that the Directory had already begun to fear the power of the General, while at the same time they knew that he was necessary to the support of themselves. Above all things, therefore, it was essential that he should not be alienated. As Bonaparte knew well how indispensable his services were to the Directory, and as it became more and more apparent that they too regarded these services as indispensable, his imperious will was held under no restraint whatever. We see, in consequence, the spectacle of a general who, though acting nominally under the orders of the Directory, followed their instructions only so far as these instructions would best subserve his pur-

* The proclamation of Napoleon on taking the field shows how completely the campaign was a war of conquest and not a war of liberty: "Soldiers, you are hungry and nearly naked. The government owes you much; it can do nothing for you. Your courage and patience do you honor, but cannot procure you either profit or glory. I come to lead you into the most fertile plains of the world. There you will find rich provisions and great towns. There you will find glory, honor, and riches. Soldiers of Italy, can your courage fail you?" Is this less barbarous than the speech which Livy puts into the mouth of Hannibal?

pose. In so important a matter even as the framing of treaties, he scarcely hesitated to act in most flagrant violation of his orders. And yet during all this high-handed work of erasing state boundaries, of overthrowing time-honored governments, and of setting up pseudo-republics, the Directory had no word of rebuke to utter. When he carried out their directions, they applauded; when he violated them, they ratified.

The process by which Napoleon acquired his strange mastery of the army it is not difficult to understand. He lost no opportunity of availing himself of the riches of which he had spoken in his first proclamation. His profound knowledge of human nature led him to take nothing for himself, while he gave unbounded opportunities to his subordinates. He knew well that it was of far more consequence to him that, on his return to Paris, he should be able to boast that he remained poor while others became rich, than that he should become possessor of millions. The scandalous fortunes which most of his generals acquired only gave him the more absolute empire over them, while they in no way weakened his popularity at home. His favorite method was to give them a mission in which large sums of money passed through their hands without any supervision; and then, if they took no advantage of these, he laughed at their scruples. When he wanted reinforcements from the army of the Alps, he wrote to Kellermann, the general in command: "Help us as promptly as possible, if you wish us to send you any more seven hundred thousand francs." Once he was offered a present of four million francs by the Duke of Modena. He replied, coldly, "No, I thank you; for such a sum I am not going to put myself into your power." He preferred to confiscate the whole, as he afterwards did; not for himself, but for those from whose hands he awaited still greater power.

If the Directory raised a complaining voice, he knew of an effectual solace. On one such occasion he sent a hundred of the finest horses in Lombardy to the Directory as a present, "to replace," as he wrote, "the middling horses now harnessed to your carriages." The government, too, was in the direst need of money; and Bonaparte kept a steady stream of it flowing toward Paris. Every city which the army approached was laid under heavy contribution. Milan, for example, perhaps in despair of making a successful resistance, ventured to put to the test the commander's magnanimity by spontaneously making the first advances toward submission. What was its reward? It had the privilege of being governed by the French for the price of twenty millions of francs. In Bonaparte's letter to the Directory on the affair are to be found these words: "The country is one of the richest in the world, but entirely exhausted by five years of war." The Directory accepted the twenty millions complacently, and bestowed upon the giver their smile of approbation.

At about the same time, Turguet, appealing to Bonaparte for contributions to the navy, said: "Let us make Italy proud of contributing to the splendor of our marine." It was much as if, when Germany, at the close of the recent war, was in the act of determining the amount of the French indemnity, Von Roon had written to Bismarck, "Let us make France proud of contributing to the splendor of our navy." It was impudence fairly sublime.

But that which better than all else reveals Bonaparte's method was his dealing with the Republic of Venice. By what Lanfrey calls the most brilliant of all his campaigns, he had obtained possession of the western portion of Northern Italy. It was not strange that he coveted the Queen of the Adriatic. Let us glance at the method by which he accomplished his purpose.

In the early part of the struggle which had been going on, Venice had succeeded in maintaining the strictest neutrality. But at length a difficulty arose which afforded a pretext for war. A French captain ventured to push his vessel up into the vicinity of the Venetian powder-magazine, in violation of a general law which had always been respected by foreign powers. The Venetian commander remonstrated, but received so insulting a reply, that he fired upon the French man-of-war. The affair could have been easily settled, but under existing circumstances it was as sure to produce an explosion as though Captain Laugier had dropped a shell into the middle of the Venetian powder-house. It afforded just the pretext that Bonaparte wanted; and therefore he would listen to no overtures for a settlement. No terms they could offer would satisfy him. At length he dismissed the envoys who had sought a settlement with these words:

"I have eighty thousand men and some gunboats. I will have in Venice no inquisition and no senate. I will prove an Attila to Venice. I will have no alliance with you. I want none of your proposals. I mean to dictate the law to you. It is of no use to deceive me to gain time. The nobles of your provinces who have hitherto been your slaves are to have a share in the government like the others, but your government is already antiquated and must tumble to pieces."

The violence of this barbarous language is easily accounted for. The protocols known as the "Preliminaries of Leoben" had already been signed, by which Bonaparte (in direct violation of the orders of his government), had entered into contract to give up to Austria all the Venetian provinces between the Oglio, the Po, and the Adriatic, together with Istria and Dalmatia, while, in consideration thereof, Belgium and Lombardy were to be given up to France. The General was certain of securing a ratification of this infamous contract only by previously involving Venice in war, and consequently no opportunity was to be lost. So precious an occasion as that just afforded could not but be eagerly seized upon. Two days after the harangue just given, Bonaparte published his manifesto, declaring war.*

Of course Venice could do nothing before the French armies. Indeed, the conquest was accomplished too soon; for the "Preliminaries of Leoben" were not yet known, and France was consequently not yet ready to turn Venice over to the Emperor. A treaty was therefore signed at Milan, the most important article of which was that the French occupation should continue until the new government was established and should declare that it had no further need of assistance.

In explaining this treaty to the Directory, Bonaparte laid bare his motives in terms which it seems to me impossible to stigmatize with too great severity. He wrote as follows:

"I had several motives for concluding the treaty. 1. To enter the town without difficulties; to have the arsenal and all else in our possession in order to take from it whatever we need under pretence of the secret articles. 2. To give us the advantage of all the strength of the Venetian territory in case the treaty with the Emperor should not be executed.

* In giving an account of this whole affair to the Directory, Bonaparte himself revealed the true character of the event. Writing on the 7th of June, he used these words: "*I have purposely devised this sort of rupture, in case you may wish to obtain five or six millions from Venice. If you have more decided intentions, I think it would be well to keep up the quarrel. The truth about the affair at Peschiera is that Beaulieu basely deceived them; he asked for a passage of fifty men, and then took possession of the town.*"—*Lanfrey*, vol. I p. 100.

3. To avoid drawing upon ourselves the odium that may attach to the execution of the preliminaries, and at the same time to furnish pretexts for them and to facilitate their execution."

For the complete execution of these purposes, Bonaparte at once despatched General Gentili to take possession of the Venetian fleet and the Venetian provinces in the Levant. In his instructions to the commanding officer he used these characteristic words: "If the inhabitants of the country should be inclined to independence, you should flatter their tastes and should not fail in your proclamations to allude to Greece, Spain, and Athens." * The commission was executed with Napoleonic despatch. At Corfu, Gentili took possession of the Venetian navy, together with five hundred guns and an immense magazine.

We now approach the climax of duplicity and hypocrisy. It is important to notice the dates of the letters and despatches. That sent to the Directory was written on the 19th of May, 1797. On the 26th of the same month he wrote to the municipality, entreating them to have full confidence in his movements. He concluded his letter with an appeal which could not fail to touch noble sentiments in those who were proud of their thousand years of mediæval glory. "Under any circumstances," wrote he, "I shall do all in my power to give you proofs of the great desire I have to

* Lanfrey, vol. I. p. 199.

guarantee your liberty, and to see this unhappy Italy free from all foreign intervention, and triumphantly placed in that rank among the great nations of the world to which by her nature, position, and destiny she is so justly entitled." *

These words were received in good faith and with acclamations of joy. It was on the strength of them that a reception of extraordinary magnificence was given to Josephine, whom Bonaparte had sent as a pledge of friendship. But what followed? These words, as we have stated, were written to the Venetian municipality on the 26th of May. It was only a few hours later, at one o'clock in the morning of May 27th, that the General wrote to the Directory: "To-day we have had our first interview on the subject of the treaty of peace, and *we have agreed to present the following propositions:* 1. The boundary of the Rhine for France. 2. Salzburg and Passau for the Emperor. 3. Cleves or its equivalent for Prussia. 4. The maintenance of the Germanic Confederation. 5. The reciprocal guaranties of these articles, and VENICE FOR THE EMPEROR."

Finally, on the same day, that is, on the very day after he had sent the mellifluous message to Venice, as if for the purpose of crowning the infamy of the affair, he wrote to his government: "Venice, which has been gradually decaying ever since the discovery of Good Hope and the rise of

* Lanfrey, vol. I. p. 200.

Trieste and Ancona, can scarcely survive the blows we have just struck. With a cowardly and helpless population, in no way fit for liberty, without territory and without rivers, it is but natural that she should go to those to whom we give the continent. We shall seize the vessels, despoil the arsenal, and carry off the guns; we shall destroy the bank and keep Corfu and Ancona for ourselves."

That these accusations against the Venetians were made merely for the purpose of justifying his monstrous conduct, is shown by the fact, that only a short time before the occurrence of these events, in writing to the Directory, the General had referred to the Venetians as "the only people among all the Italians who were worthy of liberty."

The last act of this drama was soon played. The treaty of Campo-Formio completed the work, already so far advanced, by ceding Venice to the Emperor, in accordance with the conditions which Bonaparte had proposed. When the imperial envoy appeared in the Ducal palace to receive the oath of allegiance of the Venetians, a death-like silence and despair was everywhere manifest. The ex-Doge Manini was forced to take the oath in the name of his countrymen. As he arose to pronounce the fatal words, he suddenly tottered and fell senseless to the floor, struck down by anguish of heart.

Thus vanished, after a long and glorious career, the foremost of the Italian republics. In the name of liberty another crime had been committed. The military agent of the French Republic had annexed to imperial Austria the state whose inhabitants he himself had but a short time before characterized as the only people among all the Italians who were worthy of liberty.

While these painful events were taking place in Italy, an act of no less importance was performed at Paris. The blind acquiescence with which the Directory submitted to the decisions of Bonaparte was not shared by the legislature. The Council of Five Hundred still contained many who had a genuine regard for the spirit of liberty; and these could not be entirely blind to the fact that the fall of Genoa and Venice, the two most prominent republics of Italy, presaged no good to the Republic of France. There was at least one man in the Council who had the courage to protest, and his name ought not to be forgotten. On the 23d of June, Dumolard ascended the tribune of the Five Hundred for the purpose of interrogating the Directory in regard to the affairs of Italy. His speech was entirely moderate in tone. He had no personal dislike of Bonaparte; on the contrary, he had often spoken of him with genuine admiration. He neither accused nor blamed the General; he addressed the Directory, and asked above all for accurate information. "How is it," he asked, "that France is at war with Venice before the Directory has consulted the legislative body, as the Constitution requires? By what authority have they dispensed with the formality of submitting to the Assembly the declaration of war?" Then coming to the acts that followed Bonaparte's entrance into Venice, he exclaimed: "Are we then no longer the same people who proclaimed and sustained by force of arms the principle, that under no pretence whatever ought foreign powers to interfere with the form of government of another state? I will not ask what fate is reserved for Venice; *I will not ask whether the invasion, meditated, perhaps, before the commission of the offences which are assigned as motives, will not figure in history as a fit pendant to the partition of Poland.*" Dumolard closed his speech by declaring in ringing words, that the result of the policy adopted would be endless wars, while France was perishing for want of peace. "*Every one*," said he, "who reflects on the nature of our government is indignant when he thinks of the blind and silent confidence required of us in everything connected with peace or war. In England, where the Constitution only gives the two houses an indirect participation in foreign affairs, we see them demand and obtain information on all events of importance, while we, republicans, to whom has been delegated the sovereign right of making war and peace, allow our rulers to draw the veil more and more closely over a dark and obscure policy."

These noble words of warning and of reproach stirred the Five Hundred. The motion was carried; but the Directory paid no heed to it whatever. It was evident that the executive was determined to ask no counsel and to receive no advice from the legislature.

When Bonaparte received news of this motion and speech of Dumolard, he was thrown into a genuine rage. What! an obscure representative, one of those lawyers of whom he was always speaking with contempt, had dared to discuss him, the chief of an army of eighty thousand men, the distributer of states, the arbiter of princes! It was too much. He wrote immediately to the Directory a letter which at once revealed the petty nature of his imperious will, and showed plainly what might be expected. He covered Dumolard with abusive epithets, and then expressed his "surprise that this manifesto, got up by an emigrant in the pay of England, should have obtained more credit in the Council of Five Hundred than his own testimony and that of eighty thousand soldiers." Together with this letter he sent a stiletto, designed, of course, to work with melodramatic effect on the excitable Parisians. He concluded by expressing a purpose to resign and to live in tranquillity, "if, indeed," said he, "the poniards of Clichy will allow me to live at all." In another letter of the same general purpose he apostrophized his enemies thus: "But I give you notice, and I speak in the name of eighty thousand soldiers, that the time when cowardly lawyers and miserable babblers guillotined soldiers is past; and if you compel them, the soldiers of Italy will come to the barrier of Clichy with their general at their head, but woe betide you if they do come."

These words, so much more characteristic of an aboriginal chief than of a military officer in civilized society, seem nevertheless to have had a genuine meaning; for a few days later he addressed a proclamation to his army as follows:

"Soldiers, I know you are deeply stirred by the dangers which threaten the country; but the country can have no real dangers to face. The same men that made France triumph over united Europe still live. Mountains separate us from France; you would cross them with the speed of an eagle, if it were necessary to uphold the Constitution, to defend liberty, to protect the government and the republicans. Soldiers, the government watches over the laws as a sacred deposit committed to them. The royalists, the moment they show themselves, will perish. Banish disquiet. Let us swear by the shades of the heroes who have died by our sides for liberty,—let us swear by our new standards, 'War implacable against the enemies of the Republic and of the Constitution of the year III.'"

Thus with the public and with the army, Bonaparte prepared the way for what was to follow. His labors in private, moreover, were scarcely less energetic or significant. The new election which had just occurred had strengthened his enemies in the Five Hundred, so that he became more and more convinced that a blow must be struck. Accordingly he sent two agents to Paris, to feel the pulse of the public. To Lavalette, one of these, he said: "See every one; keep clear of party spirit; give me the truth, and give it free from all passion."

A mind so upright and enlightened as Lavalette's had no difficulty in comprehending the situation. He seems to have seen the mischief involved in the plot of the Directory, and he warned Bonaparte against it:

"You will tarnish your reputation if you give your support to measures of such unjust violence, measures which the position of the government in no way justifies. You will not be forgiven for uniting with the Directory in an effort to overthrow the Constitution and liberty. The proscriptions proposed are directed against the national representation, and against citizens of tried virtue, who are to be punished without trial. The odium of such tyranny would fall, not only on the Directory, but on the whole system of republican government."

But what was to be done? A *coup d'état* seemed necessary to save the Directory, and yet there might be a reaction which would ingulf all its prominent supporters. Bonaparte did not hesitate. He told Lavalette to offer to Barras, the chief of the Directory, three million francs in case the movement should succeed. At the same time he sent Augereau to Barras, as the fittest officer to execute a *coup de main*; writing to Lavalette meanwhile, "Don't trust Augereau: he is a seditious man." Thus he encouraged Barras to make the attempt, while he furnished him with the means by which he was least likely to be permanently successful. It is in the highest degree probable that Bonaparte was willing the affair should miscarry; for in case of an attempt and a failure, who but himself and his army could decide the question in dispute between the two branches of government?

But there was to be no failure. At one o'clock on the morning of September 4th (the 18th Fructidor), Augereau with twelve thousand troops surrounded the Tuileries, where the legislative body held its sessions. No resistance was made, and therefore the palace was taken possession of without the firing of a single shot. Vigorous protests were made, but they were useless. The proscribed members were placed under arrest; the others were convoked in another part of the city to ratify the will of the Directors. And this remnant of the legislature, it must be said, was not slow to confirm with the mockery of a legislative indorsement all that had been done. They voted for the transportation of a great number of their colleagues, including some of the most irreproachable citizens of their time. With these were also included the editors, writers, proprietors, managers, and conductors of forty-two public journals. They annulled the elections in the forty-eight departments which had dared to name deputies opposed to the Directory; they renewed the laws against priests and emigrants; they destroyed all liberty of the press by giving to the Directory the right to suppress journals at pleasure; they abolished all judicial power in the forty-eight departments declared to be seditious, and assigned the appointment of new judges to the Directory; finally they gave to the Directors two new colleagues, and conferred upon the executive power thus arranged the right to reform or dissolve all political societies at pleasure, as well as the right to proclaim a state of siege and to delay to an indefinite period the organization of the National Guard. It should be added, as a fit close to the record of this infamous work, that the men condemned to banishment were thrown into iron cages and sent to Rochefort, whence they were embarked for the pestilential shores of Cayenne. Half of them died speedily, thus paying with their lives for the offence of having opposed the schemes of Bonaparte and Barras. This action, more than anything else in the whole history of the Revolution, reveals the political degeneracy—I had almost said the *hopeless* political degeneracy—of the times. That the street rabble was violent was not an occasion for especial wonder. That the executive was corrupt and base is explained by the simple fact that corrupt and base men were chosen as Directors. But that an assembly of five hundred men, embodying as it did the political intelligence and political virtue of the nation, could be guilty of such monstrous excesses can only be explained on the supposition that the poison had penetrated to every part of the body politic.

The *coup d'état* of the 18th Fructidor opened the way completely for a military dictatorship. Was the nation ready to accept Bonaparte as a master, or was further preparation necessary? That the General himself inclined to the latter opinion we have the declaration of his own words. In his *Mémoires* he declares: "*In order that I might be master of France, it was necessary for the Directory to experience reverses during my absence, and for my return to restore victory to the French flag.*"

This sentence, though written years after the event, probably reveals one of the two great motives of the General in undertaking the expedition into Egypt. But whether such was actually one of his motives or not, it is certain that he could not have planned in a manner more likely to involve the Directory in difficulties that were inextricable. The moment the government ceased to receive money from the Italian army, the finances fell into the old confusion. In order to raise money for the Egyptian campaign, Bonaparte, as his correspondence reveals, advised and urged that the Directory seize upon Switzerland and Rome. On the very eve of the departure of his expedition, therefore, this act was done, and with a consequence which it would have been easy to anticipate. The outrage was felt in every corner of

Europe. War was instantly declared by the coalition against France, and the nation at once began to suffer from a double disadvantage. In the first place, Bonaparte had with him all the best officers of the army as well as his old veterans; in the second, the French frontier, by the annexations, had been so lengthened that it now extended from Amsterdam to Naples. In consequence of these two circumstances, the French armies all along the frontier were crushed, and Italy together with several of the provinces was lost. Surely the reverses which Bonaparte had deemed it necessary that the Directory during his absence should experience must have been in the highest degree satisfactory.

Moreover, affairs in Paris were in hopeless confusion. The government was fast sinking into contempt; the people saw their armies defeated and the provinces slipping away; they remembered the glorious days of the Italian campaign, and sighed for a sight of the Little Corporal.

The same favoring fortune, however, did not follow Bonaparte in the affairs of the East. Not content with an effort to reduce Egypt to the condition of a French colony,—a project which had been more or less familiar to France ever since it was proposed by Leibnitz to Louis XIV.,—Bonaparte was ambitious to revolutionize the whole of the Eastern world. He talked of ruining the English settlements in India; of chasing the Turks from Constantinople and driving them into Asia by means of a rising of the Greek and Christian populations, and then of returning to Europe, "*la prenant à revers.*"

The "moderate preliminary," as he called it, of the occupation of Egypt was no very difficult task. In Syria, however, the obstacles were insurmountable, and the aggressive force of the expedition was completely broken. After a long siege of Saint Jean d'Acre, and after as many as fourteen assaults upon the city had been made in vain, Bonaparte learned that the Turks were about to turn the tables upon him by making an attack upon Lower Egypt. Nothing but a prompt withdrawal of his army could save him from the greatest peril. Reluctantly but promptly he gave the order to retreat. At Saint Helena he was accustomed to say that a grain of sand had thwarted all his projects. He often repeated the assertion, that if Saint Jean d'Acre had fallen, he should have changed the face of the world, and been Emperor of the East.

The disasters of the retreating march were only exceeded by the mendacity of the commander in reporting them. The bulletins declared every movement a success, and transformed every reverse into an astounding victory. But concerning the true nature of that retreat from Palestine to Egypt there can no longer be any doubt. The roads were strewn with the sick and the wounded, who were left under the scorching sun to die. At one time the troops, exasperated by the distress of their companions, who reproached them with outstretched arms for their desertion, rose in mutiny. Bonaparte ordered all the cavalry to dismount, that the horses might be devoted to the conveyance of the sick and the wounded. When his equerry came to ask which horse he desired to have reserved for his own use, he replied, with a cut of his riding-whip, "Every one on foot! did you not hear the order?"

When Bonaparte, by means of the bundle of papers which Sidney Smith caused to find their way through the French lines, learned of the condition of affairs in Europe, there was but one course consistent with his character for him to pursue. There was nothing more to be done in Egypt; there was everything to be done in France. If he were to lead his army back, even in case he should, by some miracle, elude the eager eyes of Lord Nelson, the act would be generally regarded as a confession of disaster. If he were to remain with the army, he could, at best, do nothing but pursue a purely defensive policy; and if the army were to be overwhelmed, it was no part of Napoleonism to be involved in the disaster. There was but one natural way in which to settle the whole matter. It would be far shrewder to throw the responsibility of the future of Egypt on another, and to transfer himself to the field that was fast ripening for the coveted harvest. Of course Bonaparte, under such circumstances, did not hesitate as to which course to pursue. Robbing the army of such good officers as survived, he left it in command of the only one who had dared to raise his voice in opposition to the work of the 18th Fructidor. Taking with him Lannes, Murat, Berthier, Marmont, Andréossi, Duroc, Bessières, Lavalette, Monge, Berthollet, Denon, he committed the diminished and prostrated army to the heroic but indignant Kléber. Was there ever a more exquisite revenge? And we might ask, was fortune ever more capricious than when she bestowed her rewards on these two men? For the one she had the poniard of a fanatic, for the other the most powerful throne in the world.

On the arrival of Bonaparte in Paris everything seemed ready to his hand. The very events which he had probably anticipated and desired, certainly those which he afterwards declared to have been necessary to his elevation, had taken place. The policy which, in the seizure of Switzerland and the Papal States, he had taken pains to inaugurate before his departure for Egypt had borne its natural fruit. As never before in the history of Europe, England, Holland, Russia, Austria, Naples, and even Turkey had joined hands in a common cause, and as a natural consequence the Directory had been defeated at every point. Nor was it unnatural for the people to attribute all these disasters to the inefficiency of the government. The Directory had really fallen into general contempt, and at the new election on the 30th Prairial it had been practically overthrown. Rewbell, who by his influence had stood at the head of affairs, had been obliged to give way; and what was quite as important, his place had been filled by one who was known not only to be hostile to the old government, but also to have in his pocket a new constitution which, if adopted, would establish quite another order of things. By the side of this fantastic statesman, Sieyès, Barras had been retained, probably for no other reason than that he was sure to be found with the majority, while the other members, Gohier, Moulins, and Roger-Ducos were men from whose supposed mediocrity no very decided opposition could be anticipated. Thus the popular party was not only revenged for the outrages of Fructidor, but it had also made up the new Directory of men who seemed likely to be nothing but clay in the hands of Bonaparte.

The full importance of this action in a political point of view can be only estimated when it is remembered that the fatal weakness of the Constitution of the year III. was of a nature to make a repetition of such a *coup d'ètat* as that of the 18th Fructidor perpetually possible. That weakness I have already pointed out to have been a want of all proper means of reconciling the differences that might arise between the legislature and the executive branches of the government. Differences had at once arisen, and as there was no provision for a mediation, an outbreak was likely to follow. The executive had been the first to begin the contest, and the events of Fructidor had secured for the executive the first victory. But now the reverse had taken place. The Directory had committed egregious blunders, and the people had in consequence demanded a change of policy. There was, however, no other way of inaugurating a change, except by violently overthrowing the Directory. In other words, the Constitution provided no means by which the legislature could lawfully enforce the will of the people; there was, therefore, nothing for the legislature to do but either to submit tamely, or to resort to the very means secretly adopted by the Directory. In choosing the latter course, the legislature fairly accepted the challenge which had previously been given. The gauntlet thrown down by the Directory on the 18th Fructidor was taken up by the Councils on the 30th Prairial, and henceforth it was to be a war *vi et armis*, in which neither party had a right to ask favor.

The changes which had been enforced by the Councils in the composition of the Directory gave a temporary advantage to the legislature; this advantage was, however, but a trifling victory, to be followed, as we shall see, by an overwhelming defeat. As was to be anticipated, the victory of the Councils was followed by a somewhat emphatic expression of popular enthusiasm. The people for a considerable time had had no voice either directly or indirectly in the policy of the nation; but now, it was hoped, a real change had taken place. The masses, therefore, responded heartily to the calls of the new government. The armies were filled, and Bernadotte, now Minister of War, found no difficulty in arousing the slumbering enthusiasm of the nation. "Young men," said he, "there will surely be found some great captains among you"; and once more a French army was seen to be made up of heroes. Holland and Belgium were regained; in a fortnight Masséna completely routed and scattered the Austrians and Russians in Switzerland; Brune defeated the Duke of York and forced him to capitulate; Championnet established a formidable barrier along the southern frontier.

It was while the nation was rejoicing over these victories that the first bulletin was received announcing the success of the French at Aboukir. In the midst of a profound silence the President read to the Assembly of Five Hundred a despatch which painted in brief but glowing terms the extent of the victory. There were reasons why the bulletin was received with unusual enthusiasm. Nothing had been known of the situation of the army in Egypt, and the mystery which hung over the expedition had created an inexpressible anxiety. All this was at once relieved. Then, too, in the heat of political partisanship, it had come to be generally believed by the populace that Bonaparte and the army had been deported to Egypt by the Directory for no other reason than jealousy of their glory. The petitions which poured into the

Council of Five Hundred abounded in expressions deploring the "*exile of Bonaparte.*" Absurd as all this impression was, it had a vast effect upon the nation at large. To Bonaparte's absence they had attributed all their disasters, and in their belief nothing but his return would reinstate their ancient military glory.

With such sentiments as these rife in the nation, it is not difficult to understand the reason of the enthusiasm with which the bulletins from Egypt were received. The despatches were contrived with all that clever artifice of theatrical device of which Bonaparte was so consummate a master. The campaign in Syria, the battle of Mt. Tabor, the pretended destruction of Acre,—these and like inglorious exploits—some of them pure fabrications—were the pabulum on which the popular enthusiasm fed and increased.

It was while Berthier, the most graceful of Napoleon's secretaries, was attempting to throw over that deplorable campaign the halo of his fine words, that the *Moniteur* published an item of intelligence before which all else appeared insignificant. It was announced that Bonaparte had actually returned to France, that he was at that very moment on his way to Paris, and that he was everywhere saluted by an unbounded enthusiasm.

The manner in which the General was received can have left no possible doubt remaining in his mind as to the strength of his hold on the hearts of the people. It must have been apparent to all that he needed but to declare himself, in order to secure a well-nigh unanimous support and following of the masses. But with the political leaders the case, for obvious reasons, was far different. From the moment when the news of his landing at Fréjus reached Paris, there were symptoms of uneasiness in the ranks of the old politicians; for it is evident that they already saw in the popular favorite a dangerous enemy. The different political parties were so evenly balanced, that the leaders of each were not without hopes of gaining an ultimate ascendency. To all such hopes the presence of Bonaparte was sure to be fatal. His popularity was so overwhelming, that in his enmity the leaders could anticipate nothing but annihilation, in his friendship nothing but insignificance.

These considerations, however, could have no weight with any except with those whose position and influence warranted them in hoping to be raised to the very head of affairs. To the politicians of the second and third rank the new ascendency brought better prospects. Bonaparte, therefore, had no difficulty in surrounding himself with men of more than respectable talent and influence, who were eager to secure his highest favor. His long absence had kept him from all party strife; therefore, he was able to secure for himself the earnest co-operation of men who to one another were mutually irreconcilable. The Rue de la Victoire extended hospitality to guests of every political shade. Talleyrand, whose diplomatic ability had already attracted attention; Réal, the able commissioner of the Department of the Seine; Cabanis, the old friend and coadjutor of Mirabeau; Volney, the illustrious and notorious savant; Bruix, the shrewd ex-Minister of the Navy; Cambacérès, the Minister of Justice; Dubois de Crancé, the Minister of War,—these and others of similar political incompatibility were greeted at Bonaparte's residence with a most friendly welcome. For once the friends of Sieyès sat quietly by the side of those of Bernadotte, and the men of the *Manège* chatted peacefully with the adherents of Barras. Most important of all is it to note that three of the five Directors--Gohier, Roger-Ducos, and Moulins—were among the most frequent visitors, and among the foremost in their assurances of devotion.

The method in which Bonaparte set about forming a working party out of this heterogeneous material forms a good illustration of his character. The member of the government who at the time, wielded most influence, was Sieyès, a man for whom personally the General had so unconquerable an aversion, that Josephine was accustomed to refer to him as her husband's *bête noire.* It was evident that Sieyès was the most formidable obstacle to the General's advance. Either the *bête noire* would have to be destroyed, or else he would have to be pacified, or, if these were both impossible, some other pathway of advancement would have to be found. The fact that Bonaparte resorted to each of these methods in quick succession shows at once how completely devoid of principle he was, and how readily he could subordinate all personal antipathies to the interests of his ambition.

He first proposed to get himself made a member of the Directory in the place of Sieyès by finding some pretext or other for disputing the legality of his opponent's election. This course he broached to Gohier and Moulins, but they scouted the idea, declaring that, in the first place, no decent pretext for overthrowing Sieyès could be found, and, in the second, that Bonaparte was not yet fifty years old, the age required by the Constitution for all members of the Directory. This proposition, though it was urged with significant persistence, singularly enough awakened no very considerable alarm. That some suspicion was aroused, however, may be inferred from the fact that an effort was made to get rid of his presence by offering him once more a military command. But Sieyès and Barras were openly of the opinion that he had already made a sufficient fortune out of his military appointments, and accordingly they expressed a decided preference that he should remain at home. These objections afforded a convenient excuse, and Bonaparte refused the appointment.

The attempt to oust Sieyès having failed, a strenuous effort was made to get control of the party in favor of a republican dictatorship. At the head of this body stood, as a kind of military triumvirate, Bernadotte, Augereau, and Jourdan. This party, without doubt, represented better than any other the ideas of Bonaparte; for it had gathered together the scattered remains of Jacobinism, and had a strong hold on the lower orders of the people. But Bernadotte remained inflexible, though he was appealed to by all the ties of friendship and even relationship. It is impossible to believe that he had any objection to a military dictatorship; we are left, therefore, to the inference that he recognized the overwhelming powers of his brother-in-law, and consequently feared that in case of an alliance his own influence would be overshadowed or overwhelmed.

As a third move, Bonaparte attempted reconciliation with Barras. There were, apparently at least, some reasons why they should be friends. Their careers had begun together at Toulon; and it was to Barras that Bonaparte owed his command on the 13th Vendémiaire. It was known that Fouché was somewhat uneasy from the fact that his patron had fallen into disrepute with the man whose star was evidently rising, and he therefore was employed to effect a reconciliation between the two former friends. He succeeded in getting Barras to take the first step by inviting Bonaparte to dine with him at the Luxembourg. But there was no heartiness in the meeting. Each treated the other with caution and reserve. Barras at length touched upon political matters in a vague and indirect manner, as if to force his rival to commit himself first. "The Republic," said he, "is falling to pieces; it cannot long continue in this state. We must make a great change and name Hédouville President. You will join the army. For my part, I am ill, unpopular, and worn out. I am only fit for private life."

Though this little speech was probably intended simply to draw out Bonaparte, it had the opposite effect. It was evident to the General that there was nothing to hope for from a man who talked of making Hédouville President; and therefore, instead of replying to his interlocutor, he simply fixed his eyes upon him and remained silent. Barras was utterly disconcerted; a few moments later his guest withdrew.

Thus Bonaparte had attempted to place himself at the head of affairs, first by an effort to remove Sieyès, and then by trying to get control in turn of the two parties which were strong enough to afford him efficient support. In all these attempts he had been unsuccessful, and there was now nothing for him to do but either to abandon the effort, or to seek an alliance with his worst enemy, Sieyès. After having failed to remove this *bête noire* from his path, and after having been equally unsuccessful in attempting to pass around him, first on the right and then on the left, perhaps there was nothing more natural than that he should attempt to tame or pacify him, and then, if possible, to use him.

This work of reconciliation, however, was beset

with even greater difficulties than would at first appear. It was universally known, that, only a few days before the time of which we are speaking, Sieyès had talked of having Bonaparte shot for deserting his military command, and that Bonaparte had reciprocated this amiable good-will by proposing to have Sieyès removed from the dictatorship because he was sold to Prussia. Talleyrand, however, with a shrewdness for which he afterwards became more famous, saw the great advantage which an alliance of the kind proposed would afford to Bonaparte, and accordingly, notwithstanding the difficulties in the way, did not hesitate to set himself assiduously at work to bring it about. The difficulty, of course, was to overcome the antipathy of Sieyès—a difficulty which appeared absolutely insurmountable, inasmuch as the Director foresaw clearly the obscurity with which such a reconciliation threatened him. That Sieyès fully understood the danger, we have the amplest evidence. Joseph Bonaparte in his *Mémoires* declares that when he and Cabanis were striving with the Director to arrange for a meeting, the latter declared emphatically, "I know the fate that awaits me in case of a union. After he has succeeded he will separate himself from his colleagues, and stand in front of them as I stand in front of you now." And suiting his movement to the word, he stepped forward, pushing his interlocutors behind him.

With Bonaparte, on the other hand, every interest called for a speedy consummation of the alliance. He had already learned that a conspiracy embracing a considerable number of powerful adherents had been formed, and he rightly conjectured that nothing was wanting to the organization but a man of prompt action like himself. This consideration, perhaps sufficiently powerful in itself, was fortified by the recollection of his repeated failures with other parties, and also by the evident fact that the moment the *coup d'ètat* had taken place, the lion's share would fall to the most popular man. Thus the advocates of Bonaparte had every motive for putting forth their most strenuous efforts.

That Sieyès finally consented to a meeting, when he clearly foresaw the usurpation that was to follow, removes every claim that he might otherwise have had upon our respect and sympathy. Unaccountable as it may seem, he finally threw off his reserve so completely, that when Bonaparte at last called upon him to make proposals, he accepted the first overtures of the General, and that in consequence, on that very night, it was agreed between them that in eight or ten days the decisive blow should be struck. It can hardly be denied that by this very action Sieyès drew upon himself the contempt and the oblivion into which he soon after fell.

Such were the preliminary negotiations which led to that dark day in French history known as the 18th Brumaire. It remained only to get absolute control of the military forces, a task at that time in no way difficult. The officers who had returned with Bonaparte from Egypt were impatient to follow wherever their master might lead. Moreau, who, since the death of Hoche, was regarded as standing next to Bonaparte in military ability, was not reluctant to cast in his lot with the others, and Macdonald as well as Serurier soon followed his example. Bernadotte alone would yield to neither flattery nor intimidation.

The last to give in his adhesion was Lefebvre. This officer was then regarded by Bonaparte as one of his relentless opponents, and therefore he was not let into the secret until the last moment. On the morning of the 18th, when a crowd of military men of every grade thronged the dwelling of Bonaparte, Lefebvre appeared among the others. He had been summoned at midnight merely to meet his fellow-officers for a review at six o'clock in the morning. Meeting a colonel, he asked for an explanation, and was referred to Bonaparte. The latter on being approached exclaimed, "Well, you are one of the supporters of the Republic, and will you leave it to perish at the hands of these lawyers? Here is the sword I wore at the Pyramids. I give it to you as a pledge of my esteem and confidence." Was any of Napoleon's officers likely to resist such an appeal? "Let us throw the lawyers into the river," responded Lefebvre.

It needs only to be added that Bernadotte, Jourdan, and Augereau were the only officers of note whose absence from the *review* attracted attention. Bernadotte was known to be actively opposed to the movement; the others had not been admitted to the secret, and had not been invited to be present. On the following day, Augereau, meeting Bonaparte, showed his uneasiness by remarking, "So then you have no use for *ton petit Augereau?*" The chief deigned no other reply than that of informing him that in future the quieter he kept the better off he would be.

While Bonaparte was thus marshalling his forces in the Rue de la Victoire, the way was opening in the Councils. A commission of the Ancients, made up of leading conspirators, had worked all night drawing up the proposed articles, in order that in the morning the Council might have nothing to do but to vote them. The meeting was called for seven o'clock, and care was taken not to notify those members whose opposition there was reason to fear. The moment there was an opportunity, Cornet, one of the most active conspirators, mounted the tribune and denounced in most plaintive terms the dangers which threatened the government. He declared that the conspirators were "waiting only for a signal to draw their poniards on the representatives of the nation." "You have but a moment," exclaimed he, "in which to save France. If you let it pass, the Republic will be lost, and its carcass will be the prey of vultures, who will quarrel over its torn members."

Now, in all this no names of conspirators were given, no persons were even hinted at. The object of Cornet and his associates was simply to convince the ignorant of the existence of a conspiracy, and then, after binding the Council as to the source of the danger, to call into supreme power the chief conspirator in order to put the conspiracy down. What was this but casting out devils by Beelzebub, the prince of devils?

When Cornet sat down, Régnier, another of the conspirators, arose and proposed to the Assembly, for the saving of the government, the adoption of the decrees which had been already prepared. As the opposition, and, indeed, the independent members of the Council, were generally absent, the articles were adopted without discussion. Those present voted, first, to remove the sessions of the Councils from Paris to Saint Cloud (a privilege which the constitution conferred upon the Ancients alone), thus putting them at once beyond the power of influencing the populace and of standing in the way of Bonaparte. They then passed a decree giving to Bonaparte the command of the military forces, at the same time inviting him to come to the Assembly for the purpose of taking the oath of allegiance to the Constitution.

These decrees were at once taken to the expectant Dictator. They reached him at about ten o'clock in the morning. They were at once read by him to the throng of officers and soldiers who, as we have just seen, had been for some hours in waiting. After he had concluded the reading of the decrees, he asked the crowd if he could count on their support in this hour of danger; to which they responded with a general flourish of swords. The General then mounted his horse and rode off at the head of the troop.

When Bonaparte arrived at the Hall of the Council, he acted the part of swearing allegiance to the Constitution in a manner that had been hardly anticipated.

"Citizen representatives," said he, "the Republic was in danger; you were informed of it, and your decree has saved it. Woe to those who seek to bring trouble and disorder into it. General Lefebvre, General Berthier, and all my comrades in arms will aid me to stop them. Do not look to the past for a clue to guide your onward march; nothing in history ever resembled the eighteenth century; nothing in the eighteenth century ever resembled the present moment. We want a Republic founded on true liberty and national representation. We will have it, I swear; I swear it in my own name and that of my companions in arms."

Thus, instead of an oath of allegiance to the Constitution, the Council had merely received an oath that the nation should have a Republic founded on true liberty and national representation. The words have a captivating jingle, but in the mouth of Bonaparte what was the meaning of the phrases "true liberty" and "national representation"? A mere bait, of course, with which to catch the popular support.

But this fraud did not pass undetected. As soon as Bonaparte had closed, Garat arose to point out the fact that the citizen-general had forgotten the nature of the oath required, which was to swear to support the Constitution. Poor innocent Garat, he little knew the resources of Bonaparte's friends. The President instantly interfered, declaring that after the action of the morning no discussion could take place, except at Saint Cloud. Thus the mockery of the oath-taking in the Council of Ancients was accomplished.

The General had now a more difficult part to perform in the Council of Five Hundred.

As the meeting of the Assembly was not to occur until twelve o'clock of the following day, Bonaparte made use of the intervening time in posting his forces and in disposing of the Directory. Lannes he placed in command of the Tuileries; Marmont, in that of the École Militaire; Serurier, at Point du Jour; Macdonald, at Versailles; and Murat, at Saint Cloud. At all of these points it was likely that nothing more than a purely defensive policy would be demanded. But there was one locality in the city where it was probable aggressive force would be required. The Luxembourg was the seat of the Directory, and the Directory must at all hazards be crushed. In case the individual Directors should refuse to yield, it would be absolutely necessary, in order to insure the success of the enterprise in hand, to take possession of the palace by force. But this would involve the arrest of the executive,—an ignominious work which any officer would shrink from performing, since it would require a positive and unmistakable array of the military against the civil authorities. But Bonaparte knew well how to turn all such ignominious service to account. In close imitation of that policy which had left Kléber in Egypt, he placed the Luxembourg in charge of the only man in the nation who could now be regarded as his rival for popular favor. Moreau fell into the snare, and by so doing lost a popularity which he was never afterward able to regain.

Having thus placed his military forces, Bonaparte turned his attention to the Directors. The resignations of Sieyès and of Roger-Ducos he already had upon his table. It remained only to procure the others. Barras, without warning, was confronted by Talleyrand and Bruix, who asked him without circumlocution to resign his office, at the same time presenting him with the paper of resignation already drawn up at the instigation of Bonaparte, and demanding his signature. Barras rubbed his eyes, and, finding that the agents of the General were determined, wrote his name, thus crowning the work of a life equally remarkable for its treachery and its cowardice. The baseness of the act is made all the more conspicuous by the fact that, only a half-hour before, Barras had promised to meet at once his colleagues Gohier and Moulins at the Luxembourg, for the purpose of uniting in a fitting protest, and, if need be, in an energetic resistance.

Three of the Directors thus disposed of, it was left to make away with the remaining two. Bonaparte met them in person and tried various devices of flattery and of intimidation, but in vain. When he finished his interview by peremptorily demanding of both their resignation, they flatly refused; but when they returned to the Luxembourg it was only to be made prisoners by Moreau. It might be said that in the course which they pursued Gohier and Moulins simply did their duty; but in view of the acts by which Bonaparte ever after his return from Egypt had been endeavoring to win them over to his purposes, their firm conduct on that fatal day in a measure justifies the French in claiming that the Republic did not fall without honor. For their conduct on that occasion they are entitled to a permanent tribute of respect. It is only to be regretted that their firmness and their integrity were not equalled by their foresight and their wisdom.

The night of the 18th passed in comparative tranquillity. The fact that there was no organized resistance is accounted for by Lanfrey with a single mournful statement, that "nothing of the kind could be expected of a nation that had been decapitated. All the men of rank in France for the previous ten years, either by character or genius or virtue, had been mown down, first by the scaffolds and proscriptions, next by war." These are indeed melancholy words to utter of any nation, but who that has studied the French Revolution is ready to declare that they are not essentially true? The only escape had seemed to be through mediocrity or silence. Sieyès, when once urging his claims to notice, was asked what he had done. His reply was a flash of wit which lights up the whole period, "*I have lived.*"

But notwithstanding the force of the reason urged by Lanfrey, it seems to me that the national apathy on this occasion had another and a far more deplorable cause,—a cause which even at the present time entails more woes upon France than almost all others combined. I refer to that condition of political demoralization which comes from repeated acts of revolutionary violence. It requires but a glance at the successive *coups de force* which had taken place within the previous ten years to enable one to perceive ample grounds for that demoralization. On the 14th of July, 1789, absolute royalty succumbed and gave place to a constitutional monarchy. On the 10th of August, 1792, this was overthrown, and in its place was established the Republic. On the 30th of May, 1793, the lawful Republic was displaced by the revolutionary government. On the 9th of Thermidor, 1794, this was in turn overthrown by the legal authority, which held its place until the 18th

Fructidor, in 1797, when the first military *coup d'état* substituted the revolutionary in the place of the legal Directory. And now at last this in turn was compelled to give way to the establishment of a military government on the 18th Brumaire.

What was all this but the experience painted so well by Lucretius?

> . . . . Et semper victus tristisque recedit;
> Nam petere imperium, quod inane est, nec datur unquam,
> Atque in eo semper durum sufferre laborem,
> Hoc est adverso nixantem trudere monte
> Saxum, quod tamen a summo jam vertice rursum
> Volvitur, et plani raptim petit æquora campi.

Within ten years there had been eight different *coups de force*, the violent establishment of eight different governments, not a single one of which had been the spontaneous expression of the national will. These repeated acts of violence had resulted in creating a popular insensibility, as well as a confusion of law and force which is fatal to all healthful political feeling and action, and which, it is to be feared, is still the worst malady that France has to overcome. *

* On this question of the fatal continuance of a revolutionary spirit in France, the following remarks by M. Paul Janet are so excellent that I cannot but quote them :

" On ne peut donc contester à la France un droit que l'on reconnaît aux autres nations ; cependant, pour qu'une insurrection soit legitime, il faut qu'elle ne soit qu'une date de délivérance, non le signal de la révolte à perpétuité,—il faut qu'elle ait pour conséquence la paix et l'ordre, et ne soit pas le déchainement illimité du droit de la force. Le jour où la France aura définitivement conquis des destinées paisibles et acceptera sans réserve le règne de la loi, elle pourra revenir sans dànger aux souvenirs de son affranchissement, elle fêtera avec joie le jour de sa dé-

But notwithstanding this demoralization of the people, it is not to be asserted that no effort was made to resist the work of usurpation. The feebleness of the movement attempted, however, clearly demonstrates that apathy of the people to which we have referred. A few deputies met in the night at Salicetti's for the purpose of organizing the opposition. As the best preliminary measure, they decided that in the morning they would repair to Saint Cloud and would pass a decree to give the command of the guard of the Five Hundred to Bernadotte. But no sooner had the meeting dissolved, than Salicetti himself betrayed the news to Bonaparte and received his reward. Measures were at once taken by the General to prevent the deputies from reaching their destination; and thus the effort miscarried.

On the following day, before the Council of Ancients was fairly organized, the General was announced. During that morning everything had gone contrary to his expectation, and he bore an anxious and irritated look. It was evident that the sudden *éclat* of his first movement had given way to a general anxiety and a desire to put to the test of examination the pretences in regard to

liverance; mais *tant que le droit de la force n'aura pas abdiqué,—et peut-on dire qu'il ait adbiqué?—tant qu'il y aura lieu de craindre que les partis ne tiennent en réserve cette arme fatale, elle verra toujours avec inquiétude cette invocation persistante d'un droit périlleux qui peut aussi bien tuer que délivrer, et qui retourne si souvent contre ceux qui l'emploient."—L'Esprit Révolutionnaire et la Souveraineté Nationale, Revue des Deux Mondes, Tome Centième, p.* 721.

a Jacobin plot. Bonaparte evidently felt himself oppressed by the change of atmosphere, and accordingly he determined to bring the whole matter to a speedy issue. He drew up a regiment in order of battle in the court, and, referring to the Council, announced to his officers "that he was going to make an end of it." Then, followed by his *aides-de-camp*, he pressed into the presence of the Assembly.

The address by which he attempted to justify his action is remarkable only for its violence and its incoherence. He affirmed the existence of a Jacobin plot to destroy the government; but when pressed for an explanation, he could only declare that Barras and Moulins had proposed to him to be the leader of a party to overthrow all men having liberal opinions. When he was adjuring the Council to save liberty and equality, one of the members added interrogatively, "And the Constitution?" "The Constitution," exclaimed Bonaparte, "you violated it on the 22d Floréal, and you violated it on the 30th Prairial. The Constitution! The Constitution is invoked by all factions, and has been violated by all; it is despised by all; the country cannot be saved by the Constitution, because no one any longer respects it."

This harangue, however eloquent it may have seemed and however truthful the assertions it contained, in the mouth of Bonaparte was simply outrageous; for no one had done so much to violate the Constitution of the year III. as Bonaparte himself. But this was not all. When he was pressed for further explanation of the plot of which he was constantly speaking, he tried to extricate himself by changing his former accusations into a violent attack on the Council of Five Hundred. After accusing the members of wishing to re-establish the scaffolds and revolutionary committees, and of having despatched emissaries to Paris to organize a rising, he completed the consternation of his friends by resorting to open threats:

"If any orator in foreign pay talks of outlawry, let him beware of levelling such a decree against himself. At the first sign I should appeal to you, my brave companions in arms; to you, grenadiers, whose caps I perceive yonder; to you, brave soldiers, whose bayonets are in sight. Remember that I go forward accompanied by the God of fortune and the God of war!"

Thus having shifted his attack, first to one quarter and then to another, he ended by making it understood that he was not there to give even plausible reasons, but simply to enforce the commands of his imperious will.

Having reduced into a submissive mood the Council of Ancients, Bonaparte repaired at once to the Council of Five Hundred. Here his friends were less numerous and less influential. The discussion took the same turn, but was carried on with considerably more warmth and urgency. In their impatience to fathom the plot which had caused their removal to Saint Cloud, they had decided on sending an address to the Council of Ancients, asking for information. The letter of resignation which had been forced upon Barras had just been received, and the Assembly was considering the question whether it was best for them then and there to name his successor, when the door was opened, and Bonaparte, surrounded by his grenadiers, entered the hall. A burst of indignation at once arose. Every member sprang to his feet. "What is this?" they cried, "swords here! armed men! Away! we will have no dictator here." Then some of the deputies, bolder than the others, surrounded Bonaparte and overwhelmed him with invectives. "You are violating the sanctity of the laws; what are you doing, rash man?" exclaimed Bigonnet. "Is it for this that you have conquered?" demanded Destrem, advancing towards him. Others seized him by the collar of his coat, and, shaking him violently, reproached him with treason.

This reception, though the General had come with the purpose of intimidating the Assembly, fairly overwhelmed him. Eye-witnesses declare that he turned pale, and fell fainting into the arms of his soldiers, who drew him out of the hall.*

* It has been often asserted that at this time daggers were drawn upon the General; but Lanfrey has shown that the story is contradicted by all trustworthy evidence. It would have been easy for his enemies to have assassinated him in a scuffle from which he escaped

The confusion that ensued in the Assembly was indescribable. One member moved that Bonaparte be deprived of his command. Another proposed that the six thousand soldiers then surrounding the hall be declared a part of the guard of the legislative body. Finally that terrible cry of *hors la loi* was raised, the cry which had overwhelmed Robespierre himself. It would have passed almost without opposition, but for the action of Lucien, who, as President of the Assembly, steadfastly refused to put the question to vote. He reminded the Assembly of his brother's services, and entreated them not to pass a hasty judgment; after which he surprised the members by resigning his office of President. This action, at first thought, would seem to have been a blunder; but its effect, as was probably designed, only increased the confusion, for no action could now be taken until a President was chosen, and the Council was in no condition whatever to proceed with an election.

But though this action tied the hands of the Assembly at the moment when it seemed upon the point of outlawing Bonaparte, it at the same time imposed upon the conspirators themselves an additional necessity of immediate action. The General

with his clothes torn. Moreover, the detailed account, which on the next day was published in the *Moniteur*, though written by one of the partisans of Bonaparte, says nothing of an attempt at assassination. The story was doubtless invented by Lucien the second day after the act, for the purpose of justifying his brother's action.

saw the importance of bringing the affair to an end before the Council should have time to recover, and he resorted, therefore, at once to the means for which he had made such ample preparation. He ordered the soldiers to clear the hall.

When the troops, however, began to advance upon the Council, for the purpose of breaking it up by armed force, there was a degree of hesitation that gave a momentary apprehension of failure. The cause of the delay was the fact that the soldiers to whom the command had been given formed a part of the guard of the Legislative Body. It seemed for a moment probable that they would remain steadfast in defence of their charge; but Lucien, who was still generally supposed to be President of the Assembly, showed himself master of the emergency. Since his resignation he had fallen into the hands of his brother, and he now raised his voice in a harangue to the troops in regard to their duty. He assured them that the Council had been crushed by brigands in the pay of England, and that the question was now how it should be rescued from so great a danger. Then drawing his sword in a theatrical manner, he turned to the General and exclaimed: "For my own part, I swear to run this through my own brother if ever he shall strike a blow at the liberties of the French."

It was probably this oratorical flourish that saved the conspiracy from being overwhelmed. The majority of the guard, still supposing that they were listening to the President of the Assembly, regarded the speech as sufficiently assuring, and instantly responded by shouting, "*Vive Bonaparte!*"

In the midst of the excitement Murat placed himself at their head and commanded the drums to beat. When they reached the doors of the Council, the members made an earnest appeal for the legislative inviolability, but to no purpose. When they refused to retire, the drums were again beat, and the grenadiers poured into the hall. A last cry of *Vive la République* was raised, and a moment later the hall was empty. Thus the crime of the conspirators was consummated, and the First French Republic was at an end.

After this action it remained only to put into the hands of Bonaparte the semblance of regular authority. The tragedy which had just ended with the death of a republic was immediately followed by a farce. A phantom of the Council of Five Hundred—Cornet, one of them, says thirty members—met in the evening and voted the measures which had been previously agreed upon by the conspirators. Bonaparte, Sieyès, and Roger-Ducos were appointed provisional consuls; fifty-seven members of the Council who had been most prominent in their opposition were excluded from their seats; a list of proscriptions was prepared; two commissioners chosen from the assemblies were appointed to assist the consuls in their work of organization; and, finally, as if to remove the last possibility of interference with the usurpers, they adjourned the legislative body until the 20th of February.

It needs, perhaps, hardly to be said, in addition, that by means of this victory Napoleonism had removed the most formidable obstacle to that complete triumph which it soon came to enjoy. At the close of the first meeting of the consuls, Sieyès said to the chief supporters of the *coup d'état*: "*Gentlemen, you have a master. Bonaparte means to do everything, knows how to do everything, and has the power to do everything.*" Time revealed that in this extravagant homage there was far too much of truth. From this moment there were, it is true, certain forms to go through with, but for the most part they were forms only. In due time Sieyès drew from his pocket that fantastic roll which he had so long carried, known as his Constitution; but, to use the happy expression of Madame de Staël, it was only to destroy very artistically the few remaining chances of liberty. The complicated provisions of the Constitution of the year VIII. furnished both water and grist for Bonaparte's mill.

It requires but few words to describe the method by which the General's purpose was accomplished. Sieyès had imagined that all legislative action should be conducted in the form of a judicial trial, and accordingly he had organized his legislature into a species of court of equity. The Council of State, as a kind of plaintiff, was entrusted with the work of proposing and supporting new laws, while the mission of the Tribunate was to oppose the arguments of the Council of State. The legislative body, "silent as a tribunal of judges," was to decide, and finally the decision was to go to the Senate as a grand court of appeal. When Bonaparte came into power as First Consul, France presented the spectacle of a legislative body divided into four parts, each part having a separate function to perform. The first proposed laws, without discussing them; the second discussed, without passing upon them; the third passed upon them, without either proposing or discussing; and the fourth had simply the power of veto. Of these four parts, Bonaparte suppressed the second and retained the remaining three, thus, at a blow, getting rid ostensibly of what he called "*the infinite babbling of the lawyers;*" in reality, of what was the only means in the nation of considering the questions proposed, or of raising even the faintest opposition. Henceforth the legislature was worse than the play of Hamlet with Hamlet left out; it was Hamlet abolished, and the rest of the players struck dumb.*

* The suppression of the Tribunate by Napoleon has been rigorously defended by his friends and apologists. The words of Lanfrey on this subject are so spirited and, as I think, so just, that I quote them. He says: "This very inoffensive disposition in a body elected and paid by the government, and deprived of all efficacious means of making its opinion prevail, was tempered by a prudence of which it would, perhaps, be impossible to find another example in the history of deliber-

Thus it came about that during all those fiery years of the Consulate and the Empire, France had no legislature that possessed even the semblance of independence. There were at times certain formalities that to the eye had a legislative appearance, but they were mere shadows, which only helped to conceal the real substance of the government. There were also, it is true, certain changes in the constitution of the legislature, but these were only varying expressions of the same nullity.

Nor had Bonaparte any greater difficulty in brushing his colleagues out of his way. When Sieyès, upon whose face Bourrienne once said was always written, "Give me money," saw that the First Consul was absorbing all power, legislative as well as executive, he ventured mildly to raise his voice in protest. Bonaparte, however, was not to be baffled. He threw at the feet of the

ative assemblies. It is only by the most audacious of mystifications that the story of a factious tribunate has been imposed on the ignorant. Never was there a more scrupulous or more moderate opposition than that of this minority of twenty or twenty-five members, who persisted after the 18th Brumaire in not despairing of French liberty. If a reproach can be cast upon them, it is that, on more than one occasion, consideration for their opponents amounted to pusillanimity. In the voluminous official reports of the sittings of the Tribunate we find no instance in which violent language was used, except the hasty expression which escaped Duveyrier on the third sitting, and which he very soon afterwards retracted. We look in vain for a single hostile manifestation; we find, on the contrary, plenty of advances and concessions, which were to remain useless. To refuse anything to him who wants everything is as certain to offend as to yield nothing."—*Lanfrey's History of Napoleon*, vol. I. p. 424.

objector the estates of Crosnes, worth a million, and thus easily consigned his last rival to an absolute silence. Sieyès became a senator, and said nothing.

It was in the session of the 7th of February, 1800, that Roederer presented to the Legislative Assembly a grand plan for the organization of the Consular establishment. Bonaparte, as we have seen, had already made himself master of the Legislature and had brought completely under his influence all the men whom he had reason to suspect or to fear. But the nation at large had not yet fallen a prey to his grasping ambition. Paris he held in his hand, but France was not yet subject to his control. It was for the purpose of completing the work so successfully begun that Roederer's scheme was brought forward. In describing the mechanism which he proposed he used a word which was new to the generation of Frenchmen that heard him, though it represented a thing that is as old as despotism itself. He spoke of *centralization*, of a centralization, too, which was to confer upon Bonaparte the power to organize a nation of thirty millions like a single regiment. It was not that elementary centralization which gives to a general government the entire control of such affairs as pertain to the interests of the nation as a whole ; but rather that plenitude of central authority which is characteristic of despotism when it is organized and provided with all the necessary machinery for the accomplishment of its purposes.

It was the centralization of Richelieu and Louis XIV. restored and brought to perfection.

But in order to understand the character and importance of this new scheme, we must constantly bear in mind the part which centralization had already played in the history of the country. In the time of Richelieu it had been resorted to for the purpose of subduing an insolent and a tyrannical nobility. The system of *intendances* of Richelieu was brought to perfection by Louis XIV., but was finally, even before the Revolution, abandoned as oppressive and useless. In the time of Turgot provincial assemblies were organized, which contributed much to the overthrow of the old *régime.* The functions of these were still further extended under the Constituent Assembly. There can be no possible question that the provincial legislature, organized by the Assembly, contributed vastly to revive something of that local energy in France which had been stifled by two centuries of centralization, but which now again began to show signs of a hopeful vitality. Furthermore it must be admitted that the *Convention*, though it ruled with an iron hand, never interfered with the local assemblies; on the contrary, it recognized the service of those assemblies in stimulating the national patriotism against united Europe. When calmer times returned, and the Constitution of the year III. was adopted, about five thousand cantonal administrations were organized and charged with the independent management of local affairs.

These administrations were created absolutely out of nothing, and consequently they labored under all the embarrassments incident to the political inexperience of the people and the chaotic condition of society; and yet they accomplished enough to show that in the hands of a statesman they might have served as a firm basis for constitutional liberty. No such decentralizing method, however, was compatible with the ideas of Napoleon. The cantonal governments, accordingly, were all swept away, and in their place nothing was substituted. Municipal governments, it is true, were re-established, but they turned out to be mere machines for keeping the people in absolute bondage; for not only the mayors, but also the members of the city council, were all nominated by the central power.

The same method of appointment prevailed in the administration of the arrondissements. These newly established geographical divisions of the country seem to have been created for the very purpose of destroying all public life, and preventing any possible concert of resistance. Their boundaries were entirely arbitrary, drawn without any regard to local manners or customs, often even uniting people speaking different dialects and separated by chains of mountains. Over these were placed prefects and sub-prefects appointed by the authorities at Paris, and it was easy for these agents of the general government (for they were nothing else) to manipulate the disorganized masses at will. Thus having obtained the power to nominate and dismiss at his pleasure the members of all local administrations, Bonaparte's control of the executive functions of the government was complete. Henceforth every tax was collected and every bridge was repaired by men who owed their position to his favor, and to his favor alone.

But this gigantic work of centralization would have been incomplete if it had not embraced the administration of justice. The government, therefore, now laid hold of this as it had already laid hold of the executive and of the legislature.

It is unnecessary to follow out in detail the process by which the work was accomplished. It is sufficient to say, on the one hand, that under the Constituent Assembly all efforts in the direction of the judiciary had sought to insure the independence of the judges; on the other, that under the constitution of the year VIII. the ministers of justice were all made dependent upon the arbitrary will of the Consul. Burke has somewhere said that the crowning work of good government is to put twelve good men into the jury-box; the crowning act of Napoleonic centralization was to subordinate the whole court to the will of the chief executive. It assigned to him the appointment of all the judges, of the president, of all the civil and criminal tribunals, of all the justices of the peace, and even of all the members of the jury.* Add to all

* The jurymen were chosen by the prefect, who was appointed by the Consul.

this the fact that the judiciary was made a regular service, in which promotion, as in the army, depended entirely upon the will of the chief, and we are able to understand something of the temptation that was held out to the unscrupulous and the ambitious. Well might Ganilh demand from the Tribune: "What will the tribunal become when the jury is chosen by the Government, when the directors of the jury, the public prosecutor, the chief justice and the judges, are all guided by the passions of the Government?" and well he might answer: "They will be simply *commissioners* of the Government."

With the centralization of the three branches of the government in a single hand, Napoleonism may be said to have been complete. What a spectacle it was! We have seen that in the time of the Revolution an honest effort was made to give the control of all local affairs into the care of local administrators; in less than five years after Bonaparte received the command of the army of Italy, he was in the possession of more absolute power than had been enjoyed by the proudest of kings under the *old régime.* If the President of the United States should have the power of appointing all the judges both federal and local, all the justices of the peace and all the jurymen, all the governors of States and the subordinate State officers, all the supervisors and tax-commissioners, all the mayors and members of city councils, all the sheriffs and constables; and if, in addition to these, he should be placed in command of a large and devoted standing army, our government would present an aspect much like that of France under the First Consul.

From the passage of the Act of Centralization, in the year 1800, up to the day when the sword of Napoleon was broken at Leipsic, there was no power in France that could for a moment stand up against his will. All seeming limitations of his authority were mere words and shadows. Sieyès might have said with a peculiar emphasis to the nation at large, what he said to the supporters of the *coup d'état,* "YOU HAVE A MASTER." There can be, perhaps, no better summation into a single phrase of the political condition of the country than that embodied in the plagiarism of Napoleon himself: *La France c'est un homme,* et cet homme, c'est moi.

THE RESTORATION.

"Au lieu d'accepter franchement les résultats acquis de la Révolution, de lui emprunter non-seulement ses serviteurs, mais surtout ses principes, ses symboles et ses emblèmes, la Restauration aima mieux déclarer à la Révolution une guerre impuisante, guerre de mots, car il n'etait pas en son pouvoir de revenir sur les choses, et elle ne pouvait qu'alarmer et irriter ses ennemis sans les détruire."—*Prevost-Paradol, La France Nouvelle,* p. 311.

CHAPTER V.

THE RESTORATION.

HISTORY never gave to man a greater opportunity than that which she presented to Napoleon the First. The work of centralization in France has often been compared with that of the Roman government at the fall of the Republic. Their points of difference, however, are not less conspicuous than their points of similarity. Julius Cæsar was called upon to administer a republic that was enfeebled and expiring, while Napoleon found himself at the head of a nation that was throbbing with the energies and possibilities of renewed manhood. Furthermore, while Rome divided her affections between Cæsar and Pompey, Napoleon was absolutely without a rival. Never has any nation given itself more completely or more heartily into the hand of a single person than France gave herself into the hand of her master. The question, then, which history properly asks, is not what Napoleon accomplished, but how does what he accomplished compare with what he ought to have accomplished?

That the emperor did much that was for the advantage of his country no impartial student of this period will be disposed to deny. The Directory was doubtless the very worst government that the French people have ever had. When it came into power it was master, not only of France, but also of a considerable portion of foreign soil. It had the most valiant armies and the most successful captains of Europe. It dictated the peace of the Continent, a peace which the whole world, England scarcely excepted, sought almost with importunity. After a turbulent existence of five years, what was its condition?

Its conquests lost, the countries of its allies invaded, its armies annihilated, its territory divided, itself in universal contempt. And within the state the condition of affairs if possible was still worse. Disorders were perpetual; *coups d'état* were incessant; banishment was the only substitution for the scaffold; forced loans had reduced all enterprise to bankruptcy; insecurity everywhere prevailed; debauchery everywhere displayed a shameless front; public property was constantly subject to pillage; private fortunes were given over to rapine; in short, the administration on the one hand was both corrupt and helpless, and society, on the other, was reduced to its last extremities. De Broglie has aptly said, that, when the First Consul came upon the stage, he had but to take the trouble to stoop down in order to pick up the republic and put it into his pocket. Everybody clapped hands, and the power passed with scarcely a struggle from the inkstand to the sword.

It is certainly no great praise of absolutism

to say that it is better than anarchy. The new Cæsar laid his powerful hand upon this chaos, and affairs seemed almost instantly relieved as if by enchantment. Domestic society, parental authority, and the sanctity of marriage were re-established. A better administration of justice, faith in contracts, the rights of property, all these were reinstated. The government assumed the character of unity; the finances were placed upon a firmer basis; commerce was relieved from its worst encumbrances; cities were cleansed and embellished; public highways became secure; places of resort were covered with monuments; mountains were pierced with roads; canals furrowed the soil; everywhere, indeed, there came to be evidence of incomparable energy as well as of incomparable genius.

But with these achievements, which *alone* would have spread a glorious halo over his name, Napoleon unfortunately was not content. They were the means rather than the end of his ambition. Instead of cherishing a pacific policy, and developing the domestic resources of the land, he conscripted every new acquisition of strength into his own service. It is true that he restored the nation, at least temporarily, from what appeared to be a fatal malady; but his subsequent course was like that of a physician who, after effecting a cure, insists that his patient shall reward him by spending his life in his service.

Where in history, it may well be asked, is there

to be found a spectacle more tragic or more touching than that of France in the last days of the Directory? Crushed by the terrible disasters of the Revolution, covered with blood, and yet restless and troubled, famishing for peace, as well as for order and for liberty, groping for her way after so many vain efforts, and asking in anguish whether all this sacrifice and all this blood, whether all this glory and all these crimes, were to be absolutely for naught, and then, to use a figure of Louis Blanc's, submitting herself to be used as a post-horse on which one man might gallop at a panting speed toward the unknown!

There was in Napoleon,—and is there not in every genius?—a strange admixture of weakness with greatness. His southern imagination, ever heated by a partial understanding of ancient history and distorted by false notions of the middle ages, kept before itself as models at one time Alexander, at another Cæsar, at another Charlemagne. He was ever dreaming of crowns and thrones and purple robes for himself and for his friends; and it was in the ignoble pursuit of these that he exhausted the best energies of his country. To employ a figure of Prevost-Paradol, France was employed as a magic rod with which to turn everything to himself. The nation was worn out in his service, and when at last united Europe turned against him, he had nothing but a broken sword with which to defend the national soil.

In the recently published Memoirs of Guizot,

there is an exceedingly vivid picture of the condition of France in the last days of the Empire, which I shall take the liberty of quoting. At the time to which the passage relates, Guizot had just won his first laurels as Professor of History in the *Collége de France*:

"While Napoleon was using up the remains of his fortune and his power in this supreme struggle, there came to him from no part of France,—neither from Paris nor from the Departments,—and no more from his opponents, than from the people at large, any opposition or any obstacle. There was absolutely no enthusiasm for his defence, and there was very little confidence in his success. No one, however, attempted any opposition; there were some malevolent conversations, some threatening monitions, some moving about in anticipation of the end; but these were all. The emperor acted with perfect freedom from all restraint, and with all the power consistent with his isolation and the moral and material exhaustion of the country. There was never seen such public inertness in the midst of so much national anxiety, never so many malcontents abstaining from all action, never so many agents impelled to disavow their master, and yet serving him with so much docility. It was a nation of embarrassed spectators, who had lost all habit of interfering with their own individual lot, and who knew not what end they ought to hope for, or to fear, to the terrible play of which they were the stake. I remained stationary in my place before this spectacle, and, not seeing when or how it would end, I resolved, near the end of March, to go to Nîmes in order to pass some weeks with my mother, whom I had not seen for a long time. I have still before my eyes the aspect of Paris. Among other things, I remember the Rue de Rivoli, which they were just beginning to construct. When I traversed it on the morning of my departure, I saw no workman, no stirring, materials thrown together in heaps, scaffolds deserted, constructions abandoned for want of money, of hands, and of confidence; everywhere new ruins. Among the population there was a universal air of uneasiness and of restless lassitude, as of men who were in want equally of labor and of repose. During my journey along the route, in the villages and in the country, there was the same appearance of inaction and of agitation, the same visible impoverishment of the country; there were many more women and children than men; young and sorrowful conscripts on the march for their corps; sick and wounded coming into the interior. It was a nation maimed and debilitated.

"And by the side of this material distress was to be noticed a general moral perplexity, the trouble arising from antagonistic sentiments; an ardent desire for peace and a violent hatred of foreigners; both irritation and sympathy toward Napoleon, who was now condemned as the author of so many sufferings, and now celebrated as both the defender of the country and the avenger of its injuries. *And that which struck me as a very grave evil, though I was far, at that time, from measuring its full importance, was the marked inequality of sentiments among the different classes of the population. Among the independent and enlightened classes there was a desire for peace, a distaste for the exigencies and the experiments of the imperial despotism, an intelligent foresight of the fall, and an evident anticipation of another political régime. The masses of the people, on the contrary, whenever they abandoned their lassitude, did it only to fall into fits of patriotic rage, or into revolutionary longings.* The imperial *régime* had disciplined the people without reforming them. They were calm in appearance, but it might have been said of the masses, as it was said of the emigrants, that they had forgotten nothing and had learned nothing. There was absolutely no moral unity in the country. There was neither common thought nor common passion, though there had been common experience and common misfortune. The nation was almost as blindly and as profoundly divided in its languor as it had recently been in its transports.

"I caught a glimpse of these bad symptoms, but I was young, and my mind dwelt rather upon hopes for the future than upon its perils. At Nîmes I learned immediately of the events that had happened at Paris; M. Royer-Collard pressed me by letter to return; I set out at once, and a few days after my arrival I was appointed general secretary of the ministry of the interior, an office which the king had conferred upon the Abbé de Montesquiou." *

This graphic picture of the general condition of France, and especially that portion of it which I have thrown into italics, reveals clearly, as it seems to me, the principal reason why the nation was willing to accept what, to a great extent at least, was a return to the old *régime.*

It may be said that there is now nothing more certain than this, that in the last days of the Empire Napoleon was abandoned by the intelligence and the wealth of the nation. If France had manifested a tithe of the enthusiasm which inspired the Republic of the early days of the Empire, Paris after the battle of Leipsic could, at least temporarily, have been saved. But there was no heart whatever in the defence. When on the 30th of March, 1814, the last show of defence was affected, the men ready to fight and ready to die were not men in citizens' dress, but men in shirt-sleeves and men in rags. The bankers, the manufacturers, the shopkeepers, the notaries, the proprietors of houses, were ready to applaud the entry of the allies. On the evening of the 30th, Marshal Marmont, his hat and his clothes pierced with balls which he had received in leading a last charge against the enemy, was obliged to listen to the entreaties of a panic-stricken bourgeoisie. Among those to whom

* *Mémoires pour servir à l'histoire de mon temps*, tome I. p. 24.

he was compelled to yield were Messieurs Perregaux and Lafitte, the Rothschilds of their time. It was found that the way for Napoleon's downfall had long been prepared. While the people of the faubourgs had vainly cried "To Arms!" the bourgeoisie either had remained silent, or had whispered, "Let him abdicate." It was revealed that those in charge had caused muskets without cartridges to be distributed at the *Hôtel de Ville*, and cartridges without muskets at the *Place de la Révolution*. King Joseph and Marshal Marmont were obliged by their own friends to yield, and that very night the programme of the funeral of the Empire was made out at a paltry village inn, in one of the suburbs of the capital. When, on the following day, Colonel Fabvier went to Essonne to report what he had seen to Napoleon, he was obliged to relate, though he did it with tears in his eyes, that the armies of the enemy were in possession of Paris, and, what was a thousand times worse, that they had been received with exultation. "But what do the people say of me?" inquired the Emperor. "Sire, I dare not repeat it to you." "Come, what is it?" "They vilify you on all hands." Thus it was that Paris, whose women, like those of Sparta, had not for centuries seen the smoke of an enemy's camp-fire, now received the hosts of the hostile kings with shouts of rejoicing.

Look again at the reception of Napoleon on his return from Elba. Twenty days were sufficient for his march from the Mediterranean to the

Seine. He caused himself to be hailed anew as Cæsar, and as he entered Paris at one gate, the Bourbon dynasty, haggard and trembling, made haste to retire in an opposite direction. There was, as we have already seen, no opposition. Then, as if at once to arouse the slumbering or paralyzed pride of France, and to testify to Napoleon's power over the world, there came the news from Vienna. The sovereigns there assembled had instantly on the landing of Napoleon sent orders to the armies which they had just discharged to wheel around and to set their faces toward Paris. Nothing could have been so well calculated to arouse the last energies of the French people; and yet the enthusiasm, if indeed it can be called such, was but faint and but temporary. The bourgeoisie, overcome by surprise at the strange news, showed a momentary flicker of enthusiasm, but immediately it recovered its self-possession, and settled sullenly back into indifference or opposition. After the battle of Waterloo, men in caps and smock-frocks were daily posted under the windows of the Elysée Bourbon to raise the cry of *Vive l'Empereur!* but it was in vain. While these feeble cries were going up, a far different one was heard in the legislative assembly, where the interests and passions of the intelligent and the rich found utterance. "Let him abdicate," was the language of every tongue. If France had been proud of Napoleon, it is evident that her pride had now taken refuge among the most wretched of her children. When the allies once more entered the capital, once more the respectability of Paris put on its gayest attire, and "profaned the turf of Tuileries" by dancing joyfully in the very presence of the enemies' cannon.*

It can hardly be doubted, I think, that of all possible arrangements after the overthrow of Napoleon, the restoration of Louis XVIII. was, on the whole, the most satisfactory that could be made. The more substantial interests of the nation were thoroughly tired of the Napoleonic policy of war; the King of Rome as Napoleon II., with Marie Louise as regent, therefore was out of the question, inasmuch as it was felt that he would be but the shadow of the emperor ruling from his place of exile. The Orleans branch of the Bourbon family was not yet sufficiently known to be a formidable rival, even if the law of primogeniture were not enough to set it aside.

* If there is any doubt in the mind of any one as to the satisfaction felt by the better classes in Paris at the fall of Napoleon, such doubt may be removed by simply reading the address in which Villemain congratulated the Emperor Alexander on his victory. It was given in the presence of the French Academy on the 21st of April, 1814. Think of the Academy listening to words like these addressed to the leader of an invading army and the conqueror of Napoleon! "*Eloquence, or rather history, will celebrate this literary urbanity, when it comes to tell of this war without ambition, this inviolable and disinterested league, this royal sacrifice to the most cherished feelings immolated to the repose of nations, and to a sort of European patriotism.* The valiant heir of Frederick has proved to us that the chances of arms do not cast down a genuine king from the throne; that he always rises again nobly, borne up on the people's arms, and that he remains invincible because he is loved."

There was no one, therefore, better qualified than Louis XVIII. to bridge over the chasm of the past twenty-five years. Just as in England, after the Great Revolution, the people called to the throne the natural heir and successor of Charles I., whom they had beheaded, so in France the people were not likely to be content to raise to the head of the nation any other than the one who would link them most closely with the government of Louis XVI. It mattered not that Louis XVIII. mounted the throne under the patronage and protection of foreigners, so long as in the hearts of the upper bourgeoisie he was without a rival. It must be conceded, I think, that so far as it is possible for a government to be made good or bad by those in immediate control of it, there appeared to Louis XVIII., on his restoration, every possibility of the best government France has ever had. As in England on the restoration of Charles II., so now in France the people were longing for anything, no matter what, that would give them rest. For this very reason they were in no mood to put conditions on their newly made king. They gave him the untrammelled opportunity of gathering up the best results of the past history of the nation and of the revolution, and of binding them into a renovated and vigorous nationality. The affairs of the country were in a chaos, longing for order, and it needed but a wise head and a skilful hand to mould them into any form that might be desired. That the restored dynasty was neither wise nor skilful we shall presently see.

The first impulse of the nation was a commercial one. Though it had been a maxim of Napoleon that war should support itself, yet the continued drain from the ordinary channels of industry of so many men and so much material and money, could not but result in the practical destruction of the commercial equilibrium. This was especially manifest during the Hundred Days. It is the baldest commonplace to say that capital demands stability; indeed, of all things, it must and will have stability, or it will hide itself away in obscurity. It was chiefly for this reason that the capitalists represented by Lafitte and Perregaux demanded the restoration of the Bourbons. And the sequel showed that in their demand they had not mistaken the commercial interests of the country. No sooner had it become certain that the crown was to be placed upon the head of Louis, than signs of an unwonted activity began everywhere to be seen.

Even before the allies evacuated Paris it was evident that a vast change had taken place. Industries which had been paralyzed by the uncertainties of the Napoleonic rule suddenly began to throb with signs of a new life. The change was at once felt in Paris, and it was soon afterwards felt in the provinces. In the *Histoire de la Restauration, par un Homme d'Etat,** it is asserted

* Vol. III. p. 64.

that "the ordinary receipts of the merchants increased tenfold; all the young officers had boxes in the theatres and dinners at Véry's. From this year, 1815, date most of the shop-keeping fortunes of Paris. It is impossible to imagine the immense expenditure of the leaders of the coalesced armies. The Grand Duke Constantine and his brother sank 1,500,000 roubles in Paris in the course of forty days. Blucher, who received three millions from the French government, mortgaged his estates and quitted Paris, ruined by the gambling-houses."

Louis Blanc, in commenting on the same period, declares with epigrammatic bitterness: "Paris sold herself at retail, after having given herself over at wholesale, and had thus not even the merit of disinterested infamy. The city had its wages largely doled out to it. The enemies of France were prodigal, and the purveyors for this mob of enchanted revellers were as eager to gather the profits of its intoxication, to the last farthing, as the mob itself was to riot to the last in pleasures and insolence." *

It has often at the present day been a matter of regret that the Capital of France concentrates in itself so completely the various instincts, interests, and passions of the whole nation. Paris is France in almost the same sense that the city of Rome was the vast empire over which she ruled. That

* *Histoire de Dix Ans*, vol. I. p. 29.

ascendency, if it did not begin in 1815, was then immensely strengthened. Paris was encircled by the allies just in proportion as the provinces had been subjected to plunder. Fields laid waste and desolate; multitudes of petty proprietors ruined; the agriculture of several provinces blasted; opulent cities crushed under the weight of hostile contributions; everything, indeed, that long-continued war and hostile occupation can do;—these were the price at which Paris was now enriched.

But this prosperity, which at first was confined to Paris, and seemed even to exist at the expense of the provinces, soon spread over the whole country. I know of nothing which shows better the possible recuperative energy of a people, after prolonged national disaster, than the growth of French industry during the years that succeeded the Restoration. If any one has ever been deluded into saying or believing that the return of our soldiers after the late war to ways of peace and industry was something unparalleled in history, I commend to such a one the example of France between 1814 and 1830. During twenty-three years the nation had been torn by almost incessant war. A million and a half of men had fallen, and nine billions of money had been lost forever. And yet in ten years from the close of the war the nation was in a condition of financial prosperity; the inhabitants of the land had increased by more than two millions; the various industries were replete with activity; in short, the scars of war seemed to have entirely disappeared, and the country was in a condition of perfect physical health.*

In view of these facts an important question arises. Why was not the nation content to remain subject to the control of the government under which so much prosperity existed? Why, in 1830, did the people deliver themselves up to revolutionary impulses, and, by the choice of Louis Philippe, establish a change of dynasty?

An answer to these questions involves a twofold discussion; the one pertaining to the character of the government, the other to that of the people.

I have already said that when Louis XVIII. ascended the throne for the second time the people were in no mood to impose upon him conditions. France, in her trouble and in her longing for rest,

* The recuperative energy shown by France since the war of 1870 had its antecedent after the wars which terminated in 1815. There are few things more remarkable in the history of the French people than the rapidity with which they recovered from the prostrating effects of the Napoleonic wars. If one would understand this subject in its completeness, one should read the pamphlet of Baron Dupin entitled *Situation Progressive des Forces de la France depuis* 1814, Paris, 1827. In this highly interesting *brochure* the author proves conclusively that in all the branches of material industry the progress of the nation had been truly remarkable. Statistics are given to show that this extraordinary prosperity was characteristic, not only of agricultural and mineral products, but also of the various branches of manufacture and commerce. The intellectual prosperity of the nation was not less marked. M. le Comte Daru, in his *Tableaux Statistiques des produits de l'imprimerie française*, shows that while in 1814 the number of sheets issued (exclusive of the journals) was 45,675,039, in 1820 it was 80,921,302, and in 1826, 144,561,094. In journalism the increase was from 46,000,000 to 668,791,518 folio sheets.—*Dupin*, p. 46.

put herself confidingly into his hand. Moreover, the form of government established by the charter of 1814 was one which had many points of excellence; some have even gone so far as to deem it the best that France had ever enjoyed.

But every form of government, however good in itself, requires the exercise of at least some degree of sense and judgment in its administration. Among every earnest people there are certain views—call them failings, call them prejudices if you will—which it is always difficult and often impossible for a ruler to overcome. If a king be either very wise, like Henry IV., or very strong, like Louis XIV., he may impose upon his people, at least temporarily, a policy directly the opposite of the one which they desire. But Louis XVIII., was neither wise nor strong. His life had been one of misfortune. He had received harsh lessons. His family, insultingly proscribed, had been sent wandering through the world to beg a contemptuous hospitality. At one time in Germany a petty king had caused to be conspicuously posted opposite where the exiled Bourbon was finding a night's lodging: "Beggars and proscribed persons must not stop here more than a quarter of an hour." These harsh lessons produced upon Louis an effect that is not uncommon under kindred circumstances. There is nothing that so displays and develops human weaknesses as a sudden transfer from very ill to very good fortune. The instantaneous throwing off of a yoke, the immediate transfer from extreme poverty to great wealth, will at once bring to the surface whatever impurities there are in one's nature. Perhaps it would not be too much to say that of all classes of people, the most obnoxious are the rich of to-day who were yesterday poor. This is but another form of saying what Carlyle has well said, that there are a hundred men who can bear adversity where there is one who can bear prosperity.

So long as Louis remained in comparative obscurity and in exile, his deportment was of a character to move men's respect as well as their sympathy; the moment he was seated on the throne, however, he seemed chiefly anxious lest his people should get too low an estimate of his magnificence. The very first thing he did was to fly in the face of public opinion by forming his household with all possible pomp. The hoarse cry for "*Equality*" had scarcely yet died away among the people, and yet the very walls which had seen the executioner lay hands upon Louis XVI., were now redecorated with more than their former magnificence. The old etiquette was re-established, and the most illustrious names in France were scarcely illustrious enough to supply the new court with its supernumerary functionaries. A grand master, a grand harbinger, a grand almoner, a grand master of the robes, a grand master of the ceremonies—such were some of the grand luminaries whose business it was, not to aid in governing the nation, but simply to throw light and splendor upon the new court. Thus, instead of devoting himself assiduously to the welfare of the country, and surrounding himself with the ablest statesmen of the land, the restored Bourbon gave himself up to the most demonstrative assurances of his power, and surrounded himself simply with magnificent nothings and nobodies.

But in this same general line of weakness the king made another mistake that was vastly more important in its effects on the nation; I refer to the establishment of a new nobility.

The document which is known as the charter of Louis XVIII. was doubtless the work of honest men who sincerely strove to establish the best possible form of government. But while they were honest, they were mere theorists. With that persistent devotion to the ideal rather than to the practicable and the possible, which has so often characterized French politics, they inquired, not what would be the best government for France in her present condition, but what is the best form of government of which any nation, under any circumstances, is capable. The question was precisely the same impracticable one that had been asked by the men of '89 and also by the men of '93; but it received a far different answer, for the reason that the people were now living under the reign of a far different political philosophy. Rousseau had passed away. The extreme democracy, of which he was the parent, had amply demonstrated its inability to rule the nation.

With the political speculators, therefore, Rousseau had gone out of fashion and Montesquieu had come in.

In the *Esprit des Lois*, the great work of Montesquieu, there was concentrated an amount of learning and an amount of political wisdom which the scholar may even now study with considerable profit. The author was a man of genius, and a genuine student of history. He had observed with satisfaction the workings of the English constitution, and he believed that he found there the happiest solution of the difficult problems which had been discussed by Cicero and Aristotle.

Those who are familiar with that "master and guide of human reason," Aristotle, well remember that he makes this observation: that, in a state where the political powers represent only one of the three elements of society, there must of necessity be a bad government. It is necessary, he affirms, that in every country the intellectual talent and the moneyed interests should stand at the head of society. If you are governed by incapable men, or men interested in disorder, your government will speedily come to an end. But if you give to capable men and to the rich *exclusive* power, your organization will be a bad form of tyranny, that is to say, an oligarchy. The people must have their place, and their voice must be heard; otherwise, the treasure and the blood of the nation are subject to abuse. If, on the other hand, you give everything to number and nothing to intelligence, you fall a prey either to the disorder of a mob or to the oppression of a master. Every government, therefore, which is unmixed, that is to say, which consists of but *one* element of society, no matter which, is exclusive and tyrannical. What is needed, therefore, is a union of all; a strong government springing from the people, the most capable men at the head of affairs, and the vote of the people on all questions of liberty and property.*

These political principles, as true and as important now as when Aristotle taught them to the youthful Alexander, were accepted by Montesquieu, as the foundation on which every good government must rest. He believed, moreover, that these conditions were best fulfilled by the government of England. It was his conviction that in no form could wealth and intelligence be so happily united, and exert so happy an influence for the conservation of a country, as by means of a hereditary peerage.

It was, of course, easy to bring about that which accorded at once with the personal taste of the king and the earnest convictions of the political philosopher then in fashion. Accordingly, in utter disregard of the general sentiments of the people at large, the new government, even before the return of Napoleon, called a hereditary aris-

* Aristotle, Politics, Bk. IV. Chaps. XII. and XIII.

tocracy into existence by the mere fiat of its will. Napoleon ridiculed what he called his "*champignons de pairs*," but he could not do without their influence, and for this reason they were not swept away.

It requires not much thought to enable one to see that few things could have been more unwise than this creation of a peerage. The question was not at all whether the wheels of government in England or in Germany move more easily with the help of a peerage or not; it was, in the first place, whether a peerage can ever be created, and if it can, whether the condition of France demanded an attempt to create one, and promised to make such an attempt successful.

Look at those nations which have been benefited or injured, whichever you choose to regard it, by a hereditary peerage: at Rome, Spain, England, any of the states of the Middle Ages. Do you ever find such a peerage *voted* into existence? Has it not in every case been the work of power, harsh, relentless, military power, and that, too, in the very beginning of the nation's history? Call to mind the fate of the Locke and Shaftsbury's scheme in our own South. It was not even dignified with a trial, and for the simple reason that where men could have their own choice, though there were enough willing to be dukes and earls, there were none willing to be anything else. There is, I think, no record of a peerage ever having been successfully created. It has either planted and rooted itself firmly at the very moment of a nation's rescue from primeval barbarism, or its subsequent efforts to take root have been unsuccessful.

These historical facts would seem to be enough to discourage any nation from making such an attempt at any time. But in France, the argument of these general facts was even reinforced by every special consideration. Before the Revolution of 1789, had there been anything so obnoxious to the masses of the people as the nobility? Was there anything for which the people had striven with more fidelity and with more zeal than for the crushing of the nobility? Of all the results of the Revolution, there was perhaps no one which the people looked upon with more satisfaction than the sweeping away of that very distinction between classes which the government now proposed to reinstate. No possible movement of the king, therefore, could have been more unpopular.

What was the result? Precisely that which was natural and which should have been foreseen. The nation, which was in a mood to be united in firm support of the new government, and which would have been united but for the inexcusable blunders of the king, was divided into irreconcilable factions.

Moreover, the personal composition of the new peerage was such as to arouse an infinite amount of jealousy and consequent disorder. The king might even have avoided a considerable portion of the difficulty by simply reinstating the old nobility, a method that would have been the part of consistency as well as the part of prudence. In all his manifestoes the king ignored completely the mighty facts of the past nineteen years. He was even so obtuse as to date his reign always from the death of Louis XVI. Consistency demanded that he should reinstate the peerage in the same manner. But no: its *personnel* was recast without scruple and without shame. Certain peers of the nation were swept away and others were retained; in short, the peerage was a new creation, and a mere mode of recompense for personal services. If the old nobility had been the most powerful enemy of the throne, what was to be awaited from the new? To give the briefest possible answer, the king not only gave offence to the bourgeoisie, the party to which he owed his crown, and to the lower orders of the people, the party in whose interests the nobility had been swept away, but he also divided the allegiance of the nobility itself by the bungling manner in which he had created it.

There were then in the nation three parties: the nobility and its supporters; the bourgeoisie, embracing merchants, bankers, land-owners, and professional men; and lastly, the lower orders of the people.

It is not necessary for me to attempt to trace the struggles of these parties through the reigns of Louis XVIII., Charles X., and Louis Philippe.

The thirty-three years which intervene between the restoration of the Bourbon dynasty and its overthrow seem to me to be far more remarkable for violent party strife than for earnest effort to gather up the best results of the Revolution and to work them into a renewed and healthy nationality.

At the beginning of the struggle, the bourgeoisie was the party in power. Through its instrumentality, at least by means of its support, the king had regained his throne. Moreover, the laws concerning elections gave to it an advantage which amounted to almost absolute legislative authority. As no one could become a member of the Assembly who did not pay a direct tax of a thousand francs, and as no one could vote who did not pay a tax of three hundred francs, the common people were excluded not only from direct power, but also from all direct influence.

The bourgeoisie, thus possessing absolute legislative supremacy, lost no opportunity to make their power felt. A struggle at once began between the throne and the legislature similar to that which had existed between the Directory and the Council before the 18th Brumaire. The preamble of the Charter, for example, stated that the whole authority of the government resided in the person of the monarch, and though the king possessed the initiative of all laws, yet the Assembly found ample means of displaying its hostility and of demonstrating its power.

First of all they succeeded in driving from power

the king's prime minister, Fouché, a man who, it is true, had twisted himself snake-like through every party, but who, nevertheless, had been deemed by the king a necessary part of the restoration. They then began a series of sharp attacks on the royal policy; and finally they sought and found an opportunity to break over the charter. This they did by means of an open exercise of the initiative brought about in this manner. The king proposed that royalist vengeance should be limited to nineteen persons of note to be given over to the tribunals, and to thirty-eight persons to be sentenced to banishment. The rage of the Chamber rose to its highest pitch at this proposed act of indulgence. Nothing could be more overbearing than the course which the legislature pursued. Without waiting for the constitutional initiative by the king, it attempted to proscribe at one blow all the marshals, all the generals, all the prefects, all the high functionaries implicated in Bonaparte's return, and to exclude forever from the soil of France all the members of the Bonaparte family. It required all the adroitness of the Duc de Richelieu to prevent the passage of this measure; and it failed, not on account of its unconstitutionality, but on account of what was finally thought its inexpediency.

An issue even more important was raised by the proposed system of elections. Two methods presented themselves: the one creating an electoral college in each district, and giving to the king the power of attaching to each college justices of the peace, mayors, vicars-general, curés, etc., appointed by himself; the other establishing a direct election in two degrees in such a manner as to give an overwhelming power to the rich. The former, it will be seen, would make the king independent by giving him virtual control over the elections; the latter would give to the bourgeoisie the entire legislative power of the nation. It was the latter which prevailed; and from that time on, there was an unequal duel between the throne and the legislature—a duel like that between Pym and Charles I., or that between Robespierre and Louis XVI.—but it was a duel in which every advantage was on the side of the Assembly.

Now, in order to appreciate the bitterness with which this struggle was carried on, one must keep in mind one or two facts concerning the real nature of the political situation. In the first place, as I just said, all the powers of the government were expressly declared in the preface of the charter to emanate from the king. But as a matter of fact the most important acts were performed by the Assembly, not only independently of the king, but even in open violation of the king's expressed will. This discrepancy furnished grounds for the loudest complaints; complaints which were far more numerous and far more bitter by reason of the peculiar composition of the Assembly. Statistics published by the ministry showed that the number of persons in the nation who paid taxes amounting to 300 francs, the sum necessary to the exercise of the franchise, was only 90,878, and to them the electoral law gave the exclusive parliamentary power. The fact clearly shows us that the Assembly not only usurped the powers which constitutionally belonged to the king, but that it usurped them in the interest of the rich, in utter disregard of the millions in whose interest the best work of the Revolution had been done.

Now, of all this could there be but one result? The evil day might be postponed, but it was sure to come, unless these conditions were to be radically changed. The Revolution had not been in vain; and though men from sheer exhaustion might for a time be prevented from an overwhelming uprising, yet it required no prescience to foresee that in the end such an uprising would be inevitable.

But while the great harvest of 1848 was thus slowly ripening, there was an abundant fruitage of a minor sort. One has but to turn over the pages of Lamartine, of Louis Blanc, or of Guizot, to see how utterly without system, I had almost said how utterly anarchic, was the history of the time. On the political surface there were discords without number. Beneath it society was full of conspiracies and treacherous instigations. Spies flitted from the capital to the rural districts, and from the rural districts to the capital. Villanous snares were laid for men's lives, arrests were incessant, and the executioner had abundant opportunity for the exercise of his craft.

And this deplorable condition of affairs was not essentially changed on the accession of Charles X. Was not changed? Rather, I should say, it was changed for the worse. The new king had been bred to the most extravagant notions of the divine right of kings, and he brought to the throne a most uncompromising determination to resist every tendency to parliamentary usurpation. The struggle, therefore, between the two discordant and contradictory elements was more hostile than ever. The most sincere and most ardent constitutionalists attempted to reconcile them, but to no purpose. Fouché, Decazes, Villèle, Richelieu, Martignac, Polignac, all alike failed to solve the problem which appeared hopeless, and perhaps now was hopeless.

At length, perhaps as an act of desperation, the king resorted to a violent and outrageous stretch of the prerogative in the five celebrated ordinances of the 25th of July. The act threw a fatal advantage into the hands of the enemy, an advantage which was seized with eagerness and used with determination. The Revolution of 1830 was the consequence. Thus Charles X. lost his throne by an explosion of materials that had long been collecting. The five ordinances were nothing but the glowing match that fired the train.

In the beginning of the reign of Louis Philippe

it seemed for a short time that the nation was likely to find repose from the turmoils which had so long distracted it. In his election the country had repudiated the venerable principle of divine right. He was called to the throne by the spontaneous voice of the people at the moment when the best interests of the nation were in peril from the rash folly of an implacable tyrant. Then, too, the antecedents of the king were such as to give promise of an auspicious reign. He was not only a genuine admirer of English institutions, but, what was even more important, he also desired to comform, as far as practicable, the constitution of France to that of England. The charter of 1815 honestly adhered to, freedom of popular election, two legislative chambers, the press substantially but not absolutely independent, such were the liberal principles with which the house of Orleans began its political career. It would seem that with the guidance of no more even than a moderate amount of political sagacity, such a programme would have satisfied the nation and would have been sufficient to heal it at least of its worst disorders.

But alas! it soon appeared that the maladies of the country were far more deep-seated and more organic than the political doctors had suspected. Scarcely was the new king seated upon his throne, when it became painfully apparent that the disease had not been cured: that it had been for a moment merely soothed and concealed. It became speedily patent that the old elements in society were as combustible as ever, and that at any moment it required but the smallest amount of friction to produce explosion and disaster.

Almost as soon as the crown had touched the brow of Louis, four ex-ministers of Charles X. were summoned for political offences to public trial before the Chamber of Peers. As the result of the trial, they were condemned to imprisonment for life, with the loss of their titles, rank, orders, and civil rights; but for no other reason than because the sentence fell short of capital penalty, the populace became so savagely exasperated, that the gravest apprehensions concerning the result were entertained. But a short time later an insurrection broke out in Lyons. After three days of desperate fighting, it was put down by the Duke of Orleans and Marshal Soult, but not until after there had been a deplorable sacrifice of life.

Thus discontents showed themselves every where. There was the party known as the Legitimist, made up of adherents of the elder branch of the Bourbons, who acknowledged allegiance to the Duke of Bordeaux (Henry V.) as their lawful sovereign; and these of course lost no opportunity to foment disorders. There was the party composed largely of the bourgeoisie, who had gained such control of affairs in the time of Louis XVIII.; and as they now saw the power slipping from their hands, they gave to the government but an indifferent support. Then, most formidable of all, there was looming up the party of Democrats—the party which saw itself deprived of all political power through the manœuvres of the law of elections—the party from which nothing but the most violent opposition was to be awaited.

These elements in the state, taken in connection with the prevailing revolutionary temper of the French people, undoubtedly formed one of the most difficult of political problems; and yet, if the ministry had been made up with due reference to the demands of the different parties, and if the law of elections had been so modified as to give to the people a reasonable voice in the government, it is difficult to detect any sufficient reason why the government might not have survived. The elements of the problem were in many respects similar to those which confronted William III. of England after the Revolution of 1688. But while in England the policy of reconciliation was the one adopted, in France the government chose the policy of defiance. The king selected his ministers exclusively from a single party—the party, of course, which was most friendly to himself. At the beginning of his reign, he commanded a decided majority in both houses of the legislature. But it soon appeared that there were misunderstandings and divisions even among the Orleanists themselves. Ere long it became painfully apparent that dissensions and jealousies were creeping in, and that the throne was in danger of being undermined by the very parties to whom it owed its existence. Its revolutionary origin, if nothing else, should have made the king constantly mindful of the fact, that if at any time the favor and support of the people should be withdrawn, he would be obliged to yield up his crown in imitation of his predecessor.

During the last years of this struggle, the management of affairs was committed to the hand of the great historian whose works were already known and admired in both hemispheres. On the 29th of October, 1840, the formation of a new cabinet was intrusted to M. Guizot. From that time until the Revolution of 1848, his policy was of so much importance that I shall devote the next chapter to its consideration.

THE MINISTRY OF GUIZOT.

"L'Action des assemblées représentatives, la libre discussion des affaires publiques au dedans et dehors de leur enceinte, la liberté électorale, la liberté religieuse, la liberté de la presse, la liberté du travail, l'égalité civile, l'indépendence judiciaire, telles sont aujourd'hui les impérieuses conditions du gouvernement libre."—*Guizot, Mémoires,* VIII. p. 3.

"L'Esprit révolutionnaire ne reconnaît pas plus les droits de la volonté d'un peuples régulièrement experimenté que celle d'un souverain. Il caractérise ces libéraux prétendus qui, soit par naïveté, soit par quelque autre raison, ne reculent pas devant l'idée contradictoire d'imposer la liberté. Ceci est une maladie morale dont le remède ne se trouve pas dans les institutions. On ne peut la guérir qu'en restaurant dans les âmes le sentiment de l'obéissance et la notion du respect dû à la loi."—*Naville, La Réforme Electorale en France,* p. 25.

CHAPTER VI.

THE MINISTRY OF GUIZOT.

THE first ten years of the reign of Louis Philippe were marked with frequent and great disorders. Expressions of discontent breaking out, now here, now there, led to frequent changes in the ministry,—changes so frequent, indeed, that it would be difficult to show that there was any one line of policy underlying and inspiring the course of the government. Périer, Soult, Thiers, Molé, each undertook the administration of affairs; but neither of them was able to reconcile the conflicting elements of the nation, or to suppress the turbulence which everywhere prevailed. The revolutionary spirit, of which I have so often spoken, was still active; and consequently no movement of the government was received with general favor.

The three parties into which the political sympathies of the people were then, just as they are still, divided were so nearly equal in strength that neither of them was able to gain and to hold a majority. If the nation had been pervaded by a conciliatory spirit this fact might not have been fatal to the prevalence of good order; but the government itself had a revolutionary origin, and the revolutionary spirit, which was all-pervasive, argued with faultless logic that it had the same right to resist the Orleanists that the Orleanists had maintained and carried out in resisting the Legitimists. The result was not only that the two parties out of power were always in the majority, but also that they were always disposed to use their advantage for the annoyance and overthrow of their opponent. Thus, whatever policy was adopted by the ministry, it was sure to be outvoted in the Chamber of Deputies. Not even the unscrupulous inconsistencies of Thiers enabled him to keep a majority in his favor, though to all appearances he could change his convictions as easily as he changed his garments.*

* Whatever may be thought of the presidency of Thiers after the close of the Franco-Prussian war, I imagine it will be difficult for any one who studies his early political career with care, to entertain for him any sincere respect. He began his career in the columns of the *National* as an apostle of extreme liberal opinions, but his views underwent a sudden change as soon as the Revolution was accomplished and he had a seat in the cabinet. He was the chief author of the famous "Laws of September," which were far more characteristic of an absolute, than of a limited, monarchy. Again, as soon as he was overthrown, he veered round to the contrary direction and strongly contested the royal prerogative. Through the vigor of his opposition, the Duke de Broglie was defeated in the Deputies (January, 1836), and he was again called into power as president of the Council. His persistent determination to interfere in Spanish affairs, however, brought him into such an attitude before the nation, that he was obliged to retire after an administration of only six months. Once more out of power, he threw himself again into the opposition, and finally busied himself politically by supporting, if, indeed, he did not originate, the banquets which resulted in the fall of Louis Philippe. In all this it is difficult to detect any political consistency whatever. He has evidently believed in nothing but success, and this fact is probably the best explanation,

On the accession of the Ministry of October, 1840, however, all this was changed. From that time on the government had a *policy*—a policy which at least had the merit of consistency, whatever may be thought to have been its weaknesses and its mistakes. It was under that government, that affairs were ripened for the Revolution, and it is with that government, therefore, that we have now especially to deal.

When the portfolio of the government was entrusted to Guizot, there seemed to be every reason to hope that new vigor and new wisdom would be imparted to the general conduct of affairs. This eminent historian and statesman brought to the task of forming the cabinet and determining its policy a most thorough knowledge of his own country and a most extensive acquaintance with those nations from whose history France had the most to learn. No man in France had studied the history of that country more thoroughly; no man had brought from his study such valuable results. He was not only most enlightened in the history of his own country; he, better than any other Frenchman, also knew the history of England. He had made an especial study of that portion of English history which, at this moment, France needed most to understand. His collection of

not only of his political career, but also of his political and historical writings. His History of the Consulate and Empire, which is little but a glorification of Napoleon in twenty volumes, has exerted on the French people a more pernicious influence, I have no doubt, than that of any other book since the *Du Contrat Social* of Rousseau.

original memoirs of the English Revolution had placed before his countrymen the best possible means of informing themselves of the details of that great event; and but a short time later, his History of the Revolution had given them a distinct view of the successes which it had achieved and of the mistakes which it had committed. In addition to all these qualifications, a long and trying experience at the court of St. James had given him a thorough insight into the practical workings of the English government. It is safe to say that no other man in France was so well qualified by ability, by study, and by experience, to direct the nation out of its troubles as was M. Guizot.

As a still further qualification for his high office, Guizot had been associated with the government of Louis Philippe from its beginning. He had carefully observed its faults and studied its weaknesses. In the light of his knowledge of the past history of France, in the light of his knowledge of the English Revolution with its successes and its mistakes, he brought to the direction of affairs a policy that was carefully and elaborately matured. As this policy was consistently pursued to the end, it is of great importance that it should be thoroughly understood.

The works of Guizot leave us in no doubt concerning the nature of his political views. What he regards as the essential characteristics of good government are carefully stated in the eighth volume of his *Mémoirs*, and they are so important that I shall make such extracts as may be necessary to place them before the reader.

First of all, in settling the question as to what a true government should be, he says:

"A great noise has been made, and is still made, over the words 'parliamentary government.' The question suggested is of more importance than the noise which it raises. It pertains to quite another thing, and to much more than that which they call 'parliamentary government.' That which France has been seeking, since 1789, above all the vicissitudes of its situation and its destiny, that which Europe demands from its confused but obstinate vows, is *free government.* Political liberty, that is to say, the intervention and the efficacious control of the people in their government, has been the need and the struggle, active or latent, of the social state which for nineteen centuries under the Christian religion, and by the natural course of modern civilization, has been developing in the European nations and which prevails wherever these nations carry their spirit with their empire. Parliamentary or not, is a government a free government, or in the course of becoming such? That is the question." *

But what are the conditions of such a free government? In answer, Guizot says:

"*The action of representative assemblies, free discussion of public affairs within and without*

* *Memoires pour servir à L'Histoire de mon temps. Edition interdite pour la France*, vol. VIII. p. 1.

such assemblies, electoral liberty, religious liberty, liberty of the press, liberty of labor, civil equality, an independent judiciary,—such are to-day the imperious conditions of free government. At the same time, diversity of social conditions, interior or exterior, has called up, has even made necessary, for a free government in different states very different forms. The republic is no longer the only possible form, the only natural form, nor even the only good form of government the state of society admits; it exacts in certain cases the form of monarchy." *

The author then proceeds to show that these "*imperious conditions*" are in fact complied with in states having very different modes of government; that they are found both in the United States of America and in England; that they have been developed under a republican form in Switzerland, while in Holland and in Belgium they flourish under the ægis of monarchy. He then adds:

"But if a free government admits of a variety of forms, it does not admit of a confusion of them. If it can receive different organizations, they are simply different means by which it attains its end, an end which is always the same, namely: liberty and a continuance under the protection of liberty. Now of all the conditions of free government, the first and the most imperative is that responsibility, —responsibility true and serious,—should attach

* *Ibid.* p. 3.

itself to the exercise of power. If power is not responsible, liberty is not guaranteed. It is especially in what pertains to the responsibility of power that the diversity of forms of free government imposes the employment of very different means. I consult experience; I interrogate anew the two governments to which I have already referred. In the republic of the United States of America responsibility of power resides in the election of president, in the short duration of his term of office, in the complete separation of his authority from that of the representative bodies by his side. Evidently such means could not be used in monarchy. The constitutional monarchy of England has accomplished the same end in another manner: it has declared in principle that the king can do no evil, and it has imposed upon counsellors all the responsibility of his government. I do not enter into a discussion and a comparison of these two different forms of free government and of the different systems of responsibility which are peculiar to them; I state the facts. The English monarchy and the American republic are two governments really free, and which satisfy all the actual exigencies of political liberty. In these two governments it is by very different means that responsibility of power—that necessary guarantee of political liberty—is established and is exercised. Although very different in nature, these means, put to the actual test, have shown themselves equally efficacious; in both of these states responsibility of power is real, and political liberties are guaranteed." *

After thus showing that political liberty may exist either under a monarchy or under a republic, Guizot adds further in regard to its necessary conditions:

"I insist first of all upon a fact which is often forgotten, but which may not be forgotten without a misunderstanding of the nature of the exigencies of a free government. One of the first liberties necessary under such a government is the liberty of its own agents, the free and voluntary action of men who exercise its important functions and direct its springs of action. Absolute power can only wish in its servants for docile instruments capable of executing those wishes which stand in the place of laws. But under a régime of liberty, where publicity and discussion are universal and where responsibility everywhere accompanies power, no minister can exercise authority with advantage to the governed unless he is free to act in accordance with his own reason and his own will. The moment action is carried beyond the domain of material things and works legally prescribed, a free government demands of the men who take part in it that their concurrence be absolutely free. In the presence of national liberty, a certain degree of conviction, and I should say of personal passion, is indispensable to the actors in

* *Ibid.* p. 6.

the political arena for their force and their success. Said M. Casimer Périer in the midst of his ardent struggle with riot and anarchy: 'It is not agents that I want, but it is accomplices.'"

"It is in consequence of this freedom of action," the author further argues, "that in all free governments, whether monarchical or republican, political parties spring up naturally and of necessity. Whether these come from a similarity of interests, of ideas, or of passions, or of all these motives united, free association in such governments is the indispensable condition of regular and efficacious political action. Such is the necessity of political parties in free government, that when once formed they maintain and perpetuate themselves in spite of all the transformations which changing centuries impose upon men and society. The whig and tory parties in England, though born in the crisis of political liberty in the seventeenth century, and though somewhat magnified, are to-day reproduced under the names *conservative* and *liberal*, and to-day preside over the destinies of their country. So in the United States, the parties which to-day struggle for the mastery are the legitimate successors of those which surrounded Washington and Jefferson." *

But it is not in the hot fires of great revolutions that these political parties are formed which are destined to become active elements of free govern-

* *Ibid.* p. 8.

ment. They belong rather to the epoch of organization after the revolution is accomplished, not to the period of military action itself. In France these parties were organized during the period of the Restoration. They were always embarrassed and often disfigured by those revolutionary and conspiring elements which perpetually mingled falsehood and discord in their constitutional contests. The Revolution of 1830 elevated and enlarged the rôle of political parties as the forces of free government. When the cabinet of October, 1840, was formed, it was at the head of an organized and consolidated party,—the very party, indeed, which had accomplished the Revolution of 1830 and placed Louis Philippe on the throne. This party had been chiefly instrumental in framing the constitution which was then in force. It had, in fact, established and shaped the government as it then existed, and as long as it maintained its majority in the nation, it was but natural that it should determine the governmental policy. Whenever Guizot at the head of the ministry should fail to command the support of a majority of the Representatives, he professed himself ready to retire; but until such a time should arrive, he maintained that his party should continue to have the direction of public affairs. The very foundation of his political action was the unvarying belief that the king in conjunction with the representatives of the nation is the ruling power, and that, in consequence of this conjunction, they must be kept in the closest harmony. Their general policy must be the same; and as the king's policy was to find expression through his ministry, it follows that whenever the ministry takes ground on any important question, it is to stand or fall according as it shall succeed or fail in securing the support of the legislative body. So long, therefore, as Guizot maintained the harmony of these conjoint branches of the government with each other, and so long as he himself enjoyed the confidence of each, it was incumbent upon him to continue in a steady adherence to the policy which he believed to be for the best good of the nation. When he failed to secure that harmony or that confidence it was evidently his duty to retire from his position. What may be called his constitutional policy was, it will be seen, identical with that now universally acted upon in England.

I have dwelt at length upon these views of Guizot, as they were absolutely necessary to a correct understanding of the part which he played. He has often been reproached for the firmness, even the stubbornness, with which he resisted the demands of the opposition. The firmness of that resistance can only be correctly explained when one understands the thorough manner in which Guizot has studied the question in all of its bearings, and studied it, too, for the very purpose of fixing upon a line of policy which ought to be pursued. His convictions were of that positive, never-doubting nature which, in a man of his intelligence, can only result from the most careful reasoning united with the most careful observation and experience.

Then, too, the character of these fundamental views receives an additional importance from the nature of the work to be performed. In times of peace and of national quiet and prosperity, the political theories of the king or of his minister in regard to the proper relations of the executive and the legislative powers may be of small importance; but when there are questions to be decided on which the very perpetuity of the government depends, the importance of such convictions can hardly be over-estimated. The questions then presenting themselves in France were the most vital that can ever come up for decision. The main question was no less than this: whether the nation should be controlled by the intelligence and the pecuniary interests of the country, in pursuance of a fixed line of policy, or whether it should be subject to the constantly changing phases of the revolutionary spirit. The Restoration, in 1814, as we have seen, was a triumph of the middle class over the proletariat. The Revolution of 1830 was the triumph of the same middle class over absolutism; and now the vital question under Guizot's administration was, whether the bourgeoisie should continue to hold their power, or whether they should give it over to their sworn enemies. That a continuance of the government was for the best interests of the nation, I think there can be very little question. Whether such a continuance was possible depended upon the real character of the French people.

Let us look for a moment at the objects which the government in the last days of Louis Philippe sought to accomplish. On turning again to Guizot's *Mémoires*, I find the following:

"The Cabinet and its political friends had one thought and one design fully established. They aspired to bring to a close in France the era of revolutions by founding a free government such as was promised to the nation in 1789, as the consequence and the political guarantee of the social revolution which was taking place. We regarded the policy which, with some vicissitudes, had prevailed in France since the ministry of Périer as the only efficacious and sure means of attaining this end. This policy was really at the same time liberal and anti-revolutionary. Anti-revolutionary without as well as within; for in its external relations it strove for the maintenance of European peace, and in its internal policy for that of constitutional monarchy; it was liberal, for it accepted and respected fully the essential conditions of free government, which are the decisive intervention of the country in its affairs, a constant and active discussion among the people, as well as in the chambers, of the ideas and the acts of those in power. In fact, from 1830 to 1848 this double end was attained. Peace was preserved, and I think to-day, as I thought twenty years ago, that neither the influence nor the power of France in Europe suffered from it. Within the nation, from 1830 to 1848, political liberty was broad and strong; from 1840 to 1848 especially, it was extended without having any new legal limitations imposed upon it. If I were to express my thoughts without reserve, I should say that not only impartial spectators, but for the most part even the old enemies of our policy, would recognize to-day, in their inmost thoughts, the truth of this double fact.

"The policy which we thus sustained and put into practice had its principal support in the preponderating influence of the middle classes: an influence at once recognized and accepted as laboring in the general interests of the country, and at the same time as subject to all the tests and conditions of general liberty. The middle classes, without either privileges or limits in the civil ranks, and constantly open in the political ranks to the ascending movement of the entire nation, were, in our opinion, the best guardians of the principles of 1789, of social order as well as of constitutional government, of liberty as well as of order, of civil liberty as well as of political liberty, of progress as well as of stability.

"As the result of several general elections, the liberty and legality of which could not be seriously contested, and under the influence of animated discussions incessantly repeated, the preponderant influence of the middle classes had established, in the chambers and in the country, a majority which approved of the policy which I have just explained; a majority which wished the maintenance of that policy, and which supported it through all the difficulties and trials interior and exterior to which it was subjected. That majority was repeatedly renewed, recruited, compacted, exercised in a public way, and from day to day was bound more closely to the government, just as the government was bound more closely to it. In accordance with the natural course of a representative and free government, it had become the conservative party of that anti-revolutionary and liberal policy, the success of which, since 1831, it had wished for and assisted.

"A parliamentary government, as a practical form of free government under a constitutional monarchy; a preponderant influence of the middle classes, as the efficacious guarantee of constitutional monarchy and political liberty under this form of government; a conservative party, as the natural representative of the influence of the middle classes, and the necessary instrument of parliamentary government; such were, in our profound conviction, the means of action and the conditions of duration of that liberal and anti-revolutionary policy which we had endeavored at heart to practise and to maintain.

"It was this policy, as we understood it and practised it, in conjunction with the harmonious concurrence of the crown, the chambers, and the electors, that the opposition desired to change; and it was for the purpose of changing it that loud calls were raised for electoral and parliamentary reforms. These reforms were less an end than a means; their advocates, provoked by the interior condition of parliament much more than by any need or appeal of the country, saw plainly that there was but one way of accomplishing their design. They would be obliged, in the Chamber of Deputies, to reduce the majority which there prevailed, and the conservative party, which it had formed, in one of two methods: either they would have to expell from it, by an extension of the law of incompatibilities, a part of the crown officers who held seats, or they would be compelled to call into it, by an extension of the right of suffrage, elements that were new and of an unknown character. We had not, in principle, any absolute and permanent objection to such reforms; the extension of the right of suffrage, and the incompatibility of certain public functions with the mission of deputy, could be and ought to be the natural and legitimate consequences of the ascending movement of society and of the prolonged exercise of political liberty. But at present these innovations, in our opinion, were neither necessary nor opportune. They were not necessary, for, during the past thirty years, events had proved that, under the actual laws and institutions, liberty and force had received the abundant intervention of the country in their behalf. They were not opportune, for they would impart new trials and new difficulties into that which was, in our eyes, the most actual and the most pressing interest of our country: namely, the exercise and the consolidation of that free government which was still so new among us. Such was at once the cause and the limit of our resistance to the immediate innovations which were demanded." *

Such was the policy of Louis Philippe's government while under the direction of Guizot. I think that, even at the present day, it would be difficult to show how it could have been better. Of all things, what France most needed was rest from the disturbing influence of party strife and revolutionary efforts. Ever since 1793, the nation had been ruled by factions. It cannot be stated too often, or with too much emphasis, that the worst feature of French politics was its extreme radical character; I mean that intensity and narrowness of party-feeling which shows itself constantly ready, not to correct, but to overthrow: not to modify, but to annihilate all opposing powers and opinions. The consequence of that intense radicalism had been, that ever after the revolution of '93, France had been ruled with what may, perhaps, best be called a spirit of desperation;—that desperation which comes from a consciousness, on the part of the faction in power, that defeat means overthrow, and that overthow means all manner of vengeance. The scourge of France has been the great number of men who

* Guizot, *Mémoires, tome* VIII. p. 521, *et seq.*

were ready to shout: " *Vive la révolution,—à bas le government,*" whenever they have seen in their rulers anything they did not approve; and, worst of all, such leaders have had in France, since the Revolution, no difficulty in finding a numerous constituency. The Revolution had brought into most conspicuous prominence the worst elements of society. Just as in the reign of Charles II. in England,

> "the scum
> That rises upmost when the nation boils,"

furnished abundant support for the ambition of the desperate and the aspiring. How often in France, in the reigns of Louis XVIII., Charles X., and Louis Philippe, occurred scenes like that portrayed in Dryden's Spanish Friar:

> "Some popular chief,
> More noisy than the rest, but cries halloo,
> And in a trice the bellowing herd come out;
> The gates are barred, the ways are barricaded:
> And one and all's the word: true cocks o' the game!
> They never ask for what or whom they fight;
> But turn 'em out, and show 'em but a foe,
> Cry liberty, and that's a cause for quarrel."

The ministry of Guizot saw clearly the evils of the revolutionary spirit that was still so prevalent, and it was firm in the conviction that this spirit could only be overcome by means of a somewhat prolonged ascendency of the middle classes. It was the expectation that in due time the way would be opened for the safe introduction of a more popular element. Their mistake was not in their theory, which was perfect, but, as in such circumstances is often the case, in their too low estimation of the strength of their opponents, and their too high estimation of the political intelligence of the masses of the French people. As we shall see, those very elements which Guizot and his coadjutors strove to avoid or to override, proved in the end to be not only far worse, but also far stronger, than he had believed them to be. Instead, therefore, of winning, the government repelled its opponents; instead of crushing them, it exasperated them. There are blows which crush and destroy, and there are blows which compact and strengthen the object hammered: and blows which would destroy a small object often strengthen a large one. Guizot's government failed to apprehend correctly the magnitude and the character of its opponents, and therefore its policy had the opposite effect from that which had been so studiously and elaborately intended. Instead of persuading the opposition into a proper subordination to law, he aroused it to a revolution, a revolution, too, that, to his undoubted astonishment, was strong enough to sweep everything before it.

It is necessary to look a little more closely into the nature of the revolutionary element. When Guizot first took up the portfolio in 1840, affairs were not without their hopeful aspect. Conspiracies and insurrections for the overthrow of the monarchy of 1830 had become much less frequent and much less formidable. An occasional attempt was made upon the life of the king, but aside from the perpetrators of such attempts and their few followers, the members of the opposition seemed disposed to transfer their contest entirely to the arena of parliamentary discussion. But the opposition had not the advantage of that unity of purpose which characterized the policy of the government. There were those, on the one hand, who declared themselves loyally in favor of a dynastic monarchy; while on the other, there were those who did not conceal their predilections for a republic. Both of these parties had their followers and supporters among the people; and though they were violently opposed to each other, they were a unit in their opposition to the conservative policy of the cabinet.

Then, too, each of these opposing parties was subdivided. The monarchists counted in their ranks men who since 1830 had often approved and sustained, and even put into practice, a conservative policy similar to that now pursued. With them were also men who, under the ministries of Périer, Thiers, and Molé, had violently combated such a policy. The first—generally men of experience, with prudent and temperate characters—now reproached the government with carrying its conservative spirit too far, with not making concessions enough to the popular imagination, and with making too much to foreigners. The second class, though still ardently desirous of maintaining the monarchy of 1830, were profoundly imbued with the republican maxims and principles of 1791, and therefore they accused the government of having thwarted the Revolution of 1830 in disappointing all hopes of a republican monarchy. Of these two parties the first was the most enlightened and the most skilful; the second, the most powerful and the most to be dreaded, inasmuch as its revolutionary instincts gave it a strong hold upon the sympathies of a considerable portion of the country.

The republican opposition was of the same composite nature. It contained one class made up of men who denounced the follies and excesses of the demagogues as the crimes of the Great Revolution, and who took the United States as their model of a republican government. Marching with these was another class composed of republican fanatics, steadfast admirers of the republic of 1793, men who found their model in the National Convention, and who persisted in worshipping the tyrants of that epoch as the saviors of France and the exemplars of all Frenchmen. Then, by the side of these two classes, there was another class consisting of visionary dreamers, audacious men who aspired not only to reform the government, but also to transform society itself. This motley crowd of socialists and communists, of which St. Simon, and Louis Blanc, and Victor Hugo, were the most conspicuous leaders, though its members were apparently all drawing in different directions, professed to strive for the accomplishment of the same end, namely, the complete reorganization of society, civil and domestic as well as political. These men were the apostles of new theories on every possible subject. Some of their notions were monarchic, others were completely anarchic. But wide apart as the poles in many of their theories, in one respect they were in harmonious unity. Despairing of a realization of their pet notions under any fixed government, they were ever ready to join hands for the overthrow of what existed, and to rush headlong into the uncertain future in sole reliance on the hopes and the passions of the populace. They all desired a republic and universal suffrage.

Such were the diverse elements of the opposition. Had they from the first been united in their demands, there is little reason to doubt that they would have been strong enough to enforce respect. But the monarchists were so little in harmony with republicans, and the better class of both monarchists and republicans found the doctrines of the socialists so repugnant, that it was long impossible for them to join their forces for the accomplishment of the same end. It was not until after years of isolated attacks and consequent failures, that their armies were joined for one simultaneous movement.

We have already seen that the English Constitution had been the model after which the charters of 1814 and of 1830 had, for the most part, been framed. In two somewhat important particulars, however, the French Constitution differed from that of their neighbors across the channel. In the first place, the right of franchise was much more limited (a direct payment of an impost of three hundred francs being a necessary qualification of the voter); in the second place, crown officers were admitted to seats in the representative body in a manner that was in England deemed incompatible with the complete independence of legislation. These two modifications were not without their good effects, inasmuch as they gave to the government greater stability at a time when it was in danger of being paralyzed from the general prevalence of a revolutionary spirit. But to insist upon maintaining permanently these two peculiarities was to ignore some of the best fruits of the Revolution. Of this the government was fully aware. In theory it constantly professed a purpose to withdraw ultimately its own functionaries from the legislature, and to extend the right of suffrage; but, as a matter of fact, whenever the subject of immediate reform was advanced, it was opposed by the government on the ground that the time for such reform had not yet arrived. The question, then, between the government and the opposition was not whether a reform was desirable; it was in regard to the time and manner of the reform. Such being the substantial unity of all parties on the main question at issue, it can hardly be considered strange that Guizot insisted upon adhering to his own policy, on the subordinate question of time and manner, so long as he could carry a majority of parliament with him. When he should fail to command the majority he was ready, as he declared, to yield.

But there was one element of the problem that is liable to be overlooked. It was claimed, and with justice too, that the vote in the representative body was not a free expression of the people, for the reason that the government, being itself represented, was able to exert a powerful influence in its own behalf. But though it must be admitted that there was ground for complaint, the importance of the fact was vastly magnified, for, as the government admitted the general desirability of reform, the opposition had only to bide its time in order to achieve a certain and a peaceful success. What, it may well be asked, is to be thought of a party or a policy that would precipitate a revolution for the sake of accomplishing at the present moment what is just on the point of coming about of its own inherent strength?

If any proof were wanting that Guizot was right in his belief that the nation would be unsafe in the hands of the opposition, such proof was afforded in tenfold measure by this willingness of the opposition to proceed to measures of violence when they were still in a constitutional minority. That they were certain in the end to succeed, nay, that it was desirable they should succeed, the government itself was free to admit. That success could not long be postponed, the history of their efforts and of the course of the government afford abundant proof.

The subject of electoral reform first assumed considerable importance in 1840, during the short primacy of Thiers. In opening the debate which decided the existence of his cabinet, this minister expressed himself in the following terms:

"On the subject of electoral reform great difficulties may arise in the future, but they do not present themselves to-day. Why? Is there, among the adversaries of electoral reform, any one who, in the presence of the electoral body, in the presence of chambers, and I might add in the presence of the charter, has said, *Never?* The charter, and I had the honor to be present at the conference when that article of the charter was discussed,—the charter excluded electoral qualifications from the articles which composed it. Why? Because it was understood that the enlarging of the right of suffrage would be the work of time and of an increase of intelligence, when the populace, more enlightened, would be fitted to participate in the management of affairs of state. No one before the electoral body or before the chambers has said, *Never.* At the same time, even among the partisans of reform, has any one of the orators said, *To-day?* No one. All have recognized the fact that the question belongs to the future, and that it does not belong to the present." *

* Guizot, *Mémories*, vol. VIII, p. 530.

The same general views were expressed by Rémusat; indeed, it may be said that the cabinet of Thiers as a whole recognized the necessity of reform, but remanded it to the future.

When the ministry of Thiers gave way to that of Guizot, and entered into the opposition, the reform party, thus reinforced, naturally became somewhat more urgent in its demands. Guizot remarks, with an evident touch of irony, that the ministry of Thiers had postponed the subject of reform to the future, and the future had speedily arrived. The question, therefore, was not allowed to rest. Between February of 1841 and April of 1847 electoral reform was introduced into the chambers and discussed no less than three times, and parliamentary reform no less than seven times. The cabinet constantly repelled the movement, as inopportune and likely to jeopard the interest of the free government which they were endeavoring to establish. Twice the whole subject of electoral reform was reviewed at length by the prime minister. On the 15th of February, 1842, and again on the 26th of March, 1847, he expounded in elaborate speeches the whole policy of the goverment, and analyzed at length the social and political conditions of the country which determined it.

Meanwhile the two wings of the opposition, the monarchists and the republicans, remained firm, and their position was well known. The monarchist opposition attacked the general policy of the cabinet in foreign affairs as well as in domestic, and advocated the two reforms as a proper means of correcting it. The republican opposition carried the question still farther; it began in 1847 to advocate universal suffrage as the only legitimate basis of the electoral laws. "It's day will come," said Garnier-Pagès, with a kind of half-threat that predicted a republic, and, if need be, a revolution. In view of such liabilities the Chamber of Deputies rejected the proposition by a considerable majority. This fact should not be overlooked, inasmuch as the vote was taken just after the general elections of 1846, and was, therefore, the most natural expression of views on the question which the country in any constitutional method could give. It should, perhaps, still further be said that though the majority in support of the government was thus decisive, there continued to be a very general conviction that both the reforms would soon command a majority, and consequently that neither of them would be very long delayed.

Now in any other nation than France, and at any other time than since the Great Revolution, what course would the advocates of reform have pursued? Surely it required but a small measure of patience and foresight to carry them, under the circumstances, to a triumphant and peaceful success. But patience and foresight found no place in the characters of many of the most influential party leaders. Perhaps it is doubtful whether many of them desired a peaceful success. Instead of *waiting* simply, the republican leaders determined to transfer the struggle to a field where they would gain a support that was wanting in the chambers; they resolved to summon to their aid a general agitation of the populace. The monarchic opposition was induced to imitate their example. With one accord they determined to transfer the question from the arena of parliamentary discussion to the field of popular passions. The toasts of the banquets succeeded the debates of the tribune.

It will be seen by every one who is familiar with the modern history of England, that the political situation in France during the last years of the reign of Louis Philippe resembled in many respects that which existed in England previous to the reform of 1832. The government in France professed its willingness to pursue the same course that had been so successfully adopted in England. During no less than fifty years, the subject of reform had been agitated in Great Britain before the House of Commons could be brought to commit itself to the support of the measure. When at last the Commons were carried, however, the ministry gave way, and the new government pushed the subject of reform to a triumphant conclusion.* Just so

* Nothing will place in more vivid contrast the reformatory spirit of these two nations than to call to mind, in this connection, the condition of England previous to the reform of 1832. For this purpose I commend to the reader's notice the following passages from May's *Constitional History of England*, American Edition, vol. I. p. 267:

"In 1793" (that is, thirty-nine years before the reform was actually brought about), "the Society of the Friends of the People were prepared

it would have been in France. The leaders of the reform understood perfectly that the moment they were able to secure a majority in the Assembly, the government would give to the reformatory measures its hearty support. Moreover, it was evident even to Guizot that the time was not distant when such a majority would be secured; but until that time should come, the government did not believe itself called upon to yield to the cries of an irresponsible proletariat.

But the government little understood the full force of these revolutionary lessons which the people of France, during fifty years and more, had been learning with so much earnestness and so much thoroughness. The revolutionary spirit, begot-

to prove that in England and Wales seventy members were returned from thirty-five places in which there were scarcely any electors at all; that ninety members were returned by forty-six places with less than fifty electors; and thirty-seven members by nineteen places having not more than one hundred electors. Such places were returning members, while Leeds, Birmingham, and Manchester were unrepresented; and the members whom they sent to Parliament were the nominees of peers and other wealthy patrons. No abuse was more flagrant than the direct control of peers over the constitution of the Lower House. The Duke of Norfolk was represented by eleven members; Lord Lonsdale by nine; Lord Darlington by seven; the Duke of Rutland, the Marquis of Buckingham, and Lord Carrington, each by six."

Aschenholz (vol. V. p. 12) relates that "a borough that had been swallowed up by the sea still continued to be represented; the owner of the beach on which it had stood rowed out in a boat with three voters and there played out the electoral farce." "At an election at Bute, only one person attended the election except the sheriff and the returning officer. He, of course, took the chair, constituted the meeting, called over the roll of freeholders, answered to his own name, took the vote as to who should preside, and elected himself. He then moved and seconded his own nomination, put the question to vote, and was unanimously returned."—*Fischel*, *English Constitution*, p. 429.

ten by false doctrines in philosophy and religion, nursed by violence and indiscretion, and encouraged by *coups d'état* without number, had grown to such proportions that it easily overcame its opponents and swept everything before it.

It is not difficult to see that mistakes were made by the ministry of Guizot, but they were mistakes of minor importance, and such that France could well have afforded to overlook them. That his general policy was the correct one, I think all the subsequent history of the nation has tended to show. But for the Revolution of 1848, a revolution that, as I think we shall see, was brought about without any adequate cause whatever on the part of the ministry, the government would doubtless have conceded one reform after another, until a parliamentary *régime* worthy of comparison with that of England had been established.

It may be said, furthermore, that by the ministry of Guizot much, very much, was actually accomplished. Those who are in the habit of judging of an effort solely by the fact of its success or its failure, will not appreciate the importance of that work; but its importance, nevertheless, is certain, and ought to be recognized. The government of 1830 was born of a revolution that was projected for the defence of the laws and the liberties of the people, and that was accomplished at the expense of absolute monarchy. The new *régime* was undertaken in the name of constitutional monarchy, and, as

Guizot declares, with these three principles as the basis of all its action :

1. The rights of national independence.
2. Respect for public laws, rights, and liberties.
3. The principles and the practice of a constitutional *régime.*

There was to be " no foreign intervention or interference in the interior affairs of France, and no laws of exception or of suspension of the public liberties." The constitutional powers were to be in full exercise, and to be always entitled to discuss and to regulate the affairs of the country.*

It is the proud, but, as it seems to me, the reasonable boast of Guizot, that these principles during his administration were faithfully applied and carried out. He shows by an overwhelming array of evidence that in all the branches of material and moral and political progress, the nation made genuine and rapid advances. He shows, furthermore, that the foreign policy of the government was such that Count Nesselrode, the Chancellor of Russia, wrote to the Russian ambassador at London, in February, 1848, that "*if peace continued,* France would surround herself on all sides by a rampart of constitutional states, organized on the French model, moved by the French spirit, and acting under French influence." And what could be higher praise than this?

At the conclusion of the final chapter of his work, in which he gives a *resumé* of the laws

* Guizot, *Mémoires*, vol. VIII. p. 597.

passed and the works accomplished during his administration, Guizot makes a declaration which I believe no array of facts has ever attempted to assail. He says: "Political order and civil order, moral order and material order, the rights of liberty and the rights of public security, the progress of prosperity and of well-being among all classes of the nation; these, for the government of 1830, were the object of a constant occupation and of an honest and efficient effort. The government comprehended its mission, and sought its object, seriously, simply, without charlatanry and without fantasy; and the good of its labors has survived the misfortune of its fall. It had essential characteristics, and it attained from day to day the essential results of a legal and a free government." * To a statesman who can seriously and intelligently and honestly utter such words as these, it is no disgrace to be involved in failure.

> "'Tis not in mortals to command success,—
> But he did more, Sempronius, he deserved it."

The most temperate and judicial of English historians has well declared that "no envy of faction, no caprice of fortune, can tear from M. Guizot the trophy which time has bestowed, that he, for nearly eight years past and irrevocable, held in his firm grasp a power so fleeting before, and fell only with the monarchy which he had sustained, in the convulsive throes of his country." †

* *Mémoires*, vol. VIII. p. 627.

† Hallam, *Preface to Supplemental Notes to View of the Middle Ages.*

THE REVOLUTION OF 1848.

"Ὅπερ γὰρ οἱ τὰς ἐγχέλεις θηρώμενοι πέπονθας·
Ὅταν μὲν ἡ λίμνη καταστῇ, λαμβάνουσιν οὐδέν·
Ἐὰν δ' ἄνω τε καὶ κάτω τὸν βόρβορον κυκῶσιν,
Αἱροῦσι· καὶ σὺ λαμβάνεις, ἢν τὴν πόλιν ταράττῃς.

—ARISTOPHANES, *Equites*, v. 843–6.

CHAPTER VII.

THE REVOLUTION OF 1848.

IN the last chapter I endeavored to portray the political condition of France during the administration of Guizot. It was my effort to show how the policy of the government was firmly directed, on the one hand, to the work of establishing upon a solid basis a constitutional government similar to that of England, and on the other, to that of resisting and overcoming the revolutionary spirit which was so prevalent throughout the country. We have now to consider the failure of those efforts as displayed in the ensuing revolution.

During the interval that passed between the session of 1847 and that of 1848, France was aroused to a somewhat feverish excitement. It cannot be said that there was a general desire, much less a general demand, for reform. Since the reformatory agitations had begun, repeated elections had taken place, and it may be affirmed with confidence, that if there had existed any such call for reform as would justify revolution, the advocates of reform would have been able to secure a majority. But such a majority had never been secured. It is a fact of infinite importance in the constitution of the question, that the legislative branch of the government was in complete harmony with the executive, and that the executive openly professed its willingness to abandon its position the moment the legislature should make the demand. In other words, it must be borne in mind that Guizot professed a readiness to follow in the footsteps of the English reform of 1832. It will be remembered that in England the government uniformly opposed the reformatory measures, until those measures were clearly demanded by a majority of the people represented in the House of Commons, after which the government favored the reform, and even urged it with all the powers of its patronage and prerogative. So it might have been in France but for that revolutionary spirit that would not wait for a majority. In England more than fifty years elapsed between the beginning and the end of the agitation which terminated in the reform of 1832. In France only eighteen years had passed since the people had fixed their form of government, and within that period important additions to the liberties and privileges of the people had taken place. Indeed, I am inclined to believe that if one were to search into the matter carefully, one would find that in the reign of Louis Philippe more was done to establish a healthy political sentiment, and to extend to the people the largest liberties that could safely be entrusted to them, than has been done in any other eighteen years since the death of Henry IV. This may not be very high praise, but the fact should not be overlooked or forgotten. It takes the responsibility of the revolution from the government and throws it upon the people.

But it may be asked: Why, then, did the revolution occur? The answer is to be found in the nature of the political parties and in the character of the political sentiments pervading the people.

France may be said to have been divided at this time into four classes, four parties, or perhaps it might be said, into four political castes.

The first of these embraced the old aristocracy and their adherents. They were the absolutists, the men who had supported Charles X., and been with him overthrown by the Revolution of 1830. The second class was the great middle class of professional men, of tradesmen, of artisans—the bourgeoisie, who came into political power at the time of the Restoration, and again at the accession of Louis Philippe. The third class was made up of the small land-owners and laborers—the great mass of the laboring population. Now these three classes were all monarchists. The first class was devoted to the elder branch of the Bourbon family, the second class to the Orleans dynasty as represented by Louis Philippe, and the third class to the Bonapartes. But in addition to these three classes there was a fourth class, that was now growing up into an unwonted importance. It was made up of the heirs of all those strange doctrines which had come down from the Great Revolution, of those men whose mission it seems to be to stir up discontent, of those revolutionary natures whose tendency is to condemn whatever *is*, and to praise and long for whatever *is not*. Now every nation has this class of people; every nation has at times experienced the benefits, and at times the evils, of the agitations which such people originate and encourage. Every nature must have in itself a certain amount of destructive energy, or it can make no headway in society. So every nation must have those who can spy out and attack the evils of social and political life. But when a man's destructive energy overbalances his creative or productive energy, society protects itself from his depredations only by means of its jails and penitentiaries. In like manner it may be said of any society, that whenever the destructive, that is to say, the revolutionary spirit, rises within it to an undue prominence, it is in danger just in proportion to the extent of that prominence. The right of revolution is, without doubt, a sacred right; and yet the nation which glorifies revolution, or even makes revolution easy, is on the high-road to ruin. For what is revolution? Is it anything more or less than the substitution of force in the place of law? That such a substitution is sometimes justifiable, there may be no question; that it is often justifiable, cannot for a moment be admitted. It may be stated as a general and universal truth, that it can never be resorted to with impunity when there is left open any possible constitutional means of accomplishing the end to be attained.

Now this revolutionary spirit of which I have spoken, and which I believe is at all times to be deprecated, had taken possession of a considerable portion of the French people. That the masses of the people were revolutionary is not true; indeed, the majority of the French people at the time of which I am speaking were decidedly anti-revolutionary in their predisposition. This very fact, moreover, paradoxical as it may seem, contributed to the success of the revolutionary party; and for the reason that with vast numbers of the people it degenerated into a *laissez-faire* policy that was equally averse to revolution and to the resistance of revolution. It has been said that where there is no passion there is no virtue; with equal truth it might be affirmed that where there is a general spirit of non-resistance there is room and opportunity for every kind of lawlessness and revolution. Now the masses of the rural population of France have, ever since the Great Revolution, been essentially conservative. They have taken very little interest in political affairs. They have said in effect, "Give us a Bonaparte, give us a Bourbon, give us an Orleanist, give us a republic, give us anything you please, but in the name of Heaven give us something that is fixed. We don't understand your politics; we don't care who is ruler; what we want is, to have our taxes light, and above all, to be assured that our homes and our children and our few acres may rest in our quiet possession." Thus among all the nations of Europe there is no people that has afforded so good a field for the work of political sharpers and political tricksters as the people of France during the last fifty years. In gross ignorance, and yet with instincts mainly correct, they have plodded on, leaving the affairs of politics to the people of Paris and of the other large cities.

The result of this condition of affairs has been to give the control of French politics almost exclusively into the hands of the Parisians. And now what was likely to be the influence of this result? How is any nation likely to be governed if it intrusts its political affairs to a great metropolitan city? Imagine all England surrendering herself to the unlimited control of London. Imagine, if possible, the United States withdrawing from all interest in political affairs, and saying to New York City, "Govern us as you please; we do not care to interfere."

Now Paris not only had its full quota of the ignorant and brutalized, but it had far more than its proportion of those revolutionary spirits to whom I have referred. The doctrines of Voltaire and Rousseau had taken deep hold of the Parisians, and had left upon them a permanent influence. These doctrines, as we have seen, were thoroughly revolutionary in their nature, and their influence permeated all the most popular writings of the day. In 1850, De Tocqueville used these words:

"If I were to give a Scriptural genealogy of our modern popular writers, I should say that Rousseau lived twenty years, and then begat Bernardin de St. Pierre; that Bernardin de St. Pierre lived twenty years, and then begat Chateaubriand; that Chateaubriand lived twenty years, and then begat Victor Hugo; and that Victor Hugo, being tempted of the devil, is begetting every day." * It would not be correct to affirm that the spirit of these men permeated all the writings of the day; and yet the literature which influenced the people in any considerable measure was filled with ideas and sentiments which were inherited from the writers of the revolutionary period. There was everywhere prevalent that scoffing spirit whose influence in politics is to revolutionize, rather than reform, that chronic fault-finding disposition which seems to have no definite aim, but which tends to weaken and destroy, without the possibility of putting anything better in the place of that which it would overthrow. It was in this revolutionary spirit that socialism and communism, now for the first time looming up into importance, had their origin and their support. It was in this same revolutionary spirit that the laws and restraints of marriage were attacked and ridiculed, that marriage without love, and love without marriage, against which Père Hyacinthe so eloquently protested as the

* De Tocqueville, *Memoirs and Remains*, vol. II. p. 116.

greatest bane of French society, came to be so general—it might be said, so nearly universal.

When all these conditions of France and of Paris are considered, the revolution of 1848 is easily explained. The possibility of revolution lay in the two facts that the masses of the French people were too apathetic to resist revolution, and that Paris was pervaded with a revolutionary spirit that was strong enough, when once provoked, to sweep everything before it.

Now let us look at the facts which precipitated the event.

When the revolutionary spirits of Paris found that it was impossible to secure a majority in the Assembly, they betook themselves to a systematic agitation of the subject by means of a series of banquets to be given in the avowed interests of reform. These were to be held in all the larger cities of the kingdom, and the toasts were designed to arouse and influence the revolutionary spirit. By means of these banquets, France, during the six months that followed the closing of the session of 1847, was kept in a fever of excitement. In nearly all the departments, in quite all the cities of importance, banquets were held by the opponents of the government, monarchist as well as republican, for the avowed purpose of creating and exciting public opinion. The greatest confusion was the result. In some instances it was agreed between royalists and republicans that the king and his adherents should be passed in complete silence; in others the monarchists insisted on a toast in honor of the king, and when the republican opposition refused it, the former withdrew to drink their toast by themselves. As time advanced, the revolutionary fires flamed up with unmistakable vigor. In several of the cities the remembrances of the Convention were called up only to be applauded, and the names of the most tyrannical and sanguinary chiefs, Danton, Robespierre, and Saint Just, were mentioned with unconcealed admiration.

At the first of the banquets the monarchists and the republicans were mutually suspicious and shy of each other. The radical chiefs among the republicans attributed their failures to their association with the monarchists, and the monarchist chiefs attributed their failure to their association with the republicans; many, therefore, refused to take part in the banquets so long as this association continued. But as time advanced, and the flames of public passion rose higher and higher, it became evident that the fruits of the movement were to be reaped by that branch of the opposition which should succeed in winning over the other. The radical chiefs, therefore, soon returned to the leadership of their respective parties. From this consolidation of forces the question was simply as to which one of the two oppositions would become the instrument and the dupe of the other. But the question was not long unsettled. Terms were agreed upon by the two parties, the monarchists virtually surrendering to their opponents. In commenting upon this act of diplomacy, Garnier-Pagès relates the following anecdote, which at least shows that the importance of the event was appreciated by the republican leaders:

"On leaving the residence of Mr. Odilon Barrot, the radical members of the meeting walked for some distance together. Arriving on the boulevard opposite the residence of the Minister of Foreign Affairs, they were on the point of separating. 'Ma foi,' said M. Pagnerre, 'I had no hope that our propositions would have a success so prompt and so complete. Did those men see where the affair would carry them? For my part, I confess that I don't see clearly; but it is not for us radicals to be frightened.' 'You see this tree?' responded Garnier-Pagès; 'well, cut in its bark a souvenir of this day. What we have just decided is a revolution.'" *

It now for the first time became evident to the government that the danger was serious. The journals, delighted to find the contest transported into the passions of the people, sustained and fomented the banquets and encouraged the agitation. So long as the opposition had remained divided the cabinet had entertained no special apprehension; but now that its ranks were closed, there could be no mistaking the fact that it was in every sense formidable and dangerous.

Guizot saw the situation, and had a long confer-

* Garnier-Pagès, *Hist. de la Rev. de* 1848, vol. IV. p. 102.

ence with the king. It was the opinion of the minister that the cabinet should retire, and that the whole question should be submitted anew to the chambers.* But to this the king was opposed. When it was urged that a change could now be made as a matter of prudence, but that in the future it might be a matter of necessity, the king responded: "That is precisely my reason for keeping you now. You know well that I am perfectly resolved not to depart from the constitutional *régime*, and to accept its necessities and its annoyances; but to-day it is not at all a matter of constitutional necessity. You have always had the majority; to whom should I yield in changing my ministers to-day? It would not be to the chambers, nor to the clear and regularly expressed views of the country; it would be to manifestations without any other authority than the tastes of those causing them—to a noise at the bottom of which there was nothing but evil designs. No, my dear minister; if the constitutional *régime* makes it *necessary* that I should separate myself from you, I will obey my constitutional duty, but I will not make the sacrifice in advance for the accommodation of ideas which I do not approve. Remain with me, and defend to the last the policy which we both believe to be good. If we are obliged to part, let those who make the separation necessary have the responsibility." †

* Guizot's *Mémoires*, vol. VIII. p. 543. † *Ibid*, p. 545.

"I do not hesitate, sire," responded Guizot. "I believed it my duty to call the attention of the king to the gravity of the situation. The cabinet would like a thousand times better to retire than to compromise the king, but it will not desert him."

Such was the situation at the opening of the session of 1848. The policy of the king and his cabinet was elaborated in a carefully prepared address of the throne. That policy was clearly summed up in these words:

"In the midst of those agitations which have excited hostile and blind passions, one conviction has animated and sustained me; it is that we possess in our constitutional monarchy, in the union of the great powers of state, the sure means of surmounting all obstacles, and of satisfying all the moral and material interests of our dear country. If we maintain firmly, according to the charter, social order and all its conditions; if we guarantee faithfully, according to the charter, public liberties and all their developments, we shall transmit intact to the generations which are to come after us the legacy which has been confided to us, and they will bless us for having founded and defended the edifice under the shelter of which they will live happy and free." *

These were noble words; the only pity is that the condition of the nation did not really justify them. Guizot in his *Mémoires* has a passage in

* Guizot, *Mémoires*, vol. VIII. p. 545.

reference to the hopeful spirit of the cabinet, in which he sadly confesses the manner in which they were all deceived. The paragraph throws a flood of light upon all the transactions of the period; it furnishes the key-note, not only of the history of the Revolution of 1848, but also of the whole modern history of France. While it explains the policy of the cabinet, it reveals the cause of all the painful misfortunes of the country. In referring to the words of the king just quoted, he says:

"I cannot recall these too confident words without an emotion of profound sorrow. My confidence was in fact great, although my apprehensions were real. Our error was common to all men who, in the ranks of the opposition and in our own, wished sincerely for the maintenance of the free government, into the possession of which the country was just entering. We had too early and too confidently counted upon that good sense and that political foresight which can become general only after the long exercise of liberty; we believed the constitutional *régime* stronger than it really was; we expected too much from its different elements, royalty, the chambers, parties, the middle class, the people; we did not sufficiently guard against their character and their inexperience. It is with nations as with individuals: the lessons of a vigorous life are slower and dearer than the presumptuous hopes of youth imagine." *

* *Mémoires*, vol. VIII. p. 545.

Over the address of the chambers to the crown, in response to the royal message, there occurred a protracted and earnest debate. The whole question was again raised by the introduction of an amendment calling for immediate reform.

In the course of the discussion, the government was invited to explain its policy. In a speech of considerable length, Guizot traversed the whole question, explaining the grounds of his course. He declared that he had no permanent hostility to the reforms proposed, but that he now considered the time for them inopportune; that he believed it improper for a conservative cabinet to concede them so long as the conservative party opposed them; that he was resolved to abandon his position as soon as the least majority in the chambers should show itself in favor of concession; that he was not willing to become the instrument of the defeat and disorganization of the majority of so long standing while it still persisted in the general policy which they had together maintained; that in the existing state of affairs, the fortunes of this policy depended upon the fortunes of that party which had pledged to it its faith and its force; that fidelity to ideas and to friends is one of the vital conditions of free government; that when ideas and alliances change, persons also must change with them; that after what had lately occurred in the country, and in the presence of what was passing in Europe, any innovation of the kind indicated, an innovation which would necessitate a dissolution of the chamber, would be both a weakness and an imprudence; that the ministry would be utterly wanting in its duty, should it take upon itself such a responsibility against the voice of the majority; that it was also unwise to make any engagement for the future, inasmuch as in such matters, to promise is more than to do (for in promising one destroys that which exists without putting anything in its place); that a wise government often can, and ought to, favor reform, but that such a government does not promise reform in advance; that when the proper moment, in its estimation, comes, it acts; but that until then it remains silent; that in England, many of the greatest reforms have been brought about by the very men who have combated them up to the moment when they believed they ought to be accomplished; and, finally, that the government, in adopting its conclusions, had taken into full account the spirit of the country and the necessity of a careful investigation of all the questions proposed. The last words of this address, so full of political wisdom, were as follows:

"The maintenance of the unity of the conservative party, the maintenance of the conservative policy and of its power, such will be the cabinet's fixed idea and its rule of conduct. The cabinet regards the unity of the force of the conservative party as the guarantee of all that which is dear and important to the country. It will make sincere efforts to maintain, to re-establish, if you please, the unity of the conservative party, in order that it may continue to be the conservative party entire which adopts and gives to the country the solution of these questions. If such a transaction in this party is possible,—if the efforts of the cabinet in this matter *can, in the nature of things, succeed,*—the transaction will take place. If this is not possible, if, on these questions, the conservative party cannot bring itself into harmonious agreement and maintain the force of the conservative policy, then the cabinet will leave to others the sad task of presiding over the disorganization of the party and the ruin of its policy. Such will be our rule of conduct. I oppose the amendment." *

Consistent to the last! Believing, with all the firmness of a deep-seated conviction reinforced by observation and experience, "that the prosperity of the country could only come from the continuance of that policy which kept the reins of power out of the hands of such fanatics as had long been and still are to a great extent the curse of the French nation, Guizot was determined by all proper means to endeavor to keep the conservative party together, and to keep it in power. Time has revealed how completely he was right in his judgment concerning the demands of the nation. His mistake was that of over-estimating the strength of

* Guizot, *Mémoires*, vol. VIII. p. 549.

the elements of order and stability, and of underestimating the strength of the elements of discord, of turbulence, and of anarchy.

It is of the greatest importance to notice the fact that the chambers approved of the policy, and showed faith in Guizot's speech. The amendment was rejected by a majority of 222 to 189, and an address was voted in accordance with the conservative policy. Thus again the government by methods of unquestionable legitimacy had been able to secure the support of the chambers.

The banquets held after the session of 1848 had manifestly failed to accomplish their purpose. All their efforts had been unable to create a majority in opposition to the government, and it would seem that now there was nothing left but for them to relapse into proper submission until they might again renew the issue at the next election. But submission was no part of their purpose. It was now determined to hold a monster banquet at Paris for the purpose of appealing directly to the passions of the populace.

It was evident that every just consideration demanded that the banquet should not be held. In the first place, the question for the discussion of which the banquet was about to take place had just been decided in the only constitutional method that was possible. It had been fairly submitted to an Assembly which had been elected after the reformatory agitation had begun, and that, too, when everybody understood that the government would yield the very moment the reformers should secure a majority of the members. If the banquet had been held before the vote in the Assembly had been taken, it might at least have had the excuse of hoping to influence the decision; but now, after the decision had been announced, there was nothing to be gained, or even hoped for, short of a revolution. Moreover, in the second place, it was known to everybody that the reform movement had a powerful hold upon the populace of Paris; a hold so powerful, indeed, that, in case the populace should be aroused, it might be able to overwhelm any military force that the government might have on hand to resist it. These considerations induced the government to endeavor to persuade the leaders of the movement to give up the banquet; but if that were impossible, to suppress it by force.

But the question at once arose as to the right of the government to interfere. Whether it had a moral right or not depended, of course, upon the extent of the danger involved. The right of self-preservation inheres in governments as well as in individuals, and consequently if the danger was of a nature to threaten seriously the peace of the nation, it was not only the right but the duty of the executive to avert it. That such danger existed the government had no doubt, and subsequent events showed that the apprehensions of the king and his cabinet were well founded. But all the commissioners appointed to arrange for the banquet denied the existence of danger to the government. An issue was thus at once created, one party maintaining that the general considerations of public safety demanded that the banquet should be suppressed, the other holding that the government had no right to suppress it, if for no other reason, because no possible danger was threatened. But, argued the government, we have, in the course we propose to take, the unquestionable authority and sanction of law. Duchâtel, the Minister of the Interior, recalled the laws of 1790 and of 1791, as well as those of the year VIII. and of the year IX., which regulated the powers of the prefect of police and sanctioned the habit of the government. Even after the Revolution of 1830, laws of a similar nature had been passed. In 1831, in 1833, and 1835, and 1840, under the cabinets of Périer, of De Broglie, and of Thiers, as well as under that of Guizot, similar legislation had taken place.

The opposition now took a new tack. It maintained, that since the Revolution of 1830 the right of meeting for political discussion was a public right superior to all legislation; that the abuse of it might indeed be punished like the abuse of any other right, but that it could never, in any case, be the object of a preventive measure. In other words, all legislation giving to the police a right to interfere for the prevention of public gatherings of any kind was contrary to the spirit of the charter, was unconstitutional. To this the government replied: "Very well; we have no desire to violate the constitution; the question has never been tested. We will make up a case for submission to the Supreme Court, which shall decide whether the government has or has not the constitutional right to interfere for the suppression of the banquet."

To this reasonable proposition the opposition leaders could not but agree. Accordingly a formal contract was entered into by a few representative men of each party for the purpose of bringing about such a decision. It was understood that the government was pledged, on the one hand, to act in accordance with the decision of the court, and that the opposition, on the other hand, was to postpone the banquet until the decision should be announced. Thus the matter seemed, for a moment, to be in the way of a settlement in a constitutional manner. Guizot declares that the king was delighted with the prospect of a constitutional solution of the question, and that the friends of the government were all hopeful that the crisis would have a tranquil issue.

But the mutual felicitations of the party leaders were soon interrupted. It became at once apparent that the great mass of the opposition in Paris would submit to no such legal and tranquil solution of the question. It was sadly evident that the more moderate members of the opposition had lost all control of the populace, and that since the union of the monarchist and republican factions, or rather since the surrender of the monarchist to the republican faction, nothing short of an out-

and-out revolutionary movement would satisfy the popular demand. Accordingly, within a few hours after the conclusion of the agreement above referred to, the government learned that the contract would be repudiated.

The commissioners in charge of the preliminary arrangements for the banquet had issued a formal invitation to the opposition members of the Legislative Assembly. On the morning of the 21st of February, the very day after the pacific agreement had been made, three of the more intense republican papers of Paris, the *National*, the *Réforme*, and the *Démocratie Pacifique*, published the following letter as their reply:

"*To the President and Commissioners of the Banquet:*

"GENTLEMEN:—We have received the invitation, with which you have honored us, to the banquet of the 12th arrondissement of Paris.

"The right of meeting for political discussion without previous authorization having been denied by the ministry in the discussion on the address, we see in this banquet a means of maintaining a constitutional right against the pretensions of arbitrary power, and of giving to this right a definite consecration.

"For this reason we regard it as an imperious duty to join in the legal and pacific manifestation which you are preparing, and to accept of your invitation."

This letter of acceptance was signed by ninety-two deputies of the opposition.

Now it may well be asked, What was the object of these deputies? The language of the letter cannot be mistaken. It was by no means for the purpose of any reformatory measures which they hoped to inaugurate; it was apparently for the purpose of defying the government, and that, too, in regard to a measure which the government had already engaged to submit to the court for legal decision. This was made all the more evident from the announcements. The same journals which published the letter of the deputies published also the programme as made out by the Commission. This document displays upon its very face the intention of its authors to arouse the people of the city. It boastfully refers to the numbers and rank of those who have signified their intention to be present for the purpose of protesting in the name of law against an illegal and arbitrary pretension. Its authors then make a significant appeal to the National Guard. They presume that the guard will be faithful to their motto, which is "*Liberty and Public Order*," and in the defence of liberty array themselves with the manifestation. They accordingly call upon the guard to arrange themselves in front of the Madeleine in two lines, between which the invited guests were to be stationed.

From these provisions, and from the terms of the proclamation of the Commission, it was evident that the National Guard was counted upon as being in general sympathy with the movement. It was also apparent that the purpose was not so much after all to create public opinion at the banquet, as to excite and arouse public opinion which already existed. The proclamation removed the last possibility of misunderstanding the nature of the demonstration. It was simply a formidable and dangerous defiance of the government in regard to a question which the cabinet had agreed to submit to the decision of the courts. Under such circumstances, no government could have been deceived in regard to its duty. The situation was one of peril, not only to public order, but also to constitutional government itself.

The French cabinet did not hesitate an instant. M. Duchâtel, Minister of the Interior, informed on the evening of the 20th of February of the proclamation that was to appear on the following morning, conferred at once with the committee that had agreed to submit the question to the courts. It became instantly apparent that the power which for six months had been gradually slipping from the hands of the more moderate members of the opposition had now completely escaped, and had taken refuge in the camp of the extreme republicans. The royalist opposition had completely lost its independence, and was simply dragged on in the train of the revolutionary leaders. There was evidently no dependence to be placed upon the contract, and the government did not hesitate to act accordingly. It would have been weak, not to say pusillanimous, to have done otherwise. The prefect of the police, acting under immediate instruction from the cabinet, interdicted the banquet. At the same time the commander-in-chief of the military forces reminded the National Guard of the laws which prevented their assembling without the command of their officers and the requisition of the civil authorities.

As a further precaution, the Prefect of Police published a proclamation to the inhabitants of Paris. After reminding the people of the disquietude that prevailed, and the desire of the government to have the question in dispute subjected to a judicial and constitutional decision, the Prefect continued in these words:

"The government persists in this desire, but the manifesto published to-day by the opposition journals announces another end as well as other intentions; it institutes another government by the side of the true government of the country, that which was founded by the charter and is supported by a majority in the chambers; it calls for a public manifestation dangerous to the repose of the city; it convokes, in violation of the law of the 22d of March, 1831, the National Guard, and in advance posts them in military order with their officers at their head. There is no longer any reason to believe in the good faith of the contract; laws the most plain and the most firmly established are violated. The government will cause the laws to be respected, for they are the foundation and the guarantee of public order.

"I invite all good citizens to conform to these laws, and not to join in any public concourse, lest they give occasion for troubles to be regretted. In the name of our institutions, in the name of public repose and the dearest interests of the city, I make this appeal to their patriotism and their reason." *

The effect of this proclamation was instantly manifest. The moderate adherents of the movement generally abandoned it, and the opposition seemed to be in a crisis of disorganization.

The government was everywhere vigilant. On the evening of the 21st, after the prohibition of the banquet had been published, the Minister of the Interior ordered the arrest of twenty-four of the revolutionary leaders.

The warrants for twenty-two had been made out when news arrived at the head-quarters of the minister, that the banquet had been abandoned. As if to leave no possible uncertainty in the minds of the ministry, this intelligence was brought by no less a personage that M. Boissel, the president of the Commission. It appeared that after a long and fiery debate an abandonment had finally been determined upon, and that M. Boissel had come with the decision to the cabinet. All lovers of good order, of course, were jubilant.

But once more it became speedily apparent that their rejoicings were premature. It was soon re-

* Guizot, *Mémoires*, vol. VIII. p. 563.

vealed that no action of the Commission would bind the populace of Paris. Just as it had happened when the leaders of both parties had agreed to submit the question to the decision of the court, so now, the mob refused to be constrained or directed by their leaders. The most fiery spirts declared that they would not submit to the decision, and that, if they could not have the banquet, they would at least indulge in a demonstration,—in a demonstration, too, which should be all the more decisive. Thus while the government had in reality gained a triumph, the attitude of the most active revolutionists was such as to rob that triumph of its legitimate results. Nay, it was such as to convert the triumph into a real disaster; for, on the one hand, it threw the government off its guard; and on the other, it transferred the control of the demonstration from the hands of the more moderate to the hands of the most fiery revolutionists. Thus the situation was even more dangerous than it had been before. The government was congratulating itself that the crisis was past, when, as a matter of fact, the control of the vast rabble of Paris had passed to conspirators and fanatic revolutionists, who had no scruples in seizing upon any and every means of accomplishing their mad designs.*

But it may well be asked: If the government enjoyed the hearty support of a majority of the legislative assembly, why was it not able to sup-

* De La Hodde, *History of the Secret Societies of France*, p. 405.

press the insurrection and prevent disturbance? If the rebellion was confined to the fanatics and the rabble of Paris, why could not the government put it down? Why, with the fair warning which it had, was it not able to preserve the peace of the city?

In answer it may be said, that however superior in force a government may be to those who would defy its power, some amount at least of judgment and discretion is necessary in order to ensure its success. I think it will be easy to show that in its attempts to get control of the Revolution, the government was wanting even in the very rudiments of political wisdom. It requires but the briefest outline of well-known facts to show that nothing could have been weaker than the course which was pursued. Twice it occurred that when the government had got the insurgents well in hand, it relaxed its grasp, and threw away all that it had gained. Let us look for a moment at some of the facts of the case.

As soon as the cabinet had received assurance that the banquet had been abandoned, it was ordered that the execution of the warrants be suspended, and that the troops be sent back to their quarters. As it was desirable to avoid all provocation, this order can hardly be thought to have been unwise. Its effect, however, was not what had been anticipated,—it simply cleared the way for the rioters. During the night a feverish excitement prevailed, and throughout the day of the 22d, places of business were everywhere closed. It became more and more apparent that the revolutionists were formidable and resolute. During the following night the excitement continued. On the morning of the 23d, the tumult throughout the city had so increased, that the royal family became alarmed, and the king himself began to hesitate. Everywhere in the city the cry of "*Down with the ministry!*" was heard, and presently the queen, frightened out of her wits, added her voice to the voice of the multitude. Other members of the royal family followed her example. The result was not altogether an unnatural one, although it was one which betrayed a deplorable weakness in the king. As we have already seen, Guizot himself had at one time been in favor of a change of ministry; the queen was now in favor of it, the king's sons were in favor of it, the mob was in favor of it;—because it was not done, indeed, the tide of insurrection was rising in every part of the city. Even at that late hour, as we shall in a moment see, vigorous measures would have reduced everything into submission. But the king was amiable, and he granted to the importunities of his wife and family what, we may well believe, he would never have granted to the cries of the insurrectionists alone. The king's weakness in being unable to answer their entreaties with a decisive No! imperilled everything. At three o'clock on the 23d, with the insurrection growing everywhere more and more formidable, the king announced that the formation of a new ministry would be entrusted to M. Molé.

The effect of this unexpected turn of affairs was the very opposite of what had been so foolishly expected. The queen and the Duke de Montpensier had been so beside themselves as to suppose, and the king so weak as to hope, that this surrender would satisfy the mob, and that they would abandon their weapons and return to their homes in peace. No supposition could have been weaker, or, indeed, more unnatural. The cry of defiance was instantly converted into a cry of victory. The ruler in any sphere, be that sphere high or low, who yields before armed resistance, is from the moment of his yielding a ruler no longer. So it proves everywhere; so it proved in Paris. Just as had happened in 1789, when the crown receded before the populace, the event was universally interpreted as a shrinking of royalty from an encounter. Like demons unchained, the denizens of the faubourgs rushed to the designated places of resort. "All," says one of the annalists, "who were in debt, all who had anything to gain by disturbance, the galley-slaves, the robbers, the burglars, the assassins, combined in one hideous *mêlée*. Some hoped for rapine and blood, others for disorder and confusion—all for selfish benefit from convulsion."

It was about three o'clock on the afternoon of the 23d when the change of ministry was proclaimed in the chambers by Guizot himself. The king, he announced, had sent for Molé, and the new cabinet would be made up as speedily as possible. The fact of this public announcement is of great importance, inasmuch as it reveals in its true light the spirit of the insurgents. The chambers at once adjourned, and the important news was speedily carried to every part of Paris.

At one o'clock on the evening of the day when the change of ministry was announced, a band of insurgents, more ragged and ferocious than the rest, armed with pikes and clubs, and headed by a wild-looking demon named Lagrange, set out from the *Place de la Bastile* and advanced to the residence of the prime minister. The mansion had been frequently threatened, and for its protection a troop of soldiers was on guard. The insurgents, with their pikes and their red flag flaming in the light of the torches which they carried, were forced to halt at the line of bayonets that barred the street. At the sight of the mob pressing up with their torches, the horse of the commander became unmanageable and created some confusion. At this moment Lagrange discharged his pistol in the direction of the troop. The soldiers, thinking themselves attacked, levelled their pieces, and by a single volley brought down fifty of the mob killed or wounded. Some such result as this had evidently been anticipated—probably desired; for the insurgents at once placed the dead upon a wagon that had followed the mob for the purpose, arranging the bodies in such a manner as to make the most tragic display of their bleeding wounds. The course pursued encourages the presumption, indeed, almost affords positive proof, that the whole affair had been premeditated simply to add to the excitement and fury of the people. When the hideous mass, crowned by a half-naked woman, was arranged in the most artistic manner for the display, the word of command was given: "To the *National!*" and thither they went, surrounded by a constantly increasing crowd shouting in the highest state of excitement. From the office of the *National* they went to that of the *Réforme*, where they were harangued by leaders who took good care to represent the bodies as having fallen under the blows of a cruel and vindictive tyranny. From the office of the *Réforme* this cortège continued its course, and all night it paraded through the streets of Paris. Surrounded by a mad crowd of howling men and women, it spread consternation wherever it went, and created everywhere a thirst for vengeance.

The result was precisely what Lagrange and his followers had probably desired. Barricades were hastily thrown up in the central parts of the city; the insurgents took possession of the principal churches as head-quarters; wagons and omnibuses were overturned to form barriers; paving-stones were torn up; gun-shops were broken open and rifled of their contents; in short, every preparation was made for a most desperate resistance. It was apparent that at daybreak a terrible shock would come.

While these preparations were going on in the streets, the greatest embarrassments prevailed at the Tuileries. Molé, who had been summoned by the king to succeed Guizot, found it impossible to form a cabinet. In this dilemma his majesty turned to his old minister for advice. "Call Thiers," was his answer; and Thiers was entrusted with the task. Whether he would succeed better was not immediately apparent. But something had to be done at once, without waiting for cabinet action. At a conference held in the middle of the night by the king and Guizot, it was determined to appoint Marshal Bugeaud to the command of the military forces, including the National Guard.

As this old hero, accompanied by Guizot, passed through the city to reach the head-quarters of the army, it was apparent that the mad tide of insurrection was everywhere rising. "What do you think of the prospect?" asked Guizot. "It is rather late," responded the marshal, "but I have never yet been defeated, and I shall not begin tomorrow." This was at two o'clock in the morning of the 24th of February.

At head-quarters he found everything in confusion. His vigor and capacity, however, gave a new inspiration. Everything was changed as if by enchantment. Chaos was reduced to order, and messengers were despatched throughout the city in every direction. Every one saw that a master-mind had taken hold of affairs. At five in the morning the whole army of twenty-five thousand men was in motion. The plan was to advance through the city in four columns, to destroy all the barricades in their passage, and to await orders when they had reached their destination. And such was the extraordinary vigor with which the orders were carried out, that in two hours after the officers had mounted the saddle, or as early as seven o'clock, the Hôtel de Ville, the Pantheon, and the whole centre of the city was occupied by the troops. The barricades had been surmounted and destroyed, and that too by the mere force of the advance, without the firing of a single shot. In five hours from the moment when Marshal Bugeaud took command, Paris was conquered and the revolution averted.

But at this moment the marshal received a note signed by M. Thiers, ordering him to cease the combat, and to withdraw his troops. With this unaccountable order he absolutely refused to comply, except at the positive command of the king. But an order from the Duke de Nemours coming directly from the cabinet, compelled him to submit.

The secret of this extraordinary change of policy at the moment when decisive success had everywhere been secured over the insurgents, was that the cabinet, which M. Thiers had at length succeeded in forming, had determined upon a policy of conciliation and concession. The appointment of Bugeaud to the command of the army was the last act of Guizot's administration; the first act of the ministry of Thiers was to surrender to the mob everything that had been gained.

The policy of Thiers was to withdraw the troops from all the positions they had won, to terminate the conflict by simple submission. Placards signed by the new ministers announced the change of policy all over the city.

The result was what, it would seem, the least knowledge of the elements of the problem would have anticipated. Shouts of triumph were raised by the revolutionists, while the friends of order were everywhere filled with dismay. All saw that the victory had been abandoned at the moment when it had been won. As the soldiers marched back over the barricades which they had just taken at the point of the bayonet, their indignation was universal. Many of the officers, in their rage, broke their swords and threw them on the pavement, while large numbers of the soldiers actually threw away their muskets, in sheer anger and disgust.

In deep dejection the columns of the army slowly wended their way back to the vicinity of the Tuileries and the Palais Royal.

In their retreat they were closely followed by the torrent of revolution, which now from all quarters rolled impetuously forward. At eight o'clock, the placards had been posted throughout the city; *at ten o'clock, the tide of excitement in consequence had risen so high, that Thiers felt that he could no longer direct the government, and accordingly besought the king to place another in his stead.* Those few hours constituted but a short administration, and yet they were long enough to make the saving of the monarchy impossible. Had the policy so happily begun by Marshal Bugeaud been carried forward, it is impossible to see why the Orleans family might not to-day have been in possession of the throne of France.

But to the cause of the government the withdrawal of the troops was absolutely fatal. The soldiers, paralyzed by the order not to fire, could oppose no resistance to the armed multitude that now surged around them. After a slight struggle they were forced to abandon the Palais Royal. In an instant the mob broke into this august edifice, and sacked and plundered it from top to bottom. The most beautiful pictures, the most splendid statues, the most gorgeous furniture shared a common destruction at the hands of the multitude. In half an hour, those magnificent apartments were nothing but a mass of destroyed splendor.

From the Palais Royal, the crowd, carrying trophies of their triumph, surged toward the Tuileries. The queen appealed to the troops from the balcony—Marie Antoinette had stood in the same place, and for the same vain purpose, on the 10th of August, 1792. The king put on his uniform, and presented himself to the National Guard; but it was only to hear with his own ears and see with his own eyes that all was lost. As he re-entered the royal apartments with pale visage, he may have remembered that Louis XVI., after a similar attempt on the fatal 10th of August, had returned to the same room. A moment after his return, Emile de Girardin appeared, and in a few short words informed the king that "nothing short of abdication would now suffice." "Nothing else?" "Sire, the abdication of the king, or the abdication of monarchy," was the reply. At these words the Duke de Montpensier, the king's son, with an interest that was indecently transparent, urged his father to abdicate rather than sacrifice the dynasty. While the king was hesitating, Marshal Bugeaud, having heard the report of the abdication, rushed into the apartments. "*Never abdicate!*" exclaimed the veteran; "*such an act will disarm the troops. The insurrection approaches: nothing remains but to combat it.*" "Sign not!" exclaimed Piscatory; "abdication is the republic in an hour."

But the shots were growing nearer and nearer, and every moment breathless messengers brought word that all was lost, and that abdication would be the only safety for the lives of the royal family. While the king still hesitated, Montpensier renewed his indecent appeals with frantic energy. At last, Louis Philippe, overcome with emotion, signed the fatal document which terminated his reign.

He was urged to declare the Duchess of Orleans regent, but he positively refused. "Others may do so if they deem it necessary, but I will not. It would be contrary to law; and since, thank God! I have never yet been guilty of violating it, I will not begin to do so at this moment." "What then!" said the Duchess of Orleans, "will you leave me here without friends, without relations, without counsel? What would you wish me to do?" "My dear Hellen," replied the king, "the dynasty and the crown of your son are at stake; remain, then, to save the crown for him." And with these words the king, the queen, and the princesses set out to leave the palace; the Duchess of Orleans and her two sons remained behind. Escaping from the Tuileries through the gardens, the royal fugitives found two cabriolets that were disengaged, and so made their escape from the city.

Thus the insurgents were rid of the king; it remained to be seen whether they would be rid of monarchy. There remained, to support the falling dynasty, the infant Count of Paris, the Princess Hellen, his mother, and the Duke of Nemours, his legal guardian. Scarcely had Louis Philippe and his companions in sorrow left the palace, when the President of the Chamber of Deputies, M. Dupin, sought an interview with the princess. "I came to tell you," said he, on being received, "that perhaps the *rôle* of Maria Theresa is reserved for you." "Lead the way," replied the princess, "my life belongs to France and to my children." "Then there is not a moment to lose; let us go instantly to the Chamber of Deputies."

No sooner had they left the Tuileries, than the

mob, now wholly unrestrained by the soldiery, rushed into the palace, and repeated the work that they had done at the Palais Royal. The insignia of royalty were torn down and destroyed, and a republic was ostentatiously proclaimed.

On arriving at the Chamber of Deputies, the princess found everything in trepidation. Only the departure of the king was known, and everybody seemed to be ready to inquire, What next? Thiers was absent, Lamartine was absent,—there was no one ready to take the lead.

In this condition of affairs, M. Dupin ascended the tribune, and declared that the king had abdicated and transmitted his rights to his grandson, and to the Duchess as regent. The report was false, inasmuch as the king's last act in his palace was to refuse to do what he deemed an illegal act. But the president doubtless judged that the princess would be the more popular, and for that reason the more successful, regent.

The announcement was received with applause; indeed, with considerable enthusiasm. The chamber at once, by acclamation, declared the Count of Paris, king, and the duchess, regent. It seemed for a moment that the throne would be saved. But it was only for a moment. The mob, which had followed the Princess and the Count of Paris, now broke into the chambers. It had begun by demanding a change of ministry as the price of quiet; and the demand had been granted. It then demanded abdication as the price of the dynasty; that too had been complied with. It was now present to demand a republic without conditions.

The events which followed the proclamation of the Count of Paris as king are of extraordinary interest, inasmuch as they show in the strongest light the extraordinary character of the Revolution. There is abundant proof that the leaders of the movement were conscious of the weakness of their course among the people of the nation. To realize how completely this consciousness prevailed, we have only to read Lamartine's account of their interview. What were they to do? was the important question which now confronted them. Were they called upon to proclaim a republic at once, or ought they, on the contrary, to acquiesce in the continuance of monarchy? Were the people ready for a republic, or were the sympathies of the people such that the proclamation of a republic would create a reaction in favor of monarchy? Would it be better to support the Count of Paris as king, to appoint a minister to control him, and to continue the agitation of republican doctrines until they should become so prevalent as to leave no chance for a reaction? These were difficult questions, but they demanded an immediate answer.

At half-past ten on the morning of the 24th, the man who was to answer these questions was, according to his own account, still at his home. He had anticipated nothing more than a change of ministry; and as he had no curiosity to hear the names of the new ministers read off in the Assembly, he was in no haste to take his seat. But he was now told that the rioters might attack the chamber, and, if there was to be any danger, he considered it his duty to be present. He relates that as he reached the gates of the palace where the chambers were in session, two generals on horseback met. "What news?" asked one. "Nothing of importance," answered the other; "the crowd is not numerous, and scatters at the least movement of my squadrons; and as for the bridge, the best troops in Europe could not force it." The response is of historical interest, inasmuch as it shows that the mob was at that moment under control.

Lamartine entered the Palace Bourbon, convinced, as he says, that he had been called by a false alarm. But he was deceived only for a moment. As he entered the vestibule, he was met by seven or eight persons who were anxiously waiting for him. They were representatives of the press, editors of the *National* and the *Réforme.* They demanded a secret conference. Lamartine took them into a distant apartment of the palace, when one of them, speaking for all, addressed him as follows:

"We are republicans, and we continue republicans; but we can postpone the republic, if France is not yet ripe for it;—if she would not yield to it without resistance; if there be more danger in launching her at once into the fulness of her destined institutions than in holding her on their brink. These are our doubts; we call on you to resolve them. The people call on you: they trust you;—what you say will be re-echoed; what you desire will be done. The reign of Louis Philippe is over. But might a temporary sovereignty, in the name of a child, in the hands of a woman, guided by a popular minister appointed by the people and esteemed by the republicans;—might such a phantom of monarchy suspend the crisis and prepare the nation for the republic? Will you be that minister? Will you be the guardian of our dying royalty and of our infant liberty, by governing the child, the woman, and the people? In our persons the republican party gives itself up to you; we formally engage to bear you to power by the irresistible impulse of the revolution which you hear roaring without. We will keep you there by our votes, by our journals, by our secret societies, and by our disciplined forces in the deepest strata of society. Your course shall be ours. France and Europe will believe you to be the minister of the Regent; *we* shall know that you are the minister of the Republic."

Such was the errand which this group of newspaper editors had been waiting to deliver. They professed then *to have the power to determine* whether France should have a monarchical or whether it should have a republican form of government, and this power of decision Lamartine does not question. They have come to ask Lamartine's advice,—rather they have come to throw the responsibility of deciding upon Lamartine himself. I imagine it would be difficult to find in all history an instance where so important a decision was formally entrusted to a single person. When to Julius Cæsar, or to Peter the Great, or to Napoleon the First, was it ever said by the representatives of a party in power, "Here is our country; determine at will whether it shall be ruled by a king or whether it shall be ruled by a president?"

And now let us ask what peculiar qualifications Lamartine had for the safe performance of so momentous a task. In my estimation they were very few.

That he had real genius of a certain kind there can be no possible question. The impress of great literary talent is to be seen in all his works. His mind, naturally ardent and enthusiastic, had been nurtured and enriched by travel and by reflection. His descriptive powers are certainly of the very highest order. His mind is at all times essentially poetical, and his poetry is remarkable for its exquisite touches of grace and delicacy. His prose is itself poetry. So completely is his mind filled with poetical images, so keen are his perceptions, so sensitive is he to the grand and the beautiful, so enthusiastic are his emotions in the presence of the elevated, that he can hardly touch the most ordinary theme without beautifying it with all the hues of romance. His mind was as fertile as its organization was exquisite. For a considerable time he wrote, it is said, six octavos a year, and they were all overflowing with an exuberance of fancy and a delicacy of expression which gave them a high place in the literature of the nation.

Now it may be remarked, that these qualities of mind and these characteristics of manner, admirable as they are in a poet and in a writer of romance, are well-nigh fatal to the value of the works of a writer of history. Ostrich plumes, and gold lace, and silver knee-buckles may be well in their place, but they are not the fit dress of hard-working men. You cannot with propriety or profit translate Legendre into iambics, or set Blackstone to music. A historian may be dramatic in his description of events, powerful in his delineation of character, generous in feeling, lofty in sentiment, and yet, if he have not sober judgment and rational views, as an instructor of his readers he is as nothing, and worse than nothing. In the portrayal of political events the fire of poetry is not a fit substitute for good sense and a practical understanding of mankind.

I speak thus because Lamartine's great influence on the French people had been not as a poet, but as a historian. He had written much history, and, to use a phrase of Chateaubriand, had covered it all with the bright charms of his light and shade. His history of the Girondists had all the excellences and all the defects of his style of composition. The almost infinite grace and brilliancy of its manner secured for it a success absolutely unknown since the days of Rousseau and Voltaire. Though published in eight volumes, fifty thousand copies of it were sold in the first year. It became the Frenchman's interpretation of the Great Revolution. It represented the heroes of that great convulsion in colors so attractive that men, and still more women, came not only to admire them, but also to be inspired with a certain longing to plunge into similar scenes of excitement themselves. Just as spirited boys sometimes become sailors from reading terrific tales of shipwreck, or soldiers from stories of heroic deeds in the deadly charge, so thousands of the French people were inspired with an indefinite longing for some such excitement as had existed in the days of the Reign of Terror. Lamartine drew no veil over the weaknesses and the ambition of the Girondists, it is true, but he surrounded them with such a halo of fine words that they became interesting in spite of their faults: nay, perhaps it should rather be said, in very consequence of their faults. The most sinister and selfish enterprises were covered with the most brilliant colors, and the deepest interest was excited in the men of fewest virtues and of greatest vices. Even the turpitude of Robespierre was made attractive by the very sublimity into which it was magnified, and for the same reason that one may struggle almost in vain against a kind of admiration for Satan as the hero of the *Paradise Lost.*

Now let us look for the tangible results. Thousands and tens of thousands of copies of the Girondists were published in cheap form and distributed at a price which the lowest workmen could afford. The picturesque vividness with which the work was written, the dark grandeur with which the revolutionary chiefs were surrounded, above all, the irresistible power with which the masses were invested, not only made the people familiar with revolt and street-war, but also inspired in ill-regulated minds a desire for excitement and a longing to reproduce scenes similar to those described. It was under an influence like this that portraits of the revolutionary chiefs were displayed on the boulevards, in the shops, and along all quays, and that prints representing the principal scenes of the Revolution were everywhere appealing to the passions and the enthusiasm of the people. Theatres were opened in which the Revolution was acted in plays that lasted for weeks. The events of the 10th of August, as thus portrayed in the Girondists of Lamartine, in the theatres, in the shop-windows, and on the bulletins, so interested the populace that they desired to see a 10th of August; and they were ready to make one. Beyond all possible doubt, Lamartine had thus exerted an immense influence in bringing about the Revolution of 1848, and in driving Louis Philippe from the throne. It would scarcely be too much to say that ever after the publication of the Girondists the *gamins* of Paris were ready for an insurrection, not, indeed, in opposition to any tyranny, but solely "by way of a lark."

Such had been Lamartine's influence. I think it not strange, therefore, that the leaders and representatives of the Revolution, when it came, looked to him for guidance. They, as we have seen, placed all their power at his disposal. He seems to have felt to some extent the terrible responsibility thrust upon him. He assures us that, when the speaker had concluded, he asked for a moment's time for reflection. Resting his elbows on the table, and burying his face in his hands, he spends five or six minutes in almost breathless thought. At length, uncovering his face, he gives expression to his decision. He canvasses the various considerations which press upon his mind. He vividly portrays what he believes the result will be in case they decide upon monarchy, and what in case they decide upon a republic. Finally he gives his voice for the latter. His concluding words in announcing this decision are worthy of quotation, partly because they are a fair specimen of his extraordinary eloquence, but chiefly because they reveal the false basis on which his reasoning was founded:

"As for myself," he said, "I see clearly the succession of catastrophies which I should prepare for my country if I were to attempt to stop the avalanche of the Revolution, on a slope on which no dynastic power can retain it, without adding to its mass and the crash of its fall. One power only can avert the danger in such a revolution as ours: it is the power of the people itself; it is the suffrage, the will, the reason, the interest, the hands, and the weapons of all—it is the republic. Yes, it is the republic which alone can save you from anarchy, from civil war, from confiscation, from the scaffold, from the overthrow of society from within, and from invasion from without. It is a heroic remedy, but in such times as these it is a policy as bold, almost as violent, as the crisis itself that is needed. Give to the people the republic to-morrow, and call it by its name, and you change its anger into joy, and its fury into enthusiasm. All who cherish in their hearts republican feelings,—all whose imaginations dwell on republican visions,—all who regret,—all who hope,—all who reason and all who meditate in France,—all the secret societies,—all the active and all the speculative republicans,—the people, the demagogues, the young men, the students, the journalists, the men of action and the men of thought,—all will utter one cry, will crowd around only one standard—at first in confusion, afterwards in disciplined order, to protect society by the government of all its members. Such power may be disturbed, but it cannot be deposed, for its base is the nation. It is the only force which can protect itself, the only force that can moderate itself, the only power that can bring the voice, the hands, the reason, the will, and the arms of all to protect, on the one hand the nation from servitude, and on the other hand property, morality, the relations of kindred and society from the deluge which is washing away the foundation of the throne.

"If anarchy can be subdued, it is by the republic. If communism can be conquered, it is by the republic. If the revolution can be guided, it is by the republic. If blood can be spared, it is by the republic. If a general war and invasion can be averted, it is by a republic. Therefore, as a rational and conscientious statesman, free from all illusion and from all fanaticism, I declare before God and before you, that if this day is big with a revolution, I will not conspire for a *half* revolution. I will conspire indeed for *none*, but I will *accept* only a complete one,—a republic.

"But," he added, rising from the table, "I still hope God will spare my country this trial. I accept revolutions: I do not make them. To assume such a responsibility, a man must be a villain, a madman, or a god."

"Lamartine is right," said one of the auditors; "he has more faith in our own ideas than we have." "We are convinced," they all cried. "Let us separate," said they to Lamartine; "do what under the inspiration of events you think best." *

At the close of this interview, Lamartine and the editors repaired immediately to the chamber.

An hour later the large door of the hall opened,

* Lamartine, *History of the Revolution of* 1848, p. 96.

and, as already described, the Duchess of Orleans, leading her sons, entered. As we have before seen, M. Dupin's motion to declare the Count of Paris king, and his mother regent, was carried by acclamation. But when they were proceeding to register the votes, a new tumult arose. The action, if consummated, would frustrate all the designs of the conspirators. Marrast, one of the editors of the *National*, suddenly left the gallery of the journalists, and went out to bring in a bolder mob. Marie ascended the tribune, and, remarking the illegality of the regency, demanded a Provisional Government. This demand was favored by Ledru Rollin, who desired, in the true style of '92, not only a Provisional Government, but also a Convention. There was now a cry for Lamartine. As we have seen, his conduct was prearranged. On ascending the tribune, he proceeded to develop his views concerning the demands of the situation. He declared that the first duty of the chamber was to appoint a Provisional Government. To this the chamber and the attendant mob responded with loud acclamations. "The first duty of such a Provisional Government," continued he, "will be to put an end to the contest which is now raging; the second, to call together the whole electoral body,—and by the whole body I mean all who are citizens, because they are men,—because they are beings endowed with an intellect and a will."

At this declaration in favor of universal suffrage

the shouts of approbation were louder than before. But at this moment Marrast entered the hall with about three hundred rioters, fresh from the sack of the Tuileries. Some of them levelled their muskets at the Princess, who, with her children, now fled for her life. No sooner were the royal personages gone, than Lamartine was called upon to name the Provisional Government. He says in one place in his book that he refused, and in another that he complied.*

The men appointed were Marie, Lamartine, Ledru Rollin, Cremieux, Dupont de l'Eure, Arago, and Garnier-Pagès. The majority of these, it may be observed, had already prepared the way for their appointment by proposing in the debate a Provisional Government. Thus it was definitely fixed that France should enter a second time on the experiment of a republic.

I have dwelt somewhat at length on the details of this Revolution, for the purpose of showing the true character of those events which immediately led to the abandonment of royalty. The facts, as I have endeavored to present them, show conclusively that the matter of the form of the new government was the result of the merest accident.† We have seen that the representatives of

* His words are, "*Il se borne a souffler tout bas aux scrutateurs les noms qui se presenteut le plus naturellement à son esprit.*" He adds that the *scrutateurs* handed the names up to the president, who proclaimed them to the mob.

† On this point we have the most positive testimony; no less an authority than De Tocqueville. He says:

"The monarchy might have been saved if the proclamation of the

the conspirators proposed to Lamartine to substitute the Count of Paris as king for Louis Philippe with the Duchess of Orleans as regent, and that he objected to the scheme as one that could not be permanent. Was Lamartine correct in his course of reasoning? Did the republic accomplish what Lamartine in the eloquent passage just quoted declared that it would accomplish? The chief reason of his deciding for a republic was a belief that a republic alone would harmonize all the turbulent elements of the nation into a compact government. What, as a matter of fact, was the result? In two days after the appointment of the Provisional Government it was on the brink of ruin from an attack of the Terrorists. Three weeks later, March 17th, it was saved from destruction merely by the hesitation of its enemies. Lamartine himself tells us that only a few days later, on the 15th of April, he burnt his papers, and that, when he went to bed, he had no expectation of surviving

Provisional Government and the retreat of the Duchess of Orleans could have been retarded for an hour. After having sat out the revolutionary scene, heard the proclamation of the republic, and seen Lamartine and Ledru Rollin set off for the Hôtel de Ville, I was quitting the chamber, and had reached the landing-place of the staircase, when I met a company of the 10th Legion with fixed bayonets led by General Oudinot, not in uniform, but brandishing his cane in military style and saying: 'En Avant! Vive le Roi et la Duchesse d'Orléans Régente.' Oudinot recognized me and caught me by the arm, crying out: 'Where are you going? Come with us and we will sweep these ruffians out of the chamber.' 'My dear general,' I answered, 'it is too late. The chamber is dissolved, the duchess has fled, and the Provisional Government is on its way to the Hôtel de Ville.'"—*De Tocqueville, Mémoires*, vol. II. p. 110.

the insurrection of the next day. Again, one month later, on the 15th of May, a new revolution was for a time triumphant. At the middle of April, a civil war of four days ended in the dictatorship of General Cavaignac. Finally the French people formally repudiated the republic by confirming Napoleon III. on the imperial throne. Such, then, proved to be the *stability* that was the basis of Lamartine's decision.

But there is one question which I have not yet asked, and which is pertinent to the history in hand. Admitting that the republic was the result of a series of chances or accidents or blunders, the question may still be asked whether France *wanted* a republic. Was the mob, which really set up the republic, a political representative of the nation? On the answer to this question our justification or condemnation of the Revolution must be founded; or rather, I ought to say, there can be no justification of the Revolution unless it can be shown that the insurgents represented the ideas generally prevailing in the nation. If republicanism means one thing more than another, it means the prevalence of the properly expressed will of the majority. Republicanism itself must admit that if such a majority desire a king rather than a president, a king they should have. Now how was it in France? This question is to be answered not by any vague guesses, but by a careful inspection of testimony.

As most important of all testimony on this question, we have the words of one whose admiration of republican institutions is known to every intelligent American. The memoirs and letters of De Tocqueville, from which I have already so often quoted, abound in the most positive assurances on this question. I quote one statement only, though it is but a representative of many. On the 27th of February, 1849, he wrote to the English historian, Grote, as follows:

"The events in France during the last year are well calculated to attract the attention of an elevated and thoughtful mind. To a foreigner, who sees the effect without understanding the causes, they must appear most extraordinary. To those who are on the spot and who have watched the inevitable progress of events, nothing can be more simple and natural. At any rate, *the nation did not wish for a revolution, still less did it desire a republic;* for, though in France there is not a particle of attachment for a particular dynasty, the opinion that monarchy is a necessary institution is almost universal. France, then, wished for neither a revolution nor a republic. That she allowed both to be inflicted upon her proceeds from two causes: from the fact that Paris, having become, during the last fifty years, the first manufacturing town, in the country, was able on a given day to furnish the republican party with an army of artisans; and, secondly, from another fact, which is the offspring of centralization, that Paris, no matter who speaks in her name, dictates to the rest of

France. These two facts taken together explain the catastrophe of February, 1848." *

Emile Thomas, who had the best means of judging, declares, in his History of the National Workshops, that "even on the evening of the 24th of February, 1848, there were not in Paris 10,000 avowed republicans." †

But the most detailed account of the republican party with which I am acquainted, is that given by M. De la Hodde in his History of the Secret Societies. This author having been initiated into all the secrets of their different organizations, gives a detailed account of their strength as follows:

"The republican party was, in February, 1848, composed of the following persons: 4,000 subscribers to the *National*, of whom only one-half were republicans, the other half belonging to the dynastic opposition, led by Garnier-Pagè's and Carnot. Of these 2,000, there were not more than 600 in Paris, and of these only 200 could be relied on in an actual conflict. The *Réforme* had 2,000 subscribers, of whom 500 were in Paris, and these would turn out to a man. The two societies, '*Des Saisons*' and '*La Société Dissidente*,' promised 1,000 combatants, though it was doubtful if they could muster 600, though the latter embraced all the communists in Paris. To these we must add 400 or 500 old conspirators, whom the first mus

* De Tocqueville, *Memoirs and Remains*, vol. II. p. 94.

† Thomas, *Histoire des Ateliers Nationaux*, p. 14.

ket-shot would recall to their old standards, and 1,500 Polish, Italian, and Spanish refugees, who would probably do the same, from the idea that it would advance the cause of revolution in their own countries. In all, then, there were 4,000 in Paris, and that was the very utmost that could be relied on in the capital, and I defy any one to prove the contrary. In the provinces there was only one real secret society, that at Lyons; Marseilles, Toulouse, and two or three other great towns professed to have such, but no reliance could be placed on them. On the whole, there might be 15,000 or 16,000 republicans in the departments, and 4,000 in Paris. In all, 19,000, or 20,000 out of 17,000,000 male inhabitants,—about one five-hundreth part of the whole,—a proportion so infinitely small, that it is evident they could never have overturned a formidable government." *

A writer in the *Edinburgh Review* for January, 1850, after stating that he had spent a considerable portion of the last two years in France, declares:

"We have mixed with persons of every class, in the provinces as well as in Paris, and with the exception of a few socialists, we never met with a theoretic republican,—that is to say, with any one who wished for that form of government, or even approved of it, or who did not consider the Revolution of 1847 a misfortune."†

* De la Hodde, *Histoire des Sociétés Secretes*, p. 402.

† *Edin. Rev.* vol. XCI., Am. Ed., p. 136.

Even the testimony of Lamartine may be arrayed in support of what has already been said. At the mutiny of the Assembly he saw the unpopularity of republican institutions, and acted accordingly. "Republican feelings," said he, "are weak in France. They are chiefly represented by men who excite horror or terror. As soon as a majority of the people,—which, in an enthusiasm of terror, threw itself into the hands of a moderate republic,—shall have recovered its presence of mind, it will accuse those who have saved it, and turn on the republicans." *

I might, in support of these views of the causes of the Revolution, quote numerous passages from Prevost-Paradol, De Broglie, Seneuil, and others, but it is unnecessary. I have preferred to cite only those who recorded their impressions at the time of the events described.

Now, in the presence of these facts, republican government in France was simply impossible. It would have been impossible even if the advocates of republicanism had been of a character to inspire natural respect. But such was far from being the case.

There is one other phase of the matter which must not be overlooked. I refer to the general condition of the masses of the people. Were they in a state of advancement such as to make republican institutions desirable or even possible?

This question, of course, for those who think

* *Révolution*, II. p. 405.

that for all time and under all circumstances a republican form is the only good form of government, will have no significance. But, on the other hand, for those who derive their impressions from the teachings of history rather than from their own desires, and who consequently recognize the fact that of all forms of government the republican needs the greatest amount of general intelligence, it is a question whose importance, in this connection, it is not very easy to exaggerate.

Baron Dupin, in his work on the "*Progressive Situation of France* in 1827," gives an array of facts which are as important as they are startling. The author writes from a hopeful point of view, and therefore cannot be justly charged with painting the picture in too dark colors. After referring to the fact that of the 36,000 communes, 14,000 were entirely without schools or schoolteachers, he says:

"France will have to put forth the greatest efforts to raise herself, by means of elementary instruction, to the simple level of those people whom we have been in the habit of regarding as ignorant. *I say boldly, that in this respect we are below the Irish and the Austrians.* This inferiority is especially noticeable in the South, which is far less advanced than the North. . . . In 1817, France (with a population of some 34,000,000) had in her primary schools only 856,712 scholars; and in 1820, the number had only increased to 1,116,777. Since 1820, the active and powerful impulses of the productive and commercial interests on the one hand, and the opposition of the adversaries of primary schools on the other, have struggled in different parts of the country with varying success. Nevertheless, in the majority of instances the number of pupils has been increased rather than diminished. . . . . Forty years ago seven millions of French knew how to read; to-day the number has been increased to twelve millions. . . . . Secondary schools, which give instruction to the intermediate classes, have been vastly strengthened since 1814, but the instruction given in these establishments has not ceased to be insufficient and without harmony with the needs of the professions. To supply these wants, various industrial schools have been founded at Paris, at Lyons, at Roville, at Toulouse, and at other cities in the realm. The reader, however, can see that there remains much to be done in order to render primary instruction tolerable and secondary instruction profitable to the kingdom." *

Such, then, according to M. Dupin, was the condition of France in 1827. From these representations, three facts stand out in bold prominence. The first is, that of 34,000,000 of inhabitants, only 12,000,000 could read; the second is, that of 86,600 communes or townships, 14,000 were without schools; and the third is, that the nation was making slow but steady advances toward an im-

* Dupin, *Situation progressive des Forces de la France depuis* 1814, p. 51.

proved condition. If it be claimed that a considerable improvement in the intellectual condition of the people took place in the reign of Louis Philippe, it must not be forgotten that the very men who controlled affairs in 1848 had been the very children for the majority of whom, during the period of which M. Dupin speaks, education was impossible.

But as a matter of fact, no considerable improvement had been made, or indeed has been made, up to the present day. Even in 1872, M. Taine, in his work on "Universal Suffrage," shows that in all France, of every one hundred male inhabitants, thirty-nine can neither write nor read; and that in general, the ignorance of the French peasantry is something incredible, except to those who have had the means of observation. These statements he fortifies with an array of facts and anecdotes that leave no room for doubt.*

An English author, as remarkable for his moderation as for his culture, after spending a number of years in provincial France, gives testimony of the same general character.

"The most parsimonious class in Europe," says he, "is the French peasantry; it is also the class most characterized by ignorance and intellectual apathy. The French peasant will not go anywhere except to the market-town, and could not pardon the extravagance of buying a book, or a candle to read it by in the evening." †

* *Du Suffrage Universel et de la Manière de voter*, p. 16, seq.

† Hamerton, *The Intellectual Life*, p. 189.

Elsewhere the same author declares:

"All men of refined sentiment in modern France lament the want of elevation in the bourgeoisie. They read nothing, they learn nothing, think of nothing but money and the satisfaction of their appetites. Their ignorance passes belief, and is accompanied by an absolute self-satisfaction. M. Renan complains that the country is sinking deeper and deeper into vulgarity, forgetting its past and its noble enthusiasms. 'Talk to the peasant, to the socialist, to the international, of France, of her past history, of her genius, he will not understand you. Military honor seems madness to him. The taste for great things, the glory of the mind, are vain dreams; money spent for art and science is money thrown away foolishly.' 'The end of the bourgeoisie commences,' says Flaubert, 'since it is coming to entertain the sentiments of the populace. I do not see that it reads other journals, that it regales itself with other music, or that its pleasures are more elevated. With both classes there is the same love of money, *the same respect for accomplished facts, the same necessity for idols in order to destroy them, the same hatred of all superiority, the same spirit of disparagement, the same sorid (crasse) ignorance.*' " *

Delord, in his admirable History of the Second Empire, remarks that though the French peasant has been emancipated from many of the customs which before the Revolution enthralled him, he is

* Hamerton, *Intellectual Life*, p. 295.

essentially the same in character as he was before that event.*

Now after this view of the condition of the country at large, let us look for a moment at the condition of Paris; for after all it was Paris, and Paris alone, that made the Revolution.

In the metropolis, as nowhere else, the doctrines and principles of the first revolution had taken root. The writings of the sensational school of the last century had been read by everybody in Paris who could read anything, and their blasting influence during the past twenty-five years had been felt there as in no other part of the nation. The natural consequence of those doctrines was the well-nigh universal disruption of the old bonds of society. There was a general fretting against all restraint, human and divine. The people repudiated Christianity and morals alike. There came to be a universal impatience of control, whether from the influence of the conscience, or the authority of law. This distinctly appeared in the style of fictitious literature, which for a quarter of a century was poured forth from the Parisian press, and which was of a character such that if read outside of France, its reading was seldom acknowledged. It appeared in the character of the French drama, that mirror of the public mind, which, during the two generations that

* "Son instruction et son education en sont restées à peu près au point où elles étaient en 89."—*Delord, Hist. du Sec. Emp.*, vol. III. p. 403.

succeeded the writers of whom I have spoken, showed the general prevalence of the same licentious feeling. Christianity was abjured, not so much because it was earnestly disbelieved, for men did not earnestly disbelieve anything, but because it was disagreeable. They did not give themselves the trouble to inquire whether it is true or false; they simply *declined* it, because it imposed a restraint on their appetites and their passions.

Now that this is no fanciful picture, there is abundant and most painful evidence. In 1848, there were in Paris 1,050,000 inhabitants, of whom more than one-third had been born out of wedlock. To be exact, the proportion, according to the census, was one hundred illegitimate to every one hundred and eighty-five legitimate. In Paris, then, there were, when the Revolution of 1848 broke out, 350,000 people of illegitimate birth. Since the Great Revolution, every third child born in Paris received its first lessons of life in a foundling hospital. This prodigious fact was both a consequence and a cause: it was a consequence of those doctrines by which, in a city abounding with temptations and overflowing with stimulants to the passions, the bonds of Christianity and morality had been sundered; it was the cause of that peculiar fondness for insurrection and revolution which had its birth in the consciousness, on the one hand, that disgrace was impossible, and on the other, that success would bring with it wealth and honor, and every means of gratifying the passions. The *énfant trouvé* when grown up becomes the *gamin de Paris*, whose peculiar nature is so graphically described by Victor Hugo in *Les Misérables*; and the *gamin* when still further developed is the proper terror of any true civilization. He has, generally, the rudiments of an education, enough to enable him to read the worst literature, that is to say, enough to enable him to imbibe temptation in every form, without enabling him to combat it. His parents are unknown to him, and his offspring are as strange to him as his parents; for they, as their father had been before them, are sent to the Foundling Hospital. "He has nothing he can call his own, except a pair of stout arms to aid in the formation of barricades, and a dauntless heart ready, at any moment, to accept the hazard of death or pleasure." There were in Paris, at the time of which I speak, eighty or ninety thousand men, in the prime of life, having such an origin and actuated by such dispositions and such passions; and there were associated with them an equal number of women, of a similar origin and of the same character.

But it is by the graphic hand of Lamartine itself that the picture of the revolutionists is best drawn.

"They were," he says, "in part composed of galley-slaves, who had no political ideas in their heads, nor social chimeras in their hearts, but who accepted a revolution as the condition of the disorder it was to perpetuate, the blood it was to shed, the terror it was to inspire. They contained also a part of that ragged scum of the population of great cities, which public commotions cause to rise to the surface before it falls back into the common sewers from which it had arisen; men who floated between the fumes of intoxication and the thirst for blood; who sniffed carnage while issuing from the fumes of debauchery; who never ceased to besiege the ears of the people till they got a victim thrown to them to devour. They were the scourings of the galleys and the dungeons."

FROM THE SECOND REPUBLIC TO THE SECOND EMPIRE.

"Diesem Ambos vergleich' ich das Land, den Hammer dem
Herscher;
Und dem Volke das Blech, das in der Mitte sich krümmt.
Wehe dem armen Blech, wenn nur willkürliche Schläge
Ungewiss treffen, und nie fertig der Kessel erscheint."

GOETHE.

CHAPTER VIII.

FROM THE SECOND REPUBLIC TO THE SECOND EMPIRE.

THE character of the Revolution of 1848 is well illustrated by the events which immediately followed the appointment of the Provisional Government. No sooner had the mob, which had taken possession of the Chamber of Deputies, ratified the names presented by Lamartine, than the new government set out to inaugurate itself at the Hôtel de Ville. Its troubles began at once. While the meeting described in the last chapter had been going on at the Chamber of Deputies, other events of importance had been taking place elsewhere. After the sack of the Tuileries, the most radical of the revolutionists had repaired to their clubs for consultation. Important meetings were held at the offices of the *Réforme* and the *National;* and at each of these meetings a Provisional Government was named.* The citizens thus appointed had repaired to instal themselves at the Hôtel de Ville, and were found in their places when Lamartine and his friends arrived. The most radical of the revolutionists, including Flocon, Louis Blanc, and Albert, had proclaimed

* *Mémoires de Caussidière,* vol. I. p. 63.

themselves members of the Provisional Government even before the arrival of the government appointed at the Chamber of Deputies.*

The collision which necessarily ensued ended in a compromise. The most conspicuous characters appointed at the clubs were added to the list named by Lamartine.

As soon as the terms of union were agreed upon, it was apparent that the new government contained within itself the most violent elements of discord. Lamartine and Garnier-Pagès, on the one hand, were earnestly desirous of pursuing a moderate policy, such as would inaugurate a system equally removed from an unlimited monarchy and an unbridled democracy; while, on the other, Flocon and Albert, as the representatives of the clubs, were earnest in their endeavors to carry out the ideas of the most radical republicans. Between these extremes there were such varied sympathies and aspirations, as afforded every opportunity for the most active and bitter intrigue. In less than forty-eight hours after the revolution, a most violent war between the moderate and the democratic portions of the Provisional Government was raging, so violent, indeed, that some of its members were thrown into despair, and thought of resigning.†

The first care devolving upon the Provisional Government, however, was not the settlement of its

* *Rapport de Crémieux*, vol. I. p. 266.
† *Mémoires de Caussidière*, vol. I. p. 90.

own inherent difficulties, but the protection of itself against the violence of the populace. During the three days of the insurrection the shops had been closed, labor had been suspended, and the laboring classes, destitute alike of capital and of credit, began to feel the pangs of hunger. On the morning of the 25th of February, just after the government was ready to begin its legitimate functions, an enormous crowd, amounting, according to every account, to more than 100,000 persons, assembled in the Place de Grève and surrounded the Hôtel de Ville. So dense was the throng, that it pressed into the building itself, and filled every passage and stairway and room, up to the very table about which the members of the government were sitting. To appease the mob, decrees were drawn up as rapidly as possible, and when they had been struck off on a press that had been set up for the purpose, they were distributed to the bystanders and thrown from the palace windows to the crowd below.

Some of these decrees were of the most frivolous character; others penetrated to the most vital interests of the nation's political existence. One of them, for example, changed the order of the colors on the tri-color flag; one abolished "*Monsieur*" and "*Madame*," and substituted in their places "*Citoyen*" and "*Citoyenne*"; one liberated all functionaries from their oaths of allegiance; one ordered that the words *Liberté*, *Égalité*, *Fraternité*, should be inscribed on all the walls of Paris; one ordered that trees of liberty should be planted in all the public squares; and one, that every person should wear a red rosette in his button-hole.

But these absurd acts of the government, so indicative of the immediate pressure under which they were drawn up, failed, of course, to give any ultimate satisfaction. What then was to be done? Everything that the mob of a hundred thousand should demand. And it called for legislation providing for all the interests of society. It demanded that royalty, under every name whatsoever—legitimacy, Bonapartism, or regency—should be formally abolished. Accordingly, a decree was published abolishing it, and declaring that the government had taken all the steps necessary to render impossible the return of the former dynasty or the accession of a new one. The authorities then by another manifesto declared that the actual government of France is republican, and that the nation will immediately be called on to ratify by its votes this resolution of the government and of the people of Paris. They then abolished all titles of nobility, forbidding any one to assume them. They set at liberty all persons detained on political grounds. Worst of all, they engaged to secure employment to all citizens, and for the purpose of carrying out this decree they ordered the immediate establishment of national workshops.*

* *Recueil des Actes du Gouvernement Provisoire, Paris*, 1848.

It would be unjust to charge the extreme folly of these decrees upon the government. All the authorities agree substantially that the gentlemen who sat in the Hôtel de Ville and wrote out the decrees did little more than act as secretaries for the vast crowd that was surging around. Lamartine himself describes most graphically the situation in which they were placed:

"No sooner," says he, "was one messenger despatched, charged with an order or a decree signed on the corner of a bit of paper with pencil, than another arrived with a similar note, announcing that the Tuileries was menaced by devastation and flames; that Versailles was surrounded by a furious mob which thirsted to destroy that last relic of royalty; another, that Neuilly was already half consumed by fire; a fourth, that all the railway stations were in flames and the bridges cut or destroyed. It was necessary to re-establish the traffic on the roads by which a capital with 1,100,000 mouths was to be fed, and huge mountains of barricades had to be cut through in order to let the convoys pass when they reached the streets. Crowds who had been famishing for three days were to be fed, the dead were to be collected, the wounded to be cared for, the soldiers to be protected against the people, the barracks to be evacuated, the arms and horses to be collected, the palaces and the museum to be protected from pillage. An insurgent populace, 300,000 in number, was to be calmed, pacified, and, if possible, sent back to their workshops in the suburbs; posts were to be everywhere established, formed of the volunteers and National Guards, to prevent pillage. In a word, the things to be done were innumerable; it was hard to say which was the most urgent, or where neglect would entail most serious evils on the republic." *

At one time a rumor was set in motion that the king was returning with an armed force, and that the fortresses in the vicinity were preparing to bombard the city with red-hot shot. Under the impulse of these terrors the rash crowd in the Place de Grève separated, a part setting out in one direction for Vincennes, and a part in the opposite for the Invalides. Finding these strongholds protected, they streamed back into the Place de Grève.

The government, to appease the people, had already sent the military force out of the capital. The mob now had everything its own way. The crowd overpowered the door-keepers and sentinels, spread themselves through every corner of the Hôtel de Ville, under pretence of searching for concealed arms, and finally inundated the hall where the government was in session. There was no power to resist anything which the crowd was disposed to demand; on the part of several members of the government there was no disposition to resist. It is the testimony of both Lamartine and Caussidière that the decree guaranteeing em-

* Lamartine, *Hist. de la Rev.*, vol. I. p. 245.

ployment to all, and bestowing on the combatants at the barricades the million of francs saved by the termination of the civil list, was extorted from the government at a moment when it had no power of resistance.*

It would doubtless be unfair to demand of any government, under such circumstances, that it should bring to the solution of the difficult problems presenting themselves either the highest wisdom or the calmest deliberation. But it must not be forgotton that the decrees had, and continued to have, all the force of law, and that for this reason they are not exempted from criticism by the circumstances of their origin. The government set to work to carry out these decrees with as much vigor as though they had resulted from the mature deliberation of the most venerable legislature. If they did not belong to the government in the strictest sense by creation, they certainly did by adoption. †

The decree which seems to me the most painfully

* Lamartine, vol. I. p. 245; Caussidière, vol. I. p. 74.

† I would not have my readers infer that the government could have resisted the passage of the decrees. On the contrary, I think it is certain that the decree providing employment saved the government from sure destruction. Lamartine had just made his noble and celebrated speech refusing to the mob the *drapeau rouge*. A general tumult arose at his intrepid words. While some applauded, others as vehemently condemned, and several muskets were levelled at him and at his friends. The barrels, however, were knocked up by some of the bystanders, and amid the tumult that ensued Lamartine was dragged within the building. The decree promising work was immediately read from the balcony, and the people, satisfied at least in a measure, gradually withdrew.—*Lamartine*, vol. I. p. 392.

absurd is the one which declares that, "the actual government of France is republican." In no modern nation has there been so great a confounding of names for things as in France; and never even in France was the absurdity of such a confusion more flagrant than in the instance referred to. The government sitting in the Hôtel de Ville was as far removed from republicanism as it is possible for a government to be. It was absolutely nothing less than a dictatorship. Eleven men, some of them appointed by a mob which had broken up the Chambers of Deputies, and some of them appointed in the office of a newspaper, ruled over the nation for three months with an absolutism of which it would be very difficult to find another example in all modern history. The most tyrannical monarch of Asia or Africa would not venture on a half of the arbitrary acts which they crowded into their reign of a hundred days. They dismissed judges who by law were irremovable; they added forty-one per cent. to the direct taxes; they declared at an end the treaties which were the foundation of international law in Europe; they abolished the press and dissolved the Chamber of Deputies; they appointed commissioners with powers as absolute as their own, and sent them on electioneering tours throughout the country; they altered the hours of labor throughout France, and subjected to heavy fines anyone who should allow his workmen to labor the customary number of hours; they added 200,000 men to the regular army, and 20,000 to the municipal army, with double the ordinary pay; they restricted the banks from specie payment, and required of them a loan of fifty millions; they conducted themselves, in short, as no government could conduct itself, save one which was under no restraint whatever, and which at the same time was working with that kind of spasmodic fury which comes from weakness and desperation. And this state of affairs, as absolute as any Turkish monarchy or any Venetian aristocracy, they had the effrontery to describe in saying that "the actual government of France is republican."

But the decrees concerning the form of the government, absurd as they were, were less mischievous than those guaranteeing employment and establishing the national workshops.

It would seem to require but the most elementary knowledge of political science, to enable one to see that such a provision would be fatal to the proper equilibrium of national industry. It was an assurance to every man that his conduct toward his old employés might be whatever he chose to make it; for there was no possibility of his being thrown out of employment. It was practically proclaiming to every man, whatever be his vices or even his crimes, that he should not in consequence of those vices come to want. It is safe in any civilized country to promise that no man shall die of hunger or of cold, for the reason that the gift of shelter and subsistence may be surrounded with such conditions, that no man will voluntarily accept them. But to promise *employment* was something far different. It was saying to the laboring people, "Quit your masters, raise your wages until they are forced to discharge you: do what you please, the government will protect you by constantly offering the resort of the national shops." Lamartine, as he declares, looked upon the Socialists with pity, and upon the Communists with horror; but De Tocqueville showed clearly that the 19th and 30th decrees, if enforced, must end in the complete domination of the one or the other. In his great speech on the Rights of Labor, the latter argued as follows:

"If the state attempts to fulfil its engagement by itself giving work, it becomes itself a great employer of labor. As it is the only capitalist that cannot refuse employment, and as it is the capitalists whose work-people are always the most lightly tasked, it will soon become the greatest, and soon after the only great, employer. The public revenue, instead of merely supporting the government, will have to support all the industry of the country. As rents and profits are swallowed up by the taxes, private property, now become a mere encumbrance, will be abandoned to the state; and subject to the duty of maintaining the people, the government will be the only proprietor. This is Communism.

"If, on the other hand, the state, in order to escape from this train of consequences, does not itself find work, but takes care that it shall always be supplied by individual power after the meeting of the constituent capitalists, it must take care that at no place and at no time there be a stagnation. It must take on itself the management of both capitalists and laborers. It must see that the members of one class do not injure one another by overtrading, and that the members of the other class do not injure themselves by competition. It must regulate profits and wages—sometimes retard, sometimes accelerate production or consumption. In short, in the jargon of the school, it must organize industry. This is Socialism." *

Now let us observe what actually occurred. Workshops were immediately opened in the outskirts of Paris. A person who wished to avail himself of the opportunity offered by the government, procured of the person with whom he lodged a certificate of habitation, and this he presented to the mayor of the arrondissement. From the latter he secured an order of admission to one of the shops. If he was received and employed, he obtained an order on the treasury for forty sous; if he found them all full and was not employed, he received an order for thirty sous,—thirty sous per day, for doing nothing.

The workmen were organized in military fashion. Every body of eleven men formed a squad known as an *escouade*. At their head an *escouadier*, elected by his companions, performed the

**Assemblée Constituente Séance du* 11*e. Sept*. 1848.

duties of lieutenant, and received ten sous a day extra. Five *escouades* formed a brigade; and the brigadier, also elected by the workmen, received three francs a day. Above the brigadiers were the captains (*chefs de compagnie*), colonels (*chefs de service*), and generals (*chefs d'arrondissement*), appointed by the government, and receiving salaries commensurate with their rank.*

The inducements held out to the laboring-class, together with the semi-military organization that was at once perfected at the workshops, raised these establishments into an importance which had not been anticipated. M. Thomas, in his History of the Workshops, informs us that in a single arrondissement, that embracing the Faubourg St. Antoine, a single bureau enrolled more than a thousand new applicants every day. As early as the 19th of May, less than three weeks after the decrees had been promulgated, the number of applications had swelled to 87,942. A month later the number amounted to 125,000,—*more than half the male population of Paris.*†

The daily cost of maintaining the shops was more than 200,000 francs. All branches of private industry were so disturbed, or rather so completely destroyed, that workmen once enrolled could not be removed from the lists. The necessaries of life arose enormously in price, while all articles of luxury fell to a fraction of their ordinary value.

* Emile Thomas, *Histoire des Atéliers Nationaux*, pp. 58, 70, and 80.

† *Ibid.*, p. 376.

"Nothing," writes Lord Normanby, "surprised me more, in the wonderful changes of the last two days, than the utter destruction of all conventional value attached to articles of luxury and display. Pictures, statues, plate, jewels, shawls, furs, laces, all one is accustomed to consider property, became as useless lumber. The scarcity of money became so great, that a sovereign passed for three or four and thirty francs." *

Meanwhile crowds of workmen besieged the workshops. The applicants had worked at different trades, but, as different employment could not be furnished, they had to be set to the same work. Nuisances were removed, barricades were levelled, dunghills were taken away, but at length nothing remained for the enormous multitude to do. No one was purchasing more than the absolute necessaries of life, therefore the manufacture of articles of luxury was out of the question. Affairs finally came to such a stagnation, that "of the 110,000 men on the pay-rolls, only about 2,000 were actually at work." †

It was easy to form a conjecture what the influence of such an army of idlers would be. The finances of the government, though administered with rare wisdom by Garnier-Pagès, were entirely inadequate to the permanent support of the workshops. To pay the workmen was coming to be impossible,—to discharge them was to incur the

* Normanby, *Year of Revolutions*, vol. I., p. 145.

† Louis Blanc, *Revue de* 1848, p. 64.

danger of a second Reign of Terror. The government at length came to appreciate the full extent of the danger, though it confessed its inability to avert it. "A thunder-cloud," says Lamartine, "was always before our eyes. It was formed by the *atéliers nationaux.* This army of 120,000 work-people, the greater part of whom were idlers and agitators, was the deposit of the misery, the laziness, the vagrancy, the vice, and the sedition which the flood of the Revolution had cast up and left on its shores. The Provisional Government had created these *atéliers* as a means of temporary relief, to prevent the unemployed work-people from plundering the rich or dying of hunger; but they never concealed from themselves that the day when this mass of *imperious idlers* was to be broken up, scattered over the country, and employed in real work, must bring a change which could not be effected without resistance, without a conflict, without formidable sedition." *

The conflict which Lamartine here foresaw and predicted was not long delayed in its coming. The course of events was what it is always likely to be when violent and extreme means are used to regulate industrial relations. The nineteenth decree recognized the right of work-people to combine, and at the same time it guaranteed employment to every citizen. The forty-second proclaimed that the Revolution had been made by the people, and for the people, and that it was time to

* *Hist. de la Rev.*, vol. II. p. 458.

put an end to the unjust sufferings of the laboring population. These two decrees were enough to drive the people into desperate measures the moment they were convinced the government was not fulfilling its promises in good faith. It was, of course, impossible for the government to fulfil its promises. Then followed the tactics with which we have since become more familiar. Unions of different trades were formed, committees were appointed, strikes were ordered, and the *ateliers nationaux* enabled the workmen to carry their orders into execution. Carlier, the Director of Police, in his testimony concerning the insurrection of the 23d of June, declared that the different committees obtained by intimidation the cessation of work in the private establishments, and then threw the workmen into the *ateliers nationaux.** In this way a stagnation of business was produced which immediately threatened the most alarming consequences. At length, and before many months, too, it became absolutely intolerable, and then it precipitated the civil war which the shops had, in the first instance, been organized to prevent.

In the meantime it was becoming apparent that a reaction was taking place in the country at large, or rather, perhaps, it should be said that the country was throwing off its indifference and beginning to display a positive hostility to the revolutionary movement. As we have already seen, the revolution was an affair in which the people of the coun-

* *Enquête sur l'insurrection du* 23*d Juin et* 15*e Mai*, tome II. p. 16.

try had taken no part. They had been simply reconciled to it by the various declarations which had emanated from the capital. They had entertained no especial attachment for the Orleans dynasty, and their taxes under the government of Louis Philippe had been unceasingly heavy. At the outbreak of the Revolution they were told, and for a time they seemed to believe, that the republican government would be so cheap that a great reduction of their taxes would take place, and even at no distant day they would cease altogether.

Such were the expectations of the people when the decree was published increasing the direct taxes by forty-five per cent. It is easy to conceive with what surprise and indignation such a decree was received by the small landed proprietors. The new government had promised a rapid diminution of their burdens; as a fact, it had inaugurated its active policy by imposing an additional tax of 190,000,000 francs. And this burden was even heavier than at first it seemed. The peculiar form in which the tax was imposed aggravated its weight. While forty-five per cent. had been added to the direct tax, the indirect tax had been for the most part removed. This latter provision was understood to be a concession to the commercial interests of the capital, while the direct tax fell chiefly upon the small landed proprietors, who were in possession of nine-tenths of the real estate of the country. When, in addition to all this, it came generally to be known that this formidable increase of their burdens was imposed chiefly for the support of an army of a hundred thousand revolutionists in Paris, who were paid 200,000 francs a day for doing nothing, their indignation was unbounded. They began to see that the Revolution was really in the interest of the mob at the capital, and that its whole tendency was to the impoverishment and ruin of the small proprietors in the country.

So far as mere feeling goes, the reaction against the Revolution was complete and overwhelming. Nothing but a want of political means in the hands of the people, whereby they might make their desires known, prevented the immediate overthrow of the Provisional Government. An additional tax of forty-five per cent., even when regularly imposed, is a thing which a people would submit to with patience only in case of the direst and most apparent necessity. That the people of France would cheerfully allow it to be added to their already heavy burdens by a committee of eleven gentlemen, appointed partly by a mob that had broken up the Chamber of Deputies, and partly by a Radical Club in a newspaper-office, was much more than could reasonably be expected.

The importance of these discontents of the people it is almost impossible to exaggerate. They furnish the full explanation of what, to many people, has continued to be a mystery, namely, the rapid change of the government from a republic to an empire, and the cheerful acquiescence of the great mass of the people in the transformation. The change was not so great, indeed, as it seemed to be; but even such as it was, it is hardly strange that the new government was more acceptable to the people than the old one had been. No change could be for the worse; any change, therefore, would have been acceptable,—any change that promised regularity and stability was especially welcome.

The government at Paris soon found that it would be impossible to rule the country without the aid of a National Assembly. Accordingly in March a decree was issued providing for an election and convoking an Assembly on the model of the Convention of 1793. It was to consist of nine hundred members. It was to be elected by universal suffrage and to convene on the 20th of April. Immediately following the decree which called for an election, it was ordered that all persons imprisoned for civil or commercial debts be set at liberty.

Before the elections could take place, however, it was found that the revolutionary *régime* had become so unpopular in the provinces, that some means must be devised by which the sentiments of the people could be counteracted. In order that this might be done the election was postponed until the 23d of April, and the meeting of the Assembly until the 4th of May,—the anniversary of the opening of the States'-General in 1789. In the meantime the government took the requisite measures to manufacture public opinion. A circular was addressed by Ledru Rollin to the electors; and four hundred commissioners, or electioneering officers, were appointed, with ample salaries, to go into the departments and bring the people to the desired way of thinking. A remarkable circular of the Minister of the Interior was quickly followed by a still more remarkable one by Carnot, the Minister of Public Instruction. "The great error," said he, "against which the inhabitants of our agricultural districts must be guarded, is this: That in order to be a representative it is necessary to enjoy the advantages of education or the gift of fortune. As far as education is concerned, it is clear that an honest peasant, possessed of good sense and experience, will represent the interests of his class in the National Assembly infinitely better than a rich and educated citizen having no experience of rural life, or blinded by interests at variance with those of the bulk of the peasantry. As to fortune, the remuneration (25 francs a day) which will be assigned to all the members of the Assembly will suffice for the maintenance of the very poorest. In a great assembly like that, the majority of the members discharge the functions of jurors. They decide affirmatively or negatively on the measures proposed by the *élite* of the members; they only require honesty and good sense; they judge, they do not invent."

But notwithstanding these circulars, the commissioners sent back word from the country districts, that the temper of the people was by no means encouraging. In some places the agents were actually chased out of the villages,—everywhere they were received with coldness or with indifference.

It was thus evident that the rural population was strongly, if not hopelessly, in the opposition; but the devices of the government to influence it were not yet exhausted. Ledru Rollin issued a third address couched in still more violent terms. This circular, which was addressed to the commissioners rather than the electors, is exceedingly curious, as it reveals the full extent of the intimidation and the corruption which the government was willing to use. It may be considered as in some respects one of the most remarkable state papers of modern times; and if we would comprehend how absolutely despotic it is possible for a government professing republicanism to be, one should study it sentence by sentence. It was addressed, it will be remembered, to the four-hundred commissioners sent out from Paris by the government for the purpose of manufacturing public opinion. It ran as follows:

"Your powers are unlimited. Agents of a revolutionary government, you are revolutionary also. The victory of the people has imposed on you the mandate to proclaim, to consolidate their work. To accomplish that task you are invested with their sovereign powers; you are responsible to no power but that of your own consciences; you are bound to do what the public safety requires. Thanks to your feelings, your mission does not require anything terrible. Hitherto you have encountered no serious resistance, and you have been enabled to remain calm in the consciousness of your strength. But you must not permit yourselves to be deluded as to the state of the country. Republican feelings require to be warmly excited, and, for that purpose, political functions should be entrusted only to earnest and sympathizing men. Everywhere the prefects and sub-prefects should be changed. In some lesser localities, the people petition to have them retained. It is for you to make them understand that we cannot preserve those who have served a power whose every act was one of corruption. You are invested with the authority of the executive; the armed force is therefore under your orders. You are authorized to require its service, direct its movements, and, in grave cases, to suspend its commanders. You are entitled to demand from all magistrates an immediate concurrence; if any one hesitates, let me know, and he shall be instantly dismissed. As to the irremovable magistracy, watch carefully over them: if any one evinces hostile dispositions, make use of the right of dismissal which your sovereign power confers. But above all, the elections are your great work; it is they which will prove the salvation of the country. It is on the composition of the Assembly that our destinies depend. Unless it is animated with the spirit of the Revolution we shall advance straight to a civil war and anarchy. Beware of those double-faced men who, after having served the king, profess themselves willing to serve the people. These men deceive you; never lend them your support. To obtain a seat in the National Assembly, the candidates must be clear of all the traditions of the past. Your rallying-cry should be everywhere, 'New men as much as possible, sprung from the ranks of the people.' It is for the workingmen to continue the revolution; without their aid it will be lost in Utopian theories or stifled under the heels of a retrograde faction. Enlighten the electors: repeat to them without ceasing, that the reign of men and of the monarchy is at an end. You may then see how great are the duties with which you are entrusted. The education of the country has not yet commenced; it is for you to guide it. Let the day of the election be the first triumph of the Revolution." *

These extraordinary instructions were energetically carried out. In order to make the courts the pliant instruments of the party at Paris, it was declared that henceforth all judges were to hold their positions during pleasure only. The highest judicial officers in the realm, namely, the presidents of the Court of Cassation, the Cour des Comptes, and the Court of Appeal, were deprived of their

* Normanby, vol. I. p. 220.

positions for no other reason than that they were not sufficiently pliant to the necessities of the new *régime.*

The policy of restraint even went so far as to interfere with the quality of instruction in the University. In order to make it more completely the fountain of extreme political notions, four of the professors in the *Collège de France* were removed, and their places were filled by four members of the government. The number of offices at the disposal of the government exceeded 130, 000, and these were all either changed by the new government and the commissioners, or were made to conform.*

Nor was the government content with sending one commissioner to each electoral district. A second was soon despatched to look after the work of the first. In necessary cases a third and even a fourth was sent; and even in addition to all these, the clubs of Paris sent out an army of secret agents to join in the same work, all paid out of funds secretly provided by the Minister of the Interior. †

While these extraordinary efforts to control the elections were going on, it began to be known

* The centralization which existed under the republic (which was, indeed, essentially the same as that of Charles X. and Louis Philippe) is well illustrated by the fact, that the number of civil officers amounted to the enormous host of 130,000. The number of civil functionaries in Great Britain in 1851, according to Gneist (*Geschicht e der Englischen Communalverfassung*, I. 581) was 64,224. According to the census of 1870, the United States employs 44,787.

† *Annuaire Historique pour* 1848, p. 127.

that the government was divided against itself. Lamartine and Garnier-Pagès appear to have had a genuine desire to pursue a moderate course, such an one, indeed, as would have been fully satisfactory to the nation at large. There was a faction, however, headed by Ledru Rollin and Louis Blanc, which was in the closest sympathy with the most radical of the clubs. On all matters of national policy, therefore, the government was sharply divided. At times this division even amounted to most violent hostility. Lamartine, and Ledru Rollin were at swords'-points.* Lamartine was popular with the country at large, because he withstood the pressure of the radicals at the capital; Ledru Rollin was popular with the clubs because he did what he could to further their designs, by furnishing them with advice as well as with arms and amunition. †

In the midst of the excitement occasioned by these events, the discord was much increased by the course which the government took with the banks. The industries of the country had been so disturbed that the savings-banks soon found themselves unable to pay their deposits. The govern-

* On the 18th of March, when the mob was pressing around the Hôtel de Ville, Ledru Rollin threatened to call upon the people to turn his colleagues into the street. He was only prevented from doing so by the pistol which Garnier-Pagès presented at his head.—*Lamartine, Hist. de la Rev.*, vol. II. 208.

† The "Club of Clubs," which took possession of a police-office on the Rue de Rivoli, was furnished with five hundred muskets and thirty thousand cartridges by the Minister of the Interior.—*Lamartine*, vol. II. p. 251.

ment was thrown into extreme embarrassment. It was found that nine-tenths of the depositors were laborers, while nearly nine-tenths of the deposits belonged to capitalists. It was of the utmost importance that the laborers should be prevented from breaking out into a second revolution. With this necessity in mind, the government issued a decree setting out with the preamble, that "the most sacred of all properties is the savings of the poor, and that it is not by words, but by deeds, that the government must show the good faith with which they meet the trust reposed in them by the working-classes." The decree then proceeded to declare the suspension of specie payments on all sums above 100 francs. Of the 355,000,000 francs deposited in the savings-banks, only 65,702,000 francs could be drawn, while the remaining 286,548,000 francs were to be paid in treasury notes at par, when they had already sunk to fifty per cent. of their nominal value.

The ill-will that resulted from this manner of settlement only added to the intensity of that party animosity which was already sufficiently obvious. A conspiracy of the most alarming character was entered into. The Socialists, under the inspiration and leadership of Ledru Rollin and Louis Blanc, had become so strong that they hoped to overthrow the existing government and establish a dictatorship in their own interests. A design to blow up the Hôtel de Ville was only frustrated by the barrels of gunpowder being discovered a few hours before the explosion was to take place.

The Socialists quarrelled among themselves. The movement had been begun with the design of making Ledru Rollin dictator; but while this leader of the radical faction was preparing the way, as he thought, for his own sure elevation by secretly supplying the clubs with arms, a design was set on foot to destroy his ascendency, and to put Blanqui in his place. Ledru Rollin, hearing of the turn affairs were taking, repaired at once to the "Club of Clubs." A bitter quarrel ensued. When the minister finally offered to give his influence to the furtherance of their designs, they answered him in these words: "Well, since you don't choose to go with us, you shall be thrown out of the window to-morrow with the rest. Reflect on this; we are in a situation to make good our words."

Upon this reply, the minister, whose unscrupulousness was only equalled by his cowardice, made haste to inform Lamartine of what was to occur, and then to hide himself away out of danger. Lamartine burnt his private papers, not expecting, as he declares, to survive the day, but determined to die at his post. He repaired at once to the Hôtel de Ville where by accident he met General Changarnier. They concerted measures to meet the emergency. Twelve horsemen were despatched at once to the sub-mayoralties of Paris to summon the National Guard. They were but just in time;

for it was only as the column of insurgents began to fill the Place de Grêve, that the soldiers, marching at double-quick, threw themselves between the mob and the Hôtel de Ville. Before night a hundred and thirty thousand troops were in their places to protect the government, and the mob, estimated at not less than a hundred and fifty-thousand, was obliged to disperse. The event is of importance as showing the formidable nature of the elements with which the government had to contend. After the danger was past, Ledru Rollin again appeared upon the scene.

The elections took place in the midst of the excitement which ensued. The efforts of the Commissioners had been so successful as to prevent the return of all, or nearly all, who did not at least profess to be republican; * but it was at once found that even among the republicans there were two distinct parties. The conservative party embraced all who at heart were royalists, and all who, though nominally republican, favored the adoption of a policy approaching a constitutional monarchy. They supported the Provisional Government, not because they thought it the best government, but because they saw in it the only barrier between the country and the communists of Paris. The democratic party, on the contrary, favored the adoption of extreme measures. Its members were ready to support any action which

* Lamartine, however, says that in reality it was "*non-r'publicain ou peu republicain.*"—II. 406.

Louis Blanc or Albert might propose. Generally speaking, the radicals were elected by the large cities, the conservatives by the provinces.

As soon as the Assembly convened, the Socialists and Communists became sensible that it would by no means encourage their designs. A conspiracy was accordingly at once formed to overthrow it. Such a policy had already been foreshadowed before the election, for the *Bulletin du Républic* had openly announced the "determination of the people of the barricades to annul the decision of a false national representation, if the returns did not secure the triumph of Socialism."

And the Socialists were as good as their word. Before the Assembly had been two weeks in session, a petition, couched in most imperative terms, was presented by a crowd of not less than a hundred thousand men. The object of the petition was nothing short of a declaration of war against Germany.

The Assembly hesitated; and for two reasons. In the first place, France was in no condition to war against Germany, to say nothing of the fact that such a declaration would be in most positive contradiction of the foreign policy which the Provisional Government had promulgated.* In the the second place, it was evident that a petition

* The Socialists clamored for a declaration of war, in the interests of Poland and in the interests of republicanism in Germany; whereas Lamartine in his first message had very pointedly taken the ground of non-interference in the social affairs of all foreign powers. It is evi-

presented by one hundred thousand men in person was not merely a petition, but, as Lamartine declared, a menace. To grant the object of the petition was to involve the nation in the greatest conceivable danger, and at the same time to surrender its iron power to a street mob. To refuse it, was to incur the risk of destruction. The Assembly chose the latter alternative, as was unquestionably its duty. A feeble attempt was made to protect it by a few regiments of the guards, but it was useless. The crowd without opposition burst into the Hall of the Assembly.

"I demand," exclaimed Barbès, their leader, "that a forced tax of a *thousand million francs* be laid upon the rich, and that whoever gives orders to beat the rappel [to call out the National Guard] should be declared a traitor to the country."

"You are wrong, Barbès," cried one of his associates; "what we want is two hours of pillage."

Then one of the most violent of the insurgents was carried on the shoulders of his comrades to the tribune, where he cried out,—

"In the name of the people, whose voice the Assembly has refused to hear, I declare the Assembly dissolved."

The president was dragged from his seat, and in utter dismay the Assembly abandoned the Hall.*

dent that a declaration of war at this time would not only have been an abandonment of the principle adopted, but would have been a virtual invitation to foreign powers to interfere in the domestic affairs of France.

* Lamartine, vol. II. p. 425. *Annuaire Historique pour* 1848, p. 187.

Having thus dispersed the Assembly, the mob proceeded, in the customary fashion of Parisian mobs, to elect a new Provisional Government. Barbès was placed at its head; Louis Blanc, Ledru Rollin, Blanqui, and Legrange were among its members. The new government, arranged in the course of a few minutes, set out for the Hôtel de Ville, where a formal installation took place. Its rule, however, was but momentary. The National Guard, true to its allegiance to Lamartine, had responded promptly to his call. A few regiments arrived in time even to chase the last of the mob out through the doors and windows of the Legislative Hall; others advanced upon the Hôtel de Ville. Preparations for a desperate resistance were made, but when the inmates of the building saw that the Guards were planting artillery with the evident purpose of breaching the walls before an assault should be made, their courage gave way. Seventy-two prisoners were taken; the rest escaped from the building and fled.*

It could hardly be said that the government had gained a triumph. It had indeed crushed the

* The wonderful powers of Lamartine as a descriptive writer are nowhere better shown than in his account of this insurrection. I think no one can read the pages which he devotes to these events (vol. II. pp. 440–453) without comprehending the source of his power over a Parisian multitude. Whenever a mob heard Lamartine it was subdued. I doubt if any modern orator has understood so perfectly the art of pleasing. He says that when he arrived at the Hôtel de Ville, "his horse walked no longer; it was lifted up and carried as far as the court of the palace." And yet, but a few hours before, the same mob had shouted, "*Assez joué de la lyre;* MORT À LAMARTINE!"

insurrection and thrown some of its leaders into prison; but on the other hand, the mob had succeeded in dispersing the Assembly and in giving new evidence of its enormous power. It became gradually but surely apparent, as these insurrections one after another sprang up to defy the government, that, before there could be permanent peace, the power of the socialists and communists must be thoroughly broken. Their doctrines were in violent antagonism against those of the nation, and it became more and more certain that they could only be suppressed by force of arms.

The elections which took place in June showed very clearly that the insurrections in Paris had not been without their effect on the country at large. It was now far more evident than it had formerly been, that the nation had no real sympathy with the Revolution. The cry for new men, which in March had been so potent, was no longer of any considerable influence. The former repugnance to the statesmen of the time of Louis Philippe had been swept away by the rashness of Parisian politics; and for the first time since the overthrow of monarchy, some of the best political talent of the nation was called forth from its seclusion. Thiers, Changarnier, Hugo, Dupin, Molé, Bugeaud, and Fould were found to have been elected from the provinces, while the chiefs of socialism, Caussidière, Proudhon, Leroux, and Legrange, were returned from the city. It was evident that the opposing sympathies of city and country were becoming more and more intense, and that nothing but the very wisest statesmanship could prevent a terrible struggle between the nation and the metropolis.

Even before the new members took their seats, the alarming state of the finances began to attract universal attention. The bitter truth began to be realized, that the effect of the Revolution had been not only to increase the expenditures enormously, but also in almost the same degree to diminish the revenues. Less than three months had elapsed since the overthrow of Louis Philippe. The Provisional Government had opened extraordinary credits to the amount of 206,183,035 francs; it had cut down woods to the extent of 25,000,000 francs; it had sold lands belonging to the state and the crown to the extent of 200,000,000 francs; it had borrowed of the Bank of France 245,000,000 francs, and now, on the first of June, the Minister of Finance found it necessary to negotiate a fresh loan of 150,000,000.*

It was with this disheartening array of figures before its eyes that the Assembly containing the new members came together. An investigation revealed the fact that this most disastrous state of the finances was owing chiefly to three causes: derangement of the national industries and consequent decline of revenues, the great increase of the army, and the maintenance of the National Workshops. The army, which had been increased from

* *Annuaire Historique*, 1848, pp. 212, 213.

about 300,000 to more than 500,000, could not, it was thought, be safely diminished.*

The industries of the nation were, of course, not subject to immediate legislative control. The only point, therefore, at which retrenchment was practicable, was the very point which it would be most dangerous to touch. The enormous difficulty of the situation is seen, when the single fact is mention that at the national workshops 118,300 men were receiving wages, while not more than 2,000 were employed in any species of work whatever, the remainder not only being paid for doing nothing, but holding themselves in readiness at the call of the clubs to overawe or overwhelm the government.†

No motion for the abolition of the workshops was actually brought forward, and yet it was evident that a majority of the Assembly had such a movement in mind. Various propositions looking to a more profitable employment of the men were advanced. Some desired that they should be put to work on the railroads: others proposed that they should be distributed over the country and employed as there might be opportunity. In the course of the discussion, Victor Hugo proposed boldly to strike at the root of the evil. He made no motion, but he expressed the evident sense of a

* The army was ordered by one of the first decrees of the Provisional Government, to be raised from 370,000 men to 580,000; and 530,000 were actually enrolled.—*Annuaire Historique*, 1848, p. 123.

† On the 20th of June, Leon Faucher, chairman of a committee to which an investigation had been entrusted, reported that 120,000 work-

majority of the Assembly when he used these words:

"The *Ateliers Nationaux* were necessary when first established; but it is now high time to remedy an evil, of which the least inconvenience is to squander needlessly the resources of the republic. What have they produced in the course of four months? Nothing. They have deprived the hardy sons of toil of employment, given them a distaste for labor, and demoralized them to such a degree, that they are no longer ashamed to beg on the streets. The monarchy had its idlers, the Republic has its vagabonds. God forbid that the enemies of the country should succeed in converting Parisian workmen, formerly so virtuous, into *lazzaroni* or pretorians. When Paris is in agony, London rejoices; its power, riches, and preponderance have tripled since our disturbances commenced." *

Such utterances as this, heard in the Assembly with evident sympathy, had a definite meaning for the clubs and the workmen. They waited for nothing more. Brigades of workmen that had been sent out, returned to Paris contrary to orders. An insurrectionary organization, exactly corresponding with the brigades and companies of the workshops, was rapidly completed. Every leader

men were daily paid by the Government, and that 50,000 more were demanding to be admitted to the workshops.—*Annuaire Historique*, 1848, p. 217.

* *Moniteur*, *June* 21st, quoted by Alison, vol. VIII. p. 300.

had his post assigned him. The orators of the clubs harangued without intermission. As early as the 23d of June, only a few days after the speech of Victor Hugo, the erection of barricades was commenced, and the work proceeded with a system and a rapidity that revealed the most thorough organization and the most determined spirit.

Meanwhile the government was not idle. Lamartine fully comprehended the magnitude of the difficulties which they had to confront. The military command was entrusted to General Cavaignac, who saw the necessity of organizing for a most formidable conflict. "Do not deceive yourselves," said Lamartine to those who viewed the insurrection as a mere riot; "it is not a riot that we have to suppress: we have to fight a battle; and not one battle only, but to go through a campaign against these formidable factions." *

In accordance with this understanding of the magnitude of the insurrection, the government called in the troops from Lille, Metz, and Rouen, as well as from the nearer points of Versailles and Orleans. On the morning of the 24th, the revolt had become so formidable, that the Assembly saw no way of meeting it but by conferring absolute power on a dictator. General Cavaignac was appointed, and within two hours after the action was known, twenty thousand men enrolled themselves as volunteers to aid the National Guard.

* Lamartine, vol. II. p. 473.

During the first days of the conflict that ensued, it seemed by no means certain that the troops would prevail. When, at the close of the four days of battle, the soldiers of Cavaignac had surmounted the last barricade, the magnitude of the contest for the first time became generally known. The insurgents had been so perfectly organized, that they had assumed the defensive in every part of the city; and they fought with such bravery, that when driven at the point of the bayonet from one barricade, they immediately fell back to another only to repeat the same stout resistance. It is no part of my purpose to describe those terrible days. To convey an adequate impression of the magnitude of the battle, it needs only to be said, that the number of barricades, nearly all of which had to be stormed, reached the almost incredible figure of *three thousand eight hundred and eighty-eight, and that the number of the dead reached nearly to twenty thousand.* Ten thousand dead bodies were recognized and buried, and it was estimated that nearly as many were thrown unclaimed into the Seine. It is well to bear the fact in mind, that this terrible strife cost France more lives than any of the battles of the empire;—that the numbers of generals, of subordinate officers, and of privates who were slain exceeded the number who fell at Austerlitz, at Borodino, or at Waterloo.*

The brutality of the revolutionists was amply

* *Annuaire Historique*, 1848, pp. 247–251. Cayley, *European Revolutions* of 1848, vol. I. p. 120.

revealed by the atrocious barbarities in which they indulged. The excesses of the communists of 1870 were scarcely more shocking than those of their antecedents in 1848. In one instance, four children in the uniform of the Garde Mobile were seized by the insurgents; pikes were stuck through their throats under the chin; then, suspending them from the windows, the insurgents fired under their legs, thinking that the troops would not return the fire. Prisoners, when they were taken, were shot down by dozens at a time. The women, as in 1870, took the lead in atrocity. One boasted that she had cut off, with her own hands, the heads of five officers who had been taken prisoners. Others armed themselves with vitriol, which they threw into the faces of the prisoners: in some instances burning them so, that they begged to be relieved by being put to death. The climax of this spirit was reached when they cut off the head of one of the *gardes* who had been taken prisoner, filled his mouth with pitch, and lighting it, sang and danced around it like a pack of cannibals or Comanches.*

Of this insurrection, perhaps the most formidable that Paris has ever seen, there were two immediate results. The first, was the confirmation of General Cavaignac as Dictator; the second, the abolition of the *Ateliers Nationaux* and of the Clubs. The remote consequences, as we shall presently see, were even more important than these.

* Cayley, vol. I. p. 121. Normanby, vol. II. p. 74.

As we have already had occasion to observe, France had been growing more and more impatient over the conduct of affairs at the capital. Nothing but such an insurrection, and such atrocities as those of June, was necessary to complete the opposition of the nation to the revolutionary *régime*. It became rapidly more and more apparent that when the nation should set aside the Provisional Government, it would be to inaugurate a strong central power,—one that would be able to keep the elements of turbulence in check; one, in short, that would have the characteristics of monarchy in substance, if not, indeed, in form. As after the Reign of Terror the people sought refuge in the Constitution of the year VIII., a constitution which conferred greater powers on the executive than those exercised at the present day by any monarch west of Russia and Turkey, so, after the insurrection in June, it was sufficiently apparent to the majority of the legislators of the land, that nothing short of a strong central power would be sufficient to ensure to the nation that tranquillity of which the masses of the people were in such imperative need. If the Revolution had nothing better for the nation than the series of insurrections that had followed close upon one another in all parts of the country since the abdication of Louis Philippe, if its promises of relief found no better fulfilment than taxation increased by forty-one per cent., and the prospect, even under this increase, of an annual deficit of three or four hundred millions;—if such were the benefits to be afforded by the revolutionists, surely it was not strange that the nation determined to assert its authority, and to take its affairs out of the hands of the few thousands who at Paris had brought about all these evils. In this state of public opinion it was that we are to look for the proper explanation of the events that ensued. "What is the cause," demanded Odillon Barrot, "of the universal uneasiness and perturbation which prevail, and the general feeling in favor of a dictatorship?" "It rests," answered he, "on the opinion, coming now to be universally admitted, that democracy cannot regulate or moderate itself." *

The conviction to which Barrot referred found its expression in the constitution adopted in September. If there had been any way of returning directly to monarchy, without placing the nation in a ridiculous position before the world, such a way would perhaps have been adopted. But such a way could not be found; there was, therefore, no more legitimate method in which to express the political ideas of the people, than to retain the *form* of a republic and to give to it the essential characteristics of a monarchy. I think no one can read studiously the Constitution of 1848 without seeing that it was not the constitution of a republic, but that it embodied all the most essential characteristics of royalty. If it limited the ordi-

* Barrot, *Speech of Sept. 27th*, *Annuaire Historique*, 1848, 312–314.

nary functions of the executive somewhat more than the Constitution of the year VIII. had done, it opened the way for every manner of usurpation, by authorizing an appeal to the people by means of the *plébiscite.**

The same general causes which led to the adoption of the Constitution of the 4th of November, led to the election of Louis Napoleon to the office of President. As a candidate, he possessed a double advantage over all his opponents. He bore a name that was held in enthusiastic reverence in every household in France, and he represented the idea of stability and firmness of rule. It was doubtless for his advantage that he had kept aloof from all parties during the revolution, for in so doing he gave offence to none. When, therefore,

* If any one doubts the correctness of the position here assumed, I would commend to his attention the analysis of §§43–70 of the constitution, as given by Kaiser in his *Französische Verfassungsgeschichte von* 1789–1852. The chapter which he entitles *Die vollziehende Gewalt in den Händen eines Einzelnen*, although it was written, as the author affirms, before the *Coup d'État* of December 2d, clearly pointed out the manner in which the president was likely to raise himself to the imperial throne. In the concluding chapter of the work, the author prefaces what he has to say on the subject with these words: "So überraschend für Viele der Staatsstreich vom 2ten December auch gewesen ist, so natürlich musste ein entscheidender Wendepunkt irgend einer Art denen nothwendig erscheinen, welche die Französische Verfassung von 1848 und die darauf folgende Gesetzgebung näher betrachteten." S. 683. The end was even predicted in the Constitutional Assembly. "If," said Barrot, "the Assembly now votes one chamber with a dependent executive, it will restore the Convention in all its ommipotence; for the executive power, which the Convention creates, must either yield obedience to the mandates of the Convention, or it must itself be destroyed.—Speech of Sept. 27th, *Ann. Hist.*, 1848, p. 313.

the contest came to be between Cavaignac and Bonaparte, it is plain to see why the nation declared itself in favor of the Napoleonic *régime*. The cause of his overwhelming majority was not so much that the people had an enthusiastic admiration of Louis Napoleon as a man, as that they found (or thought they found) in his name and promises the fairest prospects of stability and good order.

On the subject of the Revolution of 1848, the words of no one are entitled to more weight than those of De Tocqueville. He predicted its occurrence in a speech which has since attained a world-wide celebrity; and he commented upon the events which followed it with a wisdom and a discrimination that can hardly fail to excite the admiration, if not the assent, of every reader. Though a majority of the historians of the period have failed utterly to detect the true relation of the events narrated, De Tocqueville, from the first, saw the direction in which affairs were tending, as well as the causes of their tendency. On the 27th of February, 1849, he recorded his convictions in a letter to the English historian, Grote. If the date of this letter be observed, it will be seen to have been written a little more than two months after the election of President Bonaparte—nearly three years before monarchy was re-established. A part of the letter I have already quoted for another purpose, but it is so important that I shall venture to repeat it. The declarations which the author makes, in the first sentences of the quotation, afford a complete explanation of what to many has been a mystery—of the willingness with which the *coup d'état* and the Empire were accepted.

"To those," he writes, "who are on the spot, and who have watched the inevitable progress of events, nothing can be more simple and natural. The nation did not wish for a revolution. Still less did it desire a republic; for though in France there is not a particle of attachment for any particular dynasty, the opinion that monarchy is a necessary institution is almost universal. France then wished neither for a revolution nor a republic. That she has allowed both to be inflicted upon her, proceeds from two causes: from the fact that Paris, having become, during the last fifty years, the first manufacturing town in the country, was able, on a given day, to furnish the republican party with an army of artisans; and, secondly, from another fact, which is the offspring of centralization—that Paris, no matter who speaks in her name, dictates to the rest of France. These two facts, taken together, explain the catastrophe of February, 1848.

"The whole of this last year has been one long and painful effort, on the part of the nation, to recover its equilibrium, and to retake, by the pacific and legal means that universal suffrage has conferred upon it, all the benefits of which it was robbed by the surprise of February. Much has been said about the versatility of the French.

They are versatile, no doubt; but, in my opinion, they never were less so than during the past year. Up to the present time, their conduct has been singularly consistent. Last March they rose up as one man to attend the elections, and, in spite of much intimidation, they elected an Assembly which, though favorable to a republic, was thoroughly anti-anarchical and anti-revolutionary. In June they armed and rushed to Paris, to prevent another revolution, even more frightful than the first. Finally, in December, they designated their ruler by a name, if not monarchical, at least significant of a strong and regular mode of government. I, for my part, deeply regret this last act, which seemed to me to go too far. I did not join in it. I refused to retain my diplomatic appointment to Brussels. But I must confess that the conduct of the nation on the 10th of December was not inconsistent. It acted under excitement, but in the same spirit which governed its actions in March and in June, and even in the petty details of every day. And now what will happen? It would be madness to attempt to predict.

"Whatever it may be, we cannot possibly be replaced in the position we were in before February. Many think that we shall be. But they are fools. They think that by tearing out a page of history, they will be able to take it up where they left off. I do not believe a word of it. The Revolution has left, in many directions, scars which will never be effaced." *

* De Tocqueville, *Memoirs and Remains*, vol. II, p. 95.

From what has been shown, I think it must appear that the opportunities presenting themselves to Louis Napoleon were practically unlimited. The instructions of Machiavelli were that "A prince who is wise and prudent cannot keep, and ought not to keep, his word, when the keeping of it is to his disadvantage, and the causes for which he promised are removed." *

The ethics of Louis Napoleon was the ethics which Machiavelli thus recommended. He took the oath of office when it was required of him; he did not hesitate to break that oath when he found "the keeping of it was to his disadvantage." The *coup d'état* of December 2d was certainly an act of atrocious perfidy; at the same time, it must never be forgotten that it was an act for which the nation itself was largely responsible. It was made possible *subjectively* by the unscrupulous spirit of the President—*objectively* by the traditions of the past and the sympathies of the present.

"How sad it is," exclaims De Tocqueville, "that, all the world over, governments are just as rascally as nations will allow them to be!" †

* "Non pio pertanto un Signore prudente, nè debbe asservare la fede, quando tale osservanzia gli torni contro, e che sono spente le cagioni che la feceno promettere."—*Machiavelli Il Principe*, Chap. XVIII.

† *Memoirs and Remains*, vol. II. p. 129.

UNIVERSAL SUFFRAGE UNDER NAPOLEON THE THIRD.

Schwarz wimmelten da in grausem Gemisch,
Zu scheusslichen Klumpen geballt,
Der stachliche Roche, der Klippenfisch,
Des Hummers gräuliche Ungestalt,
Und dräuend wies mir die grimmigen Zähne
Der entsetzliche Hai, des Meeres Hyäne.—SCHILLER.

Il est trop clair qui'ici le plébiscite, l'appel au peuple, l'invitation à voter sur la forme du gouverenment n'est qu'un tour de passe-passe, une pure duperie.—TAINE, *Du Suffrage Universel*, p. 23.

CHAPTER IX.

UNIVERSAL SUFFRAGE UNDER NAPOLEON THE THIRD.

UPON no other feature of the government of Napoleon III. has so great stress been laid by his apologists and supporters as upon that of universal suffrage. The position has often been taken, that, whatever charges may be preferred and sustained against the Second Empire, the fact is undeniable that the Emperor received the hearty support of the people,—of the people, too, in the enjoyment of universal suffrage. Many even who themselves have no words of favor for some of the features of that government, claim that it was entitled to support on the very principles of republicanism itself, inasmuch as the result of repeated elections showed that it was the government which a vast majority of the people desired. In the light of such recent authorities as have come to us, it may be well to examine the correctness of the claims thus advanced. Let us, therefore, first inquire into the views of Napoleon concerning the political rights of the masses of the people, and then try to ascertain how far these views were carried out when he came into actual power.

During those turbulent years which intervened between the Revolution of 1830 and the *coup d'état* of 1851, Louis Napoleon took care that the people of France should not be ignorant of his political opinions. Scarcely was Louis Philippe seated on his throne when the publication of the "Political Reveries," embodying Napoleon's "Ideas of a Constitution," made the nation fully aware that Napoleonism had still a living representative, and that this representative entertained definite and positive ideas in regard to the manner in which France should be governed. One who, at the present day, looks over that pamphlet, is surprised that it left no more permanent impression upon the minds of the French people. And yet we cannot help reflecting that, in the days of the Republic, when the people needed to know what Napoleon had written, there was no freedom of the press, and consequently no revelation and discussion of the thoughts and purposes that the president was entertaining. At the present day it is easy to see that the people had, from the first, abundant reason to anticipate the ultimate estabment of an empire; for, whatever may be thought of the means by which the imperial throne was set up, it must be admitted that the *fact* of its establishment was entirely consistent with the views which, from the beginning of his literary career, Napoleon had advocated. In his first sketch of a constitution, published as early as 1832, the whole scheme of his government was foreshadowed.*

* This essay reminds one of the *Souper de Beaucaire* written by Napoleon I. while he was yet a student at the Military Academy. Both

It may seem at first thought the most singular characteristic of the Revolution of 1848, that the people who had at least interposed no opposition to the overthrow of monarchy, were now anxious to entrust the destinies of the republic to the hands of one who was so pronounced an imperialist. But the explanation of the fact is not difficult. I have already shown, by reference to numerous authorities, that the people were by no means republican in their sympathies. The Revolution had enormously increased their burdens, without bringing them any advantage whatever. The country was in perpetual turmoil; and of all things, that which the masses most heartily longed for, was the establishment of something like stability and order. It should be said, moreover, that although the leaders of political opinion in France have been exceedingly radical, the masses of the people, ever since the overthrow of the First Empire, have shown themselves to be eminently conservative. Amid all the revolutions and political discords that have distracted the country, one feeling has been dominant in the hearts of the peasantry, one ambition has inspired them, one impulse has directed them. Whatever innovation has been forced upon the country, they have accepted it willingly, provided it has brought, or even promised to bring, security to their possessions

of these productions, though inherently very unlike each other, sketched out with considerable accuracy the courses which their authors were in the future respectively to pursue.

and their earnings. This fact was the supreme element of strength in the cause of Napoleon III. He early discovered it, and he kept it constantly in view. Of all the Napoleonic family, as Delord assures us, this nephew of the first Emperor alone had faith in the restoration of the dynasty; and this faith, it might be added, was founded on a thorough understanding of the desires and sympathies of the great mass of the French people. Inspired by this understanding of the peasantry, and encouraged by this confidence in the future destiny of his family, he had no difficulty in determining what course to pursue. It was only necessary that he should keep himself and his political doctrines before the people; the time would evidently come when both he and his theories, if acceptable to the nation, would be called into action. He took good care that the necessary conditions should be fulfilled.

In the early political essays of Louis Napoleon, two dominant ideas prevail: the first, that the people are the supreme authority in the nation; the second, that the reins of government should be in the hands of an emperor. Beginning with the saying of Montesquieu, that "the people, in whom is the sovereign power, ought to do by itself all that it can," * he proceeds to show how the will of the people has been stifled, and how the welfare of the nation depends upon its being set free. All political power, he argues, must emanate from the

* *Esprit des Lois*, lib. II. chap. 2.

people, and yet, to prevent its abuse, it must be under the constant guidance of a controlling hand. There are two things to be dreaded in France: absolute power, on the one hand, and the reign of terror, on the other. Under the name of Napoleon there is no occasion to dread the latter: under the shadow of a republic there can be no apprehension of the former. What France needs, then, is a form of government in which the whole people, without distinction, should take part in the election of representatives of the nation. The "masses, which can never be corrupted, and which can never flatter nor dissemble, must be made the constant source from which all power should emanate." "From the opinions which I advance," he says, "it will be seen that my principles are entirely republican." * "If, in my scheme of a constitution," he continues, "I give preference to the monarchical form of government, it is because I consider that such a government would be best adapted to France; because it would give greater guarantees of tranquillity, greater strength, and greater liberty than any other." Again he says: "At the accession of each new emperor, the sanction of the people will be required. If the sanction is refused, the two chambers will propose another sovereign in his place. As the people will not have the right of election, but only that of approval, this law will not only prevent the inconveniences of an elective monarchy, which have

* *Life and Works of Louis Napoleon Bonaparte*, vol. I. p. 170.

always been a source of discussion; it will also be a security against political convulsions." Then, coupled with these privileges of the people, there must be the "right of expressing their thoughts and opinions, both through the medium of the press and in every other manner; as well as the right of peaceably assembling, and of the free exercise of divine worship."

"*No one may be accused, arrested, or detained except in the cases determined by the law, and according to the form prescribed by it.* Every procedure adopted against a man, except in the cases and according to the forms which the law provides, is arbitrary and tyrannical; and he against whom it is intended to be executed by means of violence, has the right to resist by force." *

As early then as 1832 the people of France were informed with considerable clearness respecting the political doctrines of Napoleon. These theories, moreover, in the course of the following sixteen years, were often reiterated, but always without important modification. In 1839, for example, the *Idées Napoléoniennes* presented the same political notions in a more elaborate form. This somewhat pretentious essay was little more than the body of the former one clad in another and more seductive costume. The profusion of ornaments brought from the glorious days of the First Empire, and paraded in contrast with the poverty-stricken degeneracy of these latter days, served only to advo-

* *Ibid*, vol. I. p. 175.

cate a return to the imperial *régime*, and to reveal the good things in store for the people in case they should avail themselves of their legitimate sovereignty.

Again, in 1841, the author took occasion to revive his favorite theme, and to elaborate more fully his ideas of the true sphere of a monarch. Guizot's History of the English Revolution had just been published. It had presented to the public in a powerful light the opinions of that eminent statesman in regard to what should be the position of a constitutional sovereign on all matters of national policy. The view advocated by Guizot was that which he afterward in the service of Louis Philippe so well exemplified, namely, that the monarch should be a moderator or manager of diverse influences in the state, rather than a leader of public opinion. Nothing could be more opposed to the Napoleonic idea of a government. It had been no part of the first emperor's policy to wait for an expression of popular opinion before he took action; it had been his habit rather to act independently of that opinion, and to trust to the moral force of the accomplished fact for its ratification. The nephew was no more inclined to follow the lead of the people than the uncle had been. When therefore Guizot's history appeared, it afforded the prisoner at Ham an opportunity which he was in no mood to neglect. It was necessary that he should keep himself before the people, and that the people should entertain what he believed to be correct notions of the proper relations of the governing and the governed.

Both of these ends he did something to obtain in the paper referred to. Reviewing the whole period of the English Revolution, he had no difficulty in finding material which he could press into the service of Napoleonism. Guizot had taken the ground that the great fault of the Stuarts was that they never recognized the spirit of the nation; in other words, they set up for themselves an ideal of royalty which was utterly repugnant to those aspirations for liberty that had now, in England at least, become all-pervasive and irresistible. The Stuarts, he maintained, should have submitted to the inevitable, should have allowed themselves to be led in the same manner as the monarchs of England are led at the present time. Bonaparte, however, arrived at a far different conclusion. While he recognized the failure of the Stuarts, he saw that they could have succeeded only by adopting a method very different from that suggested by Guizot. They should have put themselves, not in the train, but at the head of the ideas of their age. It was the part of monarchy to lead, not to be led. The English Revolution should have resulted in the establishment of royalty upon a firmer basis, not chiefly through the efforts of the people dragging on the monarchs, but through the exertions of the monarchs, supported and encouraged by the people. "Revolutions conducted by a chief," said he, "generally turn exclusively to the advantage of the people; for to ensure success, the chief is obliged to give himself up to the national spirit; and to support himself he must remain faithful to the interests which secured his triumph; while on the contrary, revolutions conducted by a multitude often turn to the profit of the chief only, for the reason that the people think on the morrow of victory that their wish is accomplished, and it is in their nature to discontinue for a long period all the efforts which were requisite to obtain that victory." It was in accordance with this general law, argued Bonaparte, that the Stuarts failed utterly, and that William succeeded. The former made war simply to support their tottering power: the latter solely to increase the influence of England. "The Stuarts ruled by means of the crowd, and beheld only confusion around them; William saw the object at once, rushed forward, and drew the crowd after him." Finally the prince sums up and concludes his essay in this *ad-captandum* manner:

"The history of England calls loudly to monarchs,—

"MARCH AT THE HEAD OF THE IDEAS OF YOUR AGE, AND THEN THOSE IDEAS WILL FOLLOW AND SUPPORT YOU.

"IF YOU MARCH BEHIND THEM THEY WILL DRAG YOU ON.

"IF YOU MARCH AGAINST THEM THEY WILL CERTAINLY CAUSE YOUR DOWNFALL." *

* *The Policy of the Stuarts: Life and Works*, vol. I. p. 549.

Thus in the early writings of Napoleon III. we find three dominant political ideas. He maintains, first, that all political power dwells in the people and emanates from the people; secondly, that the official to be at the head of the French people should be not a president, but an emperor; and, thirdly, that the initiative of all political innovations should be taken, not by the people or by their legislative representatives, but by the monarch.

Now in these three propositions taken conjointly, are there not embodied all the evils that came upon France during the public career of Napoleon III.? They do not, perhaps, embody the possibility of his first acquiring power,—that depended in large measure upon the character of the government already existing,—but when once the power was in his hands, did they not open to him every possibility of usurpation?

It may be answered that according to his "*Ideas of a Constitution*" the people were to have the reserved power of a negative upon his acts, and that therefore they were always to have in their own hands the means of restraining him. This answer is somewhat specious, and yet it is fraught with sophistry and error. In every nation where the government alone has the right of initiative according to the Napoleonic idea, the sole power of the people is to choose whether to the appeal of the government for support it will say Yes, or whether it will say No. All the provisions of a constitution, be that constitution ever so complicated or ever so simple, can, in such a government, do nothing more for the nation than to provide a means whereby the people may give a categorical answer to such questions as the emperor may see fit to propound. Under circumstances ideally favorable an honest expression of public opinion on a question so proposed might be secured; but under ordinary circumstances such an expression would always be impossible. A political question might be made by the authorities to assume a form that would be regarded by the people as a new choice between two evils. In such a case, whatever the merits of the question pending, it would almost invariably be decided in the affirmative, simply by that universal disposition of human nature that

> "makes us rather bear those ills we have,
> Than fly to others that we know not of."

It is readily admitted that such a method of voting may, for certain purposes, be quite legitimate and entirely unobjectionable. Such would generally be the fact in all cases where it would be equally easy to foresee the results of a negative and those of an affirmative vote. But in a nation where the government alone has the initiative, the result of a negative vote can never be foretold with any degree of certainty. In a land, too, like that of France, where to a large extent the peasantry own their own homes, such uncertainty is especially intolerable. The consequence is that whenever the French people have been appealed to by *plébiscite*, they have not only in every case answered in the affirmative, but their majority has amounted often almost to unanimity.*

These facts were perfectly understood by Louis Napoleon. In his "Napoleonic Ideas" he placed these figures in array, not indeed for the purpose of showing the only thing which they are capable of showing, but in order to convince the people of the extraordinary popularity of his uncle's political ideas. It is certain that he was familiar with the results of the appeals that had been made, and it is impossible to suppose that he had not interpreted their true meaning. No one knew better than he that the French people, if asked to give either their assent to *un fait accompli*, or their dissent from it, would, in all probability, support it with an overwhelming majority. History and human nature both pointed to the same result. He must have seen, therefore, that he needed only to secure a position from which he could appeal to the nation. With the sole right of initiative once in his possession, and with that almost absolute certainty of support which the situation necessarily

* The following figures will serve to show the force of the circumstances to which I have alluded:

	Yes.	*No.*
Constitution of 1791 (not submitted to the people).		
" " 1793	1,801,018	11,600
" " the year III	1,057,390	49,977
Temporary Consulate	3,011,007	1,562
Consulate for Life	3,568,888	8,374
Hereditary Empire (1804)	3,521,675	2,579
Presidency of Ten Years	7,439,216	646,737

secured, there could be no further obstacle in his way.

We have thus seen that the political sovereignty of the country would practically pass into the hands of Napoleon in case of his elevation to power. This, however, does not prove that such a change would be disadvantageous to the nation. Whether it would or would not depends upon the character of the ruler and the political condition of the people. If in any given case the masses of the people are so devoid of political ability as to take no serious interest in political affairs, or if indeed for any reason they are unable to govern themselves as well as they would be likely to be governed, the only practical question then is, who should govern them? Shall it be a person upon whom are imposed certain practicable constitutional restraints, or shall it be one who takes the power into his own hands, leaving with the people only so much as they can never use? There would appear to be no doubt that the choice of the former would always be the safer; and yet it must be admitted that under conceivable circumstances the latter might be deliberately and advantageously chosen as the only possible cure for anarchy. Did such circumstances exist in France? Whatever others may think, it is certain that every Frenchman would answer the question with an emphatic negative. It would not for a moment be admitted that Louis Napoleon was chosen because the nation despaired of governing itself; on the contrary, it has always been vigorously maintained that he was accepted as the best *means* of governing itself. He was chosen as President for no other reason than because he had captivated the people with his name, his ideas, and his promises.

We have glanced at the fundamental character of his political ideas; it may be well to look for a moment at the nature of his promises.

The necessity of assurances of more than ordinary force were doubtless apparent to the mind of Napoleon. He must have apprehended that the nation would not readily deliver itself over into the hands of a master, until it was at least convinced that the proposed master would not abuse his power. Accordingly, not only in his essays, but also in his letters, we have the most emphatic declarations which it would be possible to make. In the essay on the "Extinction of Pauperism," which he wrote when imprisoned at Ham, a plausible appeal was made to the masses of the nation. The author draws a vivid picture of the deplorable condition of the working-classes:

"Industry has now neither rule, nor organization, nor aim. It is an engine which works without a regulator. It cares nothing for the human force it employs, crushing men and materials equally under its wheels. It depopulates the country; conglomerates the people into small spaces without room to breathe; weakens the mind as well as the body, and afterwards throws these men on the world, when she no longer requires them,—men who have sacrificed their strength, their youth, and their existence to her service. Industry devours her children and lives only by their destruction; she is the true Saturn of labor. Must we, then, to remedy these defects, place her under a yoke of iron, rob her of this liberty which is her sole existence: in a word, kill her because she is a murderess, without profiting by the immense benefits which she confers? We think it is sufficient to cure those she has wounded, and to protect her from wounds." *

Having thus stated the case, the essayist proceeds to show how all the benefits of good society might be disseminated among the working-classes. There is a great array of figures to demonstrate how large a part of the lands of France remain uncultivated, how on a sort of joint-stock principle the unemployed laborers might be formed by the government into affluent communities, and how in this manner "pauperism might be extirpated, if not entirely, at least in a great measure." The plan proposed was a kind of socialism, exactly fitted to captivate that large class of people in France which is ever waiting for some new phantasm,—the same class which, a generation before, had gone into ecstasies over the dreams of Mably and Saint-Just. From this presentation of Bonaparte's views, the common people had a right to regard him as pledged to the rapid amelioration of their condition in case of his elevation to power.

* Louis Napoleon, *Life and Works,* vol. II. p. 96.

But other and more definite assurances were not wanting. The numerous letters with which he regaled his friends were filled with articles of political faith, all teaching and enforcing the same doctrine. In public and in private he apparently neglected no opportunity to make his views known. In September of 1840, when he was brought to trial for the affair of Boulogne, he founded his defence exclusively on the fact that the people in the nation were sovereign, and that in their sovereign capacity they had elevated his family to supreme political power. That sovereignty, he assured his judges, had been consecrated by the most powerful revolution in history. It had expressed itself in favor of the Constitution of the Empire with suffrages almost unanimous. That grand act of sovereignty the nation had never revoked; and, as the Emperor had declared, "Whatever has been done without its authority is illegal."

Here, it will be seen, was an open defiance of the authority of Louis Philippe. The declaration clearly meant, if it meant anything, that the Empire was at that moment the legally established government in France. To his assertions on that point he added these words:

"At the same time do not allow yourselves to believe that, led away by the impulses of a personal ambition, I have wished by these acts to attempt in France a restoration of the Empire. I have been taught too noble lessons, and have lived with too noble examples before me, to do so. I was born the son of a king who descended without regret from a throne on the day when he had reason to believe that it was no longer possible to conciliate with the interests of France, those of the people whom he had been called to govern. The Emperor, my uncle, preferred to abdicate the empire, rather than accept by treaty the restricted frontier, while he could not but expose France to the insults and the menaces in which foreign nations to this day permit themselves to indulge. I have not lived a single day forgetful of these lessons. In 1830, when the people recognized their sovereignty, I expected that the policy of the following days would be as loyal as the conquest itself, and that the destinies of France would be established forever. Instead of this the country has undergone the melancholy experiences of the past ten years. Under such circumstances, I consider that the vote of four millions of my countrymen, which had elevated my family to supreme power, imposed upon me the duty, at least, of making an appeal to the nation, in order to ascertain its will." *

This address, cleverly compounded of truth and falsehood, and spoken in the ears of all Frenchmen, when stripped of its conventional circumlocution proclaimed these political doctrines: The people of France are sovereign. In their sovereign capacity they chose the hereditary empire of Napoleon as their government, and they have never revoked that choice. That empire, therefore, is now

* Louis Napoleon, *Life and Works*, vol. I. p. 51.

de jure the government of France, and I am *de jure* the Emperor. That I abstain from claiming the imperial throne is not because I have no right to it, but because I have learned from the examples of my father and my uncle to practise self-denial when the welfare of the nation requires it.

Now, it is difficult to conceive how any more dangerous doctrine could have been enunciated. There was embodied in it the perpetual right to wage war upon the government for the recovery of lost possessions. Under ordinary circumstances such a declaration would, of course, be of no importance; but in view of the dissatisfied condition of the nation, in view of that great stress which Bonaparte had laid upon the sovereignty and welfare of the people, by which he had already secured great popularity with the masses, and, above all, in view of the powerful spell which the name of Napoleon continued to work upon the nation, it is strange beyond measure that the danger was not more fully comprehended. It would seem that ordinary intelligence must have perceived that there was needed only the factor of unscrupulousness to make the conditions of every evil possibility complete. In case an opportunity should come within reach, everything would depend upon the integrity of a man who had as yet given no proof of political virtue, and whose ideal, furthermore, was the hero of the 18th Brumaire.

Bonaparte did not fail to guard against the fears which would be naturally aroused by these various circumstances. His writings abound in expressions calculated to allay them. He gives a sufficient amount of assurance and expresses a becoming horror of political dishonesty. To the editor of the *Journal du Loiret*, he wrote from Ham, in October of 1843:

"I have never claimed any other rights than those of a French citizen, and I never shall have any other desire than to see the whole people legally convened, choosing fully the form of government which they might think it best to have. As a member of a family which owes its elevation to the sufferings of the nation (sic!) I should belie my origin, my nature, and what is more, I should do violence to common-sense, if I did not admit the sovereignty of the people as the fundamental basis of all political organization." *

In commenting upon this letter the editor of the *Journal du Loiret* used these words:

"It is an evidence of the all-powerful virtue of the democratic principle, and it is also an evidence of high-mindedness, to see a man of royal blood, heir to a throne, a young prince, intelligent and proud, popular for the name he bears and the glorious souvenirs which that name recalls, thus ridding himself of monarchical prejudices, abdicating the privileges of his race, and paying a solemn homage to the sovereignty of the people. We highly compliment Prince Louis for the noble sentiments expressed in this letter."

* Louis Napoleon, *Life and Works*, vol. I. p. 67.

Such expressions as these, though rather too suggestive of Sir Peter Teazle, are of some value as showing how the prince's professions were regarded. Strictly speaking, there was at that moment no Napoleonic party in France, and for that reason, perhaps, the comments of the journals should be regarded as reflecting all the more correctly the sentiments of the public.

Again in 1848, when the prince learned that it was proposed in the Assembly to retain the law of exile as regarding him alone, he wrote to the Representative Body an appeal, which concluded as follows:

"The same reasons which made me take up arms against the government of Louis Philippe would lead me, if my services were required, to devote myself to the defence of the Assembly, the result of universal suffrage. In the presence of a king elected by two hundred deputies, I might have recollected that I was heir to an empire founded on the consent of four millions of Frenchmen. In the presence of the national sovereignty, I can and I will claim no more than my rights as a French citizen; but these I will demand with that energy which an honest heart derives from the knowledge of never having done anything unworthy of its country." *

These words would seem to be sufficiently assuring, but others were more so. In July of the same year, the Prince, then at London, received word

* Louis Napoleon, *Life and Works*, vol. I. p. 86.

that he had been elected to the National Assembly by the people of Corsica. It is evident that he was hoping for something better. He immediately wrote to the President of the Assembly a letter which is a curious mixture of arrogance and humility. After declaring that the same reasons which had compelled him to refuse other demands imposed upon him the necessity of another sacrifice, he added:

"Without renouncing the idea of the honor of being one day a representative of the people, I consider it to be my duty to wait before returning to the bosom of my country, till my presence in France may not in any way serve as a pretext for the enemies of the republic. *I wish that my disinterestedness should prove the sincerity of my patriotism; I wish that those who charge me with ambition should be convinced of their error.*

"Have the goodness, Monsieur le President, to inform the Assembly of my resignation and of my regret at not being able yet to participate in its labors, and of my ardent wishes for the happiness of the Republic." *

The "disinterestedness" by which he wished to "prove the sincerity of his patriotism," appears in a strong light when we find that only a few days later he wrote to his friend, General Piat, at Paris, that, if he were again elected, he should accept. This declaration was duly noted, and consequently in September he was chosen by the

* *Life and Works*, vol. I. p. 95.

electors of four different departments. He determined to sit for the capital; and thus the "sacrifice" by which he wished to "prove the sincerity of his patriotism," while it deprived him of Corsica, gave him Paris.

On the 26th of September, Louis Napoleon took his seat in the Assembly in the midst of a scene of considerable agitation. He at once mounted the Tribune and read a short but carefully prepared speech. It was the first official act of his life, and was a most solemn profession of devotion to the Republic.

"I feel it incumbent on me," said he, "to declare openly, on the first day I am allowed to sit in this hall, the real sentiments which animate, and have always animated, me. After being proscribed during thirty-three years, I have at last recovered a country and the rights of citizenship. The Republic has conferred on me that happiness. *I offer it now my oath of gratitude and devotion, and the generous fellow-countrymen who sent me to this hall may rest certain that they will find me devoted to the double task which is common to us all, namely, to assure order and tranquillity, the first want of the country, and to develop the democratical institutions which the people have a right to claim.* During a long period I could only devote to my country the meditations of exile and captivity. To-day a new career opens to me. Admit me to your ranks, dear colleagues, with the sentiment of affectionate sympathy which animates me. *My conduct, you may be certain, shall ever be guided by a respectful devotion to law. It will prove, to the confusion of those who have attempted to slander me, that no man is more devoted than I am, I repeat, to the defence of order and the consolidation of the Republic.*" *

This address was heard with every mark of approbation and satisfaction. It was almost universally accepted as a sufficient pledge of good faith. In the course of the ensuing discussions on the Constitution, it was only at rare intervals that a word indicative of suspicion or distrust was uttered; and even then assurance was restored by the unfailing tact of the Prince. While that portion of the Constitution which pertains to the Presidency was under consideration, Thouret proposed the insertion of a proviso, that no member of either of the families which had reigned over France should be elected President or Vice-President of the French Republic. The amendment was opposed by Lacaze and others, who urged that it proposed a law of proscription unworthy of a great people, and that the chief of the imperial family, against whom the amendment was particularly directed, had come forward, and from the tribune protested his devotion to the Republic. This opened the way to the Prince himself, who said: "That he was too grateful to the nation for restoring him to his rights as a citizen to have any other ambition. It was not in his own name,

* *Life and Works*, vol. I. p. 96.

but in the name of three hundred thousand electors, that he protested against the appellation of 'Pretender,' which was continually flung in his face."

"These words," says the report, "were followed by the greatest agitation." Finally, Thouret arose and said: "*In consequence of what has been said by Monsieur Louis Bonaparte, I withdraw the amendment.*"

While these discussions were going on, Socialist banquets were taking place in various parts of the realm, and the name of Louis Napoleon was beginning to be talked of in connection with the Presidency. This fact introduced into the Assembly an instantaneous element of discord. It was evident that there were some, at least, who were not altogether satisfied with the Prince's fair promises as to his future. Monsieur Clement Thomas inveighed against the new candidate in the most violent terms. In the course of his speech he did not hesitate to charge him with covering the country with emissaries recommending his candidature to the peasantry. Finally, he startled the Assembly by declaring: "Louis Napoleon is not a candidate for the Presidency, *but for the Imperial Dignity.*"

The instantaneous effect of this prophetic outburst was the suspension of the session, and a challenge from Monsieur Pierre Bonaparte; the less immediate, but more important, result was another speech from the Prince, containing other "satisfactory assurances."

In the meantime his candidacy for the position of President was declared, and it was necessary that he should attend to his interests with the people. Accordingly he lost no time in publishing an address to his fellow-citizens. He reiterated his doctrines concerning the sovereignty of the people, the rights of labor, and the relief of poverty. Then, for the purpose of allaying any doubts which might be entertained concerning himself and his future, he crowned all his assurances by using these words:

"I am not an ambitious man, who dream at one time of the empire and of war, at another of the adoption of subversive theories. Educated in free countries, and in the school of misfortune, I shall always remain faithful to the duties which your suffrages and the will of the Assembly may impose upon me. If I am elected President, I shall not shrink from any danger or from any sacrifice to defend society which has been so audaciously attacked. *I shall devote myself wholly, without mental reservation, to the confirming of a republic, which has shown itself wise by its laws, honest in its intentions, great and powerful by its acts. I pledge my honor to leave to my successor, at the end of four years, the executive power strengthened, liberty intact, and a real progress accomplished.*" *

Such were the assurances which Louis Napoleon gave to the French people. I have dwelt upon the subject thus at length for the purpose of

* Louis Napoleon, *Life and Works*, vol. I. p. 101.

showing not only that the people of the nation had every means of making themselves familiar with his political doctrines, but also that he was pledged in the most formal and definite manner to a given line of policy. Early in life he perceived the spell with which the name of his uncle bound the mass of Frenchmen who had forgotten the disasters of 1815, and he saw how that spell might be turned to his own advantage. He comprehended how, under a system of universal suffrage, the peasantry would be the governing body, and how, if secured in their prosperity, they would always be ready to adhere to a strong executive. He saw, also, that once in possession of an opportunity, with the sole right of the initiative in his hand, there would open before him every possibility of power. Finally, he did not hesitate to give every possible assurance, and to hold out every possible inducement in order that the opportunity might be conferred upon him.

It is unnecessary to comment on the events which transferred Louis Napoleon from the President's chair to the imperial throne. That they were the natural outgrowth of Napoleon's political creed in no way detracts from the perfidious villany of an act to which it would be difficult to find a parallel since the days of Louis XI. It should, however, be borne in mind, that the acceptance by the French nation of Louis Napoleon and his political creed was the practical acceptance of a personal in distinction from a constitutional government.

No matter what the details of a plan of government may be, if it gives the sole power of initiative into the hand of a single man, then hedges the people about with executive restraints so that they can never know what the result of a negative vote would be, it is not only a personal government, but a personal government of the worst form. It is the worst form, because, in addition to all the evils which characterize the other species, it is a deception and a fraud. It is commonplace to say that an evil which is known to be such may be avoided or guarded against; while one that arrays itself in the garb of virtue, carries with it a weapon which it is always difficult and sometimes impossible to avoid. Even political poisons are not very dangerous if they are properly labelled. The very worst feature of Napoleonism was the fact that, while it carried in its essential nature the ready means of violating any law with impunity, it professed that reverence for law as a fixed rule of action, both for governments and for individuals, without which there can be neither liberty nor order. It is probable that neither of the Napoleons would have hesitated to adopt in theory even that ideal devotion to legal authority which the genius of Plato has so beautifully illustrated in his account of the last conversation and the death of Socrates; and yet it would be easy to show that in all essential characteristics the Second Empire was a government of men and not of laws, of will and not of reason, of arbitrary and not of limited and legal power.

The favorite argument of the adherents of Napoleon has been, that under a system of universal suffrage it was necessarily impossible for the Emperor to impose upon the nation a system of government that was repugnant to the majority of the people. It has often been asserted, that, even admitting what is said about the servility of France in obeying the head of the State, she has done it with her own free will. After a solemn appeal made to the whole population, she chose Napoleon as her ruler; and "she possesses in the *Corps Legislatif* an organ through which her voice may be heard, with less chance of being mistaken than even the public voice in the Parliament of England; for there the right of suffrage is restricted to a few, whereas in France it belongs to the whole adult male population." In a word, whenever it has been asserted that the power of Napoleon rested on the bayonet, the reply has been an appeal to the testimony of the ballot.

Now the strength of this argument, it will be universally admitted, can be understood only when the character of the ballot in France is known. Is the ballot, then, a truthful witness? Is the testimony which it gives a reality or a sham? These questions can be answered only by an inspection of such facts as come within reach. If it can be demonstrated that the people have absolute freedom of choice at the elections, the force of the argument will have to be admitted; if, on the contrary, it becomes manifest that the French executive exercises such an influence over the elections as to make a free choice impossible, the position will readily be conceded to have no strength whatever.

Now it requires only the simplest presentation of facts to show that the process of elections in France under the Second Empire was nothing less than a gigantic swindle. It was a mere device with which to entrap a people into giving their assent to propositions which would not be assented to either by lawful representatives or by electors in the exercise of absolute freedom of choice. It was a palpable cheat, which, but for the gravity of its results, would have become a laughing-stock in proportion as the facts concerning it came to be known and understood.

The result obtained by the ballot under the Second Empire no more represented the wishes of the people of France than it would have done if they had been marched up to the poll under military escort, and compelled at the point of the bayonet to vote in accordance with the dictates of the Emperor.

I have stated the case strongly, and I desire not to be misunderstood. I do not here express an opinion whether the government of Napoleon III. was inherently a good government or a bad one; I only affirm that in so far as it rested for its justification, upon universal suffrage, it rested upon a pretence and a fraud. If there are any who think that a government can rest upon such a basis and still be a good government, to them, of course, my argument will have no meaning. Those, however, who think that the Second Empire must have been a good government *because* it rested upon universal suffrage, should know definitely what universal suffrage under the Second Empire was. In support of the theses which I just gave, therefore, I shall cite examples enough, as I think, to establish their correctness.

It will aid us in our estimation of these facts, if we bear in mind one of the important characteristics of government in France, as distinguished from government in England or America. In our own country we have of late heard something of executive interference in affairs of a local nature, and yet it must be admitted that the distinctive feature of that liberty of which we boast is entire freedom from such interference; in other words, is self-government. Our numerous municipal and local corporations manage a vast amount of public business with as little interference of the executive as would be possible if that executive did not exist. But the very reverse of this is the case in France. An English writer of learning and critical discrimination has so well expressed this difference, that I use his words:

"The government there, under whatever form, whether that of Directory, Consulship, Empire, Restoration, Monarchy of the Barricades, Republic, or the Army, which is its present phase, has always been essentially despotic in its character. It has ruled by a system of paid *employés* in immediate dependence upon itself. The provincial functionaries, such as prefects and sub-prefects and mayors of arrondissements, are mere puppets, whose strings are pulled by the executive in Paris. In no country is the system of police surveillance and espionage more thoroughly understood or constantly practised. No public meetings are convened, as in England, to take into consideration the measures of government, and, if necessary, organize a peaceful opposition to them. The people are not, except in the solitary instance of dropping their individual votes into the ballot-box when the period of an election comes round, made parties to the management of their own interests. Hence there is, properly speaking, no public opinion in France the influence of which can be felt by statesmen, and enable them to forecast the measures which will be best suited for the wants, and most in accordance with the real wishes, of the nation. Hence also results the startling paradox that the French, of all people in the world, are the most impatient of constitutional control, and the most servilely submissive to despotic power." *

From the characteristics of the French method of administration so well described, it will be seen that the executive has at hand the means of exerting an influence such as it would be impossible to

* Forsyth, *History of Trial by Jury*, p. 143.

exert in a country with a government like that of England, or like that of America. The nature of this influence it is now my purpose to examine.

It will be unnecessary to refer at length to the *plébiscite* proper, for the reason that its true character is already universally understood. Only in irony can that be called an election which merely asks the people to say *Yea* or *Nay* to an act which has already been adopted with the aid of military power. Concerning the other elections, however, the case is different. In all constitutional governments, even in all governments merely professing to be constitutional, there are certain questions to be submitted to the people of a nature calculated to afford absolute freedom of choice,—questions which present ordinarily a fair alternative between two or more propositions, or between two or more candidates. It is not universally understood that under the Second Empire even in elections of this character the same system of fraud prevailed as in case of the *plébiscite*; and it is for this reason that I shall describe, somewhat in detail, the methods in which the elections were conducted. The two examples which I have chosen for this purpose may be fairly regarded as typical of the whole.

One of the most characteristically iniquitous measures of the Napoleonic *régime* was that by which Nice and Savoy were transferred from Italy to France. During the Italian war men were somewhat curious to know how Napoleon was to be rewarded for his service to Victor Emmanuel.

Their waiting curiosity, however, was soon gratified. As soon as it became certain that the issue of the war was no longer doubtful, the Emperor proceeded to make his policy known. Though up to that moment there had been no intimation that territorial compensation would be demanded, it was suddenly announced at the Italian court that Nice and Savoy must be transferred to France, or that the French army would be at once withdrawn.*

The smaller principalities of Italy had not yet given their allegiance to the King of Piedmont, and to deny the demand of the Emperor would have been simply to abandon all the fruits of the contest. Cavour resisted as long as resistance was possible. Ideville declares that he gave a formal promise to the English ambassador, Sir James Hudson, that he would resist the demand to the last, at the same time assuring him of his hopes that France would renounce its determination. It soon became apparent, however, that the King must either give up Nice and Savoy, or give up all else. With this alternative before him, so wise a statesman as Cavour could not hesitate. He probably saw moreover, that since Italy was obliged to yield, it were better to yield cheerfully, so as to conciliate the

* So successfully had the French government masked its design up to this point, that the English journals were completely deceived. D'Ideville, from whom a large portion of the following facts are derived, in commenting on this point, uses these words: "L'Angleterre n'avait pas assez d'eloges à adresser à cette nation généreuse (France), pleine d'initiative, qui seule, en Europe, sachant 'combattre pour une idée,' n'attachait de prix qu'à la gloire."—*Journal d'un Diplomate en Italie*, vol. I. p. 109.

good-will of Napoleon, than to incur his displeasure by making it apparent to all Europe that the cession was granted under compulsion.

It was well known that the measure would be extremely unpopular; and for this reason the negotiations were carried on with the utmost secrecy. Benedetti, as special envoy, was sent from Paris to conduct the cause of the French, and so successfully was the affair concealed from the other powers and from the people of the city, that all the details were arranged, and the treaty was actually signed, before it became known that a second plenipotentiary had arrived.*

When the details of the Treaty became known, an intense indignation on the part of the Italian people was at once aroused. This indignation would undoubtedly have been overwhelming, and would have prevented the ratification of the Treaty but for two reasons: first, that there was universal and unbounded confidence in the patriotism and statesmanship of Cavour; and secondly, that he assured them that the vote to be taken on the

* The details of this whole affair are given with admirable clearness and vivacity by D'Ideville in his *Journal d'un diplomate en Italie:* Turin, 1859–1862, p. 109, seq. He relates that on the evening of March 24th, the day on which the Treaty had actually been signed, it was whispered around at the clubs that such an issue might in the end be possible, and that in consequence of this rumor, the ministers of Prussia and Russia came to him with anxious inquiries whether it was true that a second plenipotentiary had been appointed and that a treaty was to be signed on the 30th! He states further that they were only anxious concerning Savoy, inasmuch as Cavour had assured Sir Henry Hudson that he would answer any demand for Nice with a categorical No!—P. 119.

question in Nice and Savoy should be entirely free ("*pienamente libero*").*

These assurances impart an additional interest to the facts which I shall now attempt to present somewhat in detail.

By the Treaty of the 24th of March, then, it was agreed between France and Italy that Savoy and Nice, "after the population had been consulted," should be ceded to France, and that Tuscany and the Romagna should also, after a similar "consultation," be annexed to Sardinia. It is necessary to bear in mind that by the terms of the treaty the annexation of these respective territories was made indirectly no less advantageous to Victor Emmanuel than to Napoleon. With Austria vindictive and powerful, and in a threatening strategical position; with the Pope outraged and desperate, and in control of an army which attached to itself a large share of the fanaticism of Europe,—there was no hope for struggling Italy but in a firmer alliance with France. In this fact alone, as we have just seen, is to be found an explanation of the willingness of the Sardinian government to part with so considerable a portion of its territory. Reasons enough existed, therefore, why King and Emperor were equally anxious that the people should vote for annexation.

The fifth article of the Sardinian Constitution

* "Lui seul pouvait braver ainsi l'impopularité à un tel acte, tant il était assuré de la confidance aveugle qu'on avait en lui."—*D'Ideville, Journal*, 117.

provides that "treaties which shall make any alteration in the territories of the state shall not take effect until after they have obtained the consent of the Chamber." In view of this provision, it was manifestly the duty of the government to submit the treaty to the Chamber for ratification before the popular vote should be taken, inasmuch as it was only by virtue of the Treaty that the people would be entitled to vote at all. But there were dangers in this method of procedure which the Sardinian government did not fail to foresee. The project of annexation was not popular in Parliament,—indeed, it was likely to fail. Garibaldi did not hesitate to raise his voice, in season and out of season, against it; and, what was of the greatest importance, as showing the untrammelled desires of the people most affected, *every one of the delegates from Nice and Savoy to Parliament had been elected with the express understanding that they were to protest against such a transfer to another power.* In the short time that permitted effort, thirteen thousand signatures were obtained to a protest against annexation. In view of these inconvenient facts, it was determined to postpone a ratification by Parliament until a popular vote, unanimous or nearly unanimous, had been secured. It seems to have been of no consequence that the Treaty, according to which the vote was to be taken, really had no existence until it was ratified by the Chamber; it was determined to proceed as though it had been ratified, and then to use the advantage gained by this procedure to secure its ratification.

Accordingly measures were instituted to secure such a popular vote as was desired. First of all, the Sardinian troops were withdrawn, and their places were filled by French garrisons. The opposition of the inhabitants of Nice to the transfer was indicated by the fact that the troops, on first entering the city, were received so roughly that they were obliged to resort to the use of the bayonet. The municipal junta sent a vote of thanks to those members of the English Parliament who had spoken in opposition to French annexation. The French Consul wrote to his government, that if a French man-of-war did not come to Villa Franca, his own life and that of his family would not be secure. After the said ship arrived, the editor of the newly established French organ, *L'Avenir de Nice*, was besieged in his house and obliged to rush down to Villa Franca for refuge.*

Such were some of the indications of public sentiment at the time when the French garrisons were taking their places. It was evident that the people were not to be easily overawed.

But the efforts of the government had only just begun. Immediately after the occupation of the

* I am indebted for these and for many of the following facts to a writer in Blackwood's Magazine (vol. LXXXVII. p. 734) who was residing at the time in Nice, and who had every facility for personal observation.

country by French troops, there was published an order transferring the civil government of the provinces to France. The French provisional governor, Lubonis, made haste to use the power thus placed in his hands for the advantage of his imperial master, and his example was speedily followed by Lachinal. Many of the mayors and local authorities were utterly opposed to the idea of French annexation, and without their co-operation it was felt that a vote of the people in favor of the measure could not be insured. Accordingly the following circular, filled out as might in each case be required, was issued :

"THE GOVERNOR OF ANNECY,

"Considering that Monsieur ——, mayor of the commune of ——, seems not to have accepted favorably the consequences of the Treaty of the 24th of March last; and considering that it is important, under the present circumstances, to have at the head of the administration of each commune men devoted to the new orders of things,

"Decrees,—

"1. Monsieur ——, present mayor of the commune of ——, is dismissed from his functions.

"2. The municipal counsellor —— is charged, until a new order, with the administration of said commune.

"3. The above will be transmitted to Messieurs —— and ——, for their guidance.

"(Signed) LACHINAL, *Governor-Regent.*

"ANNECY, *April*, 1860."

In commenting upon this transfer of civil authority to the sole interests of the Emperor, the French journals gave evidence of abundant zeal. One of them, *Le Bon Sens*, remarked:

"A very important thing for the success of the great votation, to which Savoy is about to be called, is to have at the head of each commune a mayor thoroughly devoted to the French annexation, for it is he who should give the impulse and preside at the electoral operations. A mayor who is devoted to Piedmont, or who has a Swiss leaning, will be altogether out of place on such an occasion. We learn with pleasure that a great purgation has already taken place in the province of Chambery, of mayors, either hostile or suspected. We ask all sincere friends of France to keep a sharp look-out upon their communal administration. We do not doubt that the governor of the province of Annecy will be ready, if such is the case, to make use of the full powers with which he is clothed, to replace in each commune all the mayors who will not loyally co-operate in the great cause of our national regeneration."

The military and civil machinery thus in order, the authorities now devoted themselves to the more immediate work of manufacturing the requisite majority. First of all, the people were informed not only that they were prohibited from holding any meetings to discuss the affairs of Nice, but also that no canvassing on the part of those opposed to French annexation would be permitted, and that no placards or circulars would be allowed to be issued by the Italian party. At the same time, documents of various kinds were issued by the officers in authority, appealing to their subordinates and to the people. The provisional governor, Lubonis, issued a proclamation, of which the following is the most important portion:

"Citizens,—All uncertainty with reference to our future has ceased. By the Treaty of the 24th of March, the gallant King Victor Emmanuel has ceded to France Savoy and the arrondissement of Nice. The most powerful motives of political necessity, the exigencies of the future of Italy, the sentiment of gratitude toward his powerful ally, and finally, the exceptional circumstances of our country, have decided our beloved sovereign to separate the provinces which have been for so many centuries intimately bound up with his dynasty. But the fate of a people does not rest exclusively with the desire of princes. Therefore the magnanimous Emperor Napoleon the Third and the King Victor Emmanuel have desired that this Treaty of cession should be strengthened by the popular adhesion. . . . . All opposition should fall powerless before the interests of the country and the sentiment of duty. Besides, it will find an insurmountable obstacle in the very wishes of Victor Emmanuel. . . . . Fellow-citizens, the mission which the king has confided to me is transitory but important. In order to fulfil my task at this extraordinary juncture, I count upon the support of your co-operation, upon your respect for law, and upon the high degree of civilization to which you have raised yourselves. Hasten, therefore, to confirm by your suffrage the reunion of your country to France. In making ourselves the echo of the intentions of the king, let us unfurl the banner of that noble and great nation which has always excited our lively sympathies. Let us rally round the throne of the glorious Emperor Napoleon the Third. Let us surround it with that same fidelity, so peculiar to our country, which we have always preserved to Victor Emmanuel. As for this august Prince, let us retain among us the worship of by-gone memories, and let us raise earnest prayers for his new and brilliant destiny. For the great Napoleon the Third, whose powerful and firm will is to open a new era of prosperity for our country, our inflexible fidelity, as well as our respectful devotion, will now commence.

"Vive la France!

"Vive L'Empereur Napoléon III.!

"*Le Gouverneur Provisioné*, LUBONIS."

A proclamation similar to that of Lubonis was issued by Malaussena, Mayor of Nice; and, finally, the Bishop came forward in the same interest, appealing to all loyal members of the church to vote for annexation. Nor, indeed, was this all. The French Committee sent to all the officials a circular bearing the government seal, and appeal-

19*

ing for support to all the authorities in town and country. Referring to the advantages to be derived from annexation, the Committee used these words:

"We are convinced that the Imperial government will recompense the people for the unanimity of their vote, and will proportion the reward according to the good disposition manifested by them. Without enumerating here the immense and incontestable advantages of every kind which our country would derive from its annexation to the great French Empire, we consider it our duty to address ourselves to all our friends and correspondents, not only to stimulate their zeal in favor of the common cause, and to engage them to use all their influence in order to ensure the success of the vote in the French interest, but also that they may carefully watch and point out to us the steps that have been taken in a contrary interest by those in opposition, in order that the necessary measures may be taken to neutralize the influences which are hostile to the interests of the country. Will you have the goodness, M.——, to acknowledge the receipt of this, and to make known to us the spirit of your population, and that of the local authorities?"

The "necessary measures" to which the Committee alluded were amply provided for. A sum of money had been placed at their disposal by the French government; and of this, it is stated, on good authority, that 3,000,000 francs were used in the direct work of bribery, exclusive of the expenses of the government, on the day of voting. Drinking-booths and *cafés* were erected especially for the purpose by the officials, and a tri-color cockade, or a voting-ticket with "*Oui*" upon it, entitled the bearer to the gratuitous enjoyment of all their privileges.

Another device which appealed to the religious zeal of the people was that of blessing the standards of the imperial party. This official blessing of the French flags was calculated to work an immense effect upon the ignorant and somewhat superstitious population. The authorization ran in this way:

"MM. les Commissaires will distribute the flags which MM. les Curés are authorized and, indeed, invited to bless. These standards will be in this case presented by the Commune at the head of the inhabitants, to MM. les Curés, who will receive them at the entry of the church. Finally you will understand the importance which I attach to this last recommendation. You will take care that official proclamations, manifestos, and notices are preserved intact. All appeals to the passions,—any notice whatever affixed without the required authorization,—will be immediately torn down."

Side by side with this was posted the following official manifesto:

"The Mayor of Bonneville hereby gives notice that the Communal Council will assist at the benediction of the flags which the Imperial government has presented to the Commune; that this religious ceremony will take place on Sunday the 22d, at seven o'clock, A. M.; that the *cortège* will leave the Hôtel de Ville to go to the church. All electors are invited to this ceremony, which will immediately precede the opening of the voting-urns. In the morning the Hôtel de Ville will be decorated with the French flag and the national colors. All the inhabitants are invited to decorate their houses with flags of the same colors.

"The Imperial government has made its *début* by a signal benefit in giving us the customs *zone* which has hitherto been refused. It assures to us the prosperity of the country. Its generosity will not end here. French engineers have explored the province, have begun to study the banks of the rivers, the state of the roads, and the public works most useful to the country. The numerous mines of Faucigny will be worked, the condition of our *collège* will be improved. Let us show our gratitude to the Emperor. Let us give a free course to our sympathies, so long restrained, and prove by a compact and unanimous vote that we are as much French as our fathers were.

"Vive l'Empereur!

"Vive la France!

(Signed) "DUFOUR, *Mayor.*"

As the day of voting approached, the Central Committee issued the following circular:

"Sir,—The Central Annexationist Committee, upon whose proceedings no restrictions were placed, has named you member of the Special Committee for the parish of ——. You will have the goodness, sir, to concert with your colleagues, MM. ——, measures which may unite and bring to the poll on Sunday next the greatest possible number of electors, and take any steps which appear expedient, *in order that the vote of the population may be a striking manifestation of its sentiments towards France and at the same time towards the Emperor.*"

In addition to all the other influences brought to bear, the local police authorities openly declared that lists of the *proscrits* would be made out, and that those who abstained from voting would be punished as soon as they became French subjects. The same authorities received orders from head-quarters, at Nice, to collect the peasants on the day of voting and march them into town, with drums beating and French flags floating at their head. An Englishman, who was at Nice at the time of the election, thus describes what he saw:

"The first object which met my view, as I entered Nice on the morning of the 15th, was a procession of country people marching into town. At the head of the procession was a fat *curé*, arm-in-arm with the village syndic and another functionary; behind were thirty or forty rustics, some of them extremely drunk, although early in the morning, carrying flags, beating drums, and cheering in a maudlin, irregular manner. The streets were crowded with persons wearing tri-colored cockades and carrying the *Oui* voting-ticket in their hats. French soldiers, of whom there was a plentiful sprinkling, mingled freely with the crowd, although one battalion had been marched to Villa Franca, to give the authorities an opportunity of saying that, in order not to influence the vote, part of the French troops had left the town. The urns were placed in the National College, and thither I repaired to watch the process of voting. The people crowded in and voted with scarcely a challenge; lists of those registered were posted up outside; but at first the votes were given too rapidly to enable the scrutineers to exercise any check. The *Oui* ticket was distributed freely in the streets—men stood at the corners as if they were advertising quack medicines, and gave you any number of "*Ouis*," but I endeavored both in the shops and in the streets to procure a "*Non*" without success. One boor I saw just about to vote two tickets. I asked him if such was his intention, and he naïvely answered, 'Why not?' 'Oh,' I said, 'it won't be fair; give me one,' which he most good-naturedly did at once. Another man to whom I spoke told me that he was strongly opposed to becoming French—that he had two sons in the Sardinian service, one in the army and the other in the navy; that he himself was a poor boatman, and that he had voted *Oui* against his inclination, because the police had told him that if he did not he would be imprisoned,—that the king whom he loved wanted it,—that England and all the powers wanted it, and that as for his voting in the opposite sense, he would simply get himself into a scrape and do no good. But he said promptly, 'I have neither cheered, nor will I wear a cockade.' As all the scrutineers were the nominees of Pietri (the French Agent of Police), and as they held the keys of the urns, there was, of course, no security against any number of *Oui* tickets being put into them in private."

The same witness wrote subsequently from Bonneville, where he happened to be on the day of the voting in Savoy.

"On the morning of the 22d I found myself once more at Bonneville in Faucigny; but a considerable change had taken place in the aspect of affairs since I had left it less than a month before. From every house, and almost every window of every house, waved French flags. The hotel, which had formerly been the head-quarters of the anti-French party, and where I had dined with the members of the committee, was tricked out in all the splendors of red, white, and blue. The bookseller's shop where I had heard sentiments strongly hostile to France, now displayed a gigantic banner; but more remarkable than all, the house of the candidate who had contested Bonneville three weeks before in the Swiss interest, as opposed to the French, was now decorated with French flags.

My old friends were nowhere to be found; the committee had evaporated, and throughout the town where party feeling had recently run so high, and anti-French annexation was rampant and openly expressed, there was not a syllable to be heard against it. A little shopkeeper, whom I knew formerly as a furious anti-Frenchman, was now with difficulty dug out of his backshop, and owned to having just voted in favor of France as an act of self-preservation. 'What could I do?' said he; 'the concièrge de la ville brought me two tickets this morning, with a message from the intendant that if I don't vote them it will be the worse for me. He also asked where my French flag was, and advised me if I valued my liberty to show one without delay. There is the flag and here is the other voting ticket—a similar one I have just voted, but this I present to you.'

'BULLETIN DE VOTATION.
La Savoie veut-elle être reunie à la France?
Oui et Zone.'

"My informant went on to tell me that every voter had received his ticket from the police authorities, and he smiled when I asked him where I could procure a '*Non*'-ticket. 'No printing-house here would venture to print one,' he said; 'you would have to get them from Geneva.' The addition of the word '*Zone*' struck me as curious, and I asked the object of its insertion in the ticket. The device was ingenious. The authorities, fear-ing that though the people had not the courage to vote *Non*, they might be bold enough to abstain from voting at all, gave it to be understood that such a course would not prevent their being annexed, but that they would thereby lose their commercial zone or free frontier with Switzerland, upon which their future prosperity would depend; in other words, by voting they would be annexed and get their zone: by abstaining they would be equally annexed, but ruined. By a recent French circular I perceive it stated that the desire of the Emperor to carry out the conditions of neutrality, as laid down in the 92d article of the treaty, has induced him to grant the Zone. It was originally invented as an election 'dodge,' and served its purpose admirably, being used either as a bribe or as a threat."

Such were the means by which the hostilities of Nice and Savoy to French annexation was converted into an almost unanimous declaration in its favor. Under any circumstances whatever such a spectacle of organized trickery would be a painful thing to contemplate. It is possible to imagine a situation in which the ruler of a country, for political reasons, might submit a question that had already been decided to the ratification of his people, with no other evil result than that which might chance to be inflicted upon the people themselves. But in the case of Savoy and Nice there was an element in the transaction which made it an outrage upon the liberal sentiments of Europe and of the world. I refer to the repeated declarations that the voting would be perfectly *free*. The first article of the Treaty declared that "it is understood between their majesties that this reunion shall be effected without any constraint upon the will of the people, and that the government of the King of Sardinia and that of the Emperor of the French will agree as soon as possible upon the best means of arriving at and of confirming the manifestation of this will." Not long after the treaty was formed a deputation from Nice waited upon Victor Emmanuel, when he assured them "that he had stipulated as a condition of this cession a votation free from any external pressure, and promised that, if a military occupation took place, or if the condition was violated in any manner, he would protest;" and again, in the proclamation by which he released his subjects in Nice and Savoy from their allegiance, he gave them this assurance: "Under no circumstances will this great change in your destiny be imposed upon you; it must be the result of your free consent. Such is my firm determination; such also is the intention of the Emperor of the French." Finally, in the Chamber of Deputies, when the vigorous protest of Garibaldi seemed likely to put an end to the whole transaction, confidence was restored only when Count Cavour assured the deputies that "the vote should be absolutely free." And yet, in view of all these most solemn assurances, what have we seen? Italian troops removed and French troops put in their places; all the important civil offices filled with Frenchmen, or men committed to the support of the French cause; official circulars and placards advocating annexation scattered everywhere, while no publication of an opposing sentiment was anywhere allowed; ballot-boxes in exclusive control of French officers; ballots in favor of annexation distributed everywhere by the police, while ballots opposed to annexation could be procured only by sending to Geneva; priests blessing the flags presented by the Emperor, and appealing to the consciences of their people in behalf of France; money, as well as general free living and drinking, furnished by the Imperial agents; and finally, the people, with French music sounding and French banners flying, marched up *en masse* to the ballot-box, with priest and mayor arm-in-arm at their head. Such was the boasted *free vote* with the sanction and help of which Nice and Savoy were annexed to France. It remains only to add that these measures succeeded in completely converting public opinion. Though at first the inhabitants of Nice and Savoy were violently opposed to annexation, they were, by means of the Imperial logic, convinced of their error, and consequently voted almost unanimously in its favor.*

It should be remembered that under the *régime* of the Second Empire there was no way of impos-

* Of 29,142 electors in Nice, 24,448 voted for annexation, and 160 against it; of 135,449 voters in Savoy, 133,533 voted *Yes*, while only 235 succeeded in voting *No.*—*D'Ideville, Journal d'un Diplomate en Italie*, p. 122.

ing any restraint upon the will of the Emperor, excepting by means of the *Corps Législatif.* As the senators and the counsellors of the state were appointed by the crown, they could in no way be regarded as in any sense representatives of the people,—they were rather representatives of the Emperor himself. The possibility of frustrating the Imperial will, that is to say, the possibility of preventing a pure absolutism, depended solely, therefore, upon the character of the representative body, while the character of that body depended upon the political intelligence of the people and the freedom of the election. If it can be shown that the elections were not substantially free, it will be unnecessary to ask whether the masses of the people do or do not possess an unusual amount of political intelligence. If there is no opportunity on the part of the people for a free exercise of the political intelligence they may possess, it is not too much to say that, for political purposes, such intelligence is of no consequence whatever. I think it will not be difficult to convince my readers that the general elections in France were no more free than was the election in Nice and Savoy; no question, therefore, concerning the intelligence of the electors is relevant, excepting, perhaps, so far as is necessary to show how the farce of the elections was continuously possible.*

* It is difficult for all those of us who are accustomed to think of the French as a highly intelligent people, to comprehend the ignorance of a large portion of the rural population. If one would get an adequate

It is difficult for an American or an Englishman to understand the political ignorance of the masses of the French peasantry; it is scarcely less so for him to comprehend the extreme centralization of the government under the Second Empire.* I have

notion of it, one should read the "Madame Bovary" of Flaubert, in which the common people of two Norman villages are portrayed. On the same subject there is ample food for meditation in the small work of Taine on universal suffrage. We must be content to make a few extracts:

"En France, sur cent personnes du sexe masculin, il y a trente-neuf illettrées c'est-à-dire ne sachant pas lire ou ne sachant pas écrire. Comme ces illettrées appartiennent presque tous à la population rurale, cela fait dans cette population trente-neuf illettrées sur soixantedix. Ainsi, l'on ne se trompe pas de beaucoup si l'on estime à sept sur quatorze, à la moitié du total, le nombre des électeurs ruraux qui n'ont pas les premiers rudiments de l'instruction la plus élémentaire. Voila déjà un indice d'après lequel on peut apprécier leur intelligence politique. Il m'est souvent arrivè de causer avec eux sur les affaires publiques. A quinze lieues de Paris, tel, cultivateur et petit propriétaire, ne savait pas ce que c'est le budget; quand je lui disais que l'argent versé chez le percepteur entre dans une caisse à Paris pour payer l'armée, les juges et le reste, qu'on tient registre de tous les recettes et dépenses, il ouvrait de grands yeux; il avait l'air de faire une découverte. Aprés les premiers emprunts du Second Empire, un fermier normand disait à un de mes amis, orléaniste: 'Ce n'est pas votre *gueux de Louis-Philippe* qui nous aurait donné de la rente à soixante-sept francs.' Après le coup-d'état, des cultivateurs me répétaient dans les Arnennes: '*Louis-Napoléon est très-riche, c'est lui qui va payer le gouvernement; il n'y aura plus d'impôts.*' Je viens de lire la correspondance de vingt-cinq à trente préfets de 1814 à 1830; l'ignorance et la crédulité des populations rurales sont étonnantes. Au moment de l'expédition d'Espagne, des maires viennent demander au préfet du Loiret s'il est vrai que les alliés vont traverser le pays pour aller en Espagne et laisser en France une nouvelle armée d'occupation. *Pendant plusieurs années dans plusieurs d'partments, au mois de mars, on croit fermement que Napol'on arrive à Brest avec quatre-cent-mille Am'ricians ou à Toulon avec quatre-cent-mille Turcs.*"—*Taine, Du Universal Suffrage*, p. 16.

* In regard to the intelligence of the people concerning the matters on which they are voting, the same author relates the following:

"Là-dessus, dans les deux ou trois élections qui ont précédé la chute

already referred to the general characteristics of what may be called the French system of administration. On the method which prevailed under Napoleon III., it is desirable to be specific, and I therefore quote the words of his latest and best historian. Comparing the administrative machinery with a polyp having an innumerable number of tentacles, this author says:

"The administrative tentacle begins with the prefect and ends with the cantonier; the judicial tentacle extends from the attorney-general and the chief justice to the village constable and the justice of the peace; the financial tentacle reaches from the secretary of the treasury to the collector of fines. Without mentioning a number of other similitudes, there are without number, licenses, customs, imposts, commissioners of roads and bridges, with which the polyp enlaces the candidate, strangles him, and suffocates him. Centralization is also an intelligent machine, complicated, and marvellously obedient to the hand that directs

du Second Empire, nous avons eu par les enquêtes des révélations étranges. Un témoin disait: 'J'avais les deux billets dans ma poche; mais, ma foi! bonnet blanc, blanc bonnet, c'etait pour moi la même chose, et j'ai pris le premier venu.' Un autre, à peu de distance de Paris, répondait à un de mes amis: 'Je ne connaissais ni l'un ni l'autre; alors, des deux, j'ai pris le bulletin qui m'allait le mieux à l'œil.' C'était la forme des lettres qui l'avait décidé. *Un troisième veut savoir quel est le bon bulletin; on le lui dit, il va le mettre dans l'urne; le lendemain on lui demande ce qu'il a fait de l'autre.* 'OH! JE L'AI DONNÉ À PIERRE, QUI EST UN MAUVAIS GARS; IL A VOTÉ AVEC; C'EST BIEN FAIT, IL LE MÉRITE.'"—*Ibid.* p. 33.

Could there be a more exquisite illustration of the manner in which voting was regarded by the ignorant?

it. There is not a single function pertaining to government, even most remotely, which cannot be included within its gearing: notaries, attorneys, bailiffs, clerks, are all embraced. Centralization, if it cannot obtain from all these a formal and hearty support, imposes upon them at least neutrality." *

In other words, if, in our own country, the governors of the States, the judges of all the courts, the sheriffs, the police officers, the county commissioners, the mayors of the cities, the appraisers, the collectors of taxes and tolls, the officers and conductors of railroads, were all appointed by the government at Washington, and were responsible to that government alone, we should have in form, if not in spirit, something like the centralization which prevailed in France. Nor, indeed, was this all. M. Delord assures his readers that the police officers, as the more immediate agents of the executive, were specially "charged to stimulate the zeal of the local authorities. They were not content to enter into the house of the peasant; they penetrated into the deliberative assembly of the municipal council, and openly reproached its members if their zeal appeared to decline. The commissioner of police acted upon the people by a kind of terror. An elector of the opposition was traversing a village on the Gironde between two gendarmes, and the

* Delord, *Histoire du Second Empire*, vol. III. p. 410.

commissioner of police cried out: 'There is a partisan of M. Decazes; that is the way we treat them.'"

The illustrations which I am about to present are all furnished by the general election in 1863. I have chosen this, not because it differed in any essential feature from the other contests of a kindred nature which took place under the Second Empire, but for the reason that the campaign was conducted on the part of the opposition with more spirit than any other, and that consequently it reveals the electoral system of the country in the strongest and clearest light. The facts presented are chiefly gathered from the third volume of "Delord's *Histoire du Second Empire*," and from "*La Lutte Electorale en* 1863, par M. Jules Ferry."

As usual, the imperial manifesto which announced the coming election, declared that it would be *free*. The prefects were called upon to address themselves only to the reason of the electors. M. de Persigny said: "Designate publicly, as in the preceding elections, the candidates who inspire the government with the most confidence. Let the people know who are the friends and who the enemies of the empire; and let them have full liberty to decide as they choose, but let it be done with a full understanding of the cause."

For a government which presents and supports a list of candidates, such an announcement would seem to be neither unnatural nor illogical; but the objectionable features of the method become glaringly apparent, when we learn that the government not only gave to the people what it called "a full understanding of the cause," but also that it threatened to withdraw all patronage from those who did not accept its conclusions. It was officially announced by Persigny himself, that his Majesty "could not allow about the electors any but men devoted actively and without mental reservation to the imperial dynasty." * Thus in the very beginning of the campaign every official was publicly informed that his continuance in office depended upon his devotion to the interests of the official candidates.

In view of these announcements, and in view of that system of centralization which brought everything within imperial reach, the people did not fail to see that it was of the greatest importance to have candidates nominated by the government who would be the least unacceptable to themselves. Accordingly, in some instances petitions were sent to the government, asking for the nomination of certain persons, a method of procedure which in itself was a complete abdication of all the principles of a free election. As early as August, 1862, "L'Echo de Vesoul" contained a petition, in which the electors of that district, despairing of being able to elect any candidate to whom the govern-

* Il ne peut appuyer auprès des électeurs que des hommes dévoués sans réserve et sans aurière-peusée à la dynastie impériale et à nos institutions.

ment was opposed, prayed the Minister of the Interior to have the goodness to designate for their suffrages the candidature of M. de La Vallette.

In due time the prefects of the departments announced the candidates, at the same time declaring that no public discussion of their merits would be allowed. The following extract from a discourse addressed to the electors of the *Haute-Loire* by the prefect of that department, will serve as an example of the way in which all free choice of candidates, as well as all discussion of their merits, was prevented:

"Under the last government, the electors, to supply the place of a general direction, which then they did not have, resorted to preliminary meetings, where the candidates declared their principles and submitted themselves to the choice of the people for nomination or rejection. To-day the administration fills, so to speak, the office of the preliminary meetings. We, the administrators, disinterested in the question, and representing only your collective interests, examine, appreciate, and judge of the candidates who are presented. After a full investigation (*mûr examen*), with the sanction of the government, we present to you the one who unites in himself the most sympathies, not as the result of our will, and still less of a caprice, but as the proper expression of your suffrages, and of your sympathies."

Numerous citations like this might be given to

show how completely the official candidates were the representatives of the Emperor. In all cases the Emperor chose the prefect, and the prefect, after conferring with the Emperor, nominated the candidate. To call the deputies who reached the *Corps Législatif* by such means, representatives of the people, is sheer absurdity. It is not so difficult to understand how Napoleon was willing to resort to such a system of duplicity, as it is to comprehend how an enlightened nation failed to be shocked and outraged by its application.

No sooner were the candidates in the field than the contest began. The overwhelming odds in favor of the official candidates now began to be seen. With free speech and a free press, the candidates of the people could at least have made a vigorous struggle; but with both of these agents taken away they are literally bound and gagged. Writing of this very election, M. Delord assures us that "the journals of the opposition had been killed almost everywhere, and there remained in each prefecture only such as were sustained by the government by means of secret subsidies and the judicial announcements." * As has already

* The *Evénement* appeared yesterday before the court of assize of the Seine, presided over by M. Perrot de Chezelles. The *Evénement* was suspended. The responsible editor was condemned to nine months imprisonment, and 3,000 francs fine. The author of the article, M. F. Victor Hugo, was condemned to 2,000 francs fine, and nine months imprisonment. The *Evénement* will have four of its editors in prison. Where will the government stop in this path? It will not stop,—it cannot. The *Reforme* has been condemned; the *Peuple* has been condemned; the *Vote Universel* has been condemned; the *Presse* has been

been shown, the general government at the very outset had prohibited meetings for the discussion of political topics. There remained, therefore, for the non-official candidates, none of the ordinary methods of publishing their views. They had sole recourse to the mails and to placards; and even these methods were constantly interfered with. The prefect, if he deemed it necessary, did not even shrink from interfering with the ordinary functions of the post in order to rob it of any hostile material. Just before the election, the suburbs of Grenoble, containing twenty-five thousand inhabitants, were deprived of all postal communication during twenty-four hours, for the sole purpose of allowing a vigorous and concerted attack to be made upon the opposition candidate, at a moment when it was impossible for him to defend himself. Scarcely was an opposition candidate announced, when the attacks of the official organs began. If he happened to reside in the district which he hoped to represent, both he and his family were placed under a surveillance which made their sojourn sometimes impossible. They were attacked with a bitter ferocity by the official journals of the locality. The candidate naturally felt the need of replying, and accordingly sought

condemned; the *Siècle* has been condemned; the *République* has been condemned; the *Assemblée National* only escaped condemnation by submission. And then came the turn of the *National*, of the *Ordre*, of the *Gazette de France*, of the *Journal des Débats*, and of the *Union*." Quoted from "*La Presse*" by Forsyth, "*History of Trial by Jury*," p. 361.

for a printer. If there happened to be two presses in the place, one of them was generally under the patronage of the prefect, and the other under that of the bishop. If by a rare chance one was found who claimed to be independent of these functionaries, he was still obliged to acknowledge his subordination to the laws for the control of the press,—laws by which his office could be closed at any moment.

But suppose, as it sometimes happened, that the candidate, by dint of management and the free use of money, surmounted all these obstacles. Three methods of distributing his documents were open to him: they could be committed to the mails; they could be distributed by hand in the street and at the places of resort; they could be put up as placards. Suppose that the candidate entrusts his fortunes to the post-office. One of two things was likely to happen: either the mass of his circulars found their way into the sewers, or, if they reached their destination, each one was accompanied with an official rejoinder. * Sometimes the candidate determined to rely chiefly or solely upon placards. In every French village the bill-poster is an official who depends upon the authorities for his position; it therefore requires more than ordinary courage in

* " On n'entendait parler de tous cotés dans les temps d'élection que de bulletins en retard, de circulaires égasées, voir même d'écrits électoraux jetés dans les égouts. Les pacquets assivaient quelquefois, mais, par un prodige singulier, entre chaque circulaire du candidat indépendent s'était glissée une circulaire du candidat officiel, et entre chaque bulletin libre un bulletin estampillé."—*Delord*, III. 407.

an *afficheur* to lead him to post the *affiche* of the independent candidate by the side of that of his opponent. Both in 1859 and 1863, it happened that candidates were reduced to the actual necessity of arming themselves with pincers and paste-pot, and putting up their own placards.

M. Clapier, a candidate in les Bouches-de-Rhone, with some faithful adherents spent the greater part of a night in flitting along the walls and dark corners of the city, and sticking up posters with their own hands. Imagine his estimate of the *freedom* of elections in France, when the next morning he found his bills covered with those of the emperor.

Another candidate, M. Aristide Dumont, of Noyen, more bold than his fellows, ventured to complain to the authorities when he found that his posters were destroyed as fast as he could put them up. His zeal subsided, however, when he was informed that, although there was indeed a law against the mutilation of posters, all complaints for violation of that law must be made by the administration itself. Thus it turned out that whether a man could be punished for destroying a placard depended upon the action of an imperial officer, and whether that officer would act depended upon the nature of the placard destroyed.

But there was one other method open to the candidate, namely, the distribution of documents at the hands of his personal friends. This service, however, required something of the spirit of a hero and martyr. The distributers were constantly assailed by the jeers and threats, and sometimes even by the blows of the officials. Commissioners, mayors, gendarmes, *gardes champêtre*, and *gardes des cantonniers* beset them at all points, and any considerable success was impossible. There are a number of authenticated instances where persons caught in this service were seized, and deprived of their liberty until after the election.

While these difficulties were besetting the non-official candidates, the candidates of the government held undisturbed possession of the field. Their posters everywhere decorated the walls of buildings, the trunks of trees, and the sign-posts at the cross-roads. The mails did for them faithful service, and the telegraph, which could never with safety be used by the opposition, was their ready and faithful messenger. The candidates themselves travelled from place to place in state, supported and protected by a retinue of officials. These latter never hesitated to take any advantage of their peculiar positions in order to accomplish their purposes. Even the inspectors of schools required of teachers not simply a passive but an active support of the official candidates.* So much for

* Numerous examples in support of this statement might be given. The Inspector of the Académie de la Côte d'Or wrote to the teachers: "Combattre les candidatures administratives, c'est combattre l'Empereur lui-même. En adopter et en patroner d'autres, c'est également servir et recruiter contre lui. *Ne pas les combattre, mais aussi ne pas les soutenir, c'est l'abandonner, c'est rester l'arme au pied dans la bataille. Votre indifférence me causerait de la surprise et du regret, votre hostilité serait à mes yeux une lâchetté coupable et sans excuse.*" The Inspector of the Académie des Vosges wrote to the teachers under his supervision in a similar strain.—*Delord*, III. 409.

what may be called the machinery of the campaign; let us now look at the means by which it was operated.

Under the system of centralization of which I have already spoken, all the public authority of a given district was under the control and direction of the prefect. Delord assures us that even the justice of the peace was his docile servant. If an elector originated or circulated any report injurious to the official candidate, the commissioner of police was directed to cause his arrest, and he was at once imprisoned. In such cases it was not even claimed that false charges were made; it was enough that they were injurious,—*une propagande gênante* being the usual expression. In vain did the non-official candidate offer bail for the good conduct and the appearance at trial of the accused; the prisoner was held until after the election, when he was generally dismissed without trial. In one instance, where the accused was no less a person than the municipal counsellor of Sainte-Foix, the prisoner was released on satisfactory assurance that he would leave the commune, and would not return until after the result of the election should have been declared.

The mayors of the cities were no less zealous than the justices of the peace. The manner in which they were expected to perform their duties may be judged of by the mandate of the prefect of La Manche, which is given merely as a sample of its kind. "Gentlemen," said he to the mayors of his province, "if you do not expect to vote for the official candidate, resign your scarf the day before election, in order that it may not be taken away from you the day after." Perhaps the threat was hardly needed; at any rate, there was no hesitation on the part of the mayors in making themselves the most active agents of the official candidate. The mayor of Ouistreham appealed to his people in these terms: "Inhabitants of Ouistreham, agents who are paid for so doing, boast of being able to make you vote against the candidate of the government. I know your spirit too well to believe that you will allow yourselves to be influenced by any means whatever. Here you have but one sincere friend, and that is I! And when I say to you: Vote for Monsieur Bertrand, it is because this vote is in your dearest interests!" The mayor of Jonvelle warned the electors of his precinct that the opposition candidate, Monsieur d'Andelarre, was "the protector of the party of the nobility and the clergy—the party which wished to see again such times as those seen when our grandfathers were obliged in turn to beat the water and thus impose silence upon the frogs in order that the sleep of this or that marquis, or this or that prior, might not be disturbed. Electors, know that in voting for Monsieur Galmich, you vote for yourselves, for your honor, for progress, for the Emperor who loves you; love him also! *Vive la France régénérée! Vive l'Empereur!*" The mayor of Kermania even mounted the pulpit on Sunday in the place of the curé; and preached in favor of the official candidate.

Illustrations might be multiplied, but it is perhaps unnecessary. In all parts of France, as might be shown by examples in abundance, the mayors brought the full weight of their official position to bear upon the result. The full significance of this interference with the free expression of the will of the people will be understood only as it is remembered that the mayors in France were not elected by the people, but were appointed by the Emperor. Moreover it must be kept in mind that the authority of the mayor over the voters of his district was in many respects similar to the authority of a custom-house officer in the United States over his subordinates. Both are officers of the general government, and both have the power to make the interests of their official inferiors depend upon the nature of their votes. If this comparison should seem to any one to be unjust to the French, I have only to refer to the array of threats and promises given in the pages of Ferry and of Delord.

But the work of the mayors, as was well understood, did not stop with threats and promises. They everywhere betook themselves to the polling-booths, in order to exercise an active *surveillance* over the work of voting. To a foreigner who simply reads the law, it would seem that ample provision had been made for the protection of the voter. It was specifically required that the election should be by *secret* ballot; a fact which would seem to be sufficient guarantee that the elector would be insured in the privilege of voting as he wished; and yet it was found to be not difficult to evade the provisions of the statute. It was necessary that those who had promised and threatened should have some means of knowing positively whether a given elector would be entitled to the promised reward, or whether, on the contrary, he would be deserving of the threatened punishment. To accomplish this end various devices were resorted to, any one of which would raise an irresistible outcry of indignation in any free country. A common method was to post along the approach to the ballot-box a double line of military and civil officers, each one of whom was commissioned to examine the ballot, and in case of need to exchange the non-official for the official.* In other places the official ballots were printed upon paper which was easily recognized.† The law that the voting should be secret was interpreted to mean that the ballot should not be

* "Les électeurs de la campagne, pour se rendre dans la salle du scrutin, sont obligés de traverser une sorte de couloir où secretaire de la mairie; officiers de pompiers, brigadiers de gendarmerie, fourriers de ville, gardes champêtres, cantonniers, sont en permanence et demandent à chaque electeur son bulletin, qu'ils remplacent par le bulletin du candidat officiel si celui qu'ils ont porte le nom du candidat de l'opposition."—*Delord*, III. 416.

† "Quelquesuns auraient bien envie de voter pour l'opposition en s'en rapportant au secret du vote guaranti par la loi, mais le candidat du gouvernement a écrit son nom sur du papier transparent, et pour plus de précaution, le maire à envoyé aux electeurs dont il se méfie le bulletin officiel piqué ou collé sur leur carte d'electeur."—*Ibid.*

opened or scrutinized by those in official charge of the election; accordingly there was no protection whatever for the elector against the interference of the mayor and those other dignitaries who had no such official connection. Even when those in charge of the boxes performed their duty faithfully, of what consequence was it after the elector had already been robbed of his non-official vote, and forced to appear before them with the government ballot only? There is the best of authority for affirming that in many instances the mayors not only seized and destroyed non-official ballots, but that they also declared that whatever the number of votes procured by the candidate of the opposition, the government candidate would be elected.* It is further to be said that the law requires the ballot-boxes to be sealed, a requirement which it would not seem very difficult to fulfil; and yet we are gravely assured that the means for carrying out this law were in many of the communes so incomplete, that the votes were actually cast, sometimes into a hat, sometimes into a soup or salad bowl, and sometimes even into the mayor's pocket, held open for that purpose by the mayor himself and by an assistant.†

* "Un grande nombre de maires ouvrent les bulletins et déchirent ceux des opponants, affirmant; d'ailleurs que quelque soit le nombre de suffrages obtenus par le candidat de l'opposition, le candidat du gouvernement sera élu, et, comme pour donner plus de poids à leur affirmation, ils offrent de parier cent contre un que les choses se passeront ainsi."—*Delord*, III. 417.

† "L'Apposition des scellés sur la boîte du scrutin ne préoccupait guère ces fonctionnaires. Ils laissaient au brigadier de gendarmerie

It would be easy to multiply examples similar to those which have already been given, but it is quite unnecessary. I should not, indeed, have prolonged the subject so far as I have already done, but for the necessity of bringing forward actual proofs of the pressure which was so constantly and so successfully used. Nothing but a presentation of facts is a sufficient answer to the arguments of those who found their support of Napoleon III. on the belief that from first to last he enjoyed the unswerving support of his people.

Now, I think there can be no question that a support gained in the manner which I have attempted to show is far worse for a nation than any open opposition to its government can be. It is making use of popular institutions as a mask behind which to hide a system of oppression and tyranny; it is prostituting the cause of freedom, and making it subordinate to the ends of despotism. If a people are to be made political slaves, let them at least be spared the mockery of sham-liberty, lest they bring all liberty into discredit, and all free institutions into contempt. It may be that an imperial government is the best government for France (though I do not believe that

ou un maitre d'école le soin de se confirmer à cette prescription de la loi, assez difficile, du reste, à remplir avec un matériel électoral tellement incomplet que *dans un grand nombre de communes on votait soit dans un chapeau, soit dans un saladier, soit dans une soupière et, à défaut de ces recipients, dans la poche du maire tenue entrebâillée* par lui et par l'adjoint ou par le garde champêtre."—*Delord*, III. 417.

such is the case); it is certain that so long as moral principles apply to the welfare of nations, as they do to the welfare of men, any government founded and sustained by such a system of *duperie*, to use the forcible word of Taine, as was that of Napoleon III., will end in weakness and ruin. What Shelley said of men as a possibility, may be said of governments as a certainty; and for the reason that with governments the end of all things is in this life:

"... . He who gains by base and armed wrong,
Or guilty fraud, or base compliances,
May be despoiled; even as a stolen dress
Is stript from a convicted thief, and he
Left in the nakedness of infamy."

But even this is not all. Not only is the government overthrown, but the political life of the nation is paralyzed. "Nous n'avons pas de vie publique en France," wrote M. Taine, two years after the fall of Paris; and the explanation of the truth is in the fact that the public has been so often duped and deceived by the government, that it no longer cares what the government is. That the nation was not cured of its political ills when monarchy was overthrown and republicanism was established, the world had startling evidence when M. Gambetta, not long since, produced in the Assembly a Circular of the Minister of the Interior, which asked the prefects for the names of such political journals as were capable of becoming friends to the government. The incident affords a new illustration of Virgil's words:

> "Facilis descensus Averno;
> Noctes atque dies patet atri janua Ditis
> Sed revocare gradum superasque evadere ad auras
> Hoc opus, hic labor est."

DECLINE AND FALL.

"We shall get rid of Napoleon in a few years, perhaps in a few months; but there is no saying how much mischief he may do in those years, or even in those months."—DE TOCQUEVILLE (in 1851), *Memoir and Remains*, II. 197.

"Plus on réfléchit sur la nature et les conditions de cet établissement, soi-disant monarchique, soi-disant constitutionel, soi-disant conservateur que le cour des choses, plus peut-être que la volonté de l'homme, nous impose aujourd'-hui, plus on demeure convaincu qu'il ne tient à rien et n'a point d'avenir; que la moindre pierre d'achoppement lui sera fatale, qu' aux approches du premier orage, des premiers embarras sérieux, du premier revers de fortune * * * * nous rentrerons, à pleines voiles, en révolution, nous verrons cette Babel crouler, a son tour, par la confusion des langues, par la discorde et la dispersion des ouvriers qui l'ont élevée."—DE BROGLIE, *Vues sur le Gouvernement de la France* (1861), p. lxvi.

CHAPTER X.

DECLINE AND FALL.

THERE are few things in history more interesting than the persistency of certain national traits. The words which, two hundred years before Christ, Cato the Elder used with peculiar felicity in describing the Gauls of his day, are equally applicable to the French of the present time.*

This same persistency, notwithstanding the numerous revolutions that have taken place, shows itself in the most fundamental relations of the governing and the governed. In England, and indeed wherever that which may be called the Anglo-Saxon idea of government prevails, the accountability of every executive officer is insisted on and acknowledged. I think it may be said that if there is any one thing which, more than all others, characterizes Anglo-Saxon institutions, it is the perpetual responsibility, under the law, of the governing to the governed. In theory, the English king can do no wrong; and yet, whenever wrong is done by the executive, the English people have a sure and a lawful remedy by means of impeachment.

* "Plera que Gallia duas res industriosissime persequitur; rem militarem et argute loqui."

Since the reign of Edward III., every English minister has known, or should have known, that no command of royal master would shield him from disgrace, or even death, in case of violation of the law. The people have kept in their own hands the means of lawfully punishing all executive transgressors, and executive transgressions have, in consequence of this fact, been comparatively infrequent.*

In France, however, a theory fundamentally different has prevailed. When the nation emerged from the middle ages, a permanent army was established, and a permanent tax for its support was imposed. These facts placed the king beyond the control of the people. As the impost appeared to be levied in no sense for the needs of the collective whole, but rather as a tribute imposed by strength upon weakness, its payment was a necessary humiliation, while successful resistance was tantamount to a title of honor. The nation, therefore, soon found itself divided into two classes: those who were strong enough to resist payment, and those who were so weak as to be obliged to pay. Sums levied upon the people belonged by right to the king, who disposed of the money received according to his fancy. Taxes were imposed upon the feeble, while the strong and the noble remained exempt from all payment. This condition of affairs, so long as it existed, was absolutely fatal to the

* This subject, as the reader will probably remember, is ably discussed by Lieber, *Civil Liberty*, chaps. V. and XXXIII.

liberty of the people; and, bad as this was, what was almost infinitely worse, it was fatal to anything like a law-abiding spirit in the nation at large. One has only to look into the history of France at any time from the accession of Louis XI. to the days of Louis XIV., to see that the element of *force* had become quite predominant over the element of *law*, and that as time progressed, matters, in this respect, were growing worse and worse.

Royal despotism attained its height in the latter half of the seventeenth century. At this period the nobles had been reduced to the condition of valets; the better class of burgesses imitated the nobles, and the lowest orders imitated the burgesses. The state was personified in the king, and the people sank into habits the most servile. The consequence was an age of feebleness, of caprice, of infatuation.

When Louis XVI. came into power he manifested the best of intentions; but he was naturally weak, and consequently was incapable of performing the difficult task set before him. He tried various reforms, always without success. His efforts only made it certain that neither the nobility, nor the clergy, nor the parliaments, nor the industrial corporations, would consent to reform; at the same time it was becoming daily more and more certain that the opinions of the people would not be satisfied without reform everywhere. Hence, when the revolution broke out, it was a revolution against institutions; and it was not unnatural that, when the former slaves became masters, they exercised the same arbitrary powers that their own masters had exercised before them. They had been schooled in a government habituated to falsehood and to the employment of *coups de force*, and they could hardly be expected, on coming into power, to abandon a habit which, confirmed by a practice of three hundred years, may be said to have become national and universal.

It was for this reason that the revolutionary government was found to afford little better security than had been afforded by that which it had overthrown. The same false ideas concerning the powers of those in office prevailed; the same lack of responsibility was everywhere manifested. Accordingly we see that, during all the turmoils which intervened between 1789 and 1851, however much the various governments differed from one another in their secondary characteristics, in this one essential feature of every good government they were all alike deficient, namely, that they afforded to the governed no guarantee whatever that their rights would be respected by the governing. The uniform effort of the person or persons in power has been, not to administer the government for the greatest good of the people, but to confirm that power in such a manner that it could be held against every emergency. That "perversion" of authority from its legitimate purpose, which, as Aristotle declared, must, under such conditions, ensue, has been the uniform result.* If we except the single reign of Louis Philippe, it may be said that the tendency after every revolution has been to allow the executive to absorb the legislative and the judicial branches of the government, and that against the abuses which have just as uniformly ensued, the people have had no remedy but the desperate remedy of revolution.

Perhaps it would have been asking too much of Napoleon III. to demand that he should form an exception to this general method; be that as it may, the thinking portion of the nation soon learned that the old process of absorption was rapidly taking place. In the last chapter I endeavored to show how the results of universal suffrage were made to subserve the imperial policy; it now remains to examine the other features of the same reign, and to point out the consequences to which they naturally and inevitably led.

There is, perhaps, nothing more essential to the existence of liberty in a nation than the freedom of the press. In the small republics of ancient times the people received political education and political knowledge in the popular assemblies. Every question of general interest was then discussed in the presence of all the people. The orator was at once the schoolmaster and the editor; the tribune was

* When the one, the few, or the many direct their policy to the common good, such states are well governed; but when the interest of the one, the few, or the many who are in office is alone consulted, a perversion takes place.—*Aristotle*, *Politics*, bk. III. chap. VII.

the school and the newspaper. It is but a truism to say that if the people at large are to take a part in the government of the nation, there must be some means by which they can learn how the government is carried on. In modern times the printing-press has taken the place of the tribune, and it is, therefore, the only means by which such information can be disseminated.

In order that the truth may be known, evidence must be sifted. There must be liberty to testify on either side of every question. The freedom to deny must be as complete as the freedom to assert. Every free government is undergoing a constant process of trial at the bar of public opinion, and the evidence on which the people are to work up their verdict comes chiefly from the emanations of the press. Books and newspapers are the main witnesses. Any intelligent people would scout at a court of justice which should permit testimony on one side only; and precisely for the same reason a people ought to insist that its press should be allowed to represent every shade of opinion. It should have absolute freedom, and then should be held accountable for the abuse of that freedom, just as a witness in a court of justice is held accountable for perjury. Under no other circumstances can a people be sure that it is receiving the truth, and hence it is, that all other liberties rest for their security upon liberty of the press. Bagehot has well said that "no state can be first-rate which has not a government by discussion," * and he might have added that no discussion is of value unless it is free.

Journalism in France has not been the result of slow growth, as it has in England. It sprang into full-armed strength from the brow of the Revolution, and it threw itself at once into the heat of the struggle. It attacked parties and powers with a ferocity absolutely unknown to the press of England or America. The almost unvarying consequence has been, that whenever the party attacked has found itself in power, it has turned the tables and annihilated its journalistic enemies.

This habit, which has long survived the Revolution, results from a confusion of the ideas of liberty and license. To recur to the simile which I used above, it is just as necessary in a court of justice that the witness should know that he can testify nothing but the truth, as that he should have liberty to testify the whole truth. It is just as essential that the perjurer should be punished, as that the witness should be allowed his liberty. For precisely the same reasons, the laws against libel should be sharply defined and vigorously carried out. It would be impossible to show that a witness who injures another by means of libellous charges is less worthy of punishment than is the witness who secures the conviction of an enemy by means of perjury. In France, however, this principle seems never to have been fully understood,

* *English Constitution*: Introduction to Second Edition, p. 71.

or at least never to have been generally admitted and applied. The press has been kept in chains. Whenever its shackles have been stricken off it has fallen into the wildest license, and then the people have demanded its destruction. The spirit which, ever since the Great Revolution, has uniformly prevailed, has been the spirit of a constant and an active supervision. It is needless to say that such a spirit is altogether incompatible with true development. Occasionally the demand for freedom from supervision has prevailed, and the result, in such cases, has been that the journals have turned upon their masters, like wild beasts broken loose from their cages. "I come to attack the true assassins of the country," cried Talot, in the Council of Five Hundred ; "I come to denounce a score of blackguards (gredins) who occupy themselves with public opinion and who are tearing the government to pieces. The clubs rendered service at the beginning of the Revolution, presently they ended in corruption and danger. Every journal is a migratory club, preaching revolt and disobedience to the laws. It is impossible that a government should subsist and establish order in the midst of such destructive elements. We must have a law to curtail the liberty of the press, or else we must give to every man the same liberty to break the head of his calumniator."*

* Il faut une loi qui réprime enfin la liberté de la presse, ou bien permettre à chacun de se servir de la même liberté pour *presser les omoplates* de son calomniateur."—*Delord, Hist. du Second Empire*, vol. II. p. 166.

The experience of the nation, after the Revolution of 1848, was of a similar nature to that indicated by the speech of Talot. The same causes once more produced the same results. The violence of the revolutionary journals was exceedingly intense, and no method revealed itself to the people by which that violence could be counteracted. They saw no method of restraining it but by imposing upon it a perpetual silence. In speaking of this very period, De Tocqueville says: "The language of the press was never more inflamed, nor their clamors more loud, than at the moment when they were to have imposed upon them fifteen years of silence. If one desires to know the true power of the press," continues he, "one must pay attention not only to what it says, but also to the manner in which it is heard. It is this very fervor which sometimes announces feebleness and presages the end. It shouts so loud only because its auditors are deaf, and it is this very deafness of the public which permits it, on occasion, to be reduced to silence with impunity."*

We are now prepared to consider the condition of the press under the Second Empire.

The law of 1852 placed all the journals under the jurisdiction of the administration. The Minister of the Interior alone had the right to appoint and dismiss editors-in-chief on the recommendation of the owners. No change in the editorial

* De Tocqueville, *Œuvres et Correspondences inédites*, quoted by Delord, vol. II. p. 169.

corps or in the proprietorship of any journal was of binding force without an authorization from the minister. Besides these conditions,—enough in themselves to stifle all journalistic enterprise,—it was decreed that the judicial decisions should be announced only in such papers as the government should designate. These announcements being in France a source of great revenue, the decree amounted to a perpetual subsidy of the journals indicated, and an enticing bait held out to journals in especial need of money. All foreign journals, excepting such as might receive authorization, were denied circulation in France.*

But even these precautions were deemed insufficient. In 1853, all newspapers were required to make a large deposit in the way of *caution-money*. The result was not only that the journals were kept in constant fear that their money would be forfeited, but also that the smaller journals, especially those in the country, were actually driven out of existence. Delord assures us that this single decree made the publication of cheap political journals impossible. It annihilated the small papers, and raised the price of the large ones.

If, at any time, the course of a journal was not satisfactory to the Minister of the Interior, some charge or other was preferred, and a trial was instituted. This investigation, in order to have the appearance of fairness, must be before a jury, but, in order that it might always issue to the satisfac-

* Delord, vol. II. p. 173.

tion of the government, the jury was selected from the correctional police.*

The circulation of any matter considered objectionable by the government brought an official warning from the minister; and after three such warnings, the paper might, at the option of the same authority, be suspended. Often this right of supervision took a preventive form. Whenever anything occurred the publicity of which seemed undesirable, the minister was authorized to prevent even its bare mention.

It would be a great mistake to suppose that this right of supervision was a mere privilege of which the government did not take occasion to avail itself. One has only to read the chapter of Delord devoted to this subject, to see that the office charged with the care of the press was far from being a sinecure. This author has given an array of evidence to show, not only that the supervision was most active and most uninterrupted, but also that it even descended to details of the most trifling and insignificant nature.†

* Delord, vol. II. p. 173.

† For example, the *Constitutionel* received its two warnings for having expressed a doubt concerning the correctness of a note in the *Moniteur*. A Protestant minister wrote in a Protestant religious journal, that "Five persons had just abjured at Edinburgh the errors of Roman Catholicism," whereupon the paper containing the notice received an immediate "warning." In the course of fourteen months under the administration of Maupas there occurred ninety-one "warnings" and three suspensions.—*Delord*, vol. II. p. 195. The same author says: "Le feuilleton de théâtre à été plus d'une fois averti d'avoir à prendre garde à ses opinions sur les pirouettes des demoiselles du corps de ballet de l'Opéra."—Vol. II. p. 198.

It would have been a marvel indeed if the amount of the caution-money exacted, and the silence imposed upon all adverse opinions, had not driven a majority of the newspapers out of existence. Most of them gave up the struggle in disgust; the few that were strong enough to continue were made to feel that the sword of Damocles was constantly over their heads.

It would be incorrect to suppose that no effort was made to change this state of affairs. From time to time a voice of protest was raised, but the result was always unsatisfactory and discouraging. In 1861, just after the Emperor had given somewhat more liberty of debate to the legislative body, Jules Favre protested against the laws controlling the press as utterly inconsistent with the pretensions of the government. "I fearlessly assert," exclaimed he, "that, as matters now stand, there is no press in France but a government press, no opinion professed except the opinion dictated or authorized beforehand by the administration itself. Liberty must be restored to the press! As long as it is withheld" (cried he, addressing the minister), "you will meet here a determined enemy, who, on every opportunity, will proclaim to the country that the wish to retain arbitrary power is in itself a confession of incurable weakness." But even these courageous words could effect nothing. "Do not imagine," said the minister in reply, "that the grand act of the 24th of November is one of those concessions under favor of which the enemy, already in the environs, finishes by penetrating into and mastering the fortress." Thus all words of protest were simply thrown away.

It needs to be said, moreover, that literature of a more substantial form was subject to the same degrading conditions. Every bookseller and every printer had to take out a government license, and this license was liable to be withdrawn in case of any offence. This fact made it impossible to carry any political work of character through the press. A process of emasculation often had to take place, before any publisher would accept the manuscript. In many instances authors, in order to get their ideas and their testimony before the world, were obliged to publish an unexpurgated edition in a foreign country.*

In the rural districts of France matters were still worse. There the book-trade is carried on exclusively through the medium of licensed pedlers. Under the pretext of moral and religious supervision, every work intended for sale had to be inspected at the Bureau of the Interior, and every volume offered had to bear the seal of imperial approbation. The law amounted to absolute interdiction of every work not acceptable to the government.

* This was the case with the *Mémoires* of Guizot,—perhaps the most important contribution to the history of France since the Revolution. That such a work should be obliged to go to Leipsic for publication, and have printed upon the title-page of every volume, "*Edition interdite pour la France*," was as great a disgrace to the nation as it was an advertisement to the work.

Now, of this policy, there could of course be but one result. As a matter of simple fact, public opinion was absolutely destroyed. When Monsieur Taine wrote, in 1870, "We have no public life in France,"* he simply recorded a natural consequence of a deliberate policy.

Under Louis Philippe, and even under the Bourbons before him, something had been done to enlighten public opinion concerning political affairs. These means of enlightenment, when suffrage was suddenly made universal, should in all reason have been increased and extended. De Tocqueville declared in 1851: "Thirty-seven years of liberty have made a free press and free parliamentary discussion necessaries to us;"† but instead of these there was imposed upon the nation a more rigid surveillance of the press than had ever been known, and consequently the people under the Second Empire were characterized by a degree of political ignorance which, to those who have not studied its causes, is absolutely marvellous. As men were ignorant of what was done by the government, they knew not what to think about it; and, as they knew not what to think, their ignorance soon lapsed into the still more deplorable phase of almost absolute indifference.

Soon after the establishment of Napoleon III. the same keen observer, whom I have so often quoted, wrote in answer to the inquiries of Beau-

* *Du Suffrage Universel*, p. 28.
† *Memoirs and Remains*, vol. II. p. 196.

mont: "It is hard to ascertain the real state of public opinion in my department, so great is the reserve with which individuals express themselves, partly from prudence, and partly from not knowing what to think. There is almost universal silence. No people, while thinking of nothing but politics, ever talked of them so little." *

In the year following he wrote to a friend in Germany: "Remember that in consequence of the loss of interest in politics, and of the liberty of the press, the country has come to be a place to which neither air nor light ever penetrate. It was always a sort of cave, and now they have stopped up the last crevice."†

Still more emphatic and striking is a passage which the same author wrote a year later. Referring to the condition of literature and of the press, he used these remarkable words: "Our present state in this respect is unlike anything one finds in the history of the last two hundred years; and of all the changes that time has effected in our habits and character, this is one of the most extraordinary. In the most literary nation of Europe, in that which has convulsed itself, and convulsed the world by means of abstract ideas taken from books, a generation has arisen up, taking absolutely no interest in anything which is written, attaching no importance to anything but events, and only to a few facts—those which are evidently,

* De Tocqueville, *Memoirs and Remains*, vol. II. p. 170.

† *Memoirs and Remains*, vol. II. p. 210.

directly, and immediately connected with physical well-being. Of all the aristocracies, that which has been most utterly destroyed by the Revolution is the aristocracy of literature." *

I turn now from the condition of the press under the Second Empire to the condition of education. It will be necessary to go into a discussion of details only so far as may be requisite to show its political influence and its political tendency.

In the reign of Louis Philippe, and under the direction of Guizot and of Villemain (each of whom was for a time Minister of Public Instruction), much was done to elevate the condition of educational institutions. The influence of the church, whose cramping hand had so long held the schools in its grasp, was at last considerably weakened. During that reign the government determined that the degree of *Bachelier-ès-Lettres* should be conferred only on those who had studied in schools open to government inspection. This decree was aimed at the schools of the Jesuits, and its influence was altogether wholesome.

On the accession of Napoleon III. this policy was reversed. The church in France since the Restoration had become more and more ultramontane.*

* *Memoirs and Remains*, vol. II. p. 247. I have quoted so largely from De Tocqueville, not because there is not abundant testimony to the same facts in the other writers, but because upon every political question which he touched, I deem his words of transcendent importance.

† "L'ultramontanisme, representé et défendu par des hommes comme de Maistre, de Bonald, Lammeunais, avait fait de notable progrès sous la Restoration."—*Delord, Hist. du Second Empire*, vol. II. p. 210.

The Revolution of 1830 was anti-Catholic in its sympathies; and largely, for that very reason, the government of Louis Philippe was never able to command the hearty sympathy of the church. Catholics welcomed the Revolution of February, 1848, with enthusiasm, * not because they saw at the time anything better in prospect, but because it overthrew an enemy, and because they believed that whatever happened, matters would not be in a worse condition. Again, the clergy did not hesitate to array themselves against the republic, and to second the efforts of Louis Napoleon. Both the clergy and the laity strove earnestly, first for his election to the presidency, and then for his support after the usurpation of December. Universal suffrage had revealed to the priests their power, and they saw that the new *régime* would put into their hands a means of influencing the government such as they had not enjoyed since the Restoration.

Napoleon did not hesitate to show his appreciation of their services in his behalf. The law of Louis Philippe to which I referred above was immediately repealed; the Jesuits were reinstated in their chairs of instruction. But this was not sufficient. It was necessary not only that there should be Jesuit schools, where instruction might be given in secret, but also that there should be adopted a method by which all instruction, public as well as private, might be controlled. Accord-

* Delord, vol. II. p. 211.

ingly, De Falloux, the first Minister of Public Instruction under the Empire, inaugurated his administration by appointing a commission to prepare a law for the reconstruction of the schools.

In due time a scheme was reported. Its most important provisions were the following: The General Council of Public Instruction was not essentially modified (probably because it was already under the direct control of the Emperor), except that in future it was to contain three archbishops or bishops, to be chosen by their colleagues. In each department a subordinate educational board, known as the Academical Council, was established; and of this, the bishop, the prefect, and the attorney-general were to be members. The academical degrees, which had hitherto been essential to all instructors, were declared to be no longer necessary either to presidents or professors or subordinate teachers. Finally, the presidents of such religious corporations as were acknowledged by the state were authorized to grant teachers' certificates without restriction.*

The consequences of this new law were twofold: on the one hand it extended vastly the powers and influence of the clergy; on the other, it completed the alliance between the clergy and the Emperor. Religious associations, devoted especially to the work of instruction, sprang up in all parts of France. The arts and the sciences came once more to be very generally taught by

* Delord, *Hist. du Second Empire*, vol. II. p. 214.

Dominicans and Benedictines. Teachers who in the time of Louis Philippe had received professional training, now found themselves without occupation; for their places were filled by men whose technical education had been acquired in the monastery and the pulpit. There were in the country eighteen hundred and thirty-six religious establishments, and these called into existence, under the new law, no less than seventeen hundred and forty-nine schools devoted to different grades of instruction. Besides these, there were established by the Jesuits sixteen colleges, which were sustained by subscription and private munificence.* When these facts are remembered, it will not be considered strange that the church was the firmest supporter of the Emperor, and that, when the latter needed a sustaining vote of the people, we find the *curé* and the *préfect* working hand in hand. Thus the new law strengthened the Emperor, while at the same time, by means of the inferior instruction for which it provided, it weakened the nation at large.*

But notwithstanding these efforts of the Imperial government to enlist the pulpit and the press in its own support, there was slowly developed in the country an opposition, which, as time advanced, became really formidable. The means

* Delord, *Hist. du Second Empire*, vol. II. p. 217.

† The spirit of the church in its relations to the press is discussed at length by Delord, in the fourteenth chapter of his fourth volume. By numerous examples he gives sufficient proof, that the church "soutenait en outre une guerre ardente et quotidienne contre la presse libérale et democratique."—Vol. IV. p. 541.

which never failed to subordinate the masses of the ignorant to the will of the Emperor, only provoked a more decided opposition from the intelligent and the educated. This opposition gradually penetrated the masses, so that, as we shall see, the hold of the Emperor upon the hearts of the nation was, toward the end of his reign, considerably weakened. The progress of this decline of popularity may be easily traced in the character and bearing of the different representative assemblies.

In order to understand this subject, it is necessary to bear in mind the fact that the Legislative Body had been degraded by the Constitution into a thing but little better than a court of record. In place of the free tribune which, in the days of Louis Philippe, had rung with the unrestrained utterances of orators like Guizot and Thiers and Lamartine, there was now only a species of representative committee empowered to approve, but not to amend, the laws proposed by the Emperor. There was a Senate, it is true, but this took no part in the work of legislation, except to decide upon the constitutionality of such laws as the Emperor might desire to propose. Finally, as if to withdraw every stimulus to oratorical effort, both the Senate and Legislative Body sat with closed doors.

The relief from fear of revolution and anarchy, so generally felt on the accession of Napoleon, and the system of official candidates adopted by the government were, when taken together, enough to secure a legislative body in which the liberal element was absolutely unrepresented. It is a remarkable fact that the first *Corps Législatif* of the Second Empire contained no element of opposition to the *régime* which had been established.

Before the election in 1857, however, this unanimity of support had been broken. The rural districts, thanks to the priests and the prefects, retained their loyalty; but the cities, where, in spite of the stringent press-laws, some intelligence of public affairs prevailed, could not be held under the yoke. The result of the canvass showed that, notwithstanding all the efforts of the government, five of its prominent candidates had been defeated, and that the course of the opposition was now to be represented by the impetuous eloquence of Picard, Ollivier, and Jules Favre.

It was not long after the election of these members before events took place which gave full play to all their powers. The attempt of Orsini upon the life of the Emperor, in January, 1858, was followed by the atrocious *loi de sureté général* which imposed fine, imprisonment, and even exile upon the utterance of opinions hostile to the Emperor or to his government. This law, followed by that system of *espionage*, which placed a secret spy in every *café* and on every street-corner, could not, with all the efforts of the government, be made acceptable. The courageous plain-speaking of the press, in the teeth of a merciless persecution, revealed to the Emperor the dangerous ground on which he was standing. The *Revue de Paris*, the *Assemblée Nationale*, and the *Manuel Général de l'Instruction Primaire* were suppressed; the *Siécle*, the *Gazette de France*, the *Constitutionel*, and the *Presse* were repeatedly warned, while the publisher of the latter was fined and imprisoned. But in spite of these vigorous measures on the part of the government, the opposition was undaunted, and the result was that the Emperor had to give way. The decree of November 24th, 1860, astonished the world by what looked like a return to parliamentary government. The Legislative Body received by this decree the right to amend bills presented by the government, to vote a reply to the address from the throne, to sit with open doors—and what was of the greatest importance—to enjoy the right of freedom of debate.

These concessions could not but excite an enthusiastic welcome on the part of the people. They were everywhere proclaimed as evidence of the Emperor's determination to promote the liberties of the nation. It was soon observed, however, that no concession of imperial power had really been made. The terms of the decree, when carefully scrutinized, will be seen to have granted nothing except freedom of debate. The *Corps Législatif* could now talk, but it could do nothing more. The right of amendment was nothing more than the right of suggestion, since the government was under no obligation to adopt any legislative measure whatever. The principal effect of the decree, therefore, was to enable the dissatisfied to make their complaints known, without giving them any means of making their power felt. Practically the only right conceded was the right to find fault. In an English Parliament or an American Congress this right is nothing to be dreaded, inasmuch as everybody knows that on the one hand, the moment the opposition can create a majority, it will have the means of enforcing its demands; and on the other, until this moment arrives, it will be practically powerless. The contest in these bodies, therefore, is at least theoretically, a contest of reason, in which the minority is constantly striving to convince the majority of its errors. In a French Assembly, where even the majority is destitute of real power, the object of discussion is altogether different. The true audience of the French legislator is not his fellow-members, whom it is of no earthly use, or of altogether secondary importance, to convert to his views, but the Emperor on the one hand and the people on the other. The consequence of this fact, taken in connection with the peculiarly ardent temperament of the typical Frenchman, is that, as Mr. Bagehot has vigorously observed,* the French assembly is far less deliberative in its character than is the representative body of either of the other great nations.

* In writing on this general subject, Mr. Bagehot says: "In the last but one of these essays I have tried to describe one of the mental con-

The Emperor in his speech from the throne, at the opening of the session in 1861, did not neglect to inform the legislature of the true import of the decree of November. "The legislative body does not, it is true," said he, "interfere in all the details of administration, but it is directly chosen by universal suffrage, and counts no functionary in its bosom. It debates measures with the most entire liberty; if they are rejected, the rejection is a warning which the government takes into account;* *but it neither gives a shock to power, arrests the course of affairs, nor forces upon the sovereign advisers in whom he cannot confide.*"

Of the freedom of debate afforded by the decree, the five members of the opposition at once availed themselves. The eloquent speech of Jules Favre on the liberty of the press, from which I have already quoted, was one of the results. The determination of the government, however, was in

ditions of parliamentary government, which I call 'rationality,' by which I do not mean reasoning-power, but rather the power of hearing the reasons of others, of comparing them quietly with one's own reasons, and then being guided by the result. But a French assembly is not easy to reason with. Every assembly is divided into parties, and in France each party—almost every section of a party—begins not to clamor, but to scream, and to scream as only Frenchmen can, as soon as it hears anything which it particularly dislikes. With an assembly in this temper, real discussion is impossible, and parliamentary government is impossible too, because the parliament can neither choose men nor measures. The French assemblies under the restored monarchy seem to have been quieter, probably because, being elected from a limited constituency, they did not contain so many sections of opinion; they had fewer irritants and fewer species of irritability."—*Walter Bagehot, The English Constitution, Second Edition; Introduction*, p. li.

"* *Un avertissement dont le gouvernement tient compte.*"

no way shaken. Driven at length to a kind of exasperation, M. Billault, speaking for his imperial master, used these defiant words: "All the foundations on which the government policy and the public security rest, the law of general safety, the control of the press, the patronage exercised by the government in the elections, are now attacked. But the very speeches we hear in this chamber prove clearly enough that the government cannot go farther without compromising itself. Gentlemen, in the presence of parties which are given to agitation, the government will not abandon the right, which it holds from the people, of preventing electoral assemblages where such meetings threaten danger; it will not abandon its right to support certain candidates in opposition to those of party nomination; it will not dissolve this chamber, which has so well served the country; it will not change the place of power conferred by the *plébéscite* of 1852."

After such an expression of imperial determination it was evident that nothing remained to be done but simply to create public opinion, and to wait until after the election of a new assembly.

The means used by the government to control the elections in 1863, I described somewhat in detail in the last chapter; it is, therefore, only necessary, in this connection, to note the results. In spite of all the efforts of prefects and priests, in spite, also, of the multitude of promises and threats which emanated from Paris and penetrated every hamlet of France, it was found, when the canvassing was completed, that the number of liberal representatives had been increased from five to thirty-six; while in Paris, of the nine opposition candidates, eight had been elected.

Still more indicative of the direction of the popular current were the facts revealed concerning the number of voters. Of an aggregate of about ten million electors, two million had been bold enough to vote for the opposition candidates, while more than two and a half millions had abstained from the polls. Of this unusual number of absentees, there could be but one explanation. No canvass had ever been conducted by the government with so much vigor. It is therefore impossible to suppose that its supporters had abstained in any considerable numbers. The absentees must have been either dissatisfied or indifferent; and as indifferentism must have generally given way before the pressure of governmental agencies, it is certain that dissatisfaction was the almost exclusive cause of absence from the polls. The result of the election afforded sufficient proof that the imperial *régime* was losing its hold on the sympathies of the people. At the present rate of departure, the government would be able to command scarcely a majority at the next election.

The gravity of this fact, however, seems to have made no impression upon the Emperor. The opposition, formidable as it had now become, was treated with an indifference bordering upon contempt. In reply to the address of the *Corps Législatif* in 1864, the Emperor administered this rebuke: "Let us each remain in our proper spheres; you, gentlemen, in enlightening and controlling the progress of the government, and taking the initiative in all that may promote the greatness and prosperity of France." That the Emperor was disposed to grant no abatement of his authority was made from time to time painfully manifest. In 1865 the *conseils généraux* of the Seine and Marne were bold enough to pass certain resolutions concerning their own interior organization, whereupon the resolutions were declared null and void by imperial decree.

During the latter part of this year the liberal party pressed vigorously their claims for reform. The relations of Prussia and Austria were becoming serious, and it was claimed with justice that a development of the decree of November 24th, 1860, would cement all parties into a firm support of the Emperor in any policy which he might find it best to pursue. They awaited anxiously, therefore, for the speech from the throne at the beginning of the new year. But all their hopes were disappointed. The imperial address contained an elaborate eulogy on the Constitution of 1852, and demonstrated clearly that no advance of liberal ideas was to be encouraged, or even tolerated. Then, too, as if to remove every possible doubt as to the purpose of the government, Persigny followed the Emperor's speech with an amplification in which he not only emphasized the eulogy, but also declared that the recent concessions which had been granted or promised were a mistake, " a violation of the true and admirable principle of authority." It thus became evident that an important reaction on the part of the government had taken place. While the nation was demanding a liberal policy in terms more and more unmistakable, the authorities were disposed to withdraw even the concessions which they had already made.

The effect of this policy was what it would seem that ordinary intelligence would have anticipated. The opposition in the legislative body, so far from being daunted, was considerably augmented. As a result of the tempestuous discussion that ensued on an amendment to the address calling for a development of the November decree, it was found that the minority of thirty-six had been increased to sixty-six. It was evident that the very parliamentary organization which the Emperor dreaded had been stimulated by the efforts which he had made to overwhelm it. " They refuse us the present, but they cannot keep from us the future," were the defiant words of the leader of the Left Centre. Following close upon these unsuccessful attempts to reform the interior administration came the war between Prussia and Austria, and all its momentous consequences. The unsuccessful efforts of the Emperor to secure, first a rectification of the Rhine boundary, and then the incorporation into France of the Duchy of Luxembourg, reinforced immensely the opposition in the French Assembly. The rise of Prussia, as the result of the war, was regarded throughout France as in some sort a disgrace to the French Government and the whole French people. This humiliation was laid at the door of the Emperor. It was categorically affirmed, during the stormy debates of 1867, that Bismarck, at the celebrated meeting at Biarritz, in 1865, had offered to the Emperor the Rhine frontier as the price of his support of Prussian policy, and that the offer had been declined, probably in expectation that the desired end would come about more naturally after the first battle had been fought. It was charged that the Emperor had anticipated the defeat of Prussia, and that he had believed an opportunity would be given for French interference and arbitration in such a manner as to lead to the coveted reward. The Emperor, it was said, had hoped to step between the combatants in order (after Prussia had received its first great disaster) to prevent too severe a punishment of the defeated nation; and he had anticipated a territorial compensation in return for this service.

All these anticipations had been frustrated. Not only had the government neglected to accept an offer which would have led to certain aggrandizement, but it had pursued a policy which had ended at once in national humiliation, and in the elevation to absolute supremacy, in Germany, of the nation's traditional enemy. A writer in the

Revue des Deux Mondes declares that the failure of the Emperor's diplomacy, and the consequent rise of Prussia, were everywhere regarded throughout France as "*une sorte de déchéance.*"

The feelings thus excited were considerably intensified by the issue of the Luxembourg affair. The Grand Duchy in question was granted by the Treaty in 1814, to the King of the Netherlands; and at the same time it was made a member of the German Confederation. To Prussia was given the important right to garrison the fortress. This right, through all the changes that had taken place in 1830 and 1837, had not been molested. When Prussia, however, in 1866, renounced her participation in the German Confederation, and that organzation in consequence was broken up, the question was raised whether Prussia should continue to exercise the right of holding the fortress. Prussia maintained the right in virtue of the fact that it had been granted to her by treaties which were in no way dependent upon the relations of Luxembourg to the Confederation. In the eyes of Napoleon, however, the territory afforded an obvious means of satisfying the national longing for additional strength on the Rhine.

Neither the Dutch king nor the Dutch nation attached much importance to the territory in question. Geographically it was completely detached from the Netherlands, and was surrounded by powers liable at any time to be more or less hostile. When, therefore, the Emperor of the French made advances to the King of the Netherlands, looking toward a purchase of the Grand Duchy, the intrigue was eagerly listened to. The private treasury of the Dutch king was always in need of supplies, and the affair, therefore, went on smoothly until it became necessary to make the negotiations public. On the side of the French government it was desired that the affair should be kept from Prussia, until the cession of the territory should be an accomplished fact; on the part of Holland, however, such a course was deemed altogether unsafe. Accordingly, on the same day that the king telegraphed to Paris that he had resolved to cede Luxembourg to France, he informed the Prussian ambassador at the Hague of his determination.

The affair caused intense excitement throughout Germany. Ever since the tenth century the Grand Duchy had in one way or another been a part of the fatherland, and public opinion was naturally outraged at the idea that it should be ceded to France. On the first day of April, Von Beuningsen of Hanover brought the matter, by means of an interpellation and a furious speech, before the North German Parliament. Bismarck replied to the excited interpellation and the fierce expressions which it called out, with most provoking calmness. He simply contented himself with regarding the parliamentary demonstration as amply justifying measures for putting the army on a war footing.

But while Germany was thus preparing for a possible emergency, the chancellor did not neglect to attempt peaceful measures. No sooner had he received information of the intrigue than he appealed to the parties of the Treaty of 1839, upon which the existence of Holland as a modern nation was founded. The result of this appeal was a conference of those powers at London on the 11th of May. Prussia consented to withdraw her garrison, whereupon the Grand Duchy was declared to be a neutral state under the collective guarantee of the powers that were parties to the Treaty. The territory was to belong to the reigning house of Nassau-Orange, and the town was to cease to be a fortress. What, then, was the real status of the question at the end of the affair? Simply that Prussia had completely frustrated the purpose of France, and had transferred the necessity of defending the Grand Duchy from herself to the leading powers of Europe.

It was while the enemies of the Napoleonic *régime* were busy in making all possible capital out of the Luxembourg question, that the sad termination of the imperial drama in Mexico was announced. On the 19th of June, 1867, while the Emperor was engaged in the ceremonies of an imperial *fête*, a despatch was handed to him containing the startling words: "Maximilian was shot to-day."

At a time when Napoleon had been confident that the United States would be permanently riven asunder, he had undertaken and accomplished the conquest of Mexico. It was soon found, however, that the exertions necessary to control the nation were altogether disproportionate to any advantages which France could hope to realize. The battle of Gettysburg, which changed the fortune of the Southern States, put a new aspect on the condition of affairs. Not only had the conquerers, at the end of 1863, failed to secure a general acknowledgment of their sway throughout the country, but they became aware that the United States, if restored, as they now seemed likely to be, would in no way tolerate a settlement of European Imperialists on the borders of the Union.

Such was the state of the question when Napoleon, to free himself from the further burden, succeeded in finding an Emperor for the young empire in the Archduke Maximilian of Austria. This prince consented to undertake the task only after the Emperor had succeeded in convincing him that he was generally desired by the Mexican people. On the 12th of June, 1864, he entered the capital of Mexico. At first he was to be supported by the French soldiers, but these were to be gradually withdrawn, and their places filled by Austrians and Belgians. The war against Juarez, the president of the legitimate Mexican Republic, dragged its weary length along and gave no promise of a termination; and yet, notwithstanding this fact, Napoleon decided, owing to the determined attitude of the government at Washington, to withdraw the French troops. Previous to the outbreak of the Austro-Prussian war, it was his purpose to accomplish the evacuation in three divisions: one to withdraw in November of 1866, one in March of 1867, and one in November of 1867.

The war in Germany, however, added a new factor to the problem, and the Emperor resolved to bring back the whole force early in 1867, urging Maximilian, meantime, to justify the act by resignation. This the Archduke declined to do; thereupon the Emperor left him to his fate.*

When the news of Maximilian's death reached Europe, the whole of France felt that her honor was affected by the sad catastrophe. The Mexican war had never been popular in the nation; and it was now claimed boldly, that under a parliamentary government, it would never have been undertaken. Those who had charged the Emperor with weakness after Sadowa, and had emphasized their charges after Luxembourg, now brought forward Mexico in the way of absolute proof of their positions. The time had been, they said, when the word of France was a power in Europe which no nation dared to disregard; but now every foreign question with which the Emperor became involved resulted only in national dishonor.

It was in the spirit of wounded pride, engendered by these several diplomatic failures, that the people of France entered upon the year 1867. Toward the Emperor there had never been so much ill-feeling; and the government saw the necessity of making concessions. On the 19th of

* Delord, *Histoire du Second Empire*, vol. IV. chap. XIII.

January Napoleon wrote to his minister a letter in which he marked out the line of policy to be pursued. "The discussions on the address to the throne," said he, "have proved nothing more than a wasteful treasury of words. They are to be abolished, and the right of ministerial interpellation, prudently regulated, is to be substituted in their place. In future the ministers are to be present in the chamber, and to take part in the debates; the law against public meetings is to be modified, and the supervision of the press is to be transferred from the discretionary power of the government to the tribunals of the correctional police."

If the Emperor had founded any hopes of a return of popular favor upon these concessions, he must have been bitterly disappointed. Neither his friends nor his enemies received them with any manifestations of satisfaction. It was at once pointed out that the right of interpellation now granted was quite identical with what had in the previous session been demanded by the minority of forty-six, and had been rejected by the supporters of the government as nothing short of an insult to the imperial power. The quick-witted Parisians were not slow to see and to point out that the Emperor, in granting what his friends had so vigorously characterized as an insult, had simply made either himself or his friends ridiculous. So far, then, as concerned the concession, it failed utterly to awaken any enthusiasm, while the suppression of freedom of debate, of course, awakened positive hostility.

The modification of the law against assembling for political discussions was scarcely less unsatisfactory. Meetings were allowed only within certain fixed dates, and even these were surrounded with so many minute regulations that no very considerable gain was realized. As if to be certain that no harm would result to the government from the new privilege, it was determined that "in any case the minister could forbid, and the prefect dissolve, such assembly at pleasure."

But the measure which attracted most attention, and which was of much the greatest importance, was the one which pertained to the control of the press. The penalties of arbitrary suspension were done away with, and in their place was substituted a system of exorbitant fines. Printers and publishers were relieved from the necessity of taking out a license; but all writers were liable to be deprived of political rights for five years,—a penality of unusual severity in France, where journalism is the principal avenue to political success. Thus it will be seen that the new law merely transferred the severity of the penalty from the publishers and printers to the writers,—a change which, though doubtless in the line of strict justice, could not but affect unfavorably the tone of the press toward the government.

The effect of the new law, however, showed that the people regarded it as of considerable importance. The mere abolition of the former arbitrary *régime* gave an immense impulse to the newspaper press. So completely had the discretionary powers of the minister crushed the provincial press in France, that seven of the largest towns, exclusive of Paris, with a population of about a million and a half, only possessed eleven daily newspapers, and the total circulation of these reached less than a hundred and thirty thousand.* In less than six weeks after the promulgation of the new law, thirty new papers had sprung up in Paris alone; and in the provinces, no less than sixty-five.

The influence of the new law was on the whole unfortunate. It was universally understood that the concession, if indeed the change was to be called such, had been made not to principle but to necessity. If greater freedom was to be granted to the press, it would seem that common-sense would have dictated that it should be done at a moment when the government was in popular favor, —at a time when it could afford to run the risk of severe criticism. As a fact, however, there had never been a period when there was so much discontent as at the moment when the press was relieved of its heaviest chains. It is impossible to conceive of anything more impolitic than the course of the Emperor in keeping the press muzzled during the days of his prosperity, and then,

* The whole subject of journalism under the Second Empire is ably treated by Delord, in vol. II. chap. IV. and vol. IV. chap. XV

when a series of political disasters had entangled him, in giving it freedom of speech. If popular feeling had been less pronounced and less intense, the folly of the action would have been less conspicuous; for under such circumstances writers would not have dared to defy inevitable conviction and excessive penalty. Now, however, no terrors of the kind daunted them. So long as a large share of the reading community regarded the Emperor as an implacable foe, writers enough were found who were ready to advance to mortal combat. The result of all was a year and more of bitter excitement, of endless press trials, of certain convictions, of excessive penalties.

The political condition to which these various mistakes, to call them by no harsher name, had brought the country at the end of the year 1868, was well calculated to excite the most serious alarm. Abroad the traditional hegemony of France was virtually gone, and at home the humiliating consciousness of this eclipse penetrated to every class and almost to every household. The rural population were wavering in their devotion to the Napoleonic name, and were beginning to despair of the future. The priesthood, generally alienated by the position of the Empire on the Roman question, stood ready at any moment "to change their blessing into an anathema, should their exclusive corporate interests so demand." The *bourgeoisie*, exasperated by the tricky, shallow, insecure, and time-serving policy of the government, held it up to scorn in contrast with their own earnest and honest struggles for the general enfranchisement. Finally the imperialist party itself, dissatisfied with the concessions made to their opponents, and distrustful of the temporizing policy of their master, seemed to be fast approaching the point of absolute dissolution. Such, in general, was the spirit of the nation when the time arrived for the election of a new assembly.

On the opening of the campaign it was found that liberal ideas had advanced so far that it was necessary to modify the ordinary methods of procedure. The official candidates, though as vigorously supported by the government as ever, were nevertheless obliged to disavow all relations with the prefects. The bribery and corruption and trickery which were resorted to, as we have seen, in 1863, were in no respect abated, though the government was obliged to throw around its operations something more of the appearance of fairness. Notwithstanding the gigantic efforts put forth in behalf of the official candidates, a counting of the ballots revealed the fact that three and a half million had dared to vote for the opposition, and that the *Corps Législatif* of 1869 would be a parliamentary body prepared to challenge the policy of the Emperor at every step. It required no power of second-sight to see how matters were drifting. In Napoleon's first *Corps Législatif* there had been no opposition whatever; in the Chamber of 1857 the opposition numbered only five members; in that of 1863, it counted forty-five; in that of 1869, it was scarcely in the minority. The situation was becoming desperate, and vigorous, if not desperate, measures had to be devised to meet it.

The course of the Emperor was the counterpart in folly, of the course he had pursued in his treatment of the press. So long as it was well disposed, he kept it chained and muzzled; when it was on the point of going mad, he unmuzzled it and turned it loose. So long as the *Corps Législatif* was overwhelmingly favorable to his *régime*, he denied it the right of the initiative; now that the number of his enemies was nearly or quite equal to that of his friends, he made haste to remove their restraints. By the decree of November 8th, 1869, he gave to the chamber the right to initiate legislation, made senators and deputies eligible to places in the cabinet, declared that each legislative body should decide upon its own internal organization, and determined that the budget should be voted on article by article rather than as a whole, and finally consented that amendments disapproved of by the government should be pronounced upon in the last appeal by the Chamber.

Had these important concessions been made at a time when the Emperor was strong enough in the legislature to control its action by legislative means, they would doubtless have subserved the real interests of the nation; under existing circumstances, however, their principal effect was to encourage the opposition by opening to it and placing in its hands a new means of making itself felt. The opportunity thus presented was not long neglected. It immediately became obvious that nothing short of most important and radical reforms would satisfy the chamber.

The programme put forward included the abolition of the laws of public safety and of official candidature, the suppression of the stamp on newspapers, the adoption of trial by jury in cases of *délits de presse*, decentralization of the government, and liberty of higher education. It was evident that if these measures should be adopted, and should be carried out with honesty and fidelity, the personal power of the Emperor would be destroyed forever. What was to be done? The Emperor did not hesitate. On the one hand, he accepted the programme of the reformatory party; on the other, he resolved to appeal to the people in the way of a *plébiscite.* By dismissing his ministry and calling Ollivier to the head of affairs, he endeavored to retain the favor of the *Corps Législatif*; by appealing to the people, he hoped to gain a new lease of power. The sixth article of the Constitution declared: "The Emperor is responsible to the French people alone, to whom he has at all times the right to appeal." To this final court of arbitration, then, Napoleon resolved to carry his case.

Up to within five days of the time when the vote was to be taken, political assemblies for discussion were allowed. The spirit with which the campaign was carried on furnished a new illustration of the saying of Milton that "when the devil tyranny hath once entered into a people, it goeth not out but with foamings and great convulsions." In one of the political meetings, Citizen Lermina "proposed that Louis Charles Napoleon Bonaparte, called Napoleon III., should be condemned to imprisonment and hard labor for life." The wretch argued the matter in all seriousness, and found a crowd of willing listeners. The proposal cost him two years of imprisonment and a fine of ten thousand francs. The affair is important simply as showing the spirit in which the campaign was carried on.

To the great assistance of the imperial party, some letters were found with a man who had just come over from England, containing allusions to a great "amputation" that was to take place. At about the same time, in one of the suburbs of Paris, a chest was discovered containing a quantity of bombs and gunpowder. These two circumstances were put together, and the police at once magnified them as a "frightful conspiracy." The opposition newspapers laughed and scouted at the matter as an absurdity, whereupon five of them were instantly confiscated. After this warning, the others with pardonable prudence allowed the spectre of the "Beaury Conspiracy" to stalk abroad unchallenged. It proved a great success. The *Presse* declared that "the object of the conspiracy was to destroy the Emperor and the whole of Paris. Whoever is not with us, is for the murderers; whoever votes *Yes*, votes against the conspirators and their bombs." * The "Left" asserted boldly that the whole affair was an invention of the government, arranged for the purpose of frightening the masses of the people with the ghost of murder and revolution into supporting it at the polls. Whether this be true or not, it is certain that the matter had an immense influence on the election. The official journals magnified the affair and the terrors to which it pointed, while the opposition journals, warned by the confiscation of their colleagues, dared not say a word. The *Red Republican Spectre* had never lost its terrors for the peasant proprietor; and now, when the question presented was not concerning this policy or that policy, but rather concerning government or anarchy, it is not strange that the people voted for government by a majority of five to one. It is to be noticed, however, that no amount of management on the part of the government was able to bring the majority up to what it had previously been, and that the proportion of those who had voted *No* had been largest in the best educated and most influential departments, and smallest

Müller. *Geschichte der Gegenwart*, 1870, s. 35.

where there was the greatest poverty and ignorance.*

Napoleon chose, of course, to interpret the result of the *plébiscite* as a new lease of personal power. He regarded it, or at least professed to regard it, as a renewed expression on the part of the people of faith in himself.

Meanwhile the *Corps Législatif* was less tractable than he desired. It seemed determined to hasten on the government along the pathway of reform in spite of itself. With the right of initiative now in full possession, it was no longer dependent on the Emperor for the introduction of political measures; and it was bold to strike out a pathway of its own. Among other innovations, it passed a bill in opposition to the Government, giving to the *Conseils Généraux* the right of political discussion. Conceal it as the Emperor and his friends might, the ugly fact still remained, that there was in the legislative body a formidable opposition which could not but inspire serious forebodings for the future.

* Immediately after the election the *Temps* published an analysis of the votes, in which it was shown that in seventeen of the best educated departments the *Noes* amounted to 26 per cent., while in the twenty-three least educated they were only 11½ per cent. In the cities, where the course of the government could be thoroughly exposed, as in Paris, Lyons, Marseilles and Bordeaux, the *Noes* even had a majority.

The votes on the three *plébiscites* of Napoleon III. resulted as follows:

		Yes.	*No.*
Presidency for ten years	(Dec. 20, 1851)......	7,437,216	646,737
Hereditary Empire	(Nov. 21, 1852)......	7,824,179	253,145
Amended constitution	(May 8, 1870)	7,210,296	1,530,610

It was at the moment when this domestic quarrel was assuming its most threatening aspect that a great foreign opportunity presented itself. All questions of family disagreement were suddenly eclipsed by the question of the Hohenzollern candidature. The military supremacy of France had been overshadowed; here was an opportunity to re-establish it in the sight of all mankind. The Second Empire had lost a great part of its prestige with the people; here was a means of regaining it. The government had been outwitted in all its diplomatic efforts to extend its boundaries to the Rhine; here was an opportunity to accomplish in the field what it had so signally failed to accomplish in the cabinet. Nothing would reinstate the hegemony of France and the prestige of the Second Empire so surely as a successful war with their hereditary enemy, Prussia; and no better occasion for war than the present was likely to occur. As for an *unsuccessful* war,—it was not to be thought of. The needle-gun, it is true, had once occasioned some anxiety, but now the *Chassepots* were ready, and so were the *mittrailleuses*. The question of arms thus disposed of, the whole matter was settled. Any one who presumed to think that those obese, drowsy, phlegmatic beings known as *ces gros Allemands* were a match for Frenchmen, was simply either a fool or a traitor. When Monsieur Thiers contended that France was not ready for a war with Germany, their answer was substantially that he must change his opinion, or they would burn his house.

But the most important question of all was the one which the government and people alike overlooked, namely, the condition of the army.

Immediately after the successes of Prussia in 1866, the French government determined to remodel its military organization. Marshal Niel was entrusted with the superintendence of the work, and he set about it with undoubted ability and vigor. The Emperor, in his speech from the throne in January, 1867, had discoursed at length upon the peaceful prospects of Europe, at the same time adding that the results of the last war pointed out the necessity of perfecting the military organization without delay. This *non-sequitur* could not but arouse the Emperor's enemies both at home and abroad. In Germany it was at once interpreted as evidence of hostile intent; and it doubtless had its influence in strengthening the German powers in their efforts to perfect the military organization. In France, however, the effect of the declaration was in great measure to weaken the hands of the government. The inconsistency of the positions assumed by the Emperor was remorselessly exposed in the *Corps Législatif.* Rouher favored the members with an elaboration of the purposes of his imperial master, whereupon Jules Favre put to him this crushing dilemma: "Either the speech you have made us is nothing but a necessary ostentation, corresponding in no way with the real political situation, or you are bound to withdraw the bill for military reorganization which you have just laid before us." "France must congratulate herself," responded Rouher, "to see the old German Confederation, an enormous mass of seventy-five millions, whose purely defensive character was a mere illusion, *broken up, as it now is, into three fragments.*" *

In the face of such weakness and such inconsistency, it was impossible for the legislative body to enter with spirit upon the work of reorganizing the army. It said practically: "If the government anticipates war, let it say so plainly, and we will furnish all needed supplies; but it declares that our foreign relations are in the fullest sense satisfactory. If this declaration is true, our army is in no need of being strengthened."

In this way it was that the hands of the government were paralyzed. By its vigorous call for a reorganization of the army, it had strengthened Prussia; by its declaration that the results of the Austro-Prussian war were satisfactory to France, it had made such a reorganization apparently unnecessary, and consequently almost impossible. Marshal Niel, therefore, labored under every dis-

* At the moment when these words were uttered, the treaty giving to Prussia the military control of the Southern German States had already been signed, but had not yet been published. Within a few days, however, Bismarck chose to give it publicity, thus proclaiming to Europe that of Rouher's "three fragments," two were virtually *one* under the control of Prussia, while the third was simply crippled Austria.

advantage. He carried on the manufacture of chassepots quite diligently, but further than this very little was accomplished. Any material increase of the size of the army was, under the circumstances, deemed unnecessary; and therefore, when an attempt was actually made to place it on such a footing that it would not compare unfavorably with that of Germany, the violence of the opposition was greatly intensified.

From this condition of affairs two results ensued. On the one hand, the impression got abroad that the French government was straining every nerve to increase the army to the highest possible efficiency; while, on the other, the government was so hampered, that any considerable *actual* increase was impossible. Thus, while the country resounded with words about "conscription" and "prepartion for war," no real preparation was actually made. Europe was thoroughly deceived.

This condition of military affairs under Marshal Niel was rendered still worse under Marshal Lebœuf. "Strange as it will now sound," says Rüstow, "the disposition of this marshal was absolutely peaceful. He wished to economize in the army, and to raise its tone through less expensive institutions." * But the very fact that the common impression prevailed that Lebœuf was warlike in his sympathies, while he was actually pacific, increased the misfortune of the nation in the direction above indicated. Military preparations practically ceased,

* Rüstow, *The War for the Rhine Frontier*, vol. I. p. 89.

though the impression prevailed abroad that the government was actively preparing for war.

In consequence of these various causes, the strength of the French army, at the outbreak of war, was much less than it was popularly believed to be, either in France or in the rest of Europe. The laws of 1867 and '68 provided for an annual contingent of 100,000 men, thus giving to France an establishment of 500,000, in active service, and 250,000, in the reserve. These laws, however, were so feebly enforced that scarcely more than half of that number were actually brought into service—a fact which is a most extraordinary commentary on the weakness of the imperial policy. On this whole subject, so eminent an authority as Rüstow, after a careful analysis of the different branches of the army, sums up his conclusions as follows:

"The French army, on the normal war footing of 1868, could place in the field 285,000 men, infantry and cavalry, and 984 guns, having in the second line, as dépôt troops, 91,000 men, infantry and cavalry. On a peace footing, the army could muster about two-thirds of these numbers; and if the calling in of these reserves was, in spite of the amendments introduced in 1868, not to be easily accomplished, the fact had to be accepted that, in case of the sudden breaking out of the war, only about 200,000 men, infantry and cavalry, would be disposable for actual service.

"The military preparations of France, expressed by these numbers, are terribly meagre when compared with her population and with her moral and material resources. This evil state of things was to be remedied by the New Service Act, which, prepared since 1866, was published on the first of February, 1868. But in reality this act wrought no essential changes, for it created no new troops or cadres for the active army; so that in the future, as in the past, in case of a serious war breaking out, every addition would have to be improvised." *

A similar analysis made by the same author shows that the military strength of the North German Confederation alone amounted to no less than 475,200 infantry, 55,000 cavalry, and 1,204 guns, exclusive of the reserves. † At the outbreak of the war, then, "Germany," says Rüstow, "could muster in field troops 518,000 men, infantry and cavalry, with 1506 guns; France could oppose to them 285,000 men, infantry and cavalry, with 964 guns—that is, but little more than the half. Germany had as reserve troops 161,000 men, infantry and cavalry; France had as dépôt troops 91,000 men. Germany had as garrison troops 187,000 men; France could show nothing as an equivalent to this, for the Mobile Guard, which was to fill their place, was simply not organized. We believe that in these round numbers we have given a true comparison of the land forces of the countries which, in the year 1870, were about to engage in

* Rüstow, *The War for the Rhine Frontier*, vol. I. p. 76.
† Ibid. p. 115, *et seq.*

an unhappy war. These numbers distinctly express the enormous military superiority of Germany on the land." *

It must also be said that the comparative size of the two hostile armies was no more to the advantage of the Germans than was their comparative condition. The German army, from the peculiar manner of its formation, as I remarked in the introductory chapter, was a fac-simile of German culture. The army of France, on the other hand, was made up largely of substitutes serving in the place of those who were able and disposed to remain at home. For this reason it contained the very dregs of society. In point of education and in point of moral taste, therefore, the difference in favor of the Germans was immeasurable. Moreover, this difference was vastly increased by the laxness of discipline which prevailed in the camp of the French. Rüstow informs us that the army regulations in France were four times changed between 1867 and 1870, and that each of the six different commanders of the imperial camp at Chalons during the same years had changed the methods of drill in accordance with his own peculiar fancy.† When these facts are contrasted

* Rüstow, *The War for the Rhine Frontier*, vol. I. p. 129.

† "As early as 1867 the infantry regulations were rewritten, then thrice revised, so that the last edition only appeared in 1870, shortly before the outbreak of the war. But nevertheless there were no comprehensive changes from former times to be remarked. In opposition to the Prussian company-column, the French held to the battalion as the only tactical unit—very likely with perfect right with their pur-

with the system and rigor for which the German military discipline has long been very justly celebrated, the result is simply to magnify vastly the difference which we have already seen to be so enormous. In the light of these comparisons we are driven to one of two conclusions: the French government must have entered upon the war either in profound ignorance of the military strength of the enemy, or in utter despair of rallying the French people in any other way.

The publication of the despatches of Count Benedetti, who was during these years the minister of France at Berlin, leaves us no possible room for doubt as to which of these conclusions is the true one. As early as the 25th of August, 1866, he sent to his government a long letter in which he gave an elaborate account of all the branches of the German army. For still more minute details he referred to an accompanying report of his military *attaché*, and concluded his letter by declaring that if the organization contemplated was completed, "the cabinet at Berlin would have at its disposal more than a million of men." * On the 18th of October following, he informed his government that the proposed military organization had been

posely weak battalions. In the camp at Chalons every commander-in-chief who governed there in succession during the years from 1867 to 1870, L'Admirault, de Failly, Lebœuf, Bazaine, Bourbaki, Froissard, manœuvred according to his own devices and fancies without going deep into detail, so that it cannot with any justice be said that a new system was established by these exercises."—*Rüstow*, *The War for the Rhine Frontier*, vol. I. p. 86.

* Benedetti, *Ma Mission en Prusse*, p. 207.

adopted. On the 18th of December of the same year, he wrote that the organization recommended by the Prussian minister was in full force, and that, in the conquered territories, the rules of the Prussian service were in process of rapid introduction. About a month later the minister reverted to the subject, using such specific words as these: "I do not believe it superfluous to repeat that the Administration of War continues exercising the greatest activity. It is carrying out without relaxation the constitution of the new *Corps d'Armée*, and it is pressing the other states of the Confederation to take, without delay, the steps which the organization of the federal army requires. It is evident, and this is the opinion of our military *attaché*, that they hold it as of the highest importance to place themselves in a condition to confront any eventuality." * In March and April, 1867, the same subject was referred to in the same vigorous manner. Again on the 5th of January, 1868, the ambassador sent a long despatch devoted to the same subject. He showed in the first place that in the event of war, France could have nothing to hope from the hostility of foreign powers to Prussia. He then reverted to the condition of the German armies. The keynote of this portion of the despatch was in its opening words: "The more I observe the conduct of the Prussian government, the more I am persuaded that all its efforts tend to extend its power

* *Ibid.* p. 208.

over the whole of Germany. I am each day more convinced that it is pursuing success in this direction, with the conviction that it cannot attain its end without making it impossible for France to place any obstacle in its way. How and by what means it seeks to obtain this twofold result is what I ask permission to explain to you to-day, by recalling and uniting in a general view the different items of information which I have already had the honor of transmitting." *

On the subject of military strength the writer then proceeds to show how the Prussian government had gained possession of the different resources of the country; how, after the last war, three new corps had been formed; how at the same time secret treaties had been formed with Bavaria, Würtemberg, and Baden; how still another engagement had been signed with Hesse and all the smaller states, by which their troops formed a part of the Prussian army; and finally how, by the law which voted the contingent for five years, the last requisite had been complied with for placing all the resources of Germany at the call and the pleasure of Prussia.† Finally, on the 14th of January, 1870, only six months before the outbreak of the war, he wrote: "The specific views which animate the king and the prime minister do not in the least prevent them from bestowing the same care that has always been shown at Berlin on the development of the military

* Benedetti, *Ma Mission en Prusse*, p. 251. † *Ibid.* p. 284.

forces of Prussia. They manifest the same solicitude for the preservation of the good relations that have been established with the Court of St. Petersburg. The solidarity of the Prussian army and an eventual alliance with Russia are looked upon at Berlin as the two guarantees necessary for the permanence of the conquests made in Germany." *

Not to prolong the discussion of this question, then, it may be stated that the despatches of Benedetti placed clearly before the Emperor these four points: first, that the military organization of Germany was most perfect and most powerful; second, that Southern Germany, as well as Northern, was under the control of Prussia; third, that the relations of Prussia and Russia were such that no hostility between them was likely to be brought about; and, fourth, that Germany had no hostile intentions toward France. No study of the causes and character of the war can yield satisfactory results unless the student remembers constantly that the French minister gave to his master detailed and reiterated information on each of these four points.

* *Ibid. et seq.*

Perhaps the most remarkable and most valuable passage in this despatch is the one in which, while he warns France against the strength of Prussia, he informs her that Prussia has no spirit of aggression. He shows that though the King had gathered in strength from every quarter, at home and abroad, until his resources were enormous, he had evidently "no intention of using them save for the purpose of compelling other nations to respect the right of Germany to control her own political affairs."—*Ibid.* p. 257.

At the outbreak of the Franco-German war, it was claimed by the friends of the French cause that the attitude of Germany toward France had long been one of hostility, and that, in consequence of this attitude, it was impossible that a war should long be postponed. When the famous "draft-treaty" was published, it was claimed that, although written indeed in the hand of the French ambassador, it had been done at the prudent dictation of the Prussian minister. That such was the fact we are given to understand by Benedetti himself, in the volume from which I have already quoted. But, unfortunately for the currency of such an explanation, the German troops, in the course of the war, took possession of the private residence of the French minister, Rouher, and with it of the correspondence which took place between Benedetti and the French government. This correspondence, or so much of it as was deemed necessary to justify the Germans, was published by Bismarck soon after the appearance of Benedetti's volume. Nothing could have been more crushing to the cause of the French. It was only a few days after the appearance of the detailed account of the French ambassador (in which it was claimed that the annexation of Belgium and the left bank of the Rhine was the proposition of Prussia) that the correspondence was given to the world.* It showed that as early as June, 1866, Benedetti was

* *Deutscher Reichs-Anzeiger und Königlich Preuszischer Staats-Anzeiger, Berlin Freitag den* 20 *Oktober, Abends, s.* 2735.

instructed to study and report upon the disposition of the Germans toward France, with special view to French aggrandizement; that he had accordingly reported that the German people were literally unanimous in the intense patriotism with which "they would resent every idea of a transaction which might involve the loss of any portion of territory whatever;" that these assurances were reiterated in the strongest possible terms; that, only a few weeks afterwards, Benedetti was instructed to demand of Prussia the cession to France of all the provinces west of the Rhine; that this proposition was indignantly rejected by Bismarck, who declared that, if pressed, it would result in a war, attended with a revolutionary crisis; * that Benedetti hereupon went to Paris, and there received formal instructions in writing to demand the cession to France, in open treaty, of Landau, Saarlouis, and Saarbrück, together with the acquiescence of Prussia in the seizure of Luxembourg by France, and a secret treaty of alliance, with the seizure of Belgium by France as its price; that the actual cession of German territory, if found unattainable, might be dispensed with, but that Belgium and Luxembourg were essential, and must be insisted on; that Benedetti, not daring to propose these terms to Bismarck, took the liberty of saying

* Faites bien observer à Sa Majesté l'Empereur qu'une guerre pareille pourrait devenir dans certaines éventualités une guerre à coups de révolution, et qu'en présence de dangers révolutionnaires les dynasties allemandes feraient preuve d'être plus solidement établies que celle de l'Empereur Napoléon.

nothing of German territory, but of confining himself to Luxembourg and Belgium; and, finally, that the Emperor had indicated his purpose by sending to Benedetti these concluding words: "If you think that the annexation of Luxembourg had better be concealed until after we lay hands on Belgium, I should be obliged by your giving your reasons in detail." *

It needs only to be said further on this subject,

Perhaps the most important part of this remarkable article is the following:

"'Zugleich wird angedeutet, dass man in Paris die Einigung Deutschlands als eine 'dans un temps prochain,' unvermeidliche Eventualität betrachte. Man dürfe indessen nicht 'solidarisèr l'article IV avec l'article III—il est bien évident, que l'extension de la suprématie de la Prusse au delà du Main nous sera une occasion toute naturelle, presque obligatoire, pour nous emparer de la Belgique; mais d'autres occasions peuvent se présenter—nous devons en rester les juges exclusifs—, la redaction trés-claire et trés-précise du projet nous maintient à cet égard une liberté précieuse.'

Wiederholt wird die Erwerbung Luxemburgs als das unmittelbare, die Belgiens als das eventuelle Ziel der Konvention festgestellt und letzteres, sowie die Offensiv- und Defensiv-Allianz sollen geheim bleiben. Es heiszt weiter:

'Cette combinaison concilie tout, elle détend l'opinion publique en France par l'obtention d'une satisfaction immédiate et l'orientation qui en résulte pour les esprits vers la Belgique. Elle maintient un secret nécessaire et sur le traité d'alliance et sur les annexions en projet. Si vous pensiez que la cession même de Luxembourg doit rester secrèt jusq'au moment de la mise sur la Belgique, je vous prierai de justifier cette appréciation par des observations détaillées. Car la suspension plus ou moins indéfinie des échanges de territoires pourrait même être une cause de précipitation malencontreuse de la question belge.'

Am Schlusz des Briefes wird Graf Benedetti ermächtigt, sich, wenn er es für nöthig halte, auf einige Zeit nach Karlsbad zu begeben. Graf Benedetti hat diesen Pariser Brief unter dem 29ten August beantwortet. In seiner Antwort spricht der französische Botschafter zum ersten Mal Zweifel aus, ob man aus Preuszen's Aufrichtigkeit in der Sache werde rechnen können; er bemerkt, dass ihm ein gewisses Misstrauen des

that since the publication of these depatches all attempts to throw upon Germany the responsibility of the war must be the dictate either of ignorance or of dishonesty. For Bismarck, in the light of these facts, to have been unprepared for war, would have been as inconsistent with wise statesmanship as it would have been fatal to German unity.

Now with all these facts before us, it is difficult to characterize with too great severity the course of the French government in bringing on the war. That the renunciation of the Hohenzollern candidature (the only thing at first demanded by France) afforded an honorable means of solving the whole difficulty must be universally admitted. France might have retired, bearing away the fruits of a real triumph; and it seems to me impossible to account for the amazing folly of the government in pushing the question farther, except by the theory of its own conscious weakness with its own people. The instructions of the Emperor to Benedetti, and the infamous address of Gramont in the *Corps Législatif*,* had inflamed the public

Grafen Bismarck darüber entgegentrete, ob der Kaiser Napoleon nicht solche Verhandlung benutzen werde, um zwischen Preussen und England Misstrauen zu erregen."

* Of this speech Charles de Mazade, in a very able and discriminating article on the origin of the war of 1870, says: "Cette déclaration, portée avec une certaine solennité au corps législatif par le ministre des affaires étrangéres, par M. le Duc de Gramont, avait et devait avoir une double conséquence. D'un côté, on mettait le feu à l'ésprit public; on ravivait des passions, des ressentiments toujours mal apaisés contre la Prusse, ... d'un autre côté parler ainsi du haut d'une tribune, devant l'Europe, à un gouvernement fier, gonflé de récess succès

sentiment of Paris until it was absolutely beyond control. The war-cry, thus first pronounced by the government, created such an excitement among the people that the Emperor and his cabinet were obliged at least to seem to lead public opinion, when in fact they were only swept along before it. From the moment when Gramont's address became generally known in the streets of Paris, it is quite probable that the real alternative was, as it certainly seemed to be, between foreign war and revolution. After reading the despatches addressed to the Emperor's government, it is impossible not to believe that he knew the risk he was running; we are driven, therefore, to conclude that the Emperor saw little hope of saving his throne but by throwing himself upon the mad current of popular opinion.*

c'était commencer par le piquer dans sons orgueil et lui rendre peut-être les concessions plus difficiles. De toute maniere, on créait une situation inextricable.—*Revue des Deux Mondes*, 1 *Jan.* 1874, p. 196.

* The desperate haste and excitement with which the negotiations just before the war were carried on by the French government will be seen by a simple enumeration of a few facts. It was on the 6th of July that Gramont, speaking for the government, pronounced his celebrated address in which he expressed the hope that the event contemplated would be averted by the "wisdom of Germany and the friendship of Spain," and that, "if it should turn out otherwise, strong in your support and in that of the nation, we shall know how to do our duty without hesitation and without feebleness." On the 8th of July (in the evening) Benedetti arrived at Ems. On the 10th Gramont complained of delays, at the same time declaring to Benedetti, that his telegraphic despatches had been mutilated ("votre dernier tellegramme chiffré d'hier soir a été trongué et denaturé"). Benedetti in his turn answered that he could decipher the despatches received from the government only imperfectly. This, however, was of no consequence; the affair must be hastened without waiting for exact infor-

It has been no part of my purpose to trace the events which followed in so rapid succession the outbreak of the war. I trust that enough has been said to show not only that the issue of the struggle could not have been other than what it was, but also that the inferiority of France was not due to any single cause alone, but to a long succession of debilitating influences. There is nothing more impressive to the student of history than the enormous cost of what we call civilization; and next to this fact in impressiveness is the difficulty of eradicating certain classes of evils when once they have taken root in society. The evils of the *old régime* had become so desperate that it was simply impossible to hold the people longer in subjection under it, and accordingly when the American Revolution set the example, and an opportunity was offered by the meeting of the

mation. "We must have an answer to-morrow," telegraphed Gramont; "day after to-morrow will be too late. Write, telegraph; if the king is unwilling to advise the prince of Hohenzollern to renounce, it is war at once, and in a few days we shall be on the Rhine" ("Et bien! c'est la guerre tout de suite, et dans quelque jours nous sommes au Rhein"). In this manner affairs were pushed. On the 12th an envoy arrived at Paris with the renunciation of the prince. At the very least this occasioned a reason for delay until a messenger should arrive on the following day from Ems. But not at all. That very evening a despatch was sent to demand an engagement of the king that the matter should never be brought forward in the future. On the 13th the king declined to make such an engagement. On the 14th it was circulated at Paris that the king had refused an audience to Benedetti (a pure fabrication, as Benedetti himself declares), and that very evening, without waiting for a messenger from Ems, war was declared in the *Corps Législatif*. On this whole subject see *Revue des Deux Mondes*, Jan. 1, 1874, p. 199.

States-General, an outbreak could not be prevented. The Revolution was, however, the uprising of an overwhelming mass of men and women who had been rendered insane by long imprisonment, rather than a revolution of rational beings who knew what liberty is, and who deliberately set about the work of acquiring it. It is undoubtedly true that a despotism of centuries had rendered the French people incapable of performing their legitimate part in the establishment of liberty; it is no less certain that the deplorable results of this tyranny remained long after their worst causes had been removed.

That the French Revolution failed to accomplish any great result can by no means be asserted; and yet it may be affirmed with positive assurance that what it accomplished was far different from that which it set out to accomplish. Nothing is now more certain than that the condition of the masses of the French peasantry made it almost, if not quite, impossible to carry out a thorough-going reform; hence the various radical attempts that have been made in this direction have miscarried, and have only served to illustrate once more the truth of the saying of Machiavelli already quoted, that "he who neglects what *is*, in order to follow what *ought to be*, will sooner learn how to ruin than how to preserve himself."

While the French peasantry have been kept by their lack of education from taking any intelligent and active part in the politics of the country, they have afforded a convenient constituency for that large class of intense partisans with which France has long been afflicted. As a rule the masses of the people have been eminently conservative. They have either abstained from politics altogether, or, if they have been forced into some degree of political activity, they have devoted themselves to the support of the party in power, whatever that party might be. This fact, paradoxical as it may seem, has afforded the best possible material for the purposes of an intense partisanship. A spirit of revolution wants nothing better to feed upon than that conservative apathy which is always ready to accept and adopt an accomplished fact. It is in great measure for this reason that France has been to such an extent the sport of faction. With a peasantry ignorant and apathetic, with no statesman of ability so pre-eminent as to be able to mould the various elements of society to one common purpose, the nation has again and again fallen a prey to the most headlong violence. Though the French Revolution taught, as a general truth and with a greater emphasis, what the English Revolution within a narrower sphere had taught a hundred years before, namely, that governments must make their policy conform to the will of the nation, it also taught that republican institutions as well as monarchical have their dangers, and that they can be prosperous and permanent only when they rest upon the basis of a general and active intelligence.

INDEX.

www.ingramcontent.com/pod-product-compliance
Lightning Source LLC
LaVergne TN
LVHW021304110826
845150LV00003B/475

* 9 7 8 1 4 2 5 5 6 0 8 1 2 *